Transforming Palliative Care in Nursing Homes

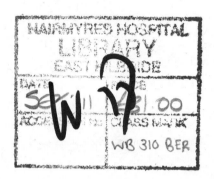

END-OF-LIFE CARE: A SERIES

End-of-Life Care: A Series
Virginia E. Richardson, Series Editor

We all confront end-of-life issues. As people live longer and suffer from more chronic illnesses, all of us face difficult decisions about death, dying, and terminal care. This series aspires to articulate the issues surrounding end-of-life care in the twenty-first century. It will be a resource for practitioners and scholars who seek information about advance directives, hospice, palliative care, bereavement, and other death-related topics. The interdisciplinary approach makes the series invaluable for social workers, physicians, nurses, attorneys, and pastoral counselors.

The press seeks manuscripts that reflect the interdisiciplinary, biopsychosocial essence of end-of-life care. We welcome manuscripts that address specific topics on ethical dilemmas in end-of-life care, death, and dying among marginalized groups, palliative care, spirituality, and end-of-life care in special medical areas, such as oncology, AIDS, diabetes, and transplantation. While writers should integrate theory and practice, the series is open to diverse methodologies and perspectives.

Joan Berzoff and Phyllis R. Silverman, *Living with Dying: A Handbook for End-of-Life Healthcare Practitioners*
Virginia E. Richardson and Amanda S. Barusch, *Gerontological Practice for the Twenty-first Century: A Social Work Perspective*
Ruth Ray, *Endnotes: An Intimate Look at the End of Life*
Terry Wolfer and Vicki Runnion, eds., *Dying, Death, and Bereavement in Social Work Practice: Decision Cases for Advanced Practice*

Transforming Palliative Care in Nursing Homes

The Social Work Role

Edited by

MERCEDES BERN-KLUG

Columbia University Press   *New York*

Columbia University Press
Publishers Since 1893
New York   Chichester, West Sussex
Copyright © 2010 Columbia University Press
All rights reserved

Library of Congress Cataloging-in-Publication Data
Transforming palliative care in nursing homes : the social work role /
edited by Mercedes Bern-Klug.
p.   cm.—(End-of-life care)
Includes bibliographical references and index.
ISBN 978-0-231-13224-4 (cloth : alk. paper)—ISBN 978-0-231-13225-1 (pbk. : alk. paper)—
ISBN 978-0-231-50707-3 (e-book)
1. Medical social work—United States. 2. Social work with older people—United States.
3. Palliative treatment—United States. 4. Nursing homes—United States.
I. Bern-Klug, Mercedes.
HV687.5.U5T73   2010
362.17'5—dc22
2009023928

Columbia University Press books are printed on permanent and durable acid-free paper.
This book is printed on paper with recycled content.
Printed in the United States of America

References to Internet Web sites (URLs) were accurate at the time of writing.
Neither the author nor Columbia University Press is responsible for URLs that may have
expired or changed since the manuscript was prepared.

This book is dedicated to my mother,
Estela Corona Bern,
who has demonstrated that each stage of life has its own purpose and beauty.

A word of thanks:
Thank you to the people and organizations who provided emotional,
financial, or inspirational support toward the development of this book:
Ginny Richardson, Rosalie Kane, Megel Klug, Rosemary Chapin, Lauren Dockett,
John Michel, Kathleen Kelly, Barbara Frank, Jim Lubben and Barbara Berkman
and the John A. Hartford Geriatric Social Work Programs. Grace Christ,
the Soros Foundation's Project on Death in America–Social Work Leadership
Award Program, the University of Iowa (UI) School of Social Work (in particular
Lorraine Dorfman, Salome Raheim, Ed Saunders, and Kate Kemp),
the UI Office of the Vice President for Research, the UI Obermann Center
for Advanced Studies–Scholar Program, and the UI Center on Aging.

I would also like to thank the nursing home staff members who welcome
researchers, and the residents and family members who are our most
important teachers.

We did the best we could with what we knew.
Now we know better; now we must do better.

—Maya Angelou

Contents

Foreword

Looking Back on the Nursing Home Experience of My Mother

MSGR. CHARLES FAHEY

My mother, age ninety-eight, drifted off from this life not one day too soon or one day too late. She had lived a full life as daughter, wife, mother, sister, aunt, teacher, volunteer, believer, and friend. Until the final days, when she slipped into a coma, she was an important part of the nursing home where she spent the final three years of her life enduring a series of debilitating medical events and concomitant disabilities as her progressive intermittent frailty reached its end point, death.

Elizabeth Fahey was a lovely person who was friend to whomever she met. During the latter part of her life, first in an assisted-living facility and then in a nursing home, she continued to be kind to and thoughtful of all with whom she came into contact. I was continually amazed and edified to experience the mutual greetings shared by staff and other residents, as I wheeled her to meals or to Mass. She had been unable to walk for several years despite excellent medical attention and efforts at physical therapy.

To my alleged expertise in the field of aging, caring for my mother and dad in their latter years added a substantial dose of reality and understanding that can only be hinted at in journal articles and textbooks. Among these is the reality that death is a social event almost anywhere and anytime it occurs. It is especially true in an institution where the community is intimate and constant. It involves both residents and staff members.

Two events illustrate the point.

Mother had been unconscious for several days, and I was not present when it was determined she had died. When I did get to her there was one of the young housekeeper boys kneeling beside her bed and saying a prayer, rising only to console me!

Though my folks were "pillars" of a parish, I decided that the wake and funeral should be at the home since this was her last community and the folks of our "broader community" including parishioners could come to it whereas the converse was not realistic.

At the well-attended funeral with people from all our communities, I noted in the homily that I had just become an orphan at age seventy-three, but in mother's final stay I, an only child, had acquired two sisters, both named Brenda, one black and the other white: the two CNAs who had cared for Elizabeth in a special way. She had become their surrogate mother and they, in turn, her surrogate daughters.

Person-centered care is something we all celebrate but that is incomplete if we do not recognize and foster the concept that an institution, large or small, should also be a person-centered community.

Msgr. Charles Fahey, current chairperson of the National Council on Aging, is the only son of Charles and Elizabeth who died at ninety and ninety-eight years of age.

Foreword

VIRGINIA RICHARDSON

When I was seeking material on end-of-life care several years ago I found almost no information about death and dying in nursing homes. I later read Mercedes Bern-Klug's seminal chapter on end-of-life care in nursing homes in Joan Berzoff and Phyllis Silverman's book, *Living with Dying: A Handbook for End-of-Life Healthcare Practitioners* (Columbia University Press, 2004), which launched the series on end-of-life care for Columbia University Press in 2004. The editors of this handbook pointed out that "in every setting there are [end-of-life] changes that may be specific to that setting" (271), and Bern-Klug's edited book is the first of several that will focus on end-of-life care in a particular setting. Bern-Klug's book spearheads a palliative-care perspective that shows how social workers and other healthcare practitioners can support a comfort-care approach toward living and dying in nursing homes. Although death is common in nursing homes, staff too often sequester dying residents away from the scrutiny of others. In this book, Bern-Klug reminds us, first, that death is natural and inevitable and, second, that even in nursing homes, dying people can thrive at the end of life when given proper care.

At the time I approached Bern-Klug about writing this book, I was unaware that she was a student. Her advisor appropriately counseled her to complete her dissertation before writing a book. When she became a pretenure assistant professor, she was appropriately advised to avoid writing a book and to focus instead on writing peer-reviewed journal articles. I remained patient but persisted. After she was awarded funds from the John A. Hartford Foundation to study end-of-life care in nursing homes, Bern-Klug was ready to write this book, which represents the most up-to-date resource on caring for terminally ill residents in nursing homes. The intent of this book is to inform social workers and other healthcare practitioners how they can help terminally ill nursing home residents and facilitate their entry through a "peaceful doorway to death."

The book is organized around eleven chapters that build on one another. Each chapter focuses on a different aspect of end-of-life care in nursing homes, and many begin with a case depicting the issues and dilemmas that are the central focus of the chapter. The authors demonstrate how social workers can help dying patients and their families prepare for death and provide appropriate comfort care to ensure that residents die peacefully.

Bern-Klug begins the book by explaining why nursing home social workers need to adopt more contemporary end-of-life-care models that integrate the fundamental principles underlying palliative care. She describes the multiple roles that nursing home social workers can take on: "context interpreters" when residents are first diagnosed with terminal conditions and need help understanding the seriousness and implications of their diagnosis; "advocates" who defend their patients' rights to decline invasive treatments, especially when residents and family members' wishes differ; "care and comfort specialists" who monitor and coordinate care to ensure that palliative and other psychosocial care is effectively administered to terminally ill persons; and "bereavement specialists" who assist family members with saying goodbye, performing death rituals, and arranging burials, cremations, funerals, or memorial services.

The book's early chapters present critical psychosocial, social, spiritual, and existential issues that arise when people struggle with chronic illnesses, and the later ones focus on specific topics. For example, in chapter 5, Ann Allegre explains the dying process and death trajectories associated with the most common terminal illnesses. Practitioners especially will appreciate the guidelines and interventions discussed here and in other chapters. Readers will resonate with the themes that consistently emerge in these chapters, such as "person-centered care," "death as a social event," "comfort care," "ethical practice," "culturally competent care," and "self-care."

Virginia Richardson

Bern-Klug looks into the future in her last chapter and identifies key palliative care issues that we still need to debate within the context of any major healthcare reforms that might occur. The baby boomers will enter late life with various chronic illnesses that will increase their frailty and vulnerability, and many will move to nursing homes, where they will need proper palliative care. Whether older people die in nursing homes, hospitals, or in their homes, healthcare practitioners must know how to deliver competent end-of-life care that will ensure dignity and tranquility. Bern-Klug and her colleagues remind us that future debates about healthcare reform must incorporate palliative and end-of-life care. According to Bern-Klug, the outcomes from these debates, ultimately, will be based on where we place our values, how we conceptualize aging, how we understand dying, and how we implement palliative care. She also acknowledges that these decisions will be based on how people feel about dependency, that is, whether it is something we are ashamed of or something we honor. The hope is that the more informed we are about palliative and end-of-life care, the better our decisions will be.

Virginia Richardson is professor in the College of Social Work at Ohio State University.

Introduction

MERCEDES BERN-KLUG

This book is dedicated to the idea that people who live in nursing homes can thrive even as they approach the end of their lives. Not only can nursing home residents thrive, but nursing homes should be designed to maximize the human potential for thriving. Excellent physical care is necessary, but it is not enough. In order for people to thrive in any setting, psychological and social needs must also be met.

The book is based on the understanding that more effort is needed to improve the quality of life in America's nursing homes; psychosocial issues are a key component of quality of life; palliative care is a philosophy of care that emphasizes quality of life and psychosocial issues; all nursing home residents deserve access to excellent palliative care, whether or not they are recognized as "dying" per se; and social workers have skills that can help transform the nursing home setting into a palliative-care setting that honors psychosocial, including spiritual, needs and thus honors the whole person. Maximum quality of life cannot be achieved if psychosocial concerns go unaddressed.

While all nursing home staff members have a hand in identifying and addressing psychosocial issues, this book invites social workers to demonstrate leadership in nursing home palliative-care needs. The book chapters can be used to help prepare nursing home social workers for an active role in transforming the nursing home setting into one in which palliative care and psychosocial care are enhanced. This book builds on the work of many practitioners, scholars, and organizations devoted to improving care for people approaching the end of life, including the Institute of Medicine's Committee on Care at the End of Life and their report "Approaching Death: Improving Care at the End of Life" (Field and Castle 1997); the Institute for the Advancement of Social Work Research's final report and blueprint for action, "Evaluating Social Work Services in Nursing Homes: Toward Quality Psychosocial Care and its Measurement" (Vourlekis, Zlotnik, and Simons 2005); the Social Work Hospice and Palliative Care Network, "Charting the Course for the Future of Social Work in End-of-Life and Palliative Care"; the National Association of Social Workers (NASW), "Standards for Social Work Services in Long-Term Care Facilities" (NASW 2003) and the "NASW Standards for Practice in Palliative and End-of-Life Care" (NASW 2004); the National Commission for Quality Long-Term Care's series of reports; and the National Consensus Project for Quality Palliative Care. The latter developed "Clinical Practice Guidelines for Quality Palliative Care" (2004) which articulated eight domains of quality palliative care. These domains were developed to apply across disciplines, settings of care, and age groups. The evidence upon which the domains were developed derives mainly from the nursing and medical literatures. In this book, we examine key concepts from these eight domains as they apply to how social workers can help to address psychosocial issues facing older adults in the nursing home setting. The eight domains of quality palliative care include:

1. Structure and processes of care
2. Physical aspects of care
3. Psychological and psychiatric aspects of care
4. Social aspects of care
5. Spiritual, religious, and existential aspects of care
6. Cultural aspects of care
7. Care of the imminently dying patient
8. Ethical and legal aspects of care

The book has been organized as a step toward building social work capacity in palliative psychosocial care in the nursing home setting. The underlying assumption is that social workers' effectiveness in extending the reach of palliative care in nursing homes—either through direct practice, administration, supervision, policy practice, or research—benefits from a broad overview of the issues that affect interdisciplinary nursing home practice. The first chapters build understanding in these areas. The book then turns to the situation facing residents, families, and staff as the end of life draws near and highlights ways in which nursing home social workers can apply their knowledge and skills to enhance the experience of living and dying. The book concludes with a chapter on future challenges and opportunities likely to affect the nursing home setting, with an eye toward the specific issue of psychosocial care at the end of life.

Specifically, chapter 1 (written by the editor) provides a review of key conceptual developments in understanding end-of-life and palliative care vis-à-vis the nursing home setting and provides definitions of key concepts used in the book. These concepts include the idea of dying trajectories, the palliative-care framework, an explanation of psychosocial issues, and an overview of the practice of nursing home social work. In chapter 2, the nurse-scholars Dr. Sarah Thompson (a former hospice nurse) and Lisa Church describe the relationship among structure, process, and outcome in terms of quality of care and then apply these concepts to the nursing home setting. Their chapter includes material related to quality psychosocial care. In chapter 3, Mike Klug, with a background in legal and technical writing related to Medicare, provides a brief explanation of nursing home care financing as a backdrop to explaining the Medicare hospice benefit, a program that can connect residents and families with additional resources at the end of life.

After providing a brief overview of the development of nursing homes, chapter 4 (written by the editor) provides background information on the characteristics of contemporary U.S. nursing homes and of the residents who receive care there. In chapter 5, the palliative-care physician Ann Allegre provides an explanation of medical concerns affecting many nursing home residents as the end of life draws near. Her chapter was written to be accessible to readers with little or no medical background. In chapter 6, the former nursing home social worker and current gerontological social work scholar Dr. Jean Munn describes the psychosocial needs of nursing home residents with advanced chronic illnesses and discusses social work interventions to address these concerns. The social worker's role with the family is the focus of chapter 7. It is written by Dr. Patricia Kolb, gerontological social worker and sociologist, who devotes part of this chapter to the need for cultural competence when working with families at the end of life in the nursing home setting. In chapter 8, the physician and public-health scholar Dr. Charles Gessert and the bioethics attorney Don Reynolds present an introduction to ethical issues as a backdrop to their argument that we need to reconsider the meaning of the principle of autonomy when dealing with people with advanced chronic illness. Especially when working with residents affected by cognitive impairment, they explain that taking a "best interest" approach toward end-of-life decision making can help support the family as medical interventions are considered.

Chapter 9, written by the social worker Peggy Sharr and the editor has two sections. In the first, Sharr discusses the importance of rituals and rites of passage related to the death of residents and weaves in examples of what practicing nursing home social workers report their nursing homes are doing to honor the death of residents. In the second, the editor provides information and ideas that social workers can use to help residents and families understand funeral-related options and costs in their local area. In chapter 10, the issue of bereavement among staff members, including the social worker, is addressed by the social workers Sara Sanders and Patti Anewalt. Dr. Sanders, a former hospice social worker and current gerontological scholar who works in the area of dementia, and Dr. Anewalt, grief and loss program director, build a case for prevention of burnout and compassion fatigue for nursing home staff members. The last chapter (written by the editor) looks toward the future and speculates on factors that will compete to enhance or diminish the experience of living and dying in the nursing home in the coming decades. Together, these chapters have been designed to broaden and deepen the practice of nursing home social work and to extend the reach of palliative care, especially palliative psychosocial care, to people facing advanced chronic illness in nursing homes.

Note

The author would like to thank Patrick Dolan of the University of Iowa Writing Center for his comments on a previous version of the introduction.

References

Field, M. J., and Castle, C. K. 1997. *Approaching Death: Improving Care at the End of Life*. Washington, D.C.: Institute of Medicine, National Academy Press.

National Consensus Project for Quality Palliative Care. 2004. "Clinical Practice Guidelines for Quality Palliative Care." http://www.nationalconsensusproject.org.

NASW. 2003. "NASW Standards for Social Workers in Long-Term Care Facilities." http://www.socialworkers.org/practice/standards/NASWLongTermStandards. pdf. Accessed June 2008.

NASW. 2004. "NASW Standards for Palliative and End-of-Life Care." http://www. naswdc.org/practice/bereavement/standards/default.asp. Accessed May 11, 2008.

National Commission for Quality Long-Term Care. 2007. "From Isolation to Integration: Recommendations to Improve Quality in Long-Term Care." http://www.qualitylongtermcarecommission.org/reports.html. Accessed September 10, 2008.

SWHPN. 2008. "Charting the Course for the Future of Social Work in End-of-Life and Palliative Care: A Report of the Second Social Work Summit on End-of-Life and Palliative Care." http://swhpn.org/lhp/. Accessed August 5, 2008.

Vourlekis, B., J. L. Zlotnik, and K. Simons, K. 2005. *Evaluating Social Work Services in Nursing Homes: Toward Quality Psychosocial Care and Its Measurement. A Report of the Institute for the Advancement of Social Work Research (IASWR).* Washington D.C.: IASWR.

[1]

The Need to Extend the Reach of Palliative Psychosocial Care to Nursing Home Residents with Advanced Chronic Illness

MERCEDES BERN-KLUG

More than any other setting, the nursing home is coming face to face with what it means to care for people who live long enough to die in old age. As a society, our expectations about the length of life have changed. Never before in human history could so high a percentage of people realistically expect to survive to reach old age. In fact, among babies born in the United States in 1900, about 12 percent could expect to reach age eighty; by the end of the twentieth century, over half (58 percent) of babies born could expect to live to at least age eighty (Uhlenberg 1996). But living into old age does not mean immortality. For most people, living into old age means dying within the context of advanced chronic illness.

In this book, the term "advanced old age" is not linked to a precise chronological number. Some people will experience "advanced old age" in their seventies and others in their nineties. The idea behind the use of the concept of "advanced old age," is not so much chronological age as functional age, which itself will be affected by factors such as genetic makeup, health-related behaviors, and environment. By the same token, we are not invoking a precise definition of "advanced chronic illness" but rather the sense that it occurs when an illness has progressed to the extent that functional abilities are clearly compromised and the individual likely requires the assistance of another person. Taken together, advanced chronic illness in the context of advanced old age means physical or mental frailty.

This chapter proposes that a philosophy of palliative care—with an emphasis on psychosocial needs—for *all* nursing home residents would increase both quality of care and quality of life. In order to explain the need to fully extend the reach of palliative care to nursing home residents, a review of end-of-life care is presented. First, an explanation of the ambiguity that surrounds much of contemporary dying is provided to underscore the mismatch between the current conceptualization of the dying role and the way that most older adults actually die. Scholarship about the trajectories of dying helps to illustrate the urgent need for changing our mindset from trying to decide who is "dying" to asking, "Who could benefit from palliative care?"

The confusion over the different uses of the term "palliative care" is then addressed followed by a clarification of what is meant by the phrase "psychosocial issues." The chapter concludes with an overview of the status of contemporary nursing home social work and a summary of examples of characteristics of nursing homes and social workers that provide excellent palliative care.

Neither this chapter nor this book assumes that the role of the nursing home and the role of the social worker as envisioned will occur within the context of the current distribution of resources. However, articulating a vision for an enhanced role for social workers in an enhanced setting for residents is necessary to broaden the current debate about quality of care and quality of life and to articulate that what social workers have to offer in terms of palliative care in the nursing home is desired, valuable, and quite possible.

The terms "nursing home" and "nursing facility" are used interchangeably in the literature. In this book, the term "nursing home" will be used because it is the most familiar to residents and family members. On the other hand, "nursing facility" is typically used by the federal government. According to the Code of Federal Regulations (2001)—a document that includes federal regulations written by government employees to address the spirit and letter of the laws enacted by Congress—"nursing facility" means a facility with three or more beds that routinely provides nursing-care services. The nursing facility is called a skilled nursing facility if meets the requirements for Medicare reimbursement (discussed in more detail in chapter 3). Nursing homes that meet the Medicaid qualifications are simply called nursing facilities.

Bridging the Chasm

The interaction of advanced old age and advanced chronic illness can blur the line between who is considered to be "dying" and who is not. This is an enormously important distinction, because under current regulatory expectations, nursing homes are expected to "maintain physical, mental, and psychosocial well-being of each resident" (Code of Federal Regulations 2001). If a resident's status declines, absent a documented medical reason, the nursing home may face a citation for deficient care. "Because nursing home regulations and reimbursement emphasize provision of restorative and rehabilitative care, nursing homes may be reluctant to embrace palliative care" (Miller and Mor 2006:51). In addition to the medical and legal implications of labeling nursing home residents as dying, there are also social implications. People who are considered to be dying have different social role expectations than people who are considered sick or those facing chronic illness (Parsons 1951; Field 1976; Estroff 1993; Singer, Martin, and Kelner 1999), as illustrated in table 1.1.

The three-role conceptualization presented in table 1.1 can present unique challenges in the context of advanced chronic illness and advanced old age. This confusion, based on the ambiguous role status (should this person be considered "dying" or not?) of many people in advanced old age with advanced chronic illness is apparent in today's healthcare system and in particular in America's nursing homes (Bern-Klug 2004). Because being labeled as dying is currently a dominant passage to the receipt of palliative care, in order to provide the best care, we need to either broaden our notion of who is dying or clarify that people who are ill can benefit from palliative care even if they are not dying. Actually, we should do both.

As we begin the twenty-first century, it is time to create new words to accompany the different types of dying. It would be helpful to have different words for different types of dying, for example, dying quickly (in weeks or months) from a newly diagnosed condition, dying as a phase of advanced chronic illness that may have challenged the person for years or decades, and dying as the end of old age. Indeed, McCue (1995) reminds us that it is natural to die in old age. The term "active dying" is currently used to label the

TABLE 1.1
Comparison of Social Expectations for Sick,
Chronic Illness, and Dying Roles

	SICK ROLE	CHRONIC ILLNESS ROLE	DYING ROLE
Expected duration in role	Short. Usually days or weeks until recovery. Generally reserved for episodes of acute illness.	Not expected to fully recover. Expected to have limited acute episodes which result in temporary sick role status.	Days, weeks, or months until death.
Responsibilities	Expected to want to recover and to follow expert's (generally physician or representative— such as director of nursing) advice and orders. Allocate resources to get well. Normal/usual (pre-sick) social role obligations relaxed until person recovers.	Expected to learn self-care for the management of the illness and to live with illness and reduced function. Allocate resources to postpone and if possible avoid, further decline. Development of a "new normal" social-role expectation now include adding self-care to usual social-role expectations.	Reconsider priorities. Not expected to follow physician orders or self-care routines if considered burdensome. Allocate resources to maximize comfort and minimize suffering.
How others should treat people in this role	Encourage help-seeking behavior and adherence to expert's advice.	Encourage self-care behavior.	Defer to the desires of the person who is dying.

final hours and days of life, when the person is clearly approaching death, but we also need words for the different processes that precede active dying.

In increasing numbers Americans are reaching advanced old age with advanced chronic illness but not meeting the Medicare definition of dying (see chapter 3). When there is confusion about whether a person is dying, there can be confusion about the care offered, as is illustrated in the case study which follows. The case is based on field notes from an ethnographic study:

Mrs. Anders was an eighty-eight-year-old widowed woman who loved ice cream. Her closest relative (in terms of both proximity and affection) was her seventy-nine-year-old brother, who admitted her to the nursing home ten years before enrolling in the study. Her chart documented that over the past year she had been losing weight, and when I met her, Mrs. Anders weighed less than ninety pounds. Mrs. Anders had no teeth or dentures and had little jaw control. It was difficult to understand her speech, although she could articulate key words well. She spent most of her day in her room, either lying in bed looking out the window or sitting in her wheelchair with the lights off. Many times during the study, Mrs. Anders told me she was hungry. On occasion, I ate supper in the nursing home dining room with Mrs. Anders. By doing so, I observed that she had difficulty swallowing. About half of what she put in her mouth she discretely regurgitated into her bib, unable to swallow. It was unclear whether the nursing staff assumed that the food missing from her plate was swallowed. A review of Mrs. Anders' medical record revealed that her code status was DNR. When asked about dying, she told me, "I am ready to die, but I like it here." From reading her medical chart, talking with her brother, and observing staff interactions with her, it was not clear what the overall goals of care were for her. Her brother relied on staff members to interpret her health status. He stated that a few years earlier the physician instructed staff and family to give Mrs. Anders anything she wanted to eat, with the hope of stabilizing her serious weight loss. The brother began bringing her chocolate bars during his weekly visits despite knowing she struggled with diabetes. After a few months she began to regain her appetite and her weight. The brother told me, "I [still] bring her two candy bars every time I come. They haven't told me not to."

Unbeknownst to them, the nursing staff was divided about "giving in" to Mrs. Anders's food requests. They all acted out of their sense of her best interest. One afternoon when her brother and I were visiting with Mrs. Anders, a certified nurse assistant was helping the roommate a few feet away. The CNA overheard Mrs. Anders ask her brother from some ice cream. The CNA said, "She is eating too much sweets." The brother replied that he thought that she could eat whatever she wanted, and the staff member said, "No. She won't eat her supper."

Later that day, I talked with the consulting dietician about Mrs. Anders's frequent comments about being hungry. The dietician responded, "Well, she is dying." I mentioned that she often requested ice cream and cookies and that some staff honored that request and others did not. The dietician replied, "Well, she can have whatever she wants." I mentioned that the week before, the staff refused to give her ice cream until she first drank a cup of water. The dietician replied, "That isn't right, and that doesn't make sense. She can have whatever she wants." The dietician walked into the kitchen and returned shortly stating, "I left a message that Mrs. Anders is to have ice cream with every dinner."

After a few days, the medical director added a note in Mrs. Anders's chart: "Resident may have food and fluids of choice at resident's discretion." The nurse notes for the same day indicated, "Resident wants ice cream and coffee throughout the day. Sometimes eats only ice cream. Order received for resident discretion in choice of foods and fluids secondary to comfort care."

However, off and on for the following two months, Mrs. Anders would tell me she was hungry and that she was not receiving ice cream. Some staff members were denying ice cream on account of her diabetes. Others were giving her ice cream because she was dying. At the end of the study, the kitchen staff reported they did not know that Mrs. Anders was on comfort care nor that she was to receive vanilla ice cream. She lived for a year after enrolling in the study.

(Excerpted from Bern-Klug 2009)

This case reveals problems that occurred because of incomplete and inconsistent documentation and communication of a resident's health status and her care-plan goals; it also shows that the resident's main concern went unaddressed: she was hungry. In this nursing home there were no clear instructions for how "comfort care" should be operationalized, and because the setting was not geared toward palliative care for all residents, effort was required to develop a specific plan for this one resident, which never successfully happened. Even if a nursing home develops a focus on palliative care, resident-specific care needs must be articulated, the difference being that in a palliative-centered nursing home, resident pain and suffering—including hunger—would be a vital concern from day one.

Indeed, until we improve our understanding of how most people in the United States die, and develop a healthcare system designed around contemporary dying, we can continue to expect social and medical confusion about the type and amount of care that is considered to be in a person's best interest, especially when that person is in advanced old age and is facing advanced chronic illnesses. And we can expect that opportunities to provide basic comfort to all nursing home residents, regardless of their dying status, will go unnoticed and therefore unaddressed. As Joanne Lynn stated, "society does not share the language to discuss what the end of life can mean" (Lynn 2003:1503).

The result of the chasm between assumptions about how people die and how people actually die is a lack of social consensus about what are appropriate care goals for people in advanced old age with advanced chronic conditions. As a result, each individual nursing home resident and his or her family (if available) must construct their own sense of when it is appropriate to focus the goals of care to emphasize palliation and comfort and how that will be operationalized. While flexibility in health care is usually good, without societal understanding of what appropriate care is, we are less likely to provide good palliative care. It is less likely that the healthcare options will be designed around the patient's preferences, and they may instead be designed around organizational financial incentives. Pritchard and colleagues (1998) reported regional differences in the settings in which people die (at home, in hospice, or in a hospital) and documented that these trends are more related to hospital bed availability than to individual wishes. Lynn and colleagues (2000) reported that many families are uncomfortable being part of medical decisions that appear to be outside the norm or other than what is considered to be the default, in part because of not wanting to feel guilty if the decision is perceived to have a hand in the person's death. Lynn and colleagues suggest that rather than having aggressive, cure-oriented care as the default for people with advanced chronic illness, the default out to be changed to palliative care (2000). This is a key idea for nursing homes: make palliative care the default.

Trajectories of Dying

Much of how we understand social interactions related to the process of dying builds on the scholarship of the sociologists Barney Glaser and Anselm Strauss (1965, 1967, and 1968). Using qualitative methods, they documented patterns of social interactions related to care for hospitalized patients (1965) and described the social consequences of the expectations for how long a patient was expected to live and how certain this prognosis was. In *Time for Dying* (1968), Glaser and Strauss emphasized that the process of dying takes place over time and that the trajectory toward death has a shape—it can be graphed. When Glaser and Strauss used the term "trajectories of dying," they did so in terms of dying's socially perceived course. In this schema, they identified such critical junctures as when the patient is defined as dying; when the patient, staff, and family make preparations for death; when there is a final descent toward death; and when death occurs. A central idea in their model is that in order for a hospital patient to be reacted to as dying, the patient must be defined as dying. Furthermore, staff and family would develop a sense of where in the trajectory the patient was and would react accordingly: "How a patient, a doctor, a nurse, or a family member defines a dying trajectory becomes the basis for his or her behavior in connection with treating and handling the patient" (1968:55). These ideas apply also to the nursing home setting. Residents who are recognized as dying have a better chance of being enrolled in hospice or the nursing home's version of "comfort care."

More recently, the concept of the trajectory of dying has also been used to illustrate the point that different causes of death have very different ways of moving toward death (Field and Cassel 1997; Lunney, Lynn, and Hogan, 2002). Figure 1.1 shows four trajectories of dying proposed by Lunney, Lynn, and Hogan (2002) based on analyzing Medicare claims data during the last year of life from about 8,000 people. Medicare is the health insurance program that covers older adults primarily, although disabled people under age sixty-five can also receive Medicare (see chapter 3 for more details about Medicare). Lunney and colleagues developed a schema for categorizing diseases with similar dying trajectories and then used Medicare data to estimate the percentage of recipients who died in each of the five categories (sudden death, frailty, organ failure, terminal, or other). The results have direct application for nursing home care, as explained later.

The death of 7 percent of Medicare recipients was classified as "sudden" if the person was under the age of eighty and had little evidence of health-care use during the last year of life. Then 22 percent of Medicare decedents were classified as "terminal" because of evidence of multiple insurance claims for cancer-related services during the last year of life. After death types had been allocated to those two groups, the organ-failure group was developed based on the presence of hospital in-patient claims and an emergency room claim with a discharge diagnosis of congestive heart failure or chronic obstructive pulmonary disease. Lunney and colleagues classified 16 percent of deaths as organ failure.

The largest number of people (47 percent) were classified as frail, based on not fitting into any other group and having at least one Medicare claim

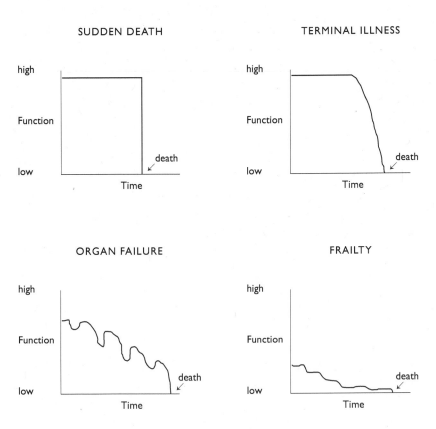

Figure 1.1   Lunney's Four Trajectories of Dying
Source: Lunney, Lynn, and Hogan (2002). Reprinted with permission.

during the last year of life associated with stroke, Alzheimer's disease, dementia, delirium, Parkinson's disease, hip fracture, incontinence, pneumonia, dehydration, syncope, or leg cellulites (Lunney, Lynn, and Hogan 2002:1109). Eight percent of the group of decedents was classified as "other" because they had diagnoses commonly billed to Medicare but not typically causing death, such as cataracts or high blood pressure.

Lunney, Lynn, and Hogan suspected that many of the people classified as frail were living in nursing homes or candidates for nursing home care based on diagnoses that suggested the need for twenty-four-hour care and help with daily living activities. They underscore that there are important differences in the end-of-life-care needs that a person will have, based on the trajectory of dying: "We must develop concepts and language for the end of life for frail people that will enhance supportive services and advance planning without diminishing the focus on active and productive living in old age. Living and dying occupy the same period, and ignoring one will not enhance the other" (Lunney, Lynn, and Hogan 2002:1112). Identifying the different trajectories of dying among older adults, based on health conditions, is an important step toward recognizing the futility of the one-size-fits-all approach to end-of-life care. But it doesn't address the issue of knowing at what point in the dying trajectory a nursing home resident's care plan should emphasize palliative care.

Field and Castle (1997) explain that people dying with fairly long periods of chronic illness punctuated by medical crises may encounter death during one of the many possible crises, although it is difficult to accurately predict which. Furthermore, it is possible that an entirely different medical problem may intervene to cause the death. People who are considered frail may be functionally "holding their own" but have limited reserve to face the flu or an injury such as a broken hip: "a relatively minor event can precipitate a catastrophic cascade of complications that lead to death" (1997:52).

Engle (1998) proposed that all permanently placed nursing home residents receive "hospice-type" services which would include the following five elements: remaining in the nursing home for death (avoiding hospitalization); adequate pain and symptom control; having spiritual and religious needs met; receipt of palliative rather than aggressive care; and withdrawal of food and fluid if this is requested by the person who is dying (1998:1172). Engle based this proposal, in part, on her research with small groups of terminally ill nursing home residents and on E. M. Pattison's (1977) model of the living-dying interval.

Figure 1.2 shows Pattison's living-dying model. He makes the point that until a person has a serious accident or receives a diagnosis for a serious disease, the person's sense of his or her own death is of something that will happen some unknown time in the future; that is, death is theoretical. With the "crisis knowledge of death" from the accident or illness, mortality is no longer theoretical, and the person becomes aware that time is limited. Pattison labels the interval of time between the crisis knowledge of death and the actual death as the "living-dying interval." The living-dying interval has three phases: the acute crisis phase, the chronic living-dying phase, and the terminal phase, which commences when the person begins to withdraw, "perhaps as a means of conserving energy" (1977:55). This model was not developed for nursing home residents, but as Engle points out, it can help guide thinking about care-plan goals. The model would apply well to nursing home residents who are no longer interested in or suited for cure-oriented care. However, some nursing home residents want to continue receiving curative care, also known as life-prolonging treatments. Being "permanently placed" in a nursing home is not synonymous with no longer benefiting from aggressive or life-prolonging care, which may continue to provide benefit and value to some people. Therefore, simply having a serious diagnosis and being in a nursing home does not mean that a resident is willing to cease receiving life-prolonging care. It is important that nursing home residents retain access to the type of care that will help them achieve their health-related goals; this care may consist of a combination of palliative and curative care.

As useful as trajectories of dying are for understanding the experience of a group of people with organ failure or frailty (the two most common trajectories for nursing home residents), they are not helpful in estimating

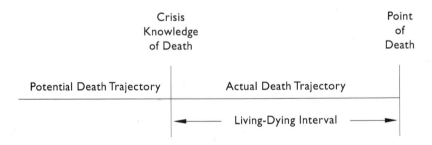

Figure 1.2   Pattison's Living-Dying Model
Source: Pattison (1977). Reprinted with permission.

the time of death for a specific individual. This is because it is not clear where on the trajectory a particular person is at a given point in time. Currently, one of the conditions for invoking hospice care (and in many nursing homes palliative care or comfort care) is that death is expected soon. In fact, the general use of the term "dying" means that there is a sense that the person will be dead soon. Most people aren't considered to be "dying" for years. Indeed currently there are social challenges related to remaining in the role of dying for "too long."

If one of the main eligibility criteria for starting hospice care is that the person has less than six months to live, and it is not easy to estimate the timing of death for a particular older adult with advanced organ failure or frailty, it is no wonder that more nursing home residents are not enrolled in hospice. It is no wonder that most nursing homes do not currently consider their main role as that of providing palliative care. The nursing home population—especially those who are "permanently placed," meaning they are not there primarily for posthospital rehabilitation—are people who are at increased risk of dying, but at a highly uncertain time. Nursing home residents with advanced organ failure or frailty are at high risk of not waking up tomorrow, yet it is entirely possible that they may be alive a year from now. Under our current use of the term, we don't usually call that "dying." Our current conceptualization of dying is not a good match for the way most nursing home residents will die, and because being recognized as dying is a common way to be seen as a candidate for hospice care, or "comfort care," most older adult nursing home residents will never experience the nursing home setting as a palliative-care setting, although most will die as nursing home residents.

We need a better way for people with advanced chronic illnesses to access palliative care, a way that does not depend upon their being labeled as "dying." Until this broader understanding of appropriate candidates for palliative care is embraced, many nursing home residents will die without their physical and emotional comfort ever being a priority. Some will die in the process of receiving aggressive life-prolonging care because they were not considered to be dying. For nursing home residents with advanced organ failure or advanced frailty, the receipt of many types of life-prolonging interventions would likely have limited effect on how long they live and could cause pain and suffering. In fact, the receipt of life-prolonging care has been shown to reduce the length of life for some residents (Connor et al. 2007) and may deprive a resident of a peaceful death.

All doors to death are not equal. Some methods of dying include more pain and suffering than others. A comfort-centered nursing home would accept that death is the end of advanced chronic illness and of old age. Death would not be sought, but neither would it be shunned. In the event that the opportunity for a peaceful doorway to death presents itself—maybe through an infection, or pneumonia, or the cessation of a beating heart—the resident, family, and staff would be prepared to consider accepting that doorway to death, with the hopes of sparing the person, who has been confirmed to be at high risk of death, a more painful death later. This is a radical concept in many healthcare settings, although the idea has been around for a long time. It is radical, in part, because people don't like the idea of being dead, and they really don't like the idea of people they love dying.

In order to accept the "peaceful doorway to death" approach, a person, a nursing home, or a society would have to accept that and behave as though people are mortal. For those who do accept that we are mortal, the thought of having anything to do with the timing of death can be extremely uncomfortable; a common refrain from family members is, "It's not my place." By way of example, focus groups of family members with a loved one in a nursing home with dementia confided that they could accept death if their loved one died in her sleep or had a heart attack, but they would struggle mightily with feelings of guilt and a sense of letting their loved one down if they were involved in making a decision that could in any way be perceived as related to the timing of their loved one's death (Gessert, Forbes, and Bern-Klug 2000). Another example comes from an ethnographic study that took place in two nursing homes. The wife of an elderly man with advanced kidney disease, who continued to receive dialysis despite the burden on him, wrestled with not wanting him to feel he had to continue with dialysis and not wanting to be in any way implicated if she encouraged him to stop dialysis and he died. She said: "I don't want him to suffer. I am not going to be one to stop dialysis. I can't make that decision. That is up to the Lord to call him home, not me" (Bern-Klug 2008a:41).

When family members are asked to help make medical decisions for nursing home residents who are approaching death, who helps them cope with the emotional ramifications of these decisions? Who helps to frame the "decisions" in such a way that family members realize that no matter what they decide, their loved one is still at a high risk of death? (This issue is presented and developed by Gessert and Reynolds in chapter 8.) More effort is needed to communicate the markers of advanced illness to residents and family members so that peaceful doorways to death can be anticipated and, if desired, accepted. How would our nursing home practice look if one of its goals was ensuring that families could look back on the experience of their loved ones' time in a nursing home with the peace of mind that comes from knowing that a painful, arduous death was spared them and that death came, as Fr. Fahey says of his mother's death in this book's foreword, "not one day too soon, nor one day too late."

Therefore, as part of understanding a resident's advanced-chronic-illness status and prognosis, physicians should be having conversations with residents and families about the likelihood of various doorways to death presenting themselves and should be helping people think through what sort of a doorway would be preferred, acceptable, or—on the other hand—worth working to avoid. If a nursing home resident (or any other person, regardless of setting) with advanced organ failure or advanced frailty develops a risk for a painful or arduous death, we should work to avoid that death experience, even if life prolongation is not this person's overarching healthcare goal. Sparing this person a painful death is of value.

What Is Palliative Care?

Palliative care is a philosophy of care that addresses the physical, mental, and emotional comfort of a person who is experiencing an illness. The goal of palliative care is the best possible quality of life. The term "palliative care" is currently used in two ways in the literature, one of which is limited to people who are considered to be dying. The other use is much broader and holds that the provision of palliative care is appropriate *throughout* the illness trajectory. In this book, as in the "Clinical Indicators for Quality Palliative Care" report (explained below), this broader concept of palliative care prevails. This book's main premise is that this broader definition of palliative care is an excellent model for the care that should be available to all nursing home residents.

It is important to distinguish the concept of "palliative care" from the concepts of "hospice" and "comfort care." Palliative care is the umbrella term. Hospice is one of the ways that palliative care can be provided to people who are considered to be at the end of life. In the United States, because of Medicare rules, hospice care is generally reserved for people who are considered to be terminally ill and approaching death (chapter 3 provides details about Medicare hospice eligibility). Furthermore, there is no consensus on how the term "comfort care" is used in nursing homes. One use of the term can be on the medical charts of nursing home residents who are candidates for hospice care, but are not enrolled in hospice, and yet want the nursing home staff to provide care that is focused on relieving pain and suffering. (Nursing home administrators should be sure to define how they want their staff members to use the terms "palliative care" and "comfort care" so as not to confuse residents and family members.)

The National Consensus Project for Quality Palliative Care (2004) reports that the target population for palliative care includes people of all ages with a life-threatening or debilitating illness, which is defined as a persistent or recurring condition that adversely affects daily functioning or will predictably reduce life expectancy, including the following groups of people, and their family:

- Children and adults with congenital injuries or conditions leading to dependence on life-sustaining treatments and/or long-term care by others for support of the activities of daily living
- People of any age with acute, serious, and life-threatening illnesses (such as severe trauma, leukemia, or acute stroke), where cure or reversibility is a realistic goal but the conditions themselves and their treatments pose significant burdens
- People living with progressive chronic conditions (such as peripheral vascular disease, malignancies, chronic renal or liver failure, stroke with significant functional impairment, advanced heart or lung disease, frailty, neurodegenerative disorders, and dementia)
- People living with chronic and life-limiting injuries from accidents or other forms of trauma
- Seriously and terminally ill patients (such as persons living with end-stage dementia, terminal cancer, or severe disabling stroke), who are unlikely to recover or stabilize, and for whom intensive palliative care is the predominant focus and goal of care for the time remaining

(Source: Adapted from National Consensus Project for
Quality Palliative Care 2004*)*

The need to improve palliative care in nursing homes and other non-hospice settings is based in part on common shortcomings in terminal care that are summarized by Conant and Lowney (1996:367) and include:

1. Inadequate physical-symptom control
2. Undiagnosed depression or anxiety
3. Unaddressed existential issues
4. Untreated psychological distress in family members
5. Untreated family fatigue
6. Lack of skill in effective communication, especially where cultural differences exist
7. Unrecognized professional healthcare provider fatigue or moral distress

Figure 1.3 illustrates how palliative care fits in with life-prolonging care. It shows palliative care being provided throughout the illness, not just at the end of life. The Medicare hospice benefit can come into play when death is expected within six months. Most nursing home residents have lived with chronic illnesses for many years before they moved to a nursing home. If we see the admission to the nursing home as somewhere in the middle of the figure, it becomes clear that palliative care is appropriate throughout the nursing home stay. In figure 1.3, the ratio of life-prolonging interventions and palliative care changes over time, yet both are available throughout the illness experience until the Medicare hospice benefit is invoked. If the palliative-care needs of nursing home residents are fully addressed throughout their stay, there is no need to "shift" to a palliative-

PALLIATIVE CARE'S PLACE IN THE COURSE OF ILLNESS

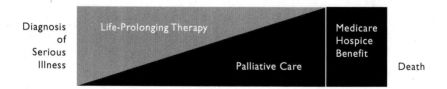

Figure 1.3 Palliative Care's Place in the Course of Illness
Source: National Consensus Project for Quality Palliative Care (2004:3).

care model toward the end of life. Instead, there would be continuity of palliative care in the face of diminished life-prolonging care. The nursing home staff would build expertise in meeting all residents' palliative-care needs throughout the nursing home stay, and the resident and family would learn that the staff can be trusted to meet the comfort-care needs of the resident.

This model of care would be appropriate for all nursing home residents because those who wish to pursue aggressive life-prolonging interventions would be supported in doing so without being required to "give up" palliative care, and vice versa. At the point that Medicare hospice is invoked, under current Medicare rules, the physician is asked to document that if the disease runs its normal course, the nursing home resident is expected to have six months or less to live. (Note that Medicare hospice does allow life-prolonging care for conditions not related to the reason that hospice was invoked.) Attention to the bereavement needs of people who are emotionally connected to the person who has died is an important aspect of palliative care.

Psychosocial Issues

Psychosocial considerations are at the heart of what it means to be a functioning human. Psychosocial issues include thoughts and feelings about one's sense of self, one's worth, and connections to people and things loved, longed-for, feared, or despised. Psychosocial issues include anxiety and depression. Spiritual issues are related to ideas and feelings of being connected to something bigger than oneself, the meaning and purpose of life, ideas about how we should treat one another, and what we can expect from our maker. In some constructs spiritual issues are incorporated into psychosocial issues, and in other constructs, the term "psychosocial spiritual" is used. Psychosocial services address psychological, social, and environmental stressors in order to enhance mental, social, and emotional well-being to promote quality of life (Bowen and Zimmerman 2009).

In his article about the psychosocial experience of dementia, Kitwood (1997) outlines domains of negative feelings that include abandonment, humiliation, a sense of being controlled or persecuted or imprisoned, frustration, sadness, anger, and bewilderment. He also discusses the psychosocial needs of people with dementia in terms of the need for attachment, comfort, identity, occupation, inclusion, and love (1997:18–19). Regardless of dementia status, people share these psychosocial needs. In the context of the nursing home, residents can be at high risk of having unmet psychosocial needs from a lack of opportunity or ability to have meaningful social interactions with others and because they are coming to terms with physical and mental changes that can accompany advanced chronic illness.

This chapter calls for a broader understanding of psychosocial issues facing nursing home residents. To fully acknowledge psychosocial issues in the nursing home means understanding that declining health and function, as well as pain, have serious psychosocial implications. This requires that social workers, and all staff, accept that medical and nursing conditions can have psychosocial consequences.

The long-term care literature, in particular the nursing home literature, is filled with documentation of the need for medical and nursing attention to address or prevent common conditions that affect people in advanced organ failure and frailty, such as incontinence, skin wounds, and malnutrition. These and other health conditions are usually framed as physical-health conditions, which, indeed they are, and yet so much more. Each of the conditions mentioned has serious psychosocial implications for the resident, and sometimes for the family. There are emotional consequences when an adult can no longer independently void in a toilet and is expected to assume that it is normal to lie in feces until staff members have time to answer the call light. There are emotional implications from being hungry or thirsty, as well as from being forced to eat when one would rather not. Bed sores and other wounds affect a person's psychosocial well-being as well as his or her health. A deep bed sore results in physical pain and can also result in anxiety, worry, and shame that the smell of the rotting flesh may be offensive to a roommate or to a grandchild. Good psychosocial care anticipates the emotional consequences of physical decline and decay and works to minimize the negative psychosocial consequences of advanced chronic illness and dying.

Because emotional issues can be antecedents to or consequences of declines in health or functional status, nursing home social workers must work with the nursing, activities, and medical staff members to address the suffering that can accompany the pain. As palliative care is also comfort care, there is enormous potential for social workers to transform the way in which health conditions are framed so that their consequences are measured not only in terms of fractures of the bone but also fractures of the heart, not only as wounds on the skin but also wounds on the soul.

The Current Status of Nursing Home Social Work

There is an enormous gulf between what the social work profession expects of nursing home social workers and what the federal government allows. The National Association of Social Workers has three documents that speak directly to the role of the nursing home social worker and palliative care: the "NASW Standards for Social Work Services in Long-Term Care," "NASW Clinical Indicators for Social Work and Psychosocial Services in Nursing Homes," and "NASW Standards for Palliative and End-of-Life Care" (all documents are available at http://www.socialworkers.org/practice/default. asp). In these documents the definition of a social worker is a person who has an undergraduate degree in social work—a BSW or BASW—from a social work program accredited by the Council on Social Work Education. For nursing home practice, the standards call for the BSW and two years of long-term care experience. According to the NASW, the social work director is viewed as an employed staff member (not a consultant) responsible for the social work program in the nursing home, and preferably has a master's degree in social work (an MSW).

Social work educational programs around the country have been actively enhancing the educational preparedness of social work students in the area of aging. Many of these initiatives have been supported through the John A. Hartford Foundation. For example, the Council on Social Work Education has been instrumental in disseminating competencies in the area of gerontological social work to be used to guide curriculum development in schools of social work. The list includes thirty-nine competencies in the areas of values, ethics, and theoretical perspectives; assessment; intervention; and aging services, programs, and policies. These competencies help to form the learning objectives for BSW and first year MSW students and are part of an effort to ensure that social work students have learned about aging issues. See http://depts.washington.edu/geroctr/Curriculum3/sub3_3_1Competencies.html.

The federal government does not require nursing homes to employ a social worker unless the nursing home has more than 120 beds (Code of Federal Regulations 2001). About two-thirds of the nursing homes in the United States have 120 or fewer beds. In a review of state administrative codes of requirements for nursing home social workers, it was determined that most state administrative codes did not exceed the federal requirements (Bern-Klug 2008b). Therefore, according to state and federal regulations, nursing homes with fewer than 121 beds need not employ a social worker, and those with more than 120 beds are required to hire one full-time qualified social worker. According to the federal government, people without a degree in social work can be considered qualified nursing home social workers, as long as they have a college degree in a related field (Code of Federal Regulations 2001). Note that the federal government does require a social work degree to be considered a qualified social worker in the following health settings: all V.A. nursing homes, home health agencies, hospice agencies, end-stage renal disease care centers, and intermediate-care facilities for people with mental retardation (Bern-Klug 2008b).

Even though nursing homes can be certified to receive Medicare and Medicaid payments without being required to hire a social worker with a degree in social work, a recent nationally representative survey found that about half of certified nursing homes do have a social work director who holds a degree in social work. The survey also found that 20 percent of U.S. nursing home social-services departments are headed by someone without a college degree in any field (Bern-Klug et al. 2009). In this nationally representative study, over half of the social service directors were the only members of the social-services department in the facility.

This discussion of the educational background of social services directors is provided as a backdrop to what nursing homes are held responsible for in terms of resident psychosocial needs. The federal government holds all certified nursing homes responsible for meeting the psychosocial needs of all residents, regardless of the number of beds in the nursing home. Nursing homes with 120 or fewer beds that do not employ a social worker can contract with a local agency for social services or hire a social worker under contract to provide services.

There is a small but growing list of resources to help nursing home social workers understand what the social work role with residents and families can be (Beaulieu 2002; Gleason-Wynn and Fonville 1993; Brody 1974). The NASW has developed and published nursing home social work clinical indicators: http://www.socialworkers.org/practice/standards/nursing_homes.asp.

In the State Operations Manual which helps guide nursing home surveyors, there is a section on the role of the social-services staff (reprinted in the appendix). There are also end-of-life resources available, including a book geared toward social workers, *Teaching Resources for End-of-Life and Palliative Care* (Csikai and Jones 2007) and another geared toward nursing home staff, *Improving Nursing Home Care of the Dying: A Training Manual for Nursing Home Staff* (Henderson, Hanson and Reynolds 2003), and numerous committee reports with important information about palliative care (see the introduction). All this is to say that although there is renewed interest in transforming nursing homes into settings that attend to quality of care and quality of life, the social worker may need to examine how his or her role could better accommodate the palliative-care needs of residents and family members.

The following chapters provide examples and ideas of what nursing home palliative psychosocial care can entail. However, it is unrealistic to expect that social workers will be able to provide excellent psychosocial care until there is a reasonable resident-to-social worker ratio, a reorganization of social work job priorities, a culture of valuing palliative care and psychosocial care, and a custom of hiring and retaining well-qualified, highly motivated staff, including social-services staff, nursing staff, and activities staff, who together provide the bulk of psychosocial care. There is much work to do in the setting for people who are committed to social services but do not yet have the background to excel in directing the department; they are valuable staff members. They deserve the education, support, and supervision to exceed in the role. Nursing home trade organizations, state offices on aging, and social work educational programs should be developing and offering training support to both social workers and others working in social-service departments. These social workers and social-service staff members are the building blocks of the provision of psychosocial care for people in advanced old age with advanced chronic illness.

It is obvious that nursing homes are settings with people who are facing depression, dementia, advanced chronic illness, and other physical and social challenges, yet we must remind ourselves that nursing homes can also be settings where older adults thrive, despite frail health. Thriving can happen as residents are incorporated into a community that exists to enhance their quality of care and quality of life. We must not allow the physical care of residents to completely dominate the setting because, after all, it is a home. The following lists provide examples of ways in which attention to comfort care and palliative issues can be demonstrated in nursing homes and in particular in the role of the nursing home social worker. I offer these lists as illustrative rather than exhaustive resources.

The nursing home as a palliative care setting:

- Residents are supported in living as fully as possible.
- The setting and staffing are designed to uphold high medical, nursing, and psychosocial standards geared toward quality of life.
- Resident's reports of pain will be honored and addressed. Residents will receive excellent pain prevention and pain alleviation care. Risks for pain will be anticipated and addressed. Pain treatment will be evaluated on an on-going basis. All staff have responsibility to notice and report pain.
- Resident's reports of suffering will be honored and addressed. Risks for psychosocial suffering will be anticipated and addressed. Treatment will be evaluated on an ongoing basis.
- Palliative care is understood to include excellent and timely care regarding incontinence, which is a human-dignity issue as well as a health concern.
- Palliative care is understood to include excellent and timely care regarding repositioning, which is a human-dignity issue as well as a health concern.
- Palliative care includes connecting people to things, ideas, and people they value and fostering resident and family meaning making.
- Dying is accepted as the end of old age.
- Dying is accepted as the last phase of advanced chronic illness.
- A peaceful death is valued.
- Palliative-centered nursing homes welcome the larger community in creating and maintaining an excellent experience for residents and families.

Palliative care and the nursing home social worker's role:

- Social workers are well prepared educationally and experientially to work with residents (including those with dementia) and their family members.
- Social workers have access to clinical supervision.
- Social workers help to gauge the extent to which the nursing home social environment is supportive of quality of life for residents,

family, and staff and are empowered to exercise leadership to enhance the setting, as appropriate, according to the needs and desires of residents, family, and staff.

- Social workers are part of a team that anticipates and addresses family members' concerns and then evaluates interventions for effectiveness.
- Social workers are part of a team that anticipates and addresses resident psychosocial concerns—including those related to declining health status—and evaluates interventions for effectiveness.
- Social workers connect residents and family members with community resources and assist residents in moving out of the nursing home if that is their wish.
- Social workers are able and willing to train fellow staff members in recognizing and addressing resident and family psychosocial challenges.
- Social workers are an active part of extending the reach of palliative-care principles and resident rights to all residents.
- Social workers identify and honor their own psychosocial needs.
- Social workers have the skills and willingness to advocate for improved palliative care at the individual, facility, community, and public-policy levels.

References

Beaulieu, E. M. 2002. *A Guide for Nursing Home Social Workers*. New York: Springer.

Bern-Klug, M. 2004. "The Ambiguous Dying Syndrome." *Health and Social Work* 29 (1): 55–65.

Bern-Klug, M. 2008a. "The Emotional Context Facing Nursing Home Residents' Families: A Call for Role Reinforcement Strategies from Nursing Homes and the Community." *Journal of the American Medical Directors Association* 9:36–44.

Bern-Klug, M. 2008b. "State Variations in Nursing Home Social Worker Qualifications." *Journal of Gerontological Social Work* 51 (3–4): 379–409.

Bern-Klug, M. 2009. "A Framework for Categorizing Social Interactions Related to End-of-Life Care in Nursing Homes." *Gerontologist* 49 (4): 495–507.

Bern-Klug, M., K. W. O. Kramer, G. Chan, R. Kane, L. Dorfman, and J. Saunders. 2009. "Characteristics of Nursing Home Social Services Directors: How Common Is a Degree in Social Work?" *Journal of the American Medical Directors Association* 10 (1): 36–44.

Bowen, S. E., and S. Zimmerman. 2009. "Understanding and Improving Psycho-social Services in Long-Term Care." *Health Care Financing Review* 30 (2): 1–4.

Brody, E. M. 1974. *A Social Work Guide for Long-Term Care Facilities.* Rockville, Md.: NIMH.

Csikai, E. L., and B. Jones. 2007. *Teaching Resources for End-of-Life and Palliative Care Courses.* Chicago: Lyceum Books.

Code of Federal Regulations. 2001. 42 CFR-Public Health, Section 483.1. Office of the Federal Register. National Archives and Records Administration: U.S. Washington D.C.: U.S. Government Printing Office.

Conant, L., and A. Lowney. 1996. "The Role of Hospice Philosophy of Care in Non-hopsice Settings." *Journal of Law, Medicine, and Ethics* 24:365–68.

Connor, S. R., B. Pyenson, K. Fitch, C. Spence, and K. Iwasaki. 2007. "Comparing Hospice and Nonhospice Patient Survival Among Patients Who Die Within a Three-Year Window." *Journal of Pain Symptom Management* 33 (3): 238–46.

Engle, V. F. 1998. "Care of the Living, Care of the Dying: Reconceptualizing Nursing Home Care." *Journal of the American Geriatrics Society* 46:1172–74.

Estroff, S.E. 1993. "Identity, Disability, and Schizophrenia." In *Knowledge, Power, and Practice: The Anthropology of Medicine and Everyday Life*, ed. S. Lindenbaum and M. Lock, 247–86. Berkeley: University of California Press.

Field, D. 1976. "The Social Definition of Illness." In *An Introduction to Medical Sociology*, ed. D. Tuckett, 334–66. London: Tavistock.

Field, M. J., and C. K. Cassel. 1997. *Approaching Death: Improving Care at the End of Life.* Institute of Medicine. Washington, D.C.: National Academy Press.

Gessert, C. E., S. A. Forbes, and M. Bern-Klug. 2000/2001. "Planning End-of-Life Care for Patients with Dementia: Roles of Families and Health Professionals." *Omega: Journal of Death and Dying* 42 (4): 273–91.

Glaser, B. G., and A. L. Strauss. 1965. *Awareness in Dying.* Chicago: Aldine.

Glaser, B. G., and A. L. Strauss. 1967. *Discovery of Grounded Theory.* Chicago: Aldine.

Glaser B. G., and A. L. Strauss. 1968. *Time for Dying.* Chicago: Aldine

Gleason-Wynn, P., and K. Fonville. 1993. *Social Work Practice in the Nursing Home Setting: A Primer for Social Workers.* LaGrange, Tex.: M and H Publishing.

Henderson, M. L., L. C. Hanson, and K. S. Reynolds. 2003. *Improving Nursing Home Care of the Dying: A Training Manual for Nursing Home Staff.* New York: Springer.

Kitwood, T. 1997. "The Experience of Dementia." *Aging and Mental Health* 1 (1): 13–22.

Lunney, J. R., J. Lynn, and C. Hogan. 2002. "Profiles of Older Medicare Decedents." *Journal of the American Geriatrics Society* 50:1108–12.

Lynn, J. 2003. "Regulating Hearts and Minds: The Mismatch of Law, Custom, and Resuscitation Orders." *Journal of the American Geriatrics Society* 51:1502–3.

Lynn, J., H. R. Arkes, M. Stevens, F. Cohn, B. Koenig, E. Fox, N. V. Dawson, R. Phillips, M. B. Hamel, and J. Tsevat. 2000. "Rethinking Fundamental Assumptions: SUPPORT's Implications for Future Reform." *Journal of the American Geriatrics Society* 48:S214–21.

McCue, J. D. 1995. "The Naturalness of Dying." *Journal of the American Medical Association* 273:1039–43.

Miller, E. A., and V. Mor. 2006. "Out of the Shadows: Envisioning a Brighter Future for Long-Term Care in America." A Brown University report for the National Commission for Quality Long-Term Care. http://www.chcr.brown.edu/PDFS/ BROWN_UNIVERSITY_LTC_REPORT_FINAL.pdf. Accessed July 17, 2008.

National Consensus Project for Quality Palliative Care. 2004. "Clinical Practice Guidelines for Quality Palliative Care." http://www.nationalconsensusproject. org. Accessed June 2008.

Parsons, T. 1951. *The Social System.* Glencoe, Ill.: The Free Press.

Pattison, E. M. 1977. *The Experience of Dying.* Englewood Cliffs, N.J.: Prentice Hall.

Pritchard, R. S., E. S. Fisher, J. M. Teno, S. M. Sharp, D. J. Reding, W. A. Knaus, J. E. Wennberg, and J. Lynn. 1998. "Influence of Patient Preferences and Local Health System Characteristics on the Place of Death. SUPPORT Investigators. Study to Understand Prognoses and Preferences for Risks and Outcomes of Treatment." *Journal of the American Geriatrics Society* 46 (10): 1242–50.

Singer, P. A., D. K. Martin, and M. Kelner. 1999. "Quality End-of-Life Care: Patient's Perspective." *Journal of the American Medical Association* 281 (2): 163–68.

Uhlenberg, P. 1996. "Mortality Decline in the Twentieth Century and Supply of Kin Over the Life Course." *Gerontologist* 36 (5): 681–85.

The Structure and Process of Advanced Chronic Illness and Palliative Care in Nursing Homes

SARAH THOMPSON AND LISA CHURCH

Many Americans express a preference for dying at home, yet 73 percent of Americans die in medical institutions, with 23 percent of these individuals dying in nursing homes (Teno 2004). Nursing homes are increasingly the site of death for older adults in the United States (Brandt et al. 2005; Johnson et al. 2005; Teno 2004). From 1989 to 2001, the rate of deaths in nursing homes increased from 17.7 percent to 23.7 percent nationally (Teno 2004). By 2010, the oldest of the baby boomers will reach age sixty-five, and by 2030 the old will outnumber the young (U.S. Department of HHS 2000). The number of Americans over the age of sixty-five grew from 3 million to 35 million during the twentieth century and is predicted to explode by the year 2050 to 87 million (Federal Interagency Forum 2006). The proportion of older adults who die in nursing homes is expected to increase to 40 percent by 2040 (Brock and Foley 1998). Furthermore, nursing homes are caring for residents who are older and have more complex illnesses, more physical and cognitive disabilities, and increased care needs (Forbes-Thompson, Leiker, and Bleich 2007; Weitzen et al. 2003).

There have been long-standing concerns about the quality of care and quality of life in nursing homes (Institute of Medicine 1986). Even though some aspects of care have improved in nursing homes, such as the decreased use of physical restraints and psychotropic medications (such as antidepressants or antianxiety drugs), serious problems persist, especially for those residents at the end of their lives. A growing body of empirical evidence portrays end-of-life care for those in nursing homes as problematic (Forbes 2001; Forbes-Thompson and Gessert 2005; Hanson 2003; Hanson and Henderson 2000; Kayser-Jones 2002; Kayser-Jones et al. 2003; Oliver, Porock, and Zweig 2004; Teno, Clarridge, et al., 2004). Problems include the failure to identify residents who are at the end of their lives, management of pain and other end-of-life symptoms, underutilization of hospice care, inappropriate hospitalizations, inadequate communication, and family members' dissatisfaction with care. As recently as 2004, a systematic review of empirical research related to end-of-life care in nursing homes did not reveal one peer-reviewed study that reported positive outcomes for residents (Oliver, Porock, and Zweig 2004). In addition, the Institute of Medicine's 1997 report recommends that organizational structures in the U.S. healthcare system, including nursing homes, direct more explicit and open attention to the manner of dying in nursing homes and improve care delivery to dying residents.

In this chapter, we review a traditional nursing home approach to care and contrast that with an approach that integrates palliative care. These approaches will be explored using Donabedian's structure, process, and outcomes (SPO) conceptual model as an organizing framework (Donabedian 1966, 1969). The traditional nursing home approach to care contains many obstacles to good end-of-life care. Understanding these obstacles will offer greater insight into the advantages of a palliative approach to care. Finally, the role of the social worker will be discussed as an essential element in delivering palliative care and improving end-of-life care for nursing home residents.

Conceptual Framework:
Nursing Home Structure, Process, and Outcomes

Donabedian (1966, 1969) suggests that to evaluate an organization's quality, in this instance nursing home care, one must examine the structures, processes, and outcomes of care. Structural components are attributes of the healthcare setting, including physical facilities, physical resources, and human resources. Examples of nursing home structural attributes include size, ownership, payment status, mission statements, and policies and procedures. Staffing characteristics, such as staff-to-resident ratios and staff skill mix, are considered structural attributes as well.

Process refers to the actions that are done to and for the residents by practitioners (e.g., resident-care activities). Process includes the hands-on care provided by staff, as well as communications and interactions related to assessing, planning, and delivering care. Processes can be interpreted as clinical (bathing a resident, assessing a resident for depression, or feeding a resident) or nonclinical (staff-to-staff communication regarding resident needs). These are all activities that have the potential to influence the quality of care a resident receives (Unruh and Wan 2004; Wan, Zhang, and Unruh 2007).

Outcomes are the end result of care in terms of the resident's health status. Outcomes represent the interaction of structure and process factors. Examples include residents' physical functioning, continence, skin condition, and satisfaction with care (Unruh and Wan 2004; Wan, Zhang, and Unruh 2007). Factors other than the care provided to residents can affect health outcomes, such as the types and extent of residents' chronic illnesses and their ages. Traditionally, Donabedian's structure, process, and outcomes framework has been interpreted as linear. Unruh and Wan (2004) suggest that the relationship among these factors is more interactive and nonlinear than previously studied.

Resident characteristics (e.g., acuity, age) interact with organizational structures and processes, thereby influencing outcomes of care. Typically, there are three types of elders who are admitted to nursing homes. First, there are those who are receiving short-term rehabilitation after an acute hospital stay and are expected to be discharged home. Second, there are those residents who are admitted when terminally ill and who die within a few days or weeks. Frequently, these residents have exceeded their ability or their family's ability to remain at home. The final category includes those residents who are chronically ill and will live the remainder of their lives in the nursing home (Fahey et al. 2003; Forbes 2001; IOM 1986). Residents who are permanently placed in nursing home settings will eventually die there or in the hospital. Permanently placed residents live in nursing homes for weeks, months, or, in some cases, years before they die.

Traditional Model of Nursing Home Delivery

Although there is no "one-size-fits-all" nursing home, the word "traditional" is used in this context to imply a common set of organizational characteristics that can be found across many nursing home settings. Nursing home organizational characteristics are influenced by the regulatory environment in which they operate. Thus, an overview of the regulatory environment is provided first, followed by an overview of common nursing home organizational characteristics.

Regulatory Environment

In 1986, a groundbreaking report by the Institute of Medicine charged that general nursing home care in the United States was "shockingly deficient" (IOM 1986). The investigations of this landmark study found abuse and neglect of residents resulting in premature death, increased disability, permanent injury, and increased fear and suffering on the part of nursing home residents. Subsequently, the impact of these findings, along with the efforts of consumer advocacy groups, led Congress to enact the 1987 Omnibus Reconciliation Act.

OBRA basically redefined nursing home care from a "warehousing," custodial model to one of skilled, licensed, rehabilitative care. By the provisions of OBRA, all nursing home facilities receiving federal funds must accent physical and mental well-being under direct care of "around-the-clock," credentialed nursing staff, for all residents. With this change, nursing homes have been required to have a registered nurse on site eight consecutive hours per day and licensed nurse (either registered or licensed practical nurse) coverage for twenty-four hours per day.

Furthermore, comprehensive assessments are mandated for all residents of nursing homes at regular intervals and at times of significant physical or mental changes (Hawes et al. 1997). The resident assessment is referred to as the "MDS" (Minimum Data Set). It is a comprehensive assessment that includes more than 500 items reflecting physical and mental needs such as disease symptoms, prevalence of events such as falls or pressure sores, bowel and bladder continence, and behavior problems. The MDS is not only a practical, functional tool for resident care but also a guided measurement used to generate "quality indicators." Quality indicators are data used by nursing home facilities for resident care planning and quality-improvement initiatives and by state surveyors to examine potential problem areas and trends in nursing home performance. Quality indicators include eleven care domains, including, for example, accidents, clinical management, infection control, nutrition and eating, and physical functioning (Zimmerman et al. 1995). Moreover, since the implementation of OBRA, additional improvements have occurred. The survey and regulatory enforcement were strengthened, and a prospective reimbursement system was designed to meet the varying needs of multi-leveled-acuity residents. The regulatory charge to provide rehabilitative care and stronger survey and enforcement processes have focused attention on the maintenance and promotion of the well-being of residents, primarily physical, often at the expense of quality end-of-life care. While the change in emphasis from custodial to rehabilitative care has improved outcomes for many nursing home residents, it leaves the most vulnerable nursing home residents, those approaching death, either neglected or receiving inappropriate, aggressive, rehabilitative care (Forbes 2001; Miller, Teno, and Mor 2004). Nursing home reforms and regulations have promoted rehabilitative care to the exclusion of palliative care (Hoffmann and Tarzian 2005; Miller, Teno, and Mor 2004).

Organizational Structures

ORGANIZATIONAL PHILOSOPHY AND MISSION

Most nursing homes explicitly state their philosophical orientation or mission as resident-centered care. These mission statements are prominently displayed on wall plaques found near main entrances. However, explicit mission statements may be quite different from implicit missions that drive the day-to-day behaviors of staff members (Forbes-Thompson and Gessert 2005; Forbes-Thompson, Leiker, and Bleich 2007). External pressures from the regulatory environment combined with financial incentives and constraints can shape an implied mission that may be focused on passing survey inspections and surviving financially as an organization. Personnel in nursing homes are frequently required to work with inadequate staffing, to keep beds full, and to cut corners when attempting to meet residents' needs. Despite the stated explicit mission, it is the implied mission that shapes care delivery to be focused on regulatory compliance and economic efficiency or to be resident-centered. Individualized, resident-centered care as a central mission of the nursing home is essential for the success of any palliative care program.

PHYSICAL FACILITIES

Many nursing homes are considering or are engaged in a culture-change movement to deinstitutionalize long-term care and radically transform nursing home environments (Doty, Koren, and Sturla 2008). Boyd and Johansen (2008) define this culture change as resident care and activities being directed by residents. Living environments are designed to be home-like rather than institutional. Close relationships among residents, family members, staff, and the community are encouraged. Work is organized to support and empower all staff to respond to residents' needs and desires. Management enables collaborative and decentralized decision making and systematic processes that are comprehensive and measurement-based and that are used for continuous quality improvement. Some of these innovative transformations are commonly referred to as the Eden Alternative, Green House projects, and Pioneer Network (www.edenalt.org; www.ncbcapitalimpact.org; www.pioneernetwork.net). Although this culture change invites alterations to physical facilities to create a more homelike atmosphere, most nursing homes have maintained their traditional, institutional appearance. The institutional design has its basis in the acute-care, medical-hospital model of care. Many nursing homes maintain hallways connected by distinctly separate, centralized nurses' stations equipped with prominently displayed medication carts, medical charts, and equipment such as telephones, computers, and fax machines. Medical treatment rooms are located nearby. Many nursing homes are organized for staff efficiency with large congregate areas such as dining rooms and activity rooms. Most have few, if any, private resident rooms. Rumbling laundry carts, overhead paging systems, and shiny linoleum floors are the norm and add to an institutional atmosphere.

POLICIES AND PROCEDURES

Since the passage of the 1987 Omnibus Reconciliation Act, nursing homes must adhere to approximately 190 federal and state regulations, which provide the impetus for many policies and procedures. This legislation has promoted a focus on resident rehabilitation and has been credited with improving the care for many residents by reducing falls, pressure ulcers, and the use of psychotropic medications. Accordingly, policies and procedures have been written around preventing and treating conditions such as weight loss, falls, skin breakdown, and declines in physical functioning. Policies outline expected routines for potential problem areas. For example, a policy on weight loss might contain instructions regarding routine monitoring of residents' weight; routine meetings to review residents' weight; steps to guard against weight loss, such as fortified snacks; increased calories added to meal items; and documentation of the amount of food eaten within a twenty-four-hour period. More recently, there has been a regulatory emphasis on the evaluation and treatment of pain. However, there is little regulatory emphasis on psychosocial needs other than a focus on depression and the use of psychotropic medications. Thus, policies and procedures to prompt palliative-care interventions such as the delivery of psycho-social-spiritual interventions are lacking.

STAFFING

Staff shortages and turnover are common problems in nursing homes and are structural obstacles to providing quality care (Bostick et al. 2006; Horn et al. 2005; Miller, Teno, and Mor 2004; Rice et al. 2004; Schnelle et al. 2004). Staff turnover occurs at all levels in nursing homes: certified nursing assistants; licensed practical nurses; registered nurses; directors of nursing; social workers; and administrators (Anderson, Issel, and McDaniel 2003; Banaszak-Holl and Hines 1996; Bowers and Becker 1992). Turnover rates for RNs, LPNs, and CNAs in one Midwestern state average 68 percent, 67 percent, and 95 percent, respectively, per year (Forbes-Thompson et al. 2005). Castle (in press) reports that nationally there are considerable differences across states for staff-turnover rates. The consequences of turnover include increased facility costs, lower job satisfaction, and lower resident quality of care (Castle and Engberg 2006; Harrington and Swan 2003). The cost of replacing a CNA is approximately $2,400 to $4,000, and for an RN, approximately $7,000 (Caudill and Patrick 1991). Job satisfaction is affected, as those who remain face increased workload until replacements are found and trained (Parsons et al. 2003). Costs of turnover deplete resources that potentially could improve resident quality of life through facility remodeling, staffing increases, or staff education.

In addition to the challenges of being short-staffed and having high staff turnover, the level of skill of current staff is problematic. Nursing homes are mandated by federal regulations to have an RN onsite for only eight consecutive hours per day; consequently, LPNs provide much of the licensed oversight of resident care. LPNs have minimal training, with frequently only a year of educational preparation. Certified nurse aides, many of whom lack a high school diploma, are the dominant care providers, typically providing up to 80 percent of resident care. Staffing ratios are usually reported as the ratio of staff to residents, the number of staff hours per resident per day, or the ratio of licensed staff to residents (Bostick et al. 2006). Studies have reported a positive association between higher staffing ratios and improved quality of resident care (Harrington et al. 2001; Rantz et al. 2004; Schnelle et al. 2004), and an increased number of licensed staff with improvements in resident quality of life (Anderson, Hsieh, and Su 1998; Bostick 2004; Harrington et al. 2001).

The situation for nursing home social workers is also challenging, as presented in chapter 1. About half of nursing home social-service departments are directed by a person who lacks a social work degree (Bern-Klug et al. 2009), and 20 percent lack a college education in any field.

Organizational Processes of Care

CARE PLANNING

Nursing homes are mandated by federal regulations to conduct individualized resident assessment and care planning at regular intervals: upon admission, quarterly, annually, and whenever there is a significant change in status. In addition, the frequency of assessment differs depending on the residents' level of care as defined by Medicare. A registered nurse must supervise the assessment and documentation of over 500 items for the Minimum Data Set, and that these data are used to inform resident care planning. Data entered into the MDS are used to generate "resident assessment protocols," which are prompts or triggers used to highlight the need for additional care planning that a particular resident may require in certain areas. For example, a RAP may trigger an evaluation of decline in physical functioning; the common intervention pathway for this trigger would be strength training, walking, range of motion, and the like. However, care-planning prompts generated by the MDS data usually are inappropriate for declining or dying residents. For example, a treatable weight loss for one resident, using prompts generated by MDS data, is difficult to differentiate from a normal weight loss associated with dying for a different resident. Many of these care-planning prompts are generated from a medically oriented model of care that focuses on rehabilitation and prevention of death (Seale 1998). Obviously these goals are inappropriate, at some point, for permanently placed residents.

Nursing homes implement the federally mandated care-planning process in different ways. The process is intended to be interdisciplinary and include social workers, activities personnel, and other individuals such as certified nurse aides and therapists, and to foster interdisciplinary communication and planning regarding individualized resident needs. Frequently, however, personnel representing disciplines such as social work, nursing, and diet complete their individual areas with little or no communication with one another. Unfortunately, traditional nursing home staff hierarchy and silos do little to create the kind of interdisciplinary input necessary to plan care for residents at the end of their lives. Ideally, staff should conduct care-planning meetings that include residents, their families, and interdisciplinary staff to determine decisions regarding care-intervention goals. Yet it is all too common for residents and their families to have little or no input into care decisions (Forbes-Thompson and Gessert 2005).

QUALITY IMPROVEMENT

Nursing homes are required to engage in quality-improvement process activities to raise the quality of care. There is tremendous variation in how and the degree to which quality-improvement strategies are initiated and implemented (Adams-Wendling and Lee 2005). MDS data are used to generate measures of quality referred to as "quality indicators and quality measures." Nursing home staff members can use their own MDS data to identify areas of needed improvement and monitor progress. State surveyors rely on MDS data to identify potential problem areas. The Centers for Medicare (www.cms.hhs.gov) use these data to compare nursing homes. As previously mentioned, the standard measures used for quality improvement focus on areas amenable to rehabilitation, such as decline in physical functioning, incontinence, falls, and decline in cognition. At some point, it becomes inappropriate to rely on these measures to assess the quality of care provided to people who are approaching death. Pain is the only indicator or quality measure currently used by the government that represents a palliative-care intervention.

NONCLINICAL PROCESSES: COMMUNICATION AND TEAMWORK

More recently, efforts to improve the quality of care in nursing homes has focused on nonclinical processes such as communication and teamwork. Staff turnover and traditional, hierarchical personnel structures impede the communication and teamwork necessary to deliver quality care (Carpenter and Thompson 2008; Forbes-Thompson, Leiker, and Bleich 2007). In fact, poor communication and teamwork regarding falls, restraint use, and wound care have been related to poor resident outcomes (Anderson, Issel, and McDaniel 2003; Berlowitz et al. 2003; Rantz et al. 2004). The lack of effective communication through both formal processes (e.g., policies) and informal processes (e.g., conversations among team members) have led to overly aggressive treatments for some nursing home residents. In some cases, the result is the provision of care that is counter to residents' stated preferences.

Nursing homes that base their structures and care processes in the more traditional, medical-oriented model have many serious obstacles to effective end-of-life communication: frequent turnover and low numbers of staff; low education levels of dominant caregivers (CNAs); differing perceptions of end-of-life care across disciplines; and regulatory and financial incentives for more aggressive care (e.g., hospitalization). Staff members' ability to communicate and work in teams is important for resident care in general and foundational to delivering palliative care (Forbes-Thompson and Gessert 2005).

ADVANCE CARE PLANNING

Advance care planning is defined as a process of communication regarding an individual's preferences and goals for end-of-life care that occurs over multiple points in time (Teno and Lynn 1996). Advance care planning, if initiated upon admission to the nursing home, begins a communication process regarding end-of-life preferences that is more likely to ensure a resident's preferences are honored even when there is no recognizable trajectory toward death. Advance care planning is a fundamental aspect to a palliative-care process and is dependent on staff education, staffing levels, communication, and teamwork. However, there is tremendous variation across nursing homes in terms of the proportion of residents with advance · directives (Degenholtz et al. 2002; Kiely et al. 2001; Teno et al. 1997). The number of advance directives and particular choices such as do-not-resuscitate orders are believed to reflect ethnic differences in end-of-life planning, as well as the establishment or absence of a palliative-care process within facilities (Gessert et al. 2000; Gessert, Curry, and Robinson 2001). Lower numbers of advance directives and, in particular, DNR orders reflect, in part, a more aggressive approach to treatment and little, if any, focus on palliative care, poorer communication and teamwork among staff, lower education of direct-care staff, and staff discomfort with discussions regarding end-of-life treatment options (Bottrell et al. 2001; Cantor and Pearlman, 2004; Happ et al. 2002).

In summary, these are but a few of the organizational structures and processes that influence the delivery of nursing home resident care and are common obstacles to the delivery of palliative care. These structures and processes are often in conflict with the needs of permanently placed residents who will inevitably die. A new way to conceptualize end-of-life care that aims to improve care and quality of life is needed. This new approach must simultaneously embrace both restorative and palliative-care interventions that begin upon admission and continue until death.

Simultaneously Embracing Both Restorative and Palliative Care

Approaches to care that include both restorative and palliative interventions will encourage care that enhances the physical and mental well-being of all residents while attending to the complex needs of residents who will inevitably decline. The World Health Organization defines palliative care as an approach to care "that improves the quality of life of patients and their families facing the problems associated with life-threatening illness, through the prevention and relief of suffering by means of early identification and impeccable assessment and treatment of pain and other problems, physical, psychosocial, and spiritual" (2002:83). The IOM (1997) states that palliative care is not restricted to only those people who are dying or are enrolled in hospice programs. Palliative care is a valuable service to those who live with chronic illnesses and to the elderly—thus, residents in nursing homes. The National Consensus Project for Quality Palliative Care (2006) reports that palliative care services need to be allocated across the entire trajectory of a patient's illness and should not be restricted to the end-of-life phase. Palliative care is and should be viewed as complementary rather than consequential to restorative treatment, as in the traditional medical model. When delivered in a simultaneous fashion, both restorative and palliative care have resident quality of life as the outcome; it is only the balance between the two care approaches that changes over time. Additionally, this simultaneous approach to care corresponds with the goals of the American Geriatric Society's "Position Statement" (2002) that advocates maintaining or improving physical and mental function, eliminating or reducing pain and discomfort, providing social involvement and recreational activities in a safe environment, and reducing unnecessary hospitalization and emergency-room visits.

In contrast to a traditional nursing home, the structure and process domains in a home with a palliative-care emphasis are based on the current empirical evidence developed by the John A. Hartford Foundation Institute for Geriatric Nursing's "Guidelines for End-of-Life Care in Nursing Facilities: Principles and Recommendations" (2001) and the National Consensus Project for Quality Palliative Care guidelines (2006).

Structure of Care

Structural attributes need to be in place to develop palliative-care programs and approaches that integrate restorative and palliative care interventions. These include a mission statement, a philosophy, policies, and procedures that embrace dying as a normal event; administrator, nursing, medical, and social work leaders trained in palliative care; nursing staff (RNs, LPNs, CNAs) and activities personnel trained in palliative care; increased ratio of licensed professionals to residents; depending on the size of the nursing home, at least one master's prepared social worker with experience working with the dying or certified in end-of-life care; access to pastoral/spiritual care; access/contracts with hospice agencies; continuing-education programs for the staff; grief-support groups for the staff, residents, and residents' families; and a quality-improvement program that evaluates not only the traditional quality indicators but outcome indicators related to end-of-life care.

MISSION STATEMENT/PHILOSOPHY OF CARE

Mission statements that explicitly state the home will provide resident-centered, quality care are not contrary to an approach that integrates restorative and palliative interventions. However, the philosophical orientation to care that will change with this integration. For homes with a strong palliative orientation, death will be viewed as a normal outcome for permanently placed residents, an outcome that is not prolonged or hastened but is planned for, expected, and met in accordance with the resident's values and preferences for treatment. Because palliative care provides aggressive care focused on comfort, quality of life, human dignity, and patient and family choice, it is appropriate for residents who enter nursing homes with multiple, chronic illnesses when symptom control is necessary and functional decline inevitable. Good palliative care is provided in a culturally competent manner.

The explicit or implicit institutional mission is a powerful force and unmistakably reflected in the policies and priorities that are used to manage daily care interventions (Forbes-Thompson and Gessert 2005). Nursing homes that embrace philosophies viewing death as normal and inevitable open the door to valuable discussions with residents and family regarding cardiopulmonary resuscitation, hospitalizations, feeding tubes, and quality of life (Froggatt 2001; Thompson and Oliver 2008). Hospitalization or the use of feeding tubes for weight loss are not the "default" care options but are chosen after careful thought and discussion. Social workers are key to these initial and ongoing discussions with residents and families.

PHYSICAL FACILITIES

Physical changes to existing buildings may be cost-prohibitive, but small changes can enhance a homelike feeling and sense of community. Physical changes that allow for resident privacy in certain areas and spaces that allow for small gatherings are examples of changes that may be created without expensive physical alterations. Spaces for worship and spaces for interacting with nature in gardens or greenhouses are important elements also. Changes that include removal of the medical-model-associated nurses' stations, chart racks, medical carts, and other institutional structures should be part of long-range planning.

POLICIES AND PROCEDURES

Policies and procedures, in and of themselves, do not change practice, but they do provide a framework and an expectation for standards of practice. In addition, policies and procedures reflect the mission and philosophy of the organization. Policies and procedures can be in place for palliative interventions such as pain management, bedside memorials, and documentation of advance care planning. Initiating, evaluating, and updating policies and procedures based on practice guidelines such as National Consensus Project for Quality Palliative Care (2006) Clinical Practice's "Guidelines for Quality Palliative Care" will ensure that standards for care are current.

STAFFING

Increasing the education level of staff and retaining staff are essential for palliative-care programs and overall quality of care in any nursing home. Of nursing homes in case-study evaluations, those whose core-leadership personnel held master's degrees (e.g., social worker, director of nursing, administrator, and activities director) demonstrated better resident care, greater job satisfaction and teamwork, more effective communication, and less staff turnover (Forbes-Thompson and Gessert 2005; Forbes-Thompson, Leiker, and Bleich 2007). Increasing the education level of core staff is necessary because of the increasing acuity level of residents and the complex issues regarding end-of-life interventions. Although increasing overall staff numbers and those with higher education qualifications is expensive, it may be effective in reducing overall costs if homes see a subsequent reduction in staff turnover (Harrington 2005).

CONTINUING EDUCATION

Many direct-care staff, such as CNAs or LPNs, have minimal formal education. Thus, nursing homes must be committed to the ongoing education of their staffs. Even staff with advanced, formal education are unlikely to have had formal training in palliative care (IOM 1997). Knowledge alone is not enough to change care practices, but it is a necessary first step. Homes that are developing or have palliative-care programs must provide access to continuing education programs either onsite or at regional and national conferences to assist their staff. Educational programs such as End-of-life Nursing Education Consortium provide licensed staff with essential information on cultural issues, communication skills, grief and bereavement, and pain and symptom management (American Association of Colleges of Nursing 2002). These modules contain information that would benefit nonnursing staff, such as social work and activities personnel, as well. Another program, entitled Palliative Care Educational Resource Team, covers important topics such as symptom management, communication skills, cultural issues, and caring for the imminently dying (Ersek, Grant, and Kraybill 2005). Both of these programs are examples of training opportunities for staff and are offered at regular intervals in regional locations. Additional educational and training opportunities for social workers are offered by the National Association of Social Workers (www.socialworkers. org). On a local level, staff can invite professionals from local hospice agencies or colleges to partner in providing in-service training. Regularly scheduled in-services on palliative care topics such as symptom management (pharmacological and nonpharmacological approaches), managing pain in cognitively impaired residents, maintaining residents' dignity, spiritual support, grief management, and coping strategies for staff are a necessary component of any palliative-care program (Wowchuk, McClement, and Bond 2007).

HOSPICE

As explained in chapter 3, hospice is a comprehensive program provided in a variety of settings, including nursing homes, that addresses the holistic needs of dying individuals and their family members (Egan and Labyak 2001). Hospice is primarily funded by the Medicare hospice benefit. Additional funding agencies include Medicaid and private insurance companies. The hospice benefit requires physician certification of a terminal diagnosis of six months or less to live. This requirement of the Medicare benefit best supports care of people with predictable dying trajectories of six months or less, such as those with end-stage cancer diagnoses, but is applicable to all terminal illnesses. Contrary to these limitations, most nursing home residents die with multiple, chronic illnesses that have unpredictable dying trajectories; their last phase of life may last months or years, making it challenging to access the Medicare hospice benefit. However, for residents who have accessed the hospice benefit, studies have shown that residents receiving hospice services have improved symptom management, decreased hospitalizations, and an overall higher degree of resident and family satisfaction (Baer and Hanson 2000; Casarett et al. 2005; Gozalo and Miller 2007). Most important, nursing homes that regularly refer residents to hospice provide a greater palliative-care focus to all residents, have lower hospitalization and feeding-tube rates, and provide better pain management, suggesting a diffusion effect of the hospice philosophy into care practices (Miller 2006; Miller, Gozalo, and Mor 2001). Contracts with hospice agencies need to be in place and an ongoing working relationship with the hospice agencies can improve care (Miller et al., 2004).

Processes of Care

QUALITY IMPROVEMENT

In the traditional nursing home, quality improvement is a process to monitor events that potentially reflect poor care and are frequently the target of state surveys, such as weight loss, pressure ulcers, and falls. Many nursing home administrators perceive they will be subject to penalty if a resident loses weight or obtains a pressure ulcer. However, some of these events may be difficult if not impossible to avoid as residents approach death. By moving toward an integrated approach to care that combines both restorative and palliative interventions, homes can use quality-improvement processes not only to evaluate and improve resident quality of life before death but also to gather and use data to protect against the perceived regulatory enforcement of restorative care. Armed with information documenting an interdisciplinary team assessment and interventions that include resident and family choice and risk negotiation, homes can provide evidence that interventions and resident changes are the result of careful evaluation and choice as opposed to neglect. Furthermore, using data for systematic evaluation will allow homes to explore the degree to which they meet resident and family goals and palliative care standards.

As nursing home staffs integrate more palliative approaches, monitoring other outcomes will be an important strategy for evaluating and improving care. Other important outcomes might include staff and family satisfaction with end-of-life interventions and bereavement follow-up with family. In short, systems are in place for nursing homes to select, evaluate, and improve upon palliative-care-performance indicators.

CARE PLANNING

The federally mandated resident care-planning process could serve as a catalyst for the discussion of preferences and goals surrounding treatment decisions. The federally mandated requirement that care-planning sessions occur both quarterly and when there is a significant change in a resident's condition offers a natural opportunity to develop resident-centered care plans that balance restorative and palliative options. As opposed to working in isolation, team members would meet to solidify an interdisciplinary approach to care, bringing together nursing, social services, diet, therapy, and activities personnel, as well as residents and their families. Certified nurse aides, who provide the most direct care to residents, are important team members; their input is crucial. Other staff, depending on their involvement, could include clergy, counselors, or pharmacists. The results of the interdisciplinary resident assessment and the team meeting would be integrated into day-to-day decisions and activities affecting the resident. Care planning becomes a seamless process of assessment, discussion, planning, intervention, and evaluation.

Interdisciplinary input into care strategies enhances communication and teamwork and offers the opportunity for exchange of ideas and spontaneous learning across disciplines. The sharing of ideas from interdisciplinary team members, especially those trained in palliative care, will allow for the incorporation of a wider array of palliative interventions. For example, interventions to manage pain could go beyond medication administration to include massage, music, and aroma therapies. Psychosocial support could include art therapy, life review, or efforts to enhance reconciliation among family members. Grief support for staff and bereaved family members are important as well (see chapter 10). These examples illustrate the need for interdisciplinary approaches to palliative care, as they extend beyond the expertise of any one discipline.

ADVANCE CARE PLANNING

Advance care planning, a process of communication regarding an individual's preferences and goals for end-of-life care, begins before admission to the nursing home. Whenever possible, potential residents and their families should visit a home before admission. For homes that embrace palliative care, the preadmission visit provides an opportunity to introduce residents and family to a care philosophy that embraces both restorative and palliative care. For residents who will be permanently placed, death is gently acknowledged through conversation or written materials that are offered to prompt reflection, conversation, and planning. Written information goes beyond what is typically provided regarding an advance-directive document to include information distinguishing restorative- and palliative-care interventions. Further, information is provided that describes how and why the balance between these two will likely change over time. Two or three case vignettes describing different scenarios can be used to illustrate changes in disease progression and palliative preferences. Vignettes are a nonthreatening way to trigger questions and foster discussion. Most individuals need the opportunity, with the support of a specially trained staff member, to think through scenarios they have never imagined. Social workers who have received training in discussions regarding advance care planning and palliative care are well suited for the initial and ongoing discussions. In addition, handouts can also be used to dispel myths related to the end of life, for example, the myth of addiction with the use of pain medication or the myth of prolongation of life with the use of feeding tubes. Scientific information on these topics, presented in lay language, can reduce the burden of guilt and from emotionally laden decisions. Finally, even though information is provided, it is unlikely that residents and family will engage in detailed conversations at preadmission or admission meetings; these are anxiety-laden events. Yet the information can be provided as a way to acknowledge the nursing home's commitment to quality of life and to send the message that the facility expects to support the resident and the family as the end of life approaches.

During admission and care-planning meetings, the nursing home's philosophy, that is, its embrace of both restorative and palliative interventions, should be openly discussed. It should be made clear that the organizational culture and individual staff members will challenge default care interventions inherent in the medical model, such as cardiopulmonary resuscitation, routine hospitalizations, and the use of feeding tubes for declining residents, yet they will honor individualized, resident-centered decisions. Advance care planning should be a standard part of all care-planning meetings.

Advance-directive documents are important but do not replace ongoing communication regarding treatment preferences and quality end-of-life care. Any resident who is permanently placed needs a plan that directs his or her end-of-life care (Travis et al. 2002). Because the end of life is so difficult to predict, someone having a durable power of attorney for health care who understands the resident's desires and views on quality of life will reduce ambiguity and foster timely decision making. However, having a DPAHC does not reduce the need for conversations.

RITUALS, MEMORIALS, AND BEREAVEMENT

Death has an impact on the nursing home community including family, staff, and residents. Rituals associated with death and dying give recognition to the deceased, comfort to the nursing home community, and offer reassurance to other residents that their final days and passing will be a meaningful event. (See chapter 9 for a more extensive discussion of using rituals to mark the death of a resident.)

Staff, especially social workers, should be well trained to provide grief-management interventions for family members and the staff who have cared for recently deceased residents. Bringing staff together within a few days of a resident's death to discuss the death event and their own personal feelings can begin a healing process. Other strategies to enhance grief management among staff members are presented in chapter 10.

Most nursing homes currently do not engage in bereavement follow-up with family members. Routine, regularly spaced, follow-ups by phone with family will aid in the bereavement period. Homes can begin bereavement support groups within their own communities or refer to local support groups. Sympathy cards, funeral visitation, and follow-up phone calls all provide support to family members as well as staff as they fondly remember the deceased and their unique relationships with them.

COMMUNICATION AND TEAMWORK

Organizational structures and processes such as a positive philosophical orientation toward the end of life, adequate staffing, the educational preparation of staff, and the establishment of quality-improvement processes are necessary for the development of palliative-care programs. However, the delivery of palliative-care interventions is dependent on communication (e.g., staff's communicating subtle changes in a resident's condition) and teamwork (e.g., disciplines' working together to meet the physical, psychological, and spiritual needs of a resident). Communication is multidimensional and includes timeliness in the transfer of information, accuracy in the transfer of information, and understanding on behalf of the receiver (Forbes-Thompson et al. 2006). Teamwork entails collaborative interaction and participation in assessing, planning, and delivering care. Teams exist when individual staff have respect for diverse opinions, are willing to assist one another with care tasks, have shared goals with a clear purpose, and are accountable to one another (Forbes-Thompson et al. 2006). Teams in nursing homes comprise multiple disciplines (e.g., nursing, social services, therapy, diet) and levels within disciplines (e.g., CNAs, LPNs, RNs, and BSWs, MSWs). Communication and teamwork are essential ingredients for quality-improvement processes and are related to resident outcomes such as falls, wound care, use of restraints, and weight loss. Poor resident outcomes are caused, in part, by communication breakdowns between leaders (directors of nursing, directors of social services) and staff regarding daily resident care activities (Forbes-Thompson and Gessert 2005). Better communication and teamwork are related to lower turnover and greater continuity in resident care. Research is in progress that will evaluate the relationships of staff communication and teamwork to resident and family outcomes at the end of life, such as pain and symptom management, resident-centered care, and caregiver strain (Forbes-Thompson 2006–2010).

Communication among providers, residents, and families is consistently identified as an essential factor in quality end-of-life care (Forbes and Daaleman 2001; Levy 2001). Staffs identify communication as a major problem with end-of-life care in nursing homes and a major impediment to timely advance care planning (Oliver, Porock, and Zweig 2005). Furthermore, the difficulty in predicting the timing of death adds tremendous complexity to communicating about and planning for resident care. Because of the difficulty of predicting the time of death, communication and teamwork, combined with a routine interdisciplinary care-planning process, advance care planning, and quality-improvement initiatives are essential for important decisions regarding interventions aimed at physical decline, weight loss, and hospitalization.

Role of the Social Worker

Current federal regulations require the provision of medically related social services in all nursing homes certified for Medicare or Medicaid payments, although only facilities with more than 120 beds are required to employ a full-time social worker, who may or may not possess a degree in social work (Wright 2001). Current regulations require the person fulfilling the social work role to have a degree in a field related to human services but not necessarily a degree in social work. The role of the social worker in a home with a strong palliative-care program is both essential and multifaceted. Social workers are vital members of the interdisciplinary team and frequently take leadership roles. They operate from the social-systems perspective, whereby residents and family are the central focus (Reese and Sontag 2001), and address a wide range of needs including the physical, psychological, spiritual, and social.

Within homes that integrate palliative-care practices, the primary responsibility for the social worker is to provide psychosocial support to residents and their family members. Related responsibilities include counseling at preadmission and admission meetings; introducing advance directives; conducting psychosocial assessments; counseling residents regarding a variety of psychosocial needs; collaborating with interdisciplinary team members regarding care planning and advance care planning; ensuring continuity of care; advocating for the needs of residents and family; offering crisis intervention; offering grief support for staff; offering bereavement services for residents' families; and assisting families to cope with issues surrounding death and dying (Cowles and Lefcowitz 1995; Dane and Simon 1991; Kulys and Davis 1986; Lacey 2006). Last but not least, documentation is essential.

Unfortunately, the ideal social work role is often in conflict with the actual role assigned in the more traditional nursing home. In homes where staff continue to work under a medical model, the social worker is frequently used to monitor compliance with regulations and is responsible for Medicaid and Medicare admissions and paperwork. Social workers frequently do preadmission screening in the community and in hospitals and may be shouldered with responsibility for keeping nursing home beds full.

The social worker has an integral role in establishing and evaluating palliative-care programs in nursing homes. The establishment of structures and processes that support quality of life for residents who will eventually die takes time. Social workers have important skills in assessment, advocacy, counseling, conflict resolution, and management that foster the implementation of creative palliative-care programs capable of surmounting the traditional modes of care in many nursing homes. For specific information about how social workers can address the palliative psychosocial needs of residents, see chapter 6. For information about the social work role with family members, refer to chapter 7.

In conclusion, nursing homes that base their structure and care processes on the traditional medical model of care may cause needless suffering for permanently placed residents. At some point in each person's life, the rehab focus is not appropriate, and a change in treatment to palliation is necessary. This needed change in nursing home culture promotes a home environment that is resident-centered. The role of the social worker as an essential team member is crucial in assuring the delivery of palliative care and a dignified end of life for nursing home residents.

References

Adams-Wendling, L., and R. Lee. 2005. "Quality Improvement in Nursing Facilities." *Journal of Gerontological Nursing* 31 (11): 36–41.

American Association of Colleges of Nursing. 2002. "Peaceful Death: Recommended Competencies and Curricular Guidelines for End-of-Life Nursing Care." www.aacn.nche.edu/Publications/deathfin.htm. Accessed October 20, 2007.

American Geriatric Society. 2002. "Position Statement: Access to High Quality End-of-Life Care in Nursing Homes." http://www.americangeriatrics.org/products/positionpapers/2006hospice.shtml. Accessed October 12, 2007.

Anderson, A., P. Hsieh, and H. Su. 1998. "Resource Allocation and Resident Outcomes in Nursing Homes: Comparisons Between the Best and Worst." *Research in Nursing and Health* 21 (4): 297–313.

Anderson, R., L. Issel, and R. McDaniel, R. 2003. "Nursing Homes as Complex Adaptive Systems: Relationship Between Management Practices and Resident Outcomes." *Nursing Research* 52 (1): 12–21.

Baer, W. M., and L. C. Hanson. 2000. "Families' Perception of the Added Value of Hospice in the Nursing Home." *Journal of the American Geriatrics Society* 48 (8): 879–82.

Banaszak-Holl, J., and M. A. Hines. 1996. "Factors Associated with Nursing Home Staff Turnover." *Gerontologist* 36 (4): 512–17.

Berlowitz, D. R., G. J. Young, E. C. Hickey, et al. 2003. "Quality Improvement Implementation in the Nursing Home." *Health Services Research* 38 (1): 65–83.

Bern-Klug, M., K. W. O. Kramer, G. Chan, R. Kane, L. T. Dorfman, and J. B. Saunders. 2009. "Characteristics of Nursing Home Social Services Directors: How Common Is a Degree in Social Work?" *Journal of the American Medical Directors Association* 10:36–44.

Bostick, J. 2004. "Relationship of Nursing Personnel and Nursing Home Care Quality." *Journal of Nursing Care Quality* 19 (2): 130–36.

Bostick, J. E., M. J. Rantz, M. K. Flesner, and C. J. Riggs. 2006. "Systematic Review of Studies of Staffing and Quality in Nursing Homes." *Journal of American Medical Directors Association* 7 (6): 366–76.

Bottrell, M. M., J. F. O'Sullivan, M. A. Robbins, E. L. Mitty, and M. D. Mezey. 2001. "Transferring Dying Nursing Home Residents to the Hospital: DON Perspectives on the Nurse's Role in Transfer Decisions." *Geriatric Nursing* 22 (6): 313–17.

Bowers, B., and M. Becker. 1992. "Nurse's Aides in Nursing Homes: The Relationship Between Organization and Quality." *Gerontologist* 32 (3): 360–66.

Boyd, C., and B. Johansen. 2008. "A Cultural Shift: Resident-Directed Care at Providence Mount St. Vincent in Seattle Places Elders at the Center of the Universe." *Health Progress* 89 (1): 37–42.

Brandt, H. E., L. Deliens, J. T. van der Steen, M. E. Ooms, M. W. Ribbe, and G. van der Wal. 2005. "The Last Days of Life of Nursing Home Patients with and Without Dementia Assessed with the Palliative Care Outcome Scale." *Palliative Medicine* 19 (4): 334–42.

Brock, D. B., and D. J. Foley. 1998. "Demography and Epidemiology of Dying in the U.S. with Emphasis on Deaths of Older Persons." *Hospice Journal* 13:49–60.

Cantor, M. D., and R. A. Pearlman. 2004. "Advance Care Planning in Long-Term Care Facilities." *Journal of the American Medical Directors Association* 5 (2 Suppl): S72–80.

Carpenter, J., and S. Thompson. 2008. "The Experience of Being a CNA: It's in My Soul." *Journal of Gerontological Nursing* 34 (9): 25–32.

Casarett, D., J. Karlawish, K. Morales, R. Crowley, T. Mirsch, and D. A. Asch. 2005. "Improving the Use of Hospice Services in Nursing Homes: A Randomized Controlled Trial." *Journal of the American Medical Association* 294 (2): 211–17.

Castle, N. G. In press. "State Differences and Facility Differences in Nursing Home Staff Turnover." *Journal of Applied Gerontology*.

Castle, N. G., and J. Engberg. 2006. "Organizational Characteristics Associated with Staff Turnover in Nursing Homes." *Gerontologist* 46 (1): 62–73.

Caudill, M. E., and M. Patrick. 1991. "Costing Nurse Turnover in Nursing Homes." *Nursing Management* 22 (11): 61–62.

Cowles, L., and M. Lefcowitz. 1995. "Interdisciplinary Expectations of the Medical Social Workers in the Hospital Setting: Part 2." *Health and Social Work* 20 (4): 279–87.

Dane, B., and B. Simon. 1991. "Resident Guests: Social Workers in Host Settings." *Social Work* 36 (3): 208–13.

Degenholtz, H. B., R. A. Arnold, A. Meisel, and J. R. Lave. 2002. "Persistence of Racial Disparities in Advance Care Plan Documents Among Nursing Home Residents." *Journal of the American Geriatrics Society* 50 (2): 378–81.

Donabedian, A. 1966. "Evaluating the Quality of Medical Care." *The Milbank Quarterly* 83 (4): 691–729.

Donabedian, A. 1969. "Some Issues in Evaluating the Quality of Nursing Care: Part 2." *American Journal of Public Health* 59 (10): 1833–36.

Doty, M. M., M. J. Koren, and E. L. Sturla. 2008. "Culture Change in Nursing Homes: How Far Have We Come?" Findings from the Commonwealth Fund 2007 National Survey of Nursing Homes, the Common Wealth Fund. May. http://www.commonwealthfund.org/publications/publications_show.htm?doc_id=684709#areaCitation. Accessed July 17, 2008.

Egan, K. A., and M. J. Labyak. 2001. "Hospice Care: A Model for Quality End-of-Life Care." In *Textbook of Palliative Nursing*, ed. B. R. Ferrell and N. Coyle, 7–26 New York: Oxford University Press.

Ersek, M., M. M. Grant, and B. M. Kraybill. 2005. "Enhancing End-of-Life Care in Nursing Homes: Palliative Care Educational Resource Team (PERT) Program." *Journal of Palliative Medicine* 8:556–66.

Federal Interagency Forum on Aging-Related Statistics. 2006. "Data Sources on Older Americans." http://agingstats.gov/agingstatsdotnet/main_site/default.aspx. Accessed September 20, 2007.

Fahey, T., A. A. Montgomery, J. Barnes, and J. Protheroe. 2003. "Quality of Care for Elderly Residents in Nursing Homes and Elderly People Living at Home: Controlled Observational Study." *British Medical Journal* 326:580–83.

Forbes, S. 2001. "This Is Heaven's Waiting Room: End of Life in One Nursing Home." *Journal of Gerontology Nursing* 27 (11): 37–45.

Forbes-Thompson, S. A. 2006–2010. "The Impact of Quality End-of-Life Care in Nursing Homes." 5R01NR009547-04 National Institute of Nursing Research.

Forbes, S. A., and T. P. Daaleman. 2001. "Physician and Nursing Perspectives on Patient Encounters in End-of-Life Care." *Journal of Family Practice* 50 (2): 155W–162W.

Forbes-Thompson, S., N. Dunton, B. Gajewski, R. Lee, M. Wrona, and R. Chapin. 2005. "The Relationship Between Staff Turnover and Nursing Home Deficiencies." Kansas Department on Aging. University of Kansas Medical Center School of Nursing.

Forbes-Thomspon, S., B. Gajewski, J. Scott-Cawiezell, and N. Dunton. 2006. "An Exploration of Nursing Home Organizational Processes." *Western Journal of Nursing Research* 28 (8): 935–54.

Forbes-Thompson, S., and C. E. Gessert. 2005. "End of Life in Nursing Homes: Connections Between Structure, Process, and Outcomes." *Journal of Palliative Medicine* 8 (3): 545–55.

Forbes-Thompson, S., T. Leiker, and M. R. Bleich. 2007. "High-Performing and Low-Performing Nursing Homes: A View from Complexity Science." *Health Care Management Review* 32 (4): 341–51.

Froggatt, K. A. 2001. "Palliative Care and Nursing Homes: Where Next?" *Palliative Medicine* 15:42–48.

Gessert, C. E., N. M. Curry, and A. Robinson. 2001. "Ethnicity and End-of-Life Care: The Use of Feeding Tubes." *Ethnicity and Disease* 11 (1): 97–106.

Gessert, C. E., M. C. Mosier, E. F. Brown, and B. Frey. 2000. "Tube Feeding in Nursing Home Residents with Severe and Irreversible Cognitive Impairment." *Journal of the American Geriatrics Society* 48 (12): 1593–1600.

Gozalo, P. L., and S. C. Miller. 2007. "Hospice Enrollment and Evaluation of Its Causal Effect on Hospitalization of Dying Nursing Home Patients." *Health Services Research* 42 (2): 587–610.

Hanson, L. C. 2003. "Creating Excellent Palliative Care in Nursing Homes." *Journal of Palliative Medicine* 6 (1): 7–9.

Hanson, L. C., and M. Henderson. 2000. "Care of the Dying in Long-Term Care Settings." *Clinics in Geriatric Medicine* 16 (2): 225–37.

Happ, M. B., E. Capezuti, N. E. Strumpf, et al. 2002. "Advance Care Planning and End-of-Life Care for Hospitalized Nursing Home Residents." *Journal of the American Geriatrics Society* 50 (5): 829–35.

Harrington, C. 2005. "Quality of Care in Home Organizations: Establishing a Health Services Research Agenda." *Nursing Outlook* 53 (6): 300–304.

Harrington, C., and J. H. Swan. 2003. "Nursing Home Staffing, Turnover, and Case Mix." *Medical Care Research and Review* 60 (3): 366–92.

Harrington, C., S. Woolhandler, J. Mullan, H. Carrillo, and D. U. Himmelstein. 2001. "Does Investor Ownership of Nursing Homes Compromise the Quality of Care?" *American Journal of Public Health* 91 (9): 1452–55.

Hawes, C., J. N. Morris, C. D. Phillips, B. E. Fries, K. Murphy, and V. Mor. 1997. "Development of the Nursing Home Resident Assessment Instrument in the USA." *Age and Ageing* 26:19–25.

Hoffmann, D. E., and A. J. Tarzian. 2005. "Dying in America—an Examination of Policies That Deter Adequate End-of-Life Care in Nursing Homes." *The Journal of Law, Medicine, and Ethics* 33 (2): 294–309.

Horn, S. D., P. Buerhaus, N. Bergstrom, and R. J. Smout. 2005. "RN Staffing Time and Outcomes of Long-Stay Nursing Home Residents: Pressure Ulcers and Other Adverse Outcomes Are Less Likely as RNs Spend More Time on Direct Patient Care." *American Journal of Nursing* 105 (11): 58–70.

Institute of Medicine. 1986. *Improving Quality of Care in Nursing Homes.* Ed. J. Takeuchi, R. Burke, and M. McGeary. Washington, D.C.: National Academy Press.

Institute of Medicine. 1997. *Approaching Death: Improving Care at the End of Life.* Washington, D.C.: National Academy Press.

John A. Hartford Foundation Institute for Geriatric Nursing. 2001. "Guidelines for End-of-Life Care in Nursing Facilities: Principles and Recommendations."

Johnson, V. M., J. M. Teno, M. Bourbonniere, and V. Mor. 2005. "Palliative Care Needs of Cancer Patients in U.S. Nursing Homes." *Journal of Palliative Medicine,* 8:273–79.

Kayser-Jones, J. 2002. "The Experience of Dying: An Ethnographic Nursing Home Study." *Gerontologist* 42:11–19.

Kayser-Jones, J., E. Schell, W. Lyons, A. E. Kris, J. Cahn, and R. L. Beard. 2003. "Factors That Influence End-of-Life Care in Nursing Homes: The Physical Environment, Inadequate Staffing, and Lack of Supervision." *Gerontologist* 43:76–84.

Kiely, D. K., S. L. Mitchell, A. Marlow, K. M. Murphy, and J. N. Morris. 2001. "Racial and State Differences in the Designation of Advance Directives in Nursing Home Residents." *Journal of the American Geriatrics Society* 49 (10): 1346–52.

Kulys, R., and M. A. Davis. 1986. "An Analysis of Social Services in Hospices." *Social Work* 31:448–56.

Lacey, D. 2006. "End-of-Life Decision Making for Nursing Home Residents with Dementia: A Survey of Nursing Home Social Services Staff." *Health and Social Work* 31 (3): 189–99.

Levy, M. M. 2001. "End-of-Life Care in the Intensive Care Unit: Can We Do Better?" *Critical Care Medicine* 29 (2 Suppl.): N56–N61.

Miller, S. C. 2006. "Workable Solutions for Successful Collaborations Between Nursing Homes and Hospices." Paper presented at NHPCO's Seventh Clinical Team Conference and Scientific Symposium. San Diego, Calif.

Miller, S. C., P. Gozalo, and V. Mor. 2001. "Hospice Enrollment and Hospitalization of Dying Nursing Home Patients." *The American Journal of Medicine* 111 (1):
38–44.

Miller, S. C., O. Intrator, P. Gozalo, J. Roy, J. Barber, and V. Mor. 2004. "Govern-
ment Expenditures at the End of Life for Short-and-Long-Stay Nursing Home
Residents: Differences by Hospice Enrollment Status." *Journal of the American
Geriatrics Society* 52 (8): 1284–92.

Miller, S. C., J. M. Teno, and V. Mor. 2004. "Hospice and Palliative Care in Nursing
Homes." *Clinics in Geriatric Medicine* 20 (4): 717–34, vii.

National Consensus Project for Quality Palliative Care. 2006. "Clinical Practice
Guidelines for Quality Palliative Care."

Oliver, D. P., D. Porock, and S. Zweig. 2005. "End-of-Life Care in U.S. Nursing
Homes: A Review of the Evidence." *Journal of the American Medical Directors
Association* 6 (3 Suppl.): S21–30.

Parsons, S. K., W. P. Simmons, K. Penn, and M. Furlough. 2003. "Determinants
of Satisfaction and Turnover Among Nursing Assistants: The Results of a Statewide Survey." *Journal of Gerontological Nursing* 29 (3): 51–58.

Rantz, M., L. Hicks, V. Grando, G. F. Petroski, R. W. Madsen, D. R. Mehr, et al.
2004. "Nursing Home Quality, Cost, Staffing, and Staff Mix." *Gerontologist* 44
(1): 24–38.

Reese, D. J., and M. Sontag. 2001. "Successful Interprofessional Collaboration on
the Hospice Team." *Health and Social Work* 26 (3): 167–75.

Rice, K. N., E. A. Coleman, R. Fish, C. Levy, and J. S. Kutner. 2004. "Factors Influencing Models of End-of-Life Care in Nursing Homes: Results of a Survey of
Nursing Home Administrators." *Journal of Palliative Medicine* 7 (5): 668–75.

Schnelle, J. F., S. F. Simmons, C. Harrington, M. Cadogan, E. Garcia, and B. M.
Bates-Jensen. 2004. "Relationship of Nursing Home Staffing to Quality of
Care." *Health Services Research* 39 (2): 225–50.

Seale, C. 1998. "Theories in Health Care and Research: Theories and Studying the
Care of Dying People." *British Medical Journal*, 317:1518–20.

Teno, J. M. 2004. "Brown Atlas of Dying." http://www.chcr.brown.edu/dying
/BROWNATLAS.HTM. Accessed October 11, 2007.

Teno, J. M., K. J. Branco, V. Mor, et al. 1997. "Changes in Advance Care Planning in
Nursing Homes Before and After the Patient Self-Determination Act: Report of
a Ten-State Survey." *Journal of the American Geriatrics Society* 45 (8): 939–44.

Teno, J. M., B. R. Clarridge, V. Casey, L. C. Welch, T. Wetle, R. Shield, and V. Mor.
2004. "Family Perspectives on End-of-Life Care at the Last Place of Care."
Journal of the American Medical Association 291 (1): 88–93.

Teno, J. M., and J. Lynn. 1996. "Putting Advance-Care Planning Into Action." *Journal of Clinical Ethics* 205 (Fall): 205–13.

Thompson, S., and D. P. Oliver. 2008. "A New Model for Long-Term Care: Balancing Palliative and Restorative Care Delivery." *Journal of Housing for the Elderly* 22:1–26.

Travis, S. S., M. Bernard, S. Dixon, W. J. McAuley, G. Loving, and L. McClanahan. 2002. "Obstacles to Palliation and End-of-Life Care in a Long-Term Care Facility." *Gerontologist* 42 (3): 342–49.

United States Department of Health and Human Services. 2000. Offices of Disease Prevention and Health Promotion. "Healthy People 2010: Objectives for Improving Health (Part A)." Washington, D.C.

Unruh, L., and T. T. Wan. 2004. "A Systems Framework for Evaluating Nursing Care Quality in Nursing Homes." *Journal of Medical Systems* 28 (2): 197–214.

Wan, T. H., N. J. Zhang, and L. Unruh. 2007. "Predictors of Resident Outcome Improvement in Nursing Homes." *Western Journal of Nursing Research* 28 (8): 974–93.

Weitzen, S., J. M. Teno, M. Fennell, and V. Mor. "Factors Associated with Site of Death." *Medical Care* 41 (2): 323–35.

World Health Organization. 2002. *National Cancer Control Programs: Policies and Managerial Guidelines.* Washington, D.C.: World Health Organization.

Wowchuk, S. M., S. McClement, and J. Bond. 2007. "The Challenges of Providing Palliative Care in the Nursing Home, Part II: Internal Factors." *International Journal of Palliative Nursing* 13 (7): 345–50.

Wright, B. 2001. "Federal and State Enforcement of the 1987 Nursing Home Reform Act." AARP Public Policy Institute. http://www.aarp.org/research/longtermcare/nursinghomes/aresearch-import-686- FS83.html. Accessed November 16, 2007.

Zimmerman, D. R., S. L. Karon, G. Arling, B. R. Clark, T. Collins, R. Ross, and F. Sainfort. 1995. "Development and Testing of Nursing Home Quality Indicators." *Health Care Financing Review* 16 (4): 107–27.

[3]

Paying for Advanced Chronic Illness and Hospice Care in America's Nursing Homes

MICHAEL KLUG

Nursing home social workers connect residents and family members with resources that include the legal, spiritual, social, mental health, and financial. This chapter is about financial and hospice services. The purpose of this chapter is to provide a general overview of how nursing home care is financed as a way to introduce the Medicare hospice benefit. When social workers understand the financial context of paying for services, they are in a better position to explain options to residents, family, and fellow staff members, and they are better able to advocate for the type of care their residents prefer. This advocacy is needed at the individual and organizational level and also at the national-policy level. By demystifying Medicare hospice eligibility and coverage, this chapter aims to help nursing home social workers connect residents with all the services they are entitled to as the end of life approaches.

It is important to begin the chapter by clarifying that the current structure of the U.S. healthcare system has been designed mainly for acute-care purposes, although there is a growing recognition that an optimal healthcare system would include a full range of preventive health measures and coverage designed for chronic-care needs (Kane et al. 2005).

Despite the fact that the healthcare system has not been designed for chronic illnesses, most of the people who use healthcare services do so in relation to chronic illnesses such as diabetes, heart conditions, and high blood pressure. "With increasing life expectancy and aging of the baby boom generation, the United States is rapidly becoming a country in which health care needs are driven by older adults with chronic diseases" (Reuben 2007:2673). Some of the people with the highest degree of chronic-illness-care needs live in nursing homes.

How Nursing Home Care Is Financed in the United States

The average annual cost of nursing home care in the United States was $70,900 in 2006 (Komisar and Thompson 2007). There is no one insurance program that covers care in nursing homes. Instead, a patchwork of programs contributes to the cost of care for nursing home residents, and if they have no insurance or their insurance coverage is limited, residents themselves are expected to pay out of pocket for care as long as their finances allow. Some people mistakenly think that Medicare covers the cost of long-term care in nursing homes. While Medicare may pay toward some short-term skilled nursing-facility stays, it does not pay for longer stays.

Table 3.1 uses data from the National Nursing Home Survey to compare the source of payment for nursing home care at two points in time, upon admission and then during data collection for the national survey. The latter can be considered cross-sectional data that answer the question, "On any given day, what is the mix of payers?" Table 3.1 shows that a higher proportion of residents are admitted with Medicare paying toward the nursing home costs, but that on any given day, Medicaid is paying toward the cost of more residents than is Medicare. The proportion of residents paid for by private and other sources remains constant. Sex, race, and marital status are all related to the percent of people in each category who receive Medicare or Medicaid payments toward the cost of their care.

Another way to address the issue is to look at the proportion of total nursing home costs—over the course of a year—by payer. The Georgetown University Long-Term Care Financing Project (Komisar and Thompson 2007) reports that in 2005, the four largest sources of payment came from Medicaid (48.9%, $100 billion), Medicare (20.4%, $42 billion), out of pocket (18%, $37 billion), and private health or long-term-care insurance (7%, $15 billion).

TABLE 3.1

Percent of Nursing Home Residents by Payment Source at Time of Admission and at Time of Interview: National Nursing Home Survey, 2004

	AT TIME OF ADMISSION				AT TIME OF NNHS STUDY			
	Private	Medicare	Medicaid	Other	Private	Medicare	Medicaid	Other
All	15.2	30.1	34.2	2.9	17.1	7.9	58.7	3.6
Age								
Under 65	4.9	12.7	55.1	5.6	5.8	4.0	68.5	6.2
Ages 65–74	8.8	27.4	40.1	3.8	9.6	8.5	63.7	4.4
Ages 75–84	13.9	34.0	32.5	3.3	15.4	9.4	57.1	3.8
Ages 85+	20.4	32.7	28.5	1.8	23.1	7.7	55.9	2.7
Sex								
Female	15.9	30.2	34.6	1.9	17.5	7.7	60.7	2.8
Male	13.5	30.1	33.3	5.5	16.1	8.6	53.6	5.8
Race								
Black*	3.7	22.1	52.7	2.3	3.1	5.9	73.5	3.3
White	17.0	31.4	31.3	3.0	19.3	8.2	56.2	3.7

(Continued on next page)

TABLE 3.1 (Continued)

Percent of Nursing Home Residents by Payment Source at Time of Admission and at Time of Interview: National Nursing Home Survey, 2004

	AT TIME OF ADMISSION				AT TIME OF NNHS STUDY			
	Private	Medicare	Medicaid	Other	Private	Medicare	Medicaid	Other
Marital status								
Married	17.7	34.1	28.4	3.7	20.8	9.7	49.4	4.6
Widowed	17.2	32.9	31.6	2.1	19.2	8.3	58.3	2.7
Divorced or separated	7.8	22.7	45.2	4.9	7.9	6.8	67.1	5.1
Single or never married	9.5	20.3	44.6	3.6	11.2	4.8	67.5	4.4

Private = private health insurance, life-care program, private pay, self, and out of pocket

Other = welfare, government assistance, and VA

Note: Includes multiple counts for residents with more than one payment source

* Because of small sample size many of these numbers have a relative standard error of 30% or more.

Source: CDC/NCHS 2008: table 9.

It is important for social workers to be familiar with the conditions under which different payers will contribute toward the cost of nursing home care, as many people—including nursing home residents, family members, and many healthcare providers—are confused. Having a basic understanding of sources of payment and conditions of payment can help prevent problems for residents and families.

What Nursing Home Costs Are Paid by Medicare?

Medicare is the federal program that provides health insurance to nearly 45 million people. In general, three groups are eligible for Medicare: people age sixty-five and older, younger people who qualify for Social Security disability benefits, and people with end-stage renal disease. While most of those who benefit from the Medicare program—called beneficiaries—are entitled to Medicare's hospital insurance because they or a spouse or parent paid a Medicare tax on wages, people sixty-five and older who are not entitled to Medicare through employment can enroll voluntarily in the program if they are citizens of the United States or resident aliens who have lived in the country for at least five years in a row before applying.

The Medicare program has four parts. Parts A, B, and D set forth the scope of Medicare's covered benefits. Part C, on the other hand, establishes several different systems for delivering Medicare's covered benefits through private insurance plans. Medicare Part A covers inpatient hospital care, *skilled nursing facility care*, home health care, and hospice care. Medicare Part B covers physician services, outpatient hospital care, durable medical equipment, ambulance services, some prevention and screening services, immunosuppressive and outpatient chemotherapy drugs, and other services and items. Taken together, Medicare Parts A and B are called original Medicare, traditional Medicare, or fee-for-service Medicare. Medicare Part D provides prescription-drug coverage through privately sponsored Medicare drug plans.

Medicare Part C created the "Medicare Advantage" program. It pays private insurance companies to deliver Medicare's covered benefits and other services through different types of MA plans, also called "Medicare health plans." These include local health maintenance organizations, local and regional preferred provider organizations, private-fee-for-service plans, special needs plans, and a few more. MA plans must cover the same benefits that the original Medicare program does, including hospice care. Medicare beneficiaries must choose to receive their benefits from either the original Medicare program or an MA plan. In 2008, 23 percent of Medicare beneficiaries belonged to Medicare Advantage plans. Beneficiary enrollment in MA plans varies greatly among the states. More than half of all MA plan members nationwide live in just six states: California, Florida, New York, Ohio, Pennsylvania, and Texas (Kaiser Family Foundation 2008). Medicare Part A pays for acute-care inpatient hospital services and for inpatient post-acute care in three settings: rehabilitation hospitals, long-term care hospitals, and skilled nursing facilities. This chapter focuses on Medicare in nursing homes.

Medicare's coverage for nursing home costs generally is limited to payments for skilled nursing facility care. Medicare Part A pays for SNF care when a beneficiary has been in a hospital for three consecutive days, enters the SNF within thirty days of hospital discharge, and then receives skilled nursing or rehabilitation services on a daily basis for a condition that is related to the hospital stay. Some examples of skilled nursing services are intravenous or intramuscular injections, intravenous feeding, and treatment of severe skin breakdown. Rehabilitation services include physical therapy, speech therapy, and occupational therapy. Beneficiaries whose SNF stays are based only on the need for rehabilitative care meet the "daily basis" requirement when they receive skilled rehabilitation services, for example, physical therapy, five days per week. Otherwise, Medicare does not cover nursing home costs when beneficiaries receive skilled care on less than a daily basis, except when a person's medical condition (e.g., extreme fatigue) requires a short break in a rehabilitation program.

When beneficiaries meet Medicare's SNF coverage criteria, Medicare Part A pays the nursing home for up to one hundred days of care in a benefit period. (A benefit period starts when a person is admitted to a hospital and ends when she has been out of a hospital or SNF for sixty days in a row; benefit periods are renewable.) Medicare's payments cover the entire cost of SNF care for the first twenty days and part of the cost for days twenty-one through one hundred. Beneficiaries owe a daily coinsurance charge after the twenty-first day ($133.50 per day in 2009). Medicare's payment rates cover the SNF's charges for bed and board, nursing services, physical therapy, speech pathology, medical social services, drugs and appliances that facilities ordinarily provide to inpatients, and other related services. As conditions of program participation, nursing facilities agree to bill Medicare directly for SNF care and to accept Medicare's payment rate as full payment. Nursing homes can bill beneficiaries with Medicare-covered stays only for the coinsurance charges for the twenty-first through one hundredth days and for services and items that Medicare excludes from payment, such as private laundry, cosmetology, and general transportation services (Medicare covers some ambulance trips).

Medicare uses a per diem prospective payment system to pay SNFs for all costs related to the services they must provide under Medicare Part A. This means that nursing homes know in advance how much Medicare will pay them for patients with certain medical conditions and skilled-care needs. Medicare adjusts its SNF payments for differences in the complexity of cases and for geographic wage variations. In 2006, Medicare Part A's average reimbursement to SNFs per discharge was $10,304. The average number of days per discharge was thirty-four. In 2005, Medicare's payments for SNF benefits comprised 16.6 percent of the nation's $129.8 billion annual spending on nursing home care (Komisar and Thompson 2007).

When Medicare beneficiaries reside in nursing homes but do not qualify for Part A's SNF coverage, Medicare Part B may still cover some of the services and items they need, for example, physical therapy sessions with an independent therapist who bills Medicare separately from the nursing home, mobile X-ray services, oral chemotherapy medications, and prosthetics. At the same time, Medicare Part D covers most prescription drugs. Significantly, Medicare Part A also covers hospice benefits for nursing home residents who do not meet the conditions for Medicare-covered SNF services, and in some situations a hospice may pay for a beneficiary's short-term nursing home stay (Medicare's hospice benefit is described later).

What Nursing Home Costs Does Private Insurance Pay?

Two types of private health insurance pay for nursing home care: supplemental insurance and long-term-care insurance. Insurance companies sell group policies and individual policies for both types. A large number of Medicare beneficiaries have some sort of supplemental insurance coverage to help cover Medicare's cost-sharing charges. In 2006, 35 percent of beneficiaries, more than 15 million people, had coverage through employer-sponsored plans for retirees, and about 8 million beneficiaries purchased

Medicare supplement (Medigap) insurance policies on an individual basis (Cubanski et al. 2008).

Employer-sponsored retiree group plans vary greatly, but many cover the daily coinsurance charge for the twenty-first through hundredth days of Medicare-covered SNF stays and other out-of-pocket costs. Some plans also cover SNF stays beyond Medicare's hundred days. Monthly premiums and other out-of-pocket costs also vary among employer-sponsored insurance plans.

Medicare beneficiaries who do not have employer-sponsored group insurance often buy individual insurance policies commonly called "Medigap insurance." State insurance agencies regulate Medigap insurance, the technical term for which is "Medicare supplement insurance." State law allows companies only to sell twelve standard policies that fill certain defined "gaps" in the original Medicare program's coverage, including the daily coinsurance charge for Medicare-covered SNF stays. The premiums for Medigap policies range widely, from about $70 to more than $400 per month, depending on such factors as the number of gaps the policy covers and the insured person's age.

In 2005, about five million individual long-term-care insurance policies and about two million group policies were in force in the United States (America's Health Insurance Plans 2007). An estimated 3.5 to 4 million people aged sixty-five and older have long-term-care insurance, roughly 10 percent of Medicare beneficiaries in that age group. Long-term-care insurance policies pay for the type of care that Medicare considers nonskilled or custodial and therefore does not cover. These policies cover some or all of the services that people need when they cannot take care of basic activities of daily living, such as bathing, dressing, toileting, cooking, and eating, on their own. Many policies available in 2008 pay for these services in a number of care settings, including nursing homes, assisted living facilities, and at home.

Unlike Medigap insurance, long-term-care insurance policies do not conform to a standard set of benefits, though many policies have common features. For example, most policies pay a set dollar amount per day, week, or month when a beneficiary receives covered services. Long-term care insurance policies commonly have an "elimination period," a set number of days before the policy starts to pay benefits. A typical elimination period is ninety days and starts when a person first meets the policy's conditions for payment. Most policies also limit the length of time they pay benefits, for example, to three or four years. The cost of long-term-care insurance varies considerably. For people aged sixty-five to sixty-nine who bought long-term-care insurance in 2005, the average annual premium was $2,003. Some of the factors that affect premiums are age at purchase, benefit (pay-out) levels and duration, and the purchase of optional features such as inflation protection. State insurance agencies regulate long-term-insurance policies and the companies that sell them. People who have concerns about a long-term-care insurance policy or company should contact the state insurance agency.

Together, supplemental insurance and long-term-care insurance covered just 7 percent of the nation's nearly $130 billion spending on nursing home care in 2005 (Komisar and Thompson 2007). That is because supplemental insurance policies generally follow Medicare Part A rules for SNF care and pay only after Medicare approves coverage for a nursing home stay, and because the vast majority of Medicare beneficiaries and current nursing home residents do not own long-term-care insurance policies.

What Nursing Home Costs Does Medicaid Pay?

The Medicaid program pays more for nursing home care in the United States than any other payer, much more than Medicare and private insurance combined. In 2005, Medicaid paid $59 billion for nursing home care, representing more than 45 percent of the nation's $129.8 billion annually spent on nursing home care, more than Medicare and private supplemental insurance and long-term-care health insurance combined (Komisar and Thompson 2007). In 2002, Medicaid helped pay for nursing home care for approximately 1.7 million people, most of whom were sixty-five or older (O'Brien 2005).

States administer the Medicaid programs under broad federal regulations, with oversight by the federal Centers for Medicare and Medicaid Services (CMS). Within certain minimum program requirements, each state can set its own eligibility rules, decide the scope and duration of services, and set payment rates, including the copayment costs that Medicaid recipients pay out of pocket. State and federal funds together finance Medicaid. The federal contribution to states varies based on per capita income, with the federal government paying a greater share of Medicaid program costs for states with low per capita income.

Because the law gives the states so much flexibility in designing their Medicaid programs, in many ways there are fifty-four different state and territorial Medicaid programs. The common thread, however, is the approach the states take to deciding who qualifies for Medicaid. Applicants must show that their income and assets are low enough to qualify. States often base their income-eligibility tests on the federal Supplemental Security Income payment level ($674 per month for one person and $1,011 per month for a married couple in 2009), though some states set higher limits. Most states also use SSI's resource standard of $2,000 for one person and $3,000 for a married couple. Generally, people who are sixty-five and older, blind, or disabled and whose countable income and assets are below these levels or whose medical expenses offset their income to the extent that they meet a qualifying income test, are eligible for Medicaid. Many nursing home residents whose monthly income exceeds the standard income level for Medicaid eligibility qualify for the program by using nursing home costs to "spend down" their income—such as Social Security and pension income—to qualifying "medically needy" or other low "special income levels."

Example: Mrs. Hanson's has monthly income of $2,080 from Social Security and a pension. The monthly semiprivate-room rate at the nursing home where she resides is $4,000. If Mrs. Hanson is a Medicaid recipient, she owes the nursing home $2,000 toward the cost of her care. The Medicaid program pays the $2,000 balance to help cover the $4,000 cost. As a Medicaid recipient, state law disregards $20 of monthly income and allows Mrs. Hanson to keep $60 as a monthly "personal allowance."

As a condition for receiving federal Medicaid payments, state programs agree to cover a set of basic mandatory benefits. These include inpatient and outpatient hospital services, physician services, rural health clinic services, and nursing facility services for those aged twenty-one and older, and more. States can also receive federal payments to provide an array of optional benefits that include optometrist services and eyeglasses, rehabilitation and physical therapy services, transportation services, and dental care to name a few.

Hospice care is another optional benefit that some state Medicaid programs provide. People who have both Medicare and Medicaid, called "dually eligible," would almost always receive hospice benefits through Medicare because Medicaid is a payer of last resort. The one exception would be the rare case where a Medicare beneficiary has Part B without Part A. Medicare Part B does not cover hospice care.

Out-of-Pocket Payments for Nursing Home Care

In 2005, people in nursing facilities and their families spent more than $32 billion out of pocket on nursing home care, roughly one-fourth of the nation's total spending on nursing homes for that year. Those who pay for nursing home care out of pocket are called "private-pay patients." The national average private-pay rate for a semiprivate room in a nursing home was $183 per day, or $66,795 per year, in 2006 (Houser 2007). Annual costs for private rooms topped $70,000 (Komisar and Thompson 2007). Without Medicare or private long-term-care insurance coverage to help pay the bill, many people exhaust their savings and other financial resources quickly.

Federal and state law enables spouses of nursing home residents to protect some of the couple's assets to prevent "spousal impoverishment." Otherwise, people who are not immediately eligible for Medicaid upon entering a nursing home spend their assets and income on nursing home costs until their remaining "countable resources" are low enough to meet Medicaid's eligibility resource level ($2,000 for one person in most states). Medicaid supports the cost of care for nearly 65 percent of nursing home residents in the United States.

The Medicare Hospice Benefit

Introduction and Background

Hospice agencies typically provide services in a person's home under Medicare's hospice benefit, but they may also provide hospice care to nursing home residents when the hospice and nursing home have a written agreement. In 2005, 28 percent of hospice beneficiaries nationwide were nursing home residents for at least part of the time they received hospice care. Compared with hospice patients in other care settings, nursing home hospice beneficiaries were more than twice as likely to have terminal diagnoses of mental disorders like dementia, Alzheimer's, and other hard to define conditions like "failure to thrive." A large percentage of these nursing home residents lived in the Midwest (Office of Inspector General 2007).

Regardless of the setting—home or nursing home—hospice care takes an interdisciplinary approach that includes social-services staff to care for terminally ill people with a focus on comfort rather than a cure. Hospice staff views the patient and family as a unit receiving care. Hospice services include pain control and counseling, including bereavement counseling for surviving family members and significant others (Federal Register 2008:32208). Given this approach, terminally ill nursing home residents and their family caregivers usually have access to some services through a hospice, such as continuous care during a medical crisis that they would not have through a nursing home alone.

Medicare's hospice coverage began in November 1983 and is available to Medicare beneficiaries whose life expectancy is six months or less. The coverage can extend for more than six months if the hospice patient lives longer. The goal of the hospice benefit is to help terminally ill people manage their pain and other symptoms. Hospice care is designed to provide palliative care not curative care. Medicare's hospice benefit also covers some support services for family members, such as respite care and bereavement counseling, not available elsewhere in the Medicare program.

The hospice benefit has had a history of public misunderstanding and underutilization. This led Congress to enact legislation in 1997 and 2003 aimed at improving access. Rates of use and payments to hospice providers have correspondingly risen in recent years. Only 16 percent of the Medicare beneficiaries who died in 1998 used Medicare's hospice benefit. Those who used hospice services typically did so only for a short time—sometimes for less than a week—before they died.

Between 2000 and 2005, however, the total number of patients receiving Medicare-covered hospice care increased more than 60 percent from 534,213 to 871,249. Average lengths of stay under Medicare-covered hospice care have slowly crept upward from a national average of 48 days in 1998 to 67 days in 2005. But the average lengths of stays vary considerably among the states, from a low of 41 days in South Dakota to a high of 122 days in Mississippi in 2005. Twenty-two states had average stays within a range of 41 to 51 days in 2004 (MedPAC 2006).

The latest data from the National Hospice and Palliative Care Organization reveal that 1.3 million people were enrolled in hospice in 2007 and that the vast majority of people who use hospice are older adults. In fact, 81.1 percent were age sixty-five or older, and about a third of all hospice patients (32.2 percent) were age eighty-six or older (NHPCO 2007). Nursing home residents accounted for about one in five (22.5 percent) hospice deaths in 2005 (NHCPO 2007:2).

While the general pubic tends to think of Medicare's hospice benefit in connection with cancer, people with other terminal diagnoses also receive Medicare coverage for hospice care. In 2005, about half (44 percent) of hospice admissions were for people with a cancer diagnosis. The second most prevalent diagnosis was heart disease, accounting for 12 percent of hospice admissions in 2006 (NHCPO 2007:3).

In 2006, the NHPCO reports there were 4,500 hospices in the United States, up from 3,100 in 2000 (NHCPO 2007:5). In 2000, 27 percent of hospice agencies were for profit. The vast majority were nonprofit organizations. That ratio is changing. As of December 2006, 46 percent of the hospice agencies were for-profit companies (NHCPO 2007:5). Steady increases in federal spending have drawn more providers to the business. Between 2000 and 2005, Medicare's annual spending on hospice care rose from $2.9 billion to over $8.1 billion. It is projected to increase at an annual rate of 9 percent through 2015 (MedPAC 2007).

Eligibility for Medicare's Hospice Benefit: Certification, Election, Revocation

As mentioned earlier in this chapter, people with Medicare Part A hospital-insurance coverage have hospice benefits available to them. Medicare pays only for hospice services that a Medicare-approved hospice provides. Medicare beneficiaries or their representatives can make a "hospice election" if the beneficiary's attending physician (if she or he has one) and the hospice medical director or another staff physician certify that a person's life expectancy is six months or less if the terminal illness runs its normal course. Medicare expects physicians to use their professional judgment in making these prognoses. The program's policy guidelines say, "Predicting of life expectancy is not always exact. The fact that a beneficiary lives longer than expected in itself is not cause to terminate benefits" (CMS 2004: chap. 9, §10). (Note: the Code of Federal Regulations [42 CFR Part 418] spells out the parameters of the Medicare hospice benefit and can be accessed through http://www.gpoaccess.gov/CFR). To see additional details about the Medicare hospice benefit, consult CMS's *Medicare Benefit Policy Manual* at http://www.cms.hhs.gov/Manuals/IOM/list/asp.

A beneficiary gives a notice of hospice election by completing a form that

- identifies the hospice agency providing care;
- acknowledges the beneficiary's understanding of what hospice care involves;
- includes a statement indicating that the beneficiary understands that she or he is accepting palliative care *for the terminal condition* and is waiving the right for Medicare services designed to cure the terminal condition (Medicare services for other unrelated conditions remain in effect);
- sets the date on which the hospice election takes effect; and
- includes the beneficiary's signature.

A beneficiary who makes a hospice election agrees to forgo Medicare payments for care that is *intended to cure the terminal condition.* This includes inpatient hospital care and emergency-room and ambulance services unless they are arranged by the hospice's medical team. It is important for patients, family members, and nursing home staff members to understand, however, that Medicare will continue to pay for medical care and services, including prescription drugs, for health conditions that are *not* related to the terminal condition. Medicare would, for example, pay to set a broken arm for a nursing home resident receiving hospice services for terminal cancer.

Some medical procedures can be considered curative or palliative. As long as the main purpose is palliation (i.e., to provide comfort) and the services are considered part of the hospice package, Medicare's hospice benefit should cover the costs. For example, people with terminal cancer may decide to accept radiation that is not aimed at curing the cancer but at shrinking the cancer and reducing the discomfort of the tumor. The Medicare hospice benefit can pay for this "palliative radiation."

Many people are confused about attempting cardiopulmonary resuscitation and Medicare hospice eligibility. Medicare does not require a "do not resuscitate" order for any beneficiary—including nursing home residents—to be enrolled in hospice. People can receive Medicare hospice benefits and either be DNR or full-code, meaning that medical personnel will use all available means to revive a patient who is in cardiac arrest. Social workers should encourage residents and family members to talk with the physician about CPR effectiveness and side effects as part of the decision-making process. Many people do not realize that attempting CPR on a person in frail health is seldom effective in keeping the person alive and often cracks ribs. CPR was never intended for people in the advanced stages of serious illness (Last Acts 2004).

Medicare Hospice Care Benefit Periods

Medicare covers hospice care in "periods of care," also called benefit periods. During a person's lifetime, he or she is eligible for two ninety-day Medicare hospice benefit periods and an unlimited number of sixty-day benefit periods. Benefit periods are important in terms of recertifying a beneficiary's terminal illness. At the start of each beneficiary period, the hospice medical director or a hospice staff physician must recertify the beneficiary's terminal illness in order to continue the hospice care. Note that the hospice benefit is unrelated to the Part A inpatient benefit period described earlier.

A beneficiary has the right to change from one hospice provider to a different provider once per benefit period. In addition, at any time, beneficiaries can cancel a hospice election and restore their eligibility for Medicare's other benefits, including curative care for the terminal condition. The revocation must be in writing, signed, dated, and filed with the hospice. When a person revokes a hospice election because, for example, her cancer is in remission and she is no longer terminally ill, she gives up the remaining days in the benefit period. If the beneficiary is terminally ill in the future, she again must submit the paperwork to make a hospice election and start a new benefit period.

A hospice agency may discharge a Medicare patient when the beneficiary

- is no longer considered to be terminally ill;
- moves away from the hospice's geographic service area;
- transfers to another hospice;

- revokes the hospice election (in other words decides to return to regular Medicare);
- behaves in a disruptive, abusive, or uncooperative manner (discharge for cause); or
- dies.

Medicare-certified hospices must have a discharge-planning process in place to address the needs of patients who stabilize or who can no longer be certified as terminally ill. Discharge planning should include necessary family counseling, patient education, and other services related to the termination of hospice care.

Medicare rules involving a discharge for cause allow hospices to discharge a patient whose behavior seriously impairs the ability of the hospice to deliver care or to operate effectively. Before a hospice agency discharges a patient for cause, it must advise the patient or representative that a discharge is being considered, make a serious effort to resolve the problem, verify that the proposed discharge is not caused by the patient's high utilization of necessary hospice services, and document in the medical record the problems and the steps taken toward resolution.

Medicare-Covered Hospice Services

Medicare covers hospice services that are reasonable and necessary for the palliation or management of a terminal illness and related conditions. In order to participate in Medicare, hospice organizations must designate an interdisciplinary group to develop a care plan and to provide or supervise the services that the hospice delivers. The group or team must include at least a doctor of medicine or osteopathy, a registered nurse, a qualified social worker, and a pastoral or other counselor (CCH Health 2008:76). Medicare rules require hospice agencies to designate an R.N. to ensure continuous assessment of each patient's and family's needs and to coordinate the implementation of patient-care plans.

Hospices must have a nurse and physician on-call at all times. Hospice agencies provide access to massage therapists, music therapists, recreation therapists, and so on on an as-needed basis. Hospice agencies also have volunteers who may perform administrative tasks or provide services to patients and their caregivers. By connecting nursing home residents to hospice services, nursing home social workers can help residents and families gain access to services that would not otherwise be paid for by Medicare, Medicaid, or private insurance.

Medicare-covered hospice services includes:

- Nursing care provided by or under the supervision of an RN
- Medical social services provided by a qualified social worker under a physician's direction
- Physician services (including nurse practitioners in the role of attending physicians)
- Counseling services (including dietary counseling and loss counseling) for the terminally ill person and family members or other caregivers to help them adjust to the approaching death
- Short-term inpatient care provided in a participating hospice inpatient unit, a participating hospital, or a skilled nursing facility to provide pain control and symptom management or respite for caregivers
- Medical appliances (equipment such as wheelchairs and other self-help and personal-comfort items)
- Medical supplies (such as bandages and catheters)
- Drugs for pain control and managing symptoms
- Home health aide and homemaker services
- Physical therapy, occupational therapy, and speech pathology for the purpose of symptom control or to maintain basic functional skills
- Bereavement counseling for the survivors for up to one year after the death
- Other services specified in the patient's care plan that are necessary for the palliation and management of the terminal illness and related conditions

MEDICAL SOCIAL WORK SERVICES THROUGH MEDICARE HOSPICE

As reported in the Federal Register, "The MSW is the standard level of care within hospice" (Federal Register 2008:32202). Medicare hospice Condition of Participation regulations were updated in June 2008 (effective December 2, 2008) and clarify that a hospice social worker must have a master's in social work degree or a bachelor's in social work or in a related field and must be supervised by a person with an MSW (Federal Register 2008:32202). The new regulations also articulate hospice beneficiary rights and require quality-assessment and performance-improvement programs for the first time.

Covered medical social services in Medicare hospice include, for example, assessment of the psychosocial factors related to the patient's illness and the person's response to treatment and adjustment to care; assessment of the relationship between the patient's medical and nursing needs and the patient's home environment; acting to obtain community resources; and services for a patient's family member or caregiver when needed to remove a barrier to the effective treatment of the patient's medical condition or rate of recovery.

Medical Crises

During periods of medical crisis, Medicare covers "Continuous Home Care," which can include nursing care on a continuous basis for up to twenty-four hours a day. The hospice benefit also provides coverage for continuous home-health-aide or homemaker services during periods of crisis as long as the nursing care predominates the services a patient needs. The hospice CHC benefit is not to be confused with the regular Medicare Part A home-health benefit, which never covers around-the-clock nursing or home-health-aide services.

Medicare's policy guidelines define a period of crisis as "a period in which the individual requires continuous care which is primarily nursing care to achieve palliation or management of acute medical symptoms." The guidelines also state that Continuous Home Care can be given when a patient is in a long-term-care facility (CMS 2004: chap. 9, §10). Medicare's base payment rate for CHC in 2009 was $816.94 per day; more than five times the $139.97 daily base rate for routine home care provided through hospice (see "Levels of Care").

Medications

As part of the hospice benefit, Medicare covers only drugs and biologicals that are prescribed to relieve pain and control symptoms related to the patient's terminal condition. Morphine is an example of a covered drug. The beneficiary is responsible for a small coinsurance payment. If a beneficiary needs medications to treat a condition other than the terminal illness, Medicare would pay through the Part D prescription-drug program.

Medicare's hospice benefit covers some services that Medicare otherwise excludes from its Part A hospital, SNF, and home-health coverage. Medicare covers respite care, homemaker services, personal-comfort items, and some custodial care for those who qualify for hospice care. Respite care is short-term inpatient care available only when necessary to relieve the caregivers who are caring for the dying person at home. A hospice may provide respite care only on an occasional basis and is not reimbursed for more than five consecutive days at a time. Hospices must offer to provide bereavement counseling to a person's family for up to one year after his or her death as a condition of participating in Medicare.

Levels of Care and Medicare Hospice Payments

The Centers for Medicare and Medicaid Services, the federal Medicare agency, pays hospices a daily rate, up to an inflation-adjusted payment cap, for four different levels or categories of care. The annual hospice payment cap was $22,386 for 2008. If the hospice's total Medicare payments divided by the total number of beneficiaries exceed the cap amount, the hospice must repay the excess to Medicare. The four levels of care and their base payment rates for 2009 are:

- Routine home care, with a payment rate of $139.97 per day
- Continuous home care, with a base payment rate of $816.94 per day
- Inpatient respite care, with a base payment rate of $144.79 per day
- General inpatient care, with a base payment rate of $622.66 per day

Continuous home care (see the "Medical Crises" section) refers to care that the patient receives during brief periods of crisis and only as needed to enable her to remain at home (including nursing homes). Medicare pays hospices for continuous home care if a patient receives at least eight hours of continuous care. If a patient receives less than eight hours of care in a day, Medicare pays at the routine home-care rate. About 95 percent of Medicare-covered hospice days are paid at the routine home-care level.

General inpatient care involves placement in an inpatient facility—a hospital, an SNF under contract with the hospice, or a hospice's own acute-care unit—for pain control or to manage acute or chronic symptoms that cannot be managed at home or in other care settings. Medicare regulations limit payments to a hospice for general inpatient care to 20 percent of the total number of days of hospice care it furnishes to beneficiaries. This means, however, that the Medicare hospice benefit may cover the room and board costs on a short-term basis for nursing home residents who need general inpatient care. Medicare guidelines give some examples of appropriate general inpatient care that include "a patient in need of medication adjustment, observation, or other stabilizing treatment such as psycho-social monitoring" (CMS 2004: chap. 9, §40.1.5).

Medicare employs contractors to make Medicare coverage decisions and process claims for hospice payment. Currently they are called regional home health intermediaries. RHHIs cover multistate and territorial regions under contracts with the Centers for Medicare and Medicaid Services. CMS is in the midst, however, of an effort called "Medicare contracting reform." In time, new home-health and hospice Medicare Administrative Contractors will handle hospice claims for four home-health and hospice regions. In the event that there is a need for clarification about some aspect of Medicare hospice eligibility or coverage, or to learn about appeal rights, the MAC is the organization to contact.

Out-of-Pocket Costs for Hospice Services

Medicare payments cover nearly all of the costs associated with hospice care. There are minimal cost-sharing charges for two hospice services, palliative medications and respite care. There is a 5 percent coinsurance charge for palliative drugs and biologicals (e.g., whole blood and blood-clotting factors), which is not to exceed $5.00 per prescription, and a 5 percent coinsurance charge for each day of respite care (estimated at $7 per day), which is capped at a total of $1,064 (in 2009). Private-pay nursing home residents with hospice care would be paying nursing home room rates in addition to these hospice copayments, as the hospice benefit does not typically pay for room and board in a nursing home. This is explained more fully below.

Medicare Advantage Plans and Hospice Care

While most people with Medicare receive their benefits through the fee-for-service original Medicare program (Medicare Parts A and B), about one-fourth of Medicare's 45 million beneficiaries are enrolled in privately administered Medicare Advantage plans. These plans contract with Medicare to deliver Medicare-covered services along with some additional benefits. MA plans include Medicare health maintenance organizations, preferred provider organizations, private-fee-for-service plans, and a few others. MA plan members can elect hospice care outside their plans under the same eligibility rules as beneficiaries in the original Medicare program.

Medicare-Covered Hospice Care in Nursing Facilities

A terminally ill Medicare beneficiary who resides in a nursing facility may elect Medicare's hospice benefit if:

- the beneficiary is paying privately for residential care; or
- the beneficiary is eligible for both Medicare and Medicaid and the state Medicaid program is reimbursing the nursing facility for the beneficiary's nonhospice care; and
- the hospice and nursing facility agree in writing that the hospice will take full responsibility for managing the beneficiary's hospice care and the facility will provide room and board.

Some residents may enter the nursing home with hospice services; others live in the nursing home for months or years before electing hospice benefits. Medicare policy guidelines confirm that a beneficiary could receive Medicare coverage for an SNF stay and for hospice care at the same time if the SNF stay is for a condition that is unrelated to the terminal condition (CMS 2004: chap. 9, §20.3).

When a person signs up for hospice, the hospice receives a certain amount of money from Medicare to meet the palliative-care needs of the terminally ill patient. The hospice agency is to cover any care the hospice patient needs to meet her pain-control and comfort-care needs. When a nursing home resident receives hospice care, there are two sources of payment involved: Medicare (for hospice) and Medicaid or private insurance (to cover room and board at the nursing home). Medicare does not pay the room and board costs of nursing home care unless the beneficiary qualifies for Medicare's SNF benefits for a condition unrelated to the terminal illness. If the nursing home resident is not eligible for Medicaid or has no private insurance, she will have to pay the nursing home room and board costs out of pocket while Medicare covers the separate cost for hospice care.

When nursing home residents who have both Medicare and Medicaid (dually eligible beneficiaries) elect the Medicare hospice benefit, the state Medicaid agency pays the hospice the daily amount for nursing home room and board while the beneficiary receives hospice care. Medicare guidelines state that the room and board services for which the nursing facility is responsible include personal care, help with activities of daily living, administering medication, maintaining a clean room for the beneficiary, and supervising and assisting the beneficiary's use of durable medical equipment and prescribed therapies (CMS 2004: chap. 9, §20.3).

Challenges and Benefits for the Nursing Home When Hospice is Involved in Care

Hospice staff members, with their expertise in end-of-life care, can provide pain and psychosocial relief to nursing home residents. But nursing home staff members have their own areas of expertise; in most cases they know the resident and the family. Sharing responsibility for resident care among the nursing home, the hospice, and the family can lead to misunderstandings if there is no infrastructure developed to clarify expectations and communicate understandings. NHPCO has developed a monograph that mentions some of the specific challenges and benefits from the nursing home/hospice partnership (http://www.nhpco.org/i4a/pages/Index.cfm?pageID=5090). Miller (2007) and colleagues have developed a model for enhancing the opportunities for successful collaboration between nursing homes and hospice as both organizations seek to address end-of-life needs. Nursing home and hospice social workers should be in close communication about resident and family status and unmet needs, as well as how to orchestrate comprehensive nursing home/hospice care for each resident.

WHEN A NURSING HOME RESIDENT GOES HOME WITH HOSPICE SERVICES

When it is clear that a nursing home resident is at the end of life, some-times it is possible for that person to leave the nursing home and die in his or her own apartment or house, with hospice services. When a nurs-ing home social worker helps a resident and family consider the option of the resident's returning home with hospice, it is important to understand what the family can expect from hospice and what hospice will expect from the family.

In a private residence, hospice enrolls only patients who have access to a caregiver. In other words, if the nursing home resident is discharged home from the nursing home, there must be someone available to provide care. The care-giving responsibility can be shared among a group of people. For example, in some retirement-care communities, people are able to leave the skilled nursing unit and return to their independent apartment with the help of volunteers (often from the same retirement community) who take turns staying with the person who is terminally ill. Nursing home social workers should encourage family and friends to contact their local hospices to find out expectations about the availability of caregivers in the home.

Nursing home social workers should also know that some people who elect hospice in their own home are entitled to short-term nursing home care. Indeed, although the most common setting for Medicare-covered hospice services is the home, the benefit includes some short-term inpa-tient care to control pain or to stabilize the patient's condition.

Medicare also pays for a hospice home-health aide to perform light cleaning and laundering tasks as long as the services are "essential to the comfort and cleanliness of the patient." Medicare does not pay for these homemaker services under its regular home-health benefit. Note also that the requirements for hospice patients, unlike the rules for home-health eligibility, do not require that hospice patients be homebound to qualify for Medicare-covered hospice home-health-aide and homemaker services.

In summary, because most nursing home residents and family members are not clear about how nursing home costs are paid, it is important for the social worker to have general familiarity with the Medicare and Medicaid programs. In addition, because hospice is considered the gold standard for end-of-life care, helping families understand the benefits available to residents under hospice and then helping to access these benefits, either in the nursing home or at home, is an important service that nursing home social workers can provide. Even if the social worker does not know all the answers, he or she should know where to begin to track them down. The Medicare website, www.medicare.gov, is a source of information and publications on Medicare's many benefits and services, including hospice care. In addition, all states and most territories have a State Health Insurance Assistance Program that help Medicare beneficiaries and their caregivers in navigating the Medicare program and private health insurance options. SHIP counselors provide free one-on-one assistance with health plan comparisons, enrollment, and problem solving. To find the contact information for a SHIP, go to the Health Assistance Partnership's SHIP Locator Web site, http://www.hapnetwork.org/ship-locator.

The author would like to thank Barbara Frank, Kansas nursing home consultant, for comments on a previous version of this chapter.

References

America's Health Insurance Plans. 2007. "Who Buys Long-Term Care Insurance? A Fifteen-Year Study of Buyers and Non-Buyers, 1990–2005." http://www.ahipresearch.org/PDFs/LTC_Buyers_Guide.pdf. Accessed August 4, 2008.

CCH Health. 2008. *2008 CCH Medicare Explained.* Chicago: Wolters Kluwer Law and Business.

CDC/NCHS. 2008. "National Nursing Home Survey." http://www.cdc.gov/nchs/about/major/nnhsd/ResidentTables_Estimates.htm#PaymentSource.

CMS. 2007. "Medicare National Utilization Summary." October. http://www.cms.hhs.gov. Accessed October 4, 2008.

CMS. 2004. *Medicare Benefit Policy Manual.* Pub. 100-02. http://www.cms.hhs.gov/manuals/Downloads/bp102c09.pdf. Accessed March 14, 2009.

Cubanski, J., T. Neuman, M. K. Strollo, A. Damico, and R. Gonzales. 2008. "Examining Sources of Coverage Among Medicare Beneficiaries: Supplemental Insurance, Medicare Advantage, and Prescription Drug Coverage: Findings from the Medicare Current Beneficiary Survey, 2006." Kaiser Family Foundation. http://www.kff.org/medicare/7801.cfm. Accessed September 29, 2008.

Federal Register. 2008. "Medicare and Medicaid Programs: Hospice Conditions of Participation." 42 CFR Part 418. Final rule published June 5, 2008, vol. 73, number 109. Accessed August 19, 2008: http://edocket.access.gpo.gov/2008/pdf/08-1305.pdf.

Houser. 2007. "Nursing Homes Fact Sheet." AARP Public Policy Institute. http://www. aarp.org/research/longtermcare/nursinghomes/fs10r_homes.html. Accessed September 29, 2008.

Kaiser Family Foundation. 2008. "Medicare Advantage Fact Sheet." September. http://www.kff.org/medicare/2052.cfm. Accessed October 4, 2008.

Kane, R. L., R. Priester, A. M. Totten, and E. Wagner. 2005. *Meeting the Challenge of Chronic Illness*. Baltimore, Md.: Johns Hopkins University Press.

Komisar, H. L. and L. S. Thompson. 2007. "National Spending for Long-Term Care: Fact Sheet." Georgetown University Long-Term Care Financing Project. http://www.ltc.georgetown.edu/pdfs/natspendfeb07.pdf. Accessed September 1, 2008.

Last Acts. 2004. "CPR, It's Not Quite Like ER." Fact sheet. http://www.rwjf.org/pr /product.jsp?id=21335. Accessed July 8, 2008.

MedPAC. 2006. "Report to the Congress: Increasing the Value of Medicare; Medicare's Hospice Benefit: Recent Trends and Consideration of Payment System Refinements." Medicare Payment Advisory Commission. www.medpac.gov. Accessed July 12, 2008.

Miller, S.C. 2007. "Nursing Home/Hospice Partnerships: A Model for Collaborative Success Through Collaborative Solutions." A report funded by the Robert Wood Johnson Foundation. http://www.oashs.rg/PDFs/070315_Nursing_Home-Hospice _Partnerships.pdf. Accessed August 10, 2008

NHPCO. 2007. "NHPCO Facts and Figures: Hospice Care in America." http://www .nhpco.org/files/public/Statistics_Research/NHPCO_facts-and-figures_Nov2007 .pdf. Accessed July 1, 2008.

O'Brien, E. 2005. "Long-Term Care: Understanding Medicaid's Role for the Elderly and Disabled." Kaiser Family Foundation. http://www.kff.org/medicaid/7428 .cfm. Accessed February 8, 2009.

Office of Inspector General. 2007. "Medicare Hospice Care: A Comparison of Beneficiaries in Nursing Facilities and Beneficiaries in Other Settings." Office of Audit Services, Department of Health and Human Services. http://oig.hhs.gov. Accessed July 12, 2008.

Reuben, D. B. 2007. "Better Care for Older People with Chronic Diseases." *Journal of the American Medical Association* 298 (22): 2673–74.

[4]

Trends in the Characteristics of Nursing Homes and Residents

MERCEDES BERN-KLUG

Examining contemporary nursing homes is like looking through a kaleidoscope. Turn it one way, and nursing homes look like the residues of attempts to solve past problems. Turn it the other way, and in today's nursing homes are the seeds of a new vision of care for people who can no longer care for themselves, most of whom are frail elders. This chapter begins with a brief overview of the history of the provision of care to frail elders and then provides an overview of demographic changes that continue to fuel the increase in the number of people in need of long-term care. The chapter then describes characteristics of today's nursing homes and concludes with the characteristics of the people who live there. By understanding the characteristics of nursing homes and residents, social workers are better able to be effective change agents who help to extend the principles of palliative care to all nursing home residents.

It is important to clearly state that the vast majority (over 80 percent) of all the people who require long-term care are receiving it outside of nursing homes (Miller and Mor 2006:10), generally in their own homes. Indeed, throughout U.S. history and including today, it is families—mainly mothers, sisters, and daughters—who have provided the bulk of long-term care to people of all ages. It is this same segment of society, women, who work as staff members in assisted living facilities, hospices, and nursing homes. Middle-aged and older women continue to be the backbone of care giving in the United States.

From the Almshouse to the *Olmstead* Decision

Holstein and Cole (1996) discuss the evolution of nonfamily care provided to people unable to care for themselves. Their work focuses on care provided in the United States over the past 200 years. The English Poor Law of 1834 was a strong influence on how early European Americans developed their understanding of the role of families and governments in providing care to people who could not care for themselves and who did not have the financial resources to buy care. This law was a revision of the 1594 Elizabethan Poor Law (Coll 1969; Holstein and Cole 1996). Then as now, society struggled to address to what lengths are families to be held responsible for care; what level of public support is appropriate for long-term care needs; what ratio of public support should be directed at people in their homes instead of group/institutional settings; what are the eligibility criteria for receiving public support; to what extent does needing support represent individual failings of caring for oneself or preparing financially for dependency; and to what extent should public funds be used to provide the infrastructure to extend the time that individuals and families can provide care outside of an institution?

Holstein and Cole explain that during the colonial period, people of all ages who had no family, or whose needs exceeded their family's capacity to care, relied on fellow townspeople for help. It was understood that small towns were responsible for meeting the needs of the people who were part of the community, and so "indigents" who were orphaned, widowed, disabled, or afflicted with mental conditions were provided sustenance because they were part of the fabric of the community; "the poor had names and faces" (1996:22).

Holstein and Cole describe the years 1820 through 1865 as "the dominance of the almshouse in an era of optimism" (1996:22). They explain that almshouses were developed as a form of "indoor relief," where people in need were housed and provided meager support for their physical needs. Their need for support was considered to be an outward sign of their moral failings; "these institutions housed the poor of all ages, as well as the sick, the retarded, the mentally ill, and the social deviant" (23).

In the mid-1800s, society began to realize that placing all the people who needed help in the same institution (the almshouse) was not the only way to provide care. Also, social reformers began to envision separate institutions for people based on separate needs. It was during this time that new institutions were developed. Orphanages became more widely available for children; asylums were developed for people with mental illness; and schools were developed for children with disabilities. Holstein and Cole explain that the development of these alternative institutions was based, in part, on new ideas related to people's capacity to learn and improve. The development of the new institutions left mainly older adults remaining in almshouses in the latter 1800s. Toward the end of the 1800s, the condition of the almshouses further deteriorated in the face of public disagreement regarding the appropriate role of government in supporting older adults who could no longer support themselves.

Lacey (1999) in her historic overview of care provided to people with Alzheimer's disease, reports that until the first half of the twentieth century, people with severe mental health conditions, including dementia, were considered to be "incurable" (105). She writes of the placement of elders with dementia in mental institutions in the early 1900s and then the challenges of "transinstitutionalization" of elders among mental institutions, nursing homes, and boarding homes decades later (109).

With the 1935 enactment of Social Security and Old Age Assistance for the aged poor, older adults had a steady stream of income that could be used to secure care in a private setting. In fact, Old Age Assistance funds were not allowed to be directed toward people in almshouses, so in order to receive this funding, the older adult needed to leave the almshouse and look for care elsewhere. This steady income inspired a market for private settings, such as living in someone's family home and paying toward room and board (Holstein and Cole 1996).

The decades following the enactment of Social Security brought a larger role for the federal government in supporting the development of nursing homes, mainly in the form of financing made available to both for-profit and not-for-profit groups to build nursing homes to house low-income frail older adults. Federal attention to health care provided in these settings became an issue after amendments to the Social Security Act established the Medicare and Medicaid programs in 1965. (Chapter 3 discusses the proportion of nursing home residents receiving Medicare and Medicaid funds and underscores that it is the Medicaid program that pays the largest proportion of nursing home costs in the United States) Because of the large amount of public money devoted to nursing homes, and the vulnerability of the people who live there, the government has a role in ensuring a decent quality of care. But it wasn't until a decade after the flow of funds, mostly from Medicaid, into nursing homes that Congress responded to public outcries for major reform.

A focus on quality of care and quality of life dominated the public discourse regarding nursing homes in the 1970s and 1980s, culminating in the Nursing Home Reform Act. The NHRA was part of the Omnibus Reconciliation Act of 1987 and is referred to as either the NHRA or OBRA'87. The NHRA was heavily influenced by a report issued by the Institute of Medicine's Committee on Nursing Home Reform, *Improving the Quality of Care in Nursing Homes* (Institute of Medicine 1986), and created a set of national minimum standards of care and rights for people living in certified nursing facilities. Key features of NHRA in OBRA 87 that continue to play a role in the daily life of nursing home residents include the establishment of resident rights, the development of the minimum data set assessment form to help guide individual care plans for each resident, and emphasis on resident quality of life as well as quality of care (NCCNHR 2007).

Throughout the later decades of the twentieth century there was a growing concern about the amount of money that the federal and state governments were directing toward nursing home care compared to funds available for services that would allow people with long-term-care needs to remain in their homes through services grouped under the term, "home and community based services." Kane, Kane, and Ladd (1998) document the wide variation among states in terms of the ratio of public spending on nursing home versus HCBS. Oregon was the only state in which more money (only slightly more) was going into HCBS than to nursing homes in 1992, while nine states had more than ten times the amount of public money going to nursing homes than to HCBS (Kane, Kane, and Ladd 1998:96). The highest proportion of funds to nursing homes occurred in Mississippi. "More than twenty times as much public money is spent on nursing homes in Mississippi than on HCBS" (97).

State variation in availability of nursing home beds persist. CMS data from 2007 reveal that the number of Medicare- or Medicaid-certified nursing home beds available per 1,000 people age eighty-five or older varies from a high of 540 beds per 1,000 in Louisiana (473 in Oklahoma, 443 in Arkansas and Missouri, and 441 in Iowa) to a low of 150 per 1,000 in

Hawaii (156 in Arizona, 170 in Alaska, 176 in Florida, and 178 in Oregon) (CMS 2008:24).

In the 1990s, the Americans with Disability Act expanded rights and access for people of all ages with disabilities. In 1999, the Supreme Court handed down a decision that called for broader access to community-based care for people with disabilities through the *Olmstead* decision. *Olmstead* upheld the right of individuals to receive care in the community as opposed to an institution whenever possible. A document issued by the National Conference of State Legislatures explains:

> The 1999 Supreme Court ruling in *L.C. and E.W. vs. Olmstead* interpreted the Americans with Disabilities Act (ADA) to mean that states must provide services in the most integrated setting appropriate to the needs of qualified individuals with disabilities. The ruling directs states to make "reasonable modifications" in programs and activities. Modifications that would "fundamentally alter" the nature of services, programs or activities, however, are not required.
>
> *(Fox-Grage, Folkemer, and Lewis 2009)*

For more information on the Olmstead Decision see the Bazelon Center for Mental Health Law (http://www.bazelon.org/issues/disabilityrights/in-court/olmstead/briefs.htm).

The government has begun to make changes in the financing of home- and community-based care. A July 26, 2006, press release announced that the Department of Health and Human Services would begin providing funds to states to use to support "elderly and disabled Medicaid recipients who wish to live in the community rather than institutions" (DHHS 2006:1). This initiative is referred to as "The Money Follows the Person" and is an attempt to rebalance the ratio of public funds from institutionalized care to community care.

Providing a summary explanation for the presence of the current type of policies related to nursing homes, Fahey (2003) points to the growth of the frail elderly population, many of whom had limited resources; public policies designed to minimize the use of acute hospitals; public policies and court decisions that minimize state mental institutions; federal funds to build facilities; and Medicaid funds to pay for care (and to a lesser extent Medicare funds). "Because this [Medicaid] is a program for the sick who are poor, the economic support of the facility will be almost always assuredly minimal out of political deference to the taxpayer and other important public priorities" (Fahey 2003:40).

Despite the reluctance of elected officials, and absent an outcry from the American public to better reimburse nursing homes on a per resident basis, it is expected that more government money will be directed to nursing homes on an aggregate basis. The increased funds will likely result because of the growing number of people who are reaching old age and experiencing the effects of advanced chronic illness and who lack the financial resources to pay upward of $70,000 per year for nursing home care.

The Democratization of Old Age and the Growing Need for Long-Term Care

There is nothing new about the possibility of a human surviving one hundred years. A "recent" example is Michelangelo, who was born more than 500 years ago and survived into his ninth decade (Heusinger 1989). What is new is the proportion of people who can expect to live long enough to die in old age.

This new demography of dying has two main consequences for the experience of living and dying in nursing homes. First, there are more people at risk for needing long-term-care services because currently with increasing age comes the propensity to develop chronic health conditions, which means that dying takes place in the context of chronic illness. Second, because of the dramatic decline in infant mortality and reductions in mortality in general, many adults lack direct experience with the death of a loved one. This is indeed a change. Uhlenberg (1980) calculated the probability that a child would experience the death of a nuclear family member before the child reached age fifteen and reports that over half (51 percent) of children born in 1900 would experience the death of a parent or a sibling before the child reached age fifteen, compared to 9 percent of children born in 1976 (1980:316). Until recently, people grew up with death.

The National Center for Health Statistics reported life expectancy for people born in the United States in 2004 was 77.8 (CDC/NCHS 2007a: table A). Life expectancy is higher for women. In 2004, it was 75.2 years for men, compared to 80.4 years for women. Life expectancy also varies by race. The life expectancy for black men born in 2004 was 69.5 years, and for black women, 76.3 years. Another use of life-table data is to calculate the age at which a certain percentage of the birth cohort is expected to have died (based on prevailing death rates for each age group). Table 4.1 shows the dramatic improvements in life expectancy in the United States over the twentieth century. For the cohort of male Americans born in 1900, about one in four was expected to have died by age seventeen. For men born in 1950 (early baby boomers) one-fourth of the birth cohort is expected to have died by age fifty-eight. For men born in 2004, about one-fourth are expected to have died by age sixty-eight. It is clear that babies born today are much more likely to live long enough to meet their grandchildren and great-grandchildren. If we focus on the age at which 75 percent of the birth cohort is expected to have died, table 4.1 shows that three-fourths of the women born in 1900 were expected to have died by age seventy-four; in 2004 that age had increased to ninety-one.

Although life expectancy has increased significantly over the twentieth century in the United States and in other developed countries, one of the results has been that a greater number of people are becoming widowed in older adulthood. This trend is expected to continue as the number of people reaching age sixty-five increases. The Social Security Administration

TABLE 4.1

Age at Which One-Quarter, One-Half, and Three-Quarters of a Birth Cohort Is Expected to Have Died, by Sex and Year of Birth: United States

	BORN IN 1900	BORN IN 1950	BORN IN 2004
	25 percent expected to have died		
Men	Age 17	Age 58	Age 68
Women	Age 23	Age 65	Age 75
	50 percent expected to have died		
Men	Age 55	Age 70	Age 79
Women	Age 58	Age 76	Age 83
	75 percent expected to have died		
Men	Age 72	Age 79	Age 87
Women	Age 74	Age 84	Age 91

Source: Author adapted data from two sources: The 1900 and 1950 data are from Social Security Administration (1983), tables 3a and 3k. The 2004 data are from CDC/NCHS (2007b), table 10 (men) and table 11 (women).

estimates that 1.5 million people will become widowed in the year 2030, including 858,269 people age seventy and older (Social Security Administration 1997). This is important to note because people who are not married are overrepresented as long-term-care residents in nursing homes.

Table 4.2 reports selected causes of death for people in different age groups. The data come from death certificates of people who died in 2005. The table reports the number of deaths to the age groups and also the percentage of deaths in each disease category that are accounted for by people age eighty-five and older. Almost two-thirds (61 percent) of Alzheimer's deaths occurred to people age eighty-five or older, as did almost half of pneumonia deaths (48 percent), and 41 percent of deaths related to hypertension. This table underscores the types of dying that most nursing home residents will face. Social workers and other nursing home staff members

TABLE 4.2

Number of Deaths for Selected Causes, by Age Group: United States, 2005

CAUSE OF DEATH	ALL AGES	AGES 65–74	AGES 85+	OF ALL DEATHS, % TO 85+
All causes	2,448,018	398,355	703,169	29%
Septicemia	34,136	6,073	9,544	28%
HIV	12,543	438	15	0%
Malignant neoplasm (cancer)	559,312	138,446	83,455	15%
Diabetes	75,119	16,183	15,903	21%
Parkinson's disease	19,544	2,414	7,322	37%
Alzheimer's disease	71,599	3,813	43,906	61%
Major cardiovascular	856,030	124,366	326,066	38%
Hypertension and hypertensive renal	24,902	3,306	10,703	43%
Cerebrovascular (stroke)	143,579	18,839	58,183	41%
Pneumonia	61,189	6,486	29,285	48%
Renal failure	42,868	7,165	14,375	34%
Accidents	117,809	8,632	14,243	12%
Falls	19,656	2,319	7,526	38%
Suicide	32,637	2,344	860	3%
Surgery complications	2,653	487	462	17%

Source: Excerpted from CDC/NCHS (2008a), table 10.

need to build their expertise in understanding the care needs of people with these conditions, including the psychosocial-care needs related to declining health from these chronic conditions.

Characteristics of Contemporary Nursing Homes

All nursing homes are required to be state licensed. In addition, they can be certified to receive Medicare, Medicaid, or both. The vast majority of nursing home beds (over 98 percent) are in nursing homes that are certified for Medicare (skilled nursing facilities) and Medicaid (nursing facilities) (American Health Care Association 2008a). In order for a nursing home to be able to collect payments from Medicare or Medicaid, it must comply with federal regulations. If the facility fails to comply with regulations, the result may be a warning, a fine, or forced closure. Nursing homes are not required to accept Medicare or Medicaid, but because of the large amount of money at stake, most facilities highly value their certification status.

Data from the "National Nursing Home Survey" show that over the past . thirty years the number of nursing homes has fluctuated between 15,700 in 1973 to 19,100 in 1985, to 16,100 in 2004 (CDC/NCHS 2007a). The number of beds increased from 1.2 million in 1973 to 1.7 million in 2004. The proportion of nursing homes with fewer than fifty beds declined dramatically from 41 percent in 1973 to 14 percent in 2004, while the proportion of nursing homes with one hundred or more beds increased from 24 percent in 1973 to 49 percent in 2004 (CDC/NCHS 2007a).

Another important change has been the increase in the number of resident discharges. The growth in the number of discharges is attributed not to resident death but rather to the receipt of sub-acute care and the return to home. In 1973, 1,077,500 people used nursing home care at some point during the year, and by 1999 the number had more than doubled to 2,522,300 (CDC/NCHS 2007a). The increase in resident turnover follows the conversion of Medicaid nursing facility beds to Medicare skilled nursing facility beds that are reimbursed at a higher level and at a higher profit level.

Aside from categorizing nursing homes based on their certification status and number of beds, they are typically classified by tax status (for profit, not for profit, or government) and chain status (part of a chain or independent). More than three-fifths (61.5 percent) of nursing homes are for profit, 30.1 percent are not for profit, and about 6.6 percent are run by state or local government (CDC/NCHS 2008b: table 1). Though the number of nursing homes with fewer than 50 beds has decreased dramatically over the past thirty years, two-thirds of certified nursing homes still have fewer than 120 beds (Bern-Klug et al. 2009). The 120-bed threshold is important because the federal government requires only nursing homes with more than 120 beds to employ a full-time qualified social worker (discussed in chapter 1).

Table 4.3 reports the number of residents in different types of nursing homes. The data are from the "National Nursing Home Survey" of the National Center for Health Statistics. The most recent NNHS collected cross-sectional data in 2004 that describe the residents who are in a nursing home at one point in time rather than over the course of the year. Table 4.3 shows that about two-thirds of residents are in for-profit nursing homes and that almost all residents (98.9%) are in a nursing home that is certified to receive Medicare or Medicaid benefits. As previously mentioned, 14 percent of nursing homes have fifty or fewer beds; table 4.3 reports that these smaller nursing homes account for only 4 percent of all residents, while two-thirds of residents are in a facility with one hundred or more beds (the NNHS does not publish the number of residents in homes with "more than 120 beds").

Table 4.3 shows the regional distribution of nursing home residents. The highest percentage is in the South and the lowest in the West. About three-fourths of nursing home residents (75.6%) are in a nursing home that is located in a metropolitan county, and a little more than half of residents (54.4%) are in a nursing home that is part of a chain of at least two nursing homes.

The "National Nursing Home Survey" also asked whether nursing homes had formal contracts with outside providers. More than 12,000 of the 16,100 U.S. nursing homes (78.1 percent) reported having a contract with at least one hospice provider, including 82.9 percent of for-profit nursing homes and 70.4 percent of not-for-profit nursing homes (CDC/NCHS 2008: table 5).

Nursing homes distinguish themselves from competitors, in part, by the type of special programs they provide. The vast majority (79.8 percent) of nursing homes report some type of special program. About one in five (18.8 percent) report a hospice end-of-life program, and another 16.7 percent report they have a palliative-care specialty program. No definitions are

TABLE 4.3

Percent of Nursing Home Residents by Various Types of
Nursing Homes: 2004

	PERCENT OF RESIDENTS
By tax status	
For-profit	61.5%
Not-for-profit, voluntary, and state and local government owned	38.5
By certification status	
Medicare or Medicaid certified	98.9
Both Medicare and Medicaid certified	92.5
Medicare certified only	1.9
Medicaid certified only	4.5
By number of beds	
Fewer than 50	4.2
50–99	28.3
100	67.5
By geographic region	
Northeast	22.2
Midwest3	30.0
South	33.6
West	14.2
By county type*	
Metropolitan statistical area	75.6
Micropolitan statistical area	13.5
"Other" (a county with no city of 10,000 or more people)	10.9
By chain affiliation status	
Part of a chain of 2 or more	54.4
Not part of a chain (i.e., "independent")	45.6

Number of residents = 1,492,200.

* A metropolitan county has at least one core urban area with at least 50,000 people; a micropolitan county has at least one city with at least 10,000 (but no more than 50,000) people, and a sparsely populated county does not have a city with at least 10,000. Each metro or micro area consists of one or more counties and includes the counties containing the core urban area, as well as any adjacent counties that have a high degree of social and economic integration (as measured by commuting to work) with the urban core. See http://www.census.gov/population/www/metroareas/metroarea.html.

Source: CDC/NCHS (2008b), table 2.

provided for what these programs entail, and it is not clear how the presence of a hospice or palliative program is related to residents becoming enrolled in Medicare hospice benefits. It is of note that 68.9 percent of nursing homes report a restorative care unit (CDC/NCHS 2008b: table 18).

Characteristics of Residents

The differences between one person and another grow with each passing year. By the time a person has lived eight decades, she or he has a wealth of positive and negative experiences and likely a collection of subtle or profound functional changes compared with a fifty-year-old and certainly with a typical twenty-year-old. Coping skills have been refined, tastes well honed, and it can be expected that the elder has experienced much joy and many losses.

Knowing the history of the development of the nursing home, someone unfamiliar with the diversity that accompanies aging may think that because most nursing home residents are older adults, most have similar needs. This is not so. The geriatrician and researcher Robert Kane classifies nursing home residents into five distinct groups, based on the type of care required from staff: people there for rehabilitation and sub-acute care; people who are chronically and physically disabled but alert; people with dementia; people in a permanent vegetative state; and people who are terminally ill (1996:149). Identifying and meeting the care needs of such a wide range of people is a challenge.

Table 4.4 uses cross-sectional data to show social and demographic characteristics of contemporary nursing home residents. While most nursing home residents are older adults, not all are. One in eight (11.7 percent) of the 1.5 million people in nursing homes in 2004 was under age sixty-five. Most are women (71.1 percent) and about half (45.25 percent) have reached age eighty-five. By race, 12.5 percent of nursing home residents were reported by staff to be black, and 85.5 percent white. Most nursing home residents are not currently married, and the majority are widowed (53.3 percent). At the time of the 2004 NNHS, 20 percent of residents had been admitted to the nursing home for less than three months, while 12 percent were admitted five or more years earlier. The median number of days in the nursing home was 463, and the mean (which is affected by extreme cases) was almost twice as long at 835 days.

TABLE 4.4

Nursing Home Residents' Demographic Characteristics: 2004

RESIDENT CHARACTERISTICS	PERCENT OF RESIDENTS
Sex	
Female	71.1
Male	28.8
Age	
Under 65	11.7
65+	88.3
65–74	11.7
75–84	31.4
85+	45.2
Race	
Black	12.5
White	85.5
Other*	2.0
Marital status	
Married	20.2
Widowed	53.3
Divorced or separated	10.2
Single or never married	14.8
Unknown	1.4
Length of time since admission**	
Less than 3 months	20.0
3–6 months	9.8
6–12 months	14.3
1 year to less than 3 years	30.3
3 years to less than 5 years	13.6
5 years or more	12.0

Number of residents = 1,492,200.

* Other includes Asian, Native Hawaiian or other Pacific Islander, American Indian or Alaska Native, and people who identify as multiple races. Hispanic/Latinos can be any race.

** Mean = 835 days; median = 463 days.

Source: CDC/NCHS (2008b), tables 1, 5, and 12.

The proportion of residents who have limitations in meeting two or more "activities of daily living" such as bathing, eating, dressing, or grooming has increased over the past twenty years. With the increasing popularity of assisted living as a residential option for people who can afford it, many people who can no longer live safely in their house or apartment move to assisted-living facilitates. By the time they reach the need for nursing home level of care, they are much more physically frail, and their financial resources have been depleted. Therefore, as a group, the people receiving long-term care in nursing homes are less functional than just a few decades ago. This suggests that their medical and psychosocial needs are more complex.

Table 4.5 indicates the percentage of nursing home residents who receive assistance with activities of daily living. The type of assistance required ranges from 24.8 percent of residents with eating needs to 82.8 percent of residents with bathing needs; the majority of residents report three of more ADL needs.

Table 4.6 shows other indicators of illness severity and need for care. The data document heavy needs in terms of medications with almost half of residents (47.9 percent) receiving nine or more medications. Almost half (43.1 percent) are incontinent of both bowel and bladder. This is an extremely important point. Although all nursing care is important,

TABLE 4.5

Nursing Home Residents Who Require "Extensive" or "Total"
Staff Assistance with Activities of Daily Living: 2004

RESIDENTS WHO NEED HELP	PERCENT OF RESIDENTS
With bathing	82.8%
With personal hygiene	59.9
With dressing	61.3
With eating	24.8
With transfers	51.4
With using the toilet room	60.5

Note: Total number of residents was 1,492,200; 97.3 percent needed help with at least one activity of daily living. These data reflect residents at the time of the NNHS interview.

Source: CDC/NCHS (2008b), table 15.

TABLE 4.6

Indications of Nursing Home Resident Care Needs: 2004

	PERCENT OF RESIDENTS
Receiving 9 or more medications	47.9%
Incontinent of both bowel and bladder	43.1
Physically restrained*	39.1
Fall or fracture during the past six months	35.0
Fractured a hip in the past 180 days	1.8
In pain during the past 7 days	22.7
Feeding tube use	5.9
Had a pressure ulcer	10.7

* 4% of all residents were trunk or limb restrained; 13.7% bedrails; 24.5% side rails; 3.4% chair; some residents had more than one type of restraint.

** Half were at stage 1, and one-half of 1 percent were at stage 4.

Number of residents = 1,492,200.

Source: CDC/NCHS (2008b): tables 16, 18, 19, 27, 29, 30, and 39.

prompt attention to incontinence is extremely important to residents and families because it is a dignity issue. Nursing homes will be considered second-class settings as long as incontinence is not prevented or addressed well, as one daughter of a nursing home resident stated: "I will never get used to coming in here and seeing her sitting in her feces. That is not right. That is not good care" (Bern-Klug and Forbes-Thompson 2008).

According to the NNHS, 23 percent of nursing home residents were in pain at some point during the seven days before data collection (CDC/NCHS 2008b: table 24). Addressing pain is a hallmark of good palliative care. All nursing home staff members, including social workers, have a role in anticipating and addressing resident pain. When social workers begin psychosocial interventions related to pain, they must evaluate the extent to which the interventions are effective, and they should also help to document overall pain levels. Excellent resources about pain are available for nursing home staff members (End-of-Life Nursing Education Consortium 2008) and specifically for social workers, such as the ACE Project at the City of Hope, an annual meeting

TABLE 4.7

Percent of Nursing Home Residents with No Advance Directive,
by Age, Sex, and Race: 2004

	PERCENT OF RESIDENTS WITH NO ADVANCE DIRECTIVE
Age	
Under 65	62.8%
65–74	47.4
75–84	34.3
85+	22.0
Sex	
Female	29.9
Male	42.7
Race/Ethnicity	
Black	62.7
White	28.9
Other*	51.3
Hispanic or Latino (can be of any race)	54.6

Note: 501,500 (33 percent) nursing home residents had no advance directive on record.

Note: In the NNHS, advance directives include a living will, DNR, DNH, feeding restriction, medication restriction, organ donation, autopsy request, and "other."

* Other race includes Asian, Native Hawaiian or other Pacific Islander, American Indian or Alaska Native, and people who identify as multiple races. Hispanic/Latinos can be any race.

Source: CDC/NCHS (2008b): table 20.

jointly sponsored by City of Hope and Southern California Cancer Pain Initiative called "Promoting Excellence in Pain Management and Palliative Care for Social Workers" (see http://sccpi.coh.org/2008%20SWC /SWCB8.pdf and http://www.cityofhope.org). Physical pain has psychosocial consequences that nursing home social workers must address if a high quality of life is to be a reality. Pain is a psychosocial as well as a medical and nursing issue.

TABLE 4.8

Percent of Nursing Home Residents Who Have a DNR or DNH in
Their Medical Chart, by Age, Sex, and Race: 2004

	PERCENT WITH DNR	PERCENT WITH DNH
All residents	55.9	3.5
Under age 65	27.8	*
Age 65–74	40.5	3.2
Age 75–84	54.3	2.8
Age 85+	68.4	4.7
Female	60.0	3.7
Male	45.9	2.9
Black	27.8	*
White	60.5	3.9
Other**	35.9	*

(Number of residents = 1,492,200)

DNR = Do not resuscitate; DNH = Do not hospitalize.

* Sample size too small to accurately report.

** Other race includes Asian, Native Hawaiian or other Pacific Islander, American Indian or
Alaska Native, and people who identify as multiple races. Hispanic/Latinos can be any race.

Note: These data reflect residents at the time of interview.

Source: CDC/NCHS (2008b): table 21.

The Patient Self-Determination Act requires health facilities, including
nursing homes, to inform patients/residents at the time of admission of
their right to have an advance directive. Table 4.7 shows that the percentage
of residents with no advance directives varies by age (a higher percentage
of people under age sixty-five have no advance directive), sex (men are less
likely), and race (a higher percentage of black and people who fit in the
"other" category have no advance directive).

The NNHS 2004 data reported in table 4.8 focus on two types of advance directives, the "do no resuscitate" order and the "do not hospitalize"
order. About half of residents (55.9 percent) had a DNR order in their medical chart compared to a much lower percentage of residents (3.5 percent)
who had a DNH. The percentage of nursing home residents with a DNR
in their medical chart varied by age group, sex, and race.

TABLE 4.9

Number and Percent of Deaths in Age Groups, By Setting: 2004

	All settings	%	Hospital	%	NH/LTC	%	Home	%
All ages	2,401,400	100	1,107,431	46	530,818	22	586,564	24
< age 45	200,220	8	111,896	56	3,939	2	45,461	23
Ages 45–64	443,478	18	235,407	53	29,313	7	141,137	32
Ages 65–74	400,445	17	208,391	52	51,469	13	117,322	29
Ages 75–84	684,839	29	318,127	46	165,612	24	162,291	24
Ages 85+	672,052	28	233,532	35	280,475	42	120,307	18

NH/LTC = in a nursing home or other long-term care setting

Note: Deaths in which the age or setting was not known are not reflected in the table, other than in the total.

Source: Author tabulation of data from CDC/NCHS 2004.

Place of Death

In 2004, 2.4 million people died in the United States. The vast majority were older adults. Almost three-fourths of the people who died in 2004 (73.1 percent) were age sixty-five or older, and 27.9 percent of all deaths occurred in people age eighty-five or older (CDC/NCHS 2004). About half of the deaths occurred in a hospital setting, and 22 percent in a nursing home or other long-term care setting. Tables 4.9 and 4.10 both show data about the place of death and the age of people who died in each setting. Each table addresses a different question. Table 4.9 addresses the percentage of people in different age groups who died in a hospital, nursing home, or the decedent's home. While 2 percent of deaths to people ages one through forty-four occurred in a nursing home in 2004, almost half (42 percent) of people older than age eighty-five who died in 2004 did so in a nursing home. This number does not include nursing home residents who died in hospital emergency rooms or as a hospital inpatient. Therefore, the actual number of people who died as nursing home residents (as opposed to in a nursing home) is higher than shown. Brock, Holmes, Foley and Holmes (1992) estimate that more than one-quarter of hospital deaths are nursing home residents transferred to the hospital days before death.

Table 4.10 looks at all the deaths that occur in each setting, and asks what percentage of deaths in each setting is accounted for by people of various age groups. A disproportionate number of deaths of people under age sixty-five occur in hospital emergency rooms. About half of deaths in hospital emergency rooms and on arrival to hospitals occur to people under the age of sixty-five (although these constitute a quarter of all deaths). Over half of nursing home deaths occur to people age over age eighty-five, and another 31 percent to people between the ages of seventy-five and eighty-four. About half of hospital inpatient deaths occur to people who have reached age seventy-five.

In summary, nursing homes continue to change, in part, in response to the growing number of frail older adults, the higher medical acuity of nursing home residents, and available financing. Fahey (2003) suggests we reconsider the merits of designing a long-term-care system based on the medical model; he believes that residents would be better served by a person-centered-care model, and so do the growing number of Pioneer Network members (http://www.pioneernetwork.net) and members of

TABLE 4.10

Number and Percent of Deaths in Various Settings, by Age Group: 2004

	All ages	Under 65	65-74	75-84	85+	Unknown
				AGE GROUP		
Total deaths	2,401,400	643,698	400,445	684,839	672,052	366
	100%	27%	17%	28%	28%	—
Hospital inpatient	903,953	249,326	172,872	275,645	206,054	56
	100%	28%	19%	30%	23%	0%
Hospital ER or outpatient	178,837	83,870	31,898	38,430	24,624	15
	100%	47%	18%	21%	14%	0%
Hospital DOA	24,641	14,107	3,621	4,052	2,854	7
	100%	57%	15%	16%	12%	0%
Hospice facility*	10,326	2,503	1,873	3,253	2,697	0
	100%	24%	18%	32%	26%	0%
Nursing home/LTC	530,818	33,252	51,469	165,612	280,475	10
	100%	6%	10%	31%	53%	0%
Decedent's home	586,564	186,598	117,322	162,291	120,307	46
	100%	32%	20%	28%	21%	0%
Other	159,415	71,813	20,207	33,698	33,471	226
	100%	45%	13%	21%	21%	0%
Don't know	6,846	2,229	1,183	1,858	1,570	6
	100%	33%	17%	27%	23%	0%

Hospital DOA = "dead on arrival"

* This category does not include people enrolled in a hospice program who die at home, in a nursing home, or in a hospital.

Source: Author tabulation of data from CDC/NCHS 2004.

the national advocacy group NCCNHR: The National Consumer Voice for Quality Long-Term Care (http://www.nccnhr.org). The call for person-centered care is part of a larger call for more emphasis on the quality of life of people who live in nursing homes. (For more information about nursing home quality of life, please see Kane et al. [2001] and Lawton [2001].) The calls for person-centered care, quality of life, and palliative care share the same core value: the vital importance of remembering that long-term care is received by a person, and the person should neither be diminished by the need for long-term care nor by the provision of long-term care.

As we continue to turn the kaleidoscope of nursing home care, a new image is emerging: a broader, more holistic understanding of the needs and desires of people who are in need of daily assistance to complete the activities of everyday living. The provision of palliative care throughout the nursing home stay is a sign of person-centered care and a means to enhance the quality of living and dying in nursing homes.

References

American Health Care Association. 2008a. "Nursing Facility Beds by Certification Type." CMS OSCAR Data Current Surveys. June 2008. http://www.ahcancal.org/research_data/oscar_data/Nursing%20Facility%20Operational%20Characteristics/NF_Beds_Certification_TypeDec2008.pdf. Accessed September 21, 2008.

American Health Care Association 2008b. "Activities of Daily Living—Toileting—Percent of Patients and Dependency." CMS OSCAR Data Current Surveys. June 2008. http://www.ahcancal.org/research_data/oscar_data/NursingFacilityPatientCharacteristics/ADL_Toiletting_Jun2008.pdf. Accessed September 21, 2008.

Bern-Klug, M., and S. Forbes-Thompson. 2008. "Family Members' Responsibilities to Nursing Home Residents: 'She's the Only Mother I Got.'" *Journal of Gerontological Nursing* 34 (20): 43–52.

Bern-Klug, M., K. W. O. Kramer, G. Chan, R. Kane, L. Dorfman, and J. Saunders. 2009. "Characteristics of Nursing Home Social Service Directors." *Journal of the American Medical Directors Association* 10:36–44.

Brock, D., M. Holmes, D. Foley, and D. Holmes. 1992. "Methodological Issues in a Survey of the Last Days of Life." In *The Epidemiologic Study of the Elderly*, ed. R. Wallace and R. Woodson, 315–32. New York: Oxford University Press.

CDC/NCHS. 2004. "Deaths by Place of Death, Age, Race, and Sex: United States, Worktable 309." www.cdc.gov/nchs/data/dvs/mortfinal2004_worktable309.pdf.

CDC/NCHS. 2007a. "National Nursing Home Survey." http://www.cdc.gov/nchs /data/nnhsd/nursinghomes1973-2004.pdf, http://www.cdc.gov/nchs/data/nnhsd /Estimates/nnhs/Estimates_Demographics_Tables.pdf#Table01. Accessed September 21, 2008.

CDC/NCHS. 2007b. "United States Life Tables, 2004." *National Vital Statistics Reports* 56, no. 9.

CDC/NCHS. 2008a. "Deaths: Final Data for 2005." *National Vital Statistics Reports* 56, no.10.

CDC/NCHS. 2008b. "National Nursing Home Survey." http://www.cdc.gov /nchs/about/major/nnhsd. Accesed January 26, 2008.

CMS. 2007. "Nursing Home Data Compendium, 2007 Edition." http://www.cms.hhs.gov/CertificationandComplianc/Downloads /2007NursingHomeDataCompendium_508.pdf. Accessed September 21, 2008.

CMS. 2008. "Nursing Home Data Compendium, 2008 Edition." http://www.cms.hhs.gov/CertificationandComplianc/Downloads /2008NursingHomeDataCompendium_508.pdf. Accessed February 14, 2009.

Coll, B. D. 1969. *Perspectives in Social Welfare: A History*. Washington, D.C.: U.S. Department of Health, Education, and Welfare.

DHHS. 2006. "HHS Provides Funding to States for Alternatives to Nursing Home Care in Medicaid." July 26. http://www.hhs.gov /news/press/2006pres/20060726.html. Accessed May 11, 2008.

End-of-Life Nursing Education Consortium. 2008. "Promoting Palliative Care in Long-Term Care Nursing." ELNEC Geriatric Training Program. City of Hope and American Association of Colleges of Nursing: http://www.aacn.nche.edu/ELNEC/.

Fahey, C. J. 2003. "Culture Change in Long-Term Care Facilities: Changing the Facility or Changing the System?" *Journal of Social Work in Long-Term Care* 2:35–51.

Fox-Grage, W., D. Folkemer, and J. Lewis. 2009. "The States' Response to the Olmstead Decision: How Are States Complying?" National Conference of State Legislatures. http://www.ncsl.org/programs/health/forum/olmsreport.htm. Accessed March 15, 2009.

Heusinger, L. 1989. *Michelangelo*. Florence, Italy: SCALA, Instituto Fotografico Editoriale.

Holstein, M., and T. R. Cole. 1996. "The Evolution of Long-Term Care in America." In *The Future of Long-Term Care: Social and Policy Issues*, ed. Binstock et al., 19–47. Baltimore, Md.: Johns Hopkins University Press.

Institute of Medicine. 1986. *Improving Quality of Care in Nursing Homes.* Ed. J. Takeuchi, R. Burke, and M. McGeary. Washington, D.C.: National Academy Press.

Kane, R.A., R. L. Kane, and R. C. Ladd. 1998. *The Heart of Long-Term Care.* New York: Oxford University Press.

Kane, R. A., K. C. Kling, B. Bershadsky, R. L. Kane, K. Giles, H. B. Degenholtz, J. Liu, and L. Cutler. 2003. "Quality of Life Measures for Nursing Home Residents." *Journal of Gerontology: Medical Sciences* 58a(3): 240–48.

Kane, R. L. 1996. "The Evolution of the American Nursing Home." In *The Future of Long-Term Care: Social and Policy Issues,* ed. Binstock et al., 145–68. Baltimore, Md.: Johns Hopkins University Press.

Lacey, D. 1999. "The Evolution of Care: A Hundred-Year History of the Institutionalization of People with Alzheimer's Disease." *Journal of Gerontological Social Work* 31 (3/4): 101–31.

Lawton, M. P. 2001. "The Physical Environment of the Person with Alzheimer's Disease." *Ageing and Mental Health* 5 (supplement): S56–S64.

Miller, E. A., and V. Mor. 2006. "Out of the Shadows: Envisioning a Brighter Future for Long-Term Care in America." A Brown University report for the National Commission for Quality Long-Term Care. http://www.chcr.brown.edu/PDFS/BROWN_UNIVERSITY_LTC_REPORT_FINAL.pdf. Accessed July 17, 2008.

NCCNHR: The National Consumer Voice for Quality Long-Term Care. 2007. "OBRA '87 Twentieth Anniversary." http://www.nccnhr.org/public/245_1265_13831.cfm#law. Accessed October 1, 2008.

Social Security Administration, Office of the Actuary. 1983. "Life Tables for the U.S.: 1900–2050." SSA Pub. No.11-11536.

Social Security Administration, Office of the Actuary. 1997. Supplemental documentation to the 1997 Trustees Report to Congress (alternative 2). Unpublished.

Uhlenberg, P. 1980. "Death and the Family." *Journal of Family History* 5:313–20.

Anticipating and Managing Common Medical Challenges Encountered at the End of Life

ANN ALLEGRE

CASE STUDY

John is a seventy-eight-year-old nursing home resident who was admitted to the facility eighteen months ago after a stroke. His stroke left him with weakness of his left side and dependence on others for care. His wife of fifty-six years, Sarah, lives in a nearby apartment. Sarah visits him daily, feeding him and encouraging him to interact with others. John was hospitalized recently for pneumonia and shortness of breath. During his hospital stay, he was diagnosed with lung cancer that had spread to the liver. He was not felt to be a candidate for chemotherapy because of his poor functional status and the small likelihood of benefit. He returned to the facility for terminal care. He and Sarah had decided that he would not have attempts at resuscitation, and a hospice program was consulted to participate in his care.

At the time he returned to the facility, John was on oxygen to help with his shortness of breath. He had been limited to a wheelchair since his stroke and had become too weak to transfer himself. He tired easily and wanted to go back to bed after about an hour in the wheelchair. He still went to the dining room for meals, but his appetite was poor and he ate less than half of the food on his plate. Sarah was concerned about his loss of weight and came to the facility for each meal to encourage him to eat. This became a source of stress for both of them as she sat beside him trying to get him to eat. She was becoming exhausted from the hours that she spent at the facility each day, and John was irritated at her for nagging him to eat constantly.

John was having moderately severe pain in his abdomen, felt to be caused by the liver metastases. The hospice nurse contacted his attending physician for orders for small doses of morphine, to be given as needed for pain. Initially, John would only get the medications when he asked for them and often would suffer for a long time in pain before the dose arrived. The hospice nurse then requested a long-acting pain medication that gave much more consistent control of his pain.

John became bed-bound and slept most of the time. He was taking in almost no food. Sarah asked the physician to have a feeding tube inserted to give him nutrition. The social worker and hospice nurse met with Sarah to help her understand that a feeding tube might increase John's discomfort and would be unlikely to help him live longer. Since the goal was John's comfort without prolonging the dying process, she accepted that he would be more comfortable with mouth care and being allowed to take bites or sips as he was able.

John reached a point of being almost completely unresponsive. From time to time, he would look around the room at unseen things, and occasionally he would reach up. Even this activity stopped, and he lay completely unconscious. Sarah continued to sit at his bedside most of the day. She was distressed when he had noisy respirations and thought he was drowning in his secretions. She became alarmed when he had long pauses in his breathing, thinking he was gone, only to have him start breathing again. She felt that he was suffering and wondered how long this stage would go on. The hospice team and nursing home staff members gave her support as John went through the dying process. Finally, he peacefully died with Sarah at his side.

Most Americans are ill informed about the natural process of dying in advanced old age or as the result of advanced chronic disease. Much of the fear and suffering experienced by dying patients and their families comes because they do not know what will happen during the process of dying. This chapter is a review of the usual process of dying and the common medical challenges encountered in that phase of life. Social workers and others who are caring for the dying will be asked about these issues and should be prepared to address them using language that nursing home residents and family members can understand. The goal of this chapter is to provide information about dying in a straightforward manner. Key medical terms are defined throughout the chapter. The person who is dying will generally be referred to as "patient" rather than "resident" because I will be examining the medical aspects of care for nursing home residents.

Misconceptions About the Process of Dying

The many images shown in American media are usually of violent or sudden deaths. In those rare occasions when people are portrayed dying of illness in the movies and television, they generally say their last words just before taking their last breath. The media portrayals rarely reveal that the process of dying is one that can last for months for most people and that people who are dying are seldom able to communicate in their final days. In contrast with the media images that we see, families are often unprepared for how long the process of real-life dying can take. Milestones in this process will be discussed in this chapter.

Many caregivers who have experienced deaths in their own families or in their work in healthcare have seen a medically altered dying trajectory rather than a more natural process. In many cases, the nursing home resident is not even recognized as dying until days or even hours before they die. Aggressive medical efforts to treat illness are often continued right up to the day of death. In other cases, the process of dying is altered by interventions such as life support and the need to make decisions on when it is appropriate to stop care such as dialysis, artificial feeding, or ventilators. The developments in life-saving or life-prolonging medical technology in recent decades have made dying much more complicated. Only a small minority of Americans (less than 10 percent) die suddenly. The rest receive medical care as they die of chronic illness. In many cases, patients or their family members will have to make decisions about whether to or when to stop pursuing aggressive life-prolonging interventions. If the decision is made to remove a patient from life support, that person may die right away or may linger for days. Family members, though, often feel that the timing and cause of death are determined by the decision to cease life support; medical professionals recognize that the death is the result of the underlying medical condition.

A common misperception about dying is the supposed choice between suffering with terrible pain or being constantly sedated by pain medications. Although pain is commonly experienced in advanced disease, we will see below that the dosage of pain medications can usually be adjusted to address the pain without causing the patient to lose all alertness. Another misconception is that pain medications hasten death. Pain medications do not hasten death when used appropriately; this is true even in the case of terminal illness.

Normal Dying Process

It is common for the process of dying to take weeks or months. As mentioned, dying is a process that takes time. The average person who dies this year will die from an illness that he or she has had for over two years. During the course of this illness, there will be efforts at curing or slowing the disease. Eventually, for most people, there will be a long period of worsening health and loss of function. This process of decline and the uncertainty of the timing of death can create severe strains on nursing home residents and family members.

It is normal to need care from another person as death approaches. One of the difficulties for many Americans, who value their independence, is that the normal dying process includes a period of time when they will need care from others. Many people say that they want to die in their sleep after a "normal" day of living. In reality, most of us will die after weeks or months of dependence on others. In addition to being difficult for the person who is dying, this can create burdens for families, who may expect to be present and available to help around the clock once the dying "begins."

It is normal for the timing of death to be somewhat uncertain and this unpredictability creates another stress and source of burden. Medical science has not produced much research on prognosis. Little is known about how to accurately predict the timing of death at the individual level. An estimate can often be given on whether the death is most likely to occur in days, months, or weeks, but even these vague estimates are often wrong. Nursing home residents and families are stressed as they try to manage their finances and other responsibilities, not knowing how long the process of dying can go on.

The trajectories of terminal illness formulated by Lunney, Lynn, and Hogan (2002) and presented in chapter 1 can be useful guides to help patients and families understand what pattern can be expected. The "terminal-illness" trajectory is the one seen in cancer patients, in whom the process of decline is somewhat steady and the timing of death is more predictable. This is the trajectory that fits best with the hospice model, with a relatively short period of full dependency.

The "organ-failure" trajectory is a more common scenario and is seen in major causes of death such as heart disease and lung disease. These patients have episodes of getting seriously ill very quickly and then improving somewhat until the next exacerbation or, in other words, until the next episode of serious illness. Their pattern of dying is much harder to predict because the length of time until the next crisis and the severity of that crisis are both unpredictable. They could die quickly during a serious exacerbation or have a slower decline at the end of a long illness. It helps patients, staff, and family members to understand this trajectory if they can recognize that the patient usually doesn't bounce back as high after each exacerbation. So even though residents and families may be focused on the periods of improvement after each crisis, they can often acknowledge that the overall course of the illness over the past months or years has been downhill.

The "frailty" trajectory is more commonly observed in the frail elderly and in many nursing home residents. These people may have a lengthy period of dependency, sometimes with long periods of total unawareness of their surroundings. As medical ethicist Dr. Bill Bartholome put it, they are nearly dead indefinitely. Predicting the time of death for people following this trajectory can also be very difficult because they could die at any time with a minor illness but they frequently hang on for months or years. Their situation also raises questions about the quality and meaning of life, which can be very difficult for families and for the professional caregivers.

Despite the differences in these trajectories and the multiple types of illnesses that cause death, there are some commonalities in the natural dying process. Increasing weakness that leading to dependence is common in natural dying. As death approaches, this increasing weakness is often accompanied by other common symptoms such as loss of appetite, increasing number and severity of physical symptoms, and changes in mental status. These changes will be reviewed in more detail below.

Pain: A Common and Feared Symptom at the End of Life

Pain is a commonly experienced symptom as the end of life approaches. The largest modern study of the experience of dying patients, known as the SUPPORT study (SUPPORT Investigators 1995) found that half the hospitalized patients who were conscious near the end of life experienced moderate or severe pain at least half the time. Other studies have reported pain occurring in 60 to 90 percent of patients with advanced cancer. Significant levels of pain also occur in about half of dying patients with most other diseases, including congestive heart failure, chronic pulmonary disease, and liver failure.

Elderly patients and nursing home residents are less likely to receive adequate pain management than younger patients. Studies in nursing homes have found that 45 to 80 percent of residents have substantial pain that affects their functional status and quality of life (Ferrell 2004). A study of elderly nursing home residents with cancer found that more than a quarter of cancer patients with daily pain did not receive any pain medication, especially those patients who were older than eighty-five (Bernabei et al. 1998). This undertreatment of pain may be related to the concerns about prescribing these medications in elderly patients because of the side effects. Furthermore, many of these patients suffer from cognitive deficits that make assessing their pain more difficult.

Results of Uncontrolled Pain

Research over the past few years has helped us to understand that uncontrolled pain can have devastating effects on patients. Their ability to function can be severely impaired. It is said that "severe pain nails you to the bed," making it impossible to do anything else. Severe pain is also linked to major depression and thoughts of suicide. Other studies have shown that uncontrolled pain can render the immune system less effective. This may be the reason that some studies have shown that cancer patients who have good pain control survive longer than cancer patients with unaddressed pain.

Recent research has also determined that the human nervous system can be dramatically affected and indeed changed from continued stimulus like chronic pain; this process of change is called neuroplasticity. In cases of chronic pain, complex changes in the central nervous system increase sensitivity to pain stimuli and cause abnormal firing of the nerves. This results in an ongoing sensation of pain long after the injury that caused the pain has resolved. One way to reduce the risk of developing this neuropathic pain is to treat pain adequately from the beginning.

Patient and Family Barriers to Effective Pain Management with Opioids

In surveys, patients and families state that their greatest fear related to taking opioids (the class of strong pain medications that includes morphine) is that they will become addicted. America is a society that has been fighting a "war on drugs" for several decades, and many people are aware of the dangers of addictive drugs. Unfortunately, this societal attention to addiction has created the misperception that use of opioid drugs will lead to addiction even for patients with terminal illness and severe pain. Yet the few available studies show a very low risk of addiction when medications are taken to control pain (less than 1 percent incidence of addiction). Even if the risk were somewhat higher, many would argue that it is appropriate for dying patients to continue the medications indefinitely because their pain is related to incurable disease and is unlikely to resolve. Especially as people are approaching the end of life, emphasis should be on control of their symptoms rather than on concern about addiction.

There is much confusion about the terms physical dependence, tolerance, and addiction to drugs. Addiction means compulsive drug use with continued craving. People who are addicted use the drug for effects other than pain relief. Physical dependence means a patient's system has adjusted to the presence of a chemical, and if that chemical is suddenly stopped, withdrawal symptoms are experienced. This happens with caffeine, alcohol, and many medications. Being physically dependent on a drug does not mean the patient is addicted. Tolerance means a larger dose of the medication is required to achieve the desired effect after chronic use. Tolerance is not a common issue in most patients when pain medications are given by mouth. An increase in the pain level usually means a change in the patient's condition (such as further growth of a cancer) rather than a loss of effectiveness of the medication. The amount of medication required to relieve the pain is also not an indication of addiction. The range of effective doses for these medications is wide, from a few milligrams to many thousands of milligrams a day, with no ceiling or upper limit on how high the dosing can go. The dosing is determined by the amount that is needed to relieve the pain or is limited by the amount that causes intolerable side effects.

Another reason that patients are reluctant to take opioid pain medications is that they are afraid of the side effects, especially mental changes such as sedation. They do not realize that a balance can usually be achieved between adequate pain control and tolerable side effects. In fact, many patients are able to be more active once their pain is controlled. Mental changes are common but usually improve quickly. Patients and family members should be told ahead of time that the opioid might temporarily affect the patient's mental condition. Drowsiness is common for the first few days after starting a new medication or after an increase in dosage. The drowsiness usually decreases after a few days. More serious mental effects, such as hallucinations, may mean that the patient cannot tolerate that particular drug. In that case, a different type of opioid may be tried. Just because a person hallucinates with one type of opioid, that does not necessarily mean he or she will hallucinate with other types of opioids.

Constipation is another side effect of opioids that occurs in nearly all patients but can be managed with laxatives. Nausea or vomiting occurs in about a third of patients in the first few days of using opioid medications. Medications for nausea can be given at the start of treatment but are not necessary in most patients after a few days. Many people have had a bad experience of nausea with one pain medication (codeine is the most likely to cause nausea) and are reluctant to try others.

Some patients and families have misconceptions about the role of opioids in the dying process. The patient might be a military veteran who remembers the medic out on the battlefield, triaging injured soldiers and giving morphine to those who were most likely to die. The veteran may have thought that the morphine was given to hasten the death, although the purpose was to relieve the pain of the dying soldier. Other families have felt that morphine or other opioids given to their dying loved one hastened the death. In reality, when the appropriate amount of opioids necessary to relieve symptoms is provided, it is unlikely that the pain medications will hasten death. Some research indicates that they may actually prolong survival. The use of opioids to relieve pain and shortness of breath in dying patients is ethical and is not considered excessively dangerous when the dosages are adjusted to treat the symptoms. The AMA Code of Medical Ethics states: "Physicians have an obligation to relieve pain and suffering and to promote the dignity and autonomy of dying patients in their care. This includes providing effective palliative treatment even though it may foreseeably hasten death" (AMA Council on Ethical and Judicial Affairs 1994).

Other patients are reluctant to take opioids because they fear that if they start taking them too early in the course of illness, the medications will not work later on when the pain gets much worse. Patients can be reassured by informing them that the dose can be increased as needed if their pain becomes more intense. The medication should be started as soon as necessary and should be continued as long as necessary to control the symptoms. In some cases that will be days, in other cases weeks, and in some cases months or even years.

A few patients are reluctant to take strong pain medications for spiritual reasons. Some people want to keep their minds clear for spiritual practice. These patients can be offered a dose that will take the edge off the pain without making them too drowsy so that they might be better able to focus on their spiritual practices. Other patients believe that their suffering helps others in the world, by removing that much suffering from the total for humankind. A person who is dying is vulnerable, and we should be careful not to strongly challenge their spiritual beliefs. It is appropriate, however, to offer them the opportunity to relieve at least part of the pain so that they can tolerate the suffering more effectively and continue to contribute to the well being of others.

Professional Caregivers' Barriers to Effective Pain Management

Physicians, nurses, and other professionals can also create barriers to effective pain management with opioids. Some of this occurs because most physicians and nurses who are now practicing had limited training in pain management when they were in school. Professional schools of medicine and nursing did not give pain control much priority until recent years. This lack of training can lead to a lack of confidence in giving the medications. Inexperience with the medications can also lead to misconceptions about the risks and harms of using opioids, further limiting adequate pain management.

Pain control has been given low priority in medical practice as well as training, which is another barrier to treatment. Physicians and nurses have learned only in the past few years that they must ask patients about the presence of symptoms of pain at each encounter. Patients in chronic pain may not show their pain by their expressions, behaviors, or vital signs, and they may be reluctant to "bother" the professional by bringing up their pain. Because pain is a subjective symptom, with no test that can indicate the presence or severity of pain "objectively," professionals are sometimes suspicious of those who say they are in pain but don't show outward signs of it. They may refuse to believe or trust the patient. Health professionals should be trained that the nursing home resident is the expert on his or her pain level.

The psychology and regulations of the "war on drugs" have also created barriers. The emphasis in regulation of controlled substances is preventing drug diversion and addiction. The professionals are concerned about being sanctioned by drug control agencies or losing their licenses to practice if they prescribe pain medications too freely. Because of these concerns, patients with serious chronic pain, especially those without a cause of pain that can be demonstrated on a test such as an X ray or those without a terminal illness, often suffer without adequate pain control. Attitudes are changing in the medical community and licensing boards, but many patients still have difficulty finding a physician who will treat their pain. Fortunately, dying patients are more likely to receive adequate treatment for their pain; nursing home residents receiving hospice services are more likely to have their pain addressed than are other residents.

The effort to control opioids has also created systematic barriers to the availability of pain medications, even when the physician is willing to prescribe them and the nurse is willing to administer them. Controlled substances usually require special handling, such as being locked up separately from other medications or needing to have a specific type of prescription form. Pharmacies that carry controlled substances may be more vulnerable to robberies, and these medications are less likely to be available in pharmacies that serve low-income areas.

In John's case, his initial difficulty in obtaining pain medications on an as-needed basis was probably related to a variety of factors. The nursing staff at the facility was not monitoring his pain by asking him frequently if he needed medications. The nurse may not have been comfortable with giving opioids. The need to handle these medications in special ways may have contributed to the delay in getting doses.

Opioids for Pain Management

Nursing home social workers who care for the dying will often be asked about pain medications; it is helpful to have at least some knowledge about the appropriate use of these medications. As mentioned, "opioid" is the name for the class of strong analgesics that includes morphine, oxycodone, hydromorphone, fentanyl, methadone, hydrocodone, propoxyphene, and codeine. Codeine and propoxyphene are weaker than the other medications and have more side effects, so they are used less frequently in end-of-life care. Hydrocodone is only available in combination with acetaminophen, which limits the dose that can be given. The other five drugs can be used over a wide range of doses and are the mainstays of pain control in end-of-life care. Other analgesic medications that are available for mild pain include acetaminophen, tramadol, and nonsteroidal anti-inflammatory drugs. These are not strong enough for moderate to severe pain and may have potentially more serious organ toxicities than the opioids.

Frequently, opioids are prescribed for patients at adequate doses, but the interval between doses is too long to maintain pain control. For most of the short-acting medications, the dose lasts about four hours. Each dose reaches its full effectiveness within one hour after the patient takes it by mouth. If the patient is still having significant pain after an hour, that dose was not strong enough. Subsequent doses of short-acting morphine or oxycodone can be given every hour until the pain is controlled. If patients have constant pain or need frequent doses to keep their pain controlled, they should be started on long-acting opioids. These provide a constant dose of the medication so that most of the pain is controlled. As Dr. Cicely Saunders, founder of the modern hospice movement, said, "Patients should not have to *earn* their pain medication by getting into pain." However, pain levels will increase from time to time, perhaps because of activity, treatments (such as wound-dressing changes), episodes of emotional distress, or for no apparent reason. A patient who is on long-acting opioids also needs a short-acting opioid to take for these episodes, called breakthrough pain. The breakthrough dose is proportional to the long-acting dose.

Other Treatments Used in Pain Control

The cause of pain should always be assessed and treated with specific treatments, such as for angina or infections. Many patients have types of pain that are best treated by a combination of an opioid and a medication that targets the specific type of pain. This targeted pain medicine is called an adjuvant. Nerve pain, which occurs when the nerves are damaged or malfunctioning and produce a pain message out of proportion to the tissue damage, can be difficult to control with opioids alone. Adjuvant medications such as anticonvulsants and tricyclic antidepressants are given with the opioids to increase their effectiveness. Bone pain, such as pain from cancer deposits in the bones, also may require the use of an anti-inflammatory drug as an adjuvant. The adjuvants alone may control mild pain, but moderate to severe pain usually requires treatment with both the opioid and the adjuvant.

Nonpharmacologic treatments can be effective for relieving pain in some patients. Repositioning the patient or gently moving stiff joints can be helpful in some cases. Heat pads or ice packs relieve some types of muscle and joint pains. Massage, acupuncture, and TENS units may also give relief. Some patients find that relaxation therapy helps them to manage their pain. Pain often leads to anxiety and the tensing of muscles around the area that hurts. Relaxation techniques may be helpful in relieving some of this pain. Other nonpharmacologic pain treatments include guided imagery or self-hypnosis if the patient is open to trying such therapies. Some patients can take their minds off their pain by using distractions such as laughter, prayer, or music. Such interventions may help the patient to feel more in control of the pain and may lower the dose of medication they need for pain control. These nonpharmacologic treatments add to pain control but are rarely effective on their own in cases of severe pain.

Monitoring Pain Control

Patients who are in acute pain usually show it by their facial and verbal expressions and their vital signs. Patients who have chronic pain often do not show it externally. Frequent assessments are needed to ensure that the patient's pain control is adequate. It is common in most hospices to have each member of the interdisciplinary team ask patients about their pain on each visit. The patient is generally asked what pain level they would find acceptable. Pain is assessed by asking whether pain is present at that moment, how many types of pain are present, the severity of the pain using a zero to ten scale or other instrument, the best and worst pain levels since the previous assessment, the location in the body, the type of pain, the duration of the pain, what factors make the pain better or worse, how the pain is interfering with the patient's function or quality of life, which medications have been tried, and how effective the medications were in relieving the pain. The patient's desired level of pain control should also be determined. Each time the medication dose is adjusted, the patient should be reassessed to determine if the dose was effective.

Changes in Appetite, Swallowing, and Intake of Food and Fluids

Loss of appetite and eventual loss of ability to swallow are parts of the normal dying process that are often distressing to both patients and families. They often feel that the patient's decline is related to the lack of nutrition or fluids and that they would be stronger or live longer if they would only eat. Until the past few decades, all persons who were dying naturally did so without artificial feeding or hydration. Technologies such as feeding tubes have been developed to provide nutrition and fluids to those who are not able to eat adequate amounts. The appropriate use of these technologies continues to be debated. Unfortunately, this issue has also become caught up with religious, legal, and political struggles, and the medical realities of nutrition and hydration at the end of life are often not acknowledged. Many people do not realize that artificial feeding and hydration usually do not prolong life in patients with advanced illness and in fact may even hasten death.

Loss of Appetite Is Normal at the End of Life

There are several factors that contribute to a loss of appetite as a serious illness progresses. The patient has a limited amount of energy and may find that eating tires them too much. Their activity levels are much lower, and they are spending more time sleeping so they are not using as many calories. Some treatments and medications may affect appetite and the taste of food. As people lose weight, their dentures may not fit, and it is more diffi-cult for them to chew and swallow. Mouth sores or infections will decrease their ability to eat, as will nausea and constipation. As the body's internal systems slow down near the end of life, the stomach and intestines are less able to absorb and process the food and fluids. Filling the stomach too much at this point can cause physical discomfort or nausea.

Research has found that factors in the immune system that are activated when the body is fighting serious illness also cause a loss of appetite. Most people are familiar with this when they are ill with a serious infection: they just don't feel like eating. The body may have its own wisdom about what level of intake is best.

As patients lose their appetite near the end of life, family members fear that they will suffer from starvation. The main symptom related to starva-tion is hunger, and these patients are simply not hungry. They feel worse if they try to force themselves to eat.

Patients who are losing their appetite often feel full with just a few bites of food. Sometimes they think a favorite food sounds good but are then able to eat only a small amount. They should be encouraged to eat small amounts of foods that appeal to them. Food can be offered more frequently throughout the day. Dietary restrictions on sodium and sugar can often be eliminated at this stage because the patient's overall intake is so lim-ited. Some patients and families who have been adherent to a diabetic diet or low-sodium diet may need counseling on appropriate management of blood pressure and diabetes at the end of life. The goal at this stage is to prevent symptoms rather than to strictly control sugars or blood pressure, measures that are indicated for long-term disease prevention. Families are encouraged to let the patient eat what is wanted but to not put all their time and effort into trying to find foods that the patient can eat. Their time is too precious to spend on this fruitless task. *The patients are not dying because they are not eating; they are not eating because they are dying.*

Swallowing Problems

Most patients with advanced illness reach a stage where they have difficulty swallowing. This may occur early with neurologic illnesses such as strokes and Parkinson's disease, later in the course of dementia, and near the end of life in nearly all patients. Many patients who are hospitalized with serious illness have periods of impaired ability to swallow. Initially, patients may have trouble swallowing solid foods and pills, or they may tend to aspirate food or fluids into the lungs rather than managing to take it down the esophagus into the stomach. Such aspiration carries bacteria into the lungs and is a major risk factor for pneumonia.

Aspiration pneumonia is a common and serious problem. In fact it is the second most common type of infection in hospitalized patients. It occurs in 13 to 48 percent of nursing home residents. The mortality rates have been reported to range from 20 to 80 percent. When a patient is diagnosed with a risk of aspiration, the past medical advice was to use a tube for feeding. Evidence from studies of patients who are fed by tubes show that they may have a higher rate of aspiration pneumonia than patients who are eating by mouth. Besides swallowing problems, other important factors that determine the risk of aspiration pneumonia include being dependent on others for feeding, the number of decayed teeth, presence of tube feeding, number of medications being taken, and smoking (Langmore et al. 1998).

Patients who have difficulty swallowing may benefit from strategies to improve their swallow. These include sitting fully upright to swallow, tucking the chin during a swallow, double swallowing, and clearing the mouth with fluids between bites of food. They should receive the consistencies of food and fluid that they can swallow most easily (often soft or pureed foods and thickened liquids). A speech therapist can be helpful in giving advice on swallow techniques and appropriate food consistencies for a given patient. Some medications can be crushed and given in applesauce or jelly if the patient is not able to swallow whole pills.

Some patients who have severe aspiration on all consistencies of food and fluids may still have a desire to eat and drink by mouth. If they were to be fed by a tube, they would be giving up one of the last pleasures available to them. As previously noted, they would still be at high risk of aspiration with a feeding tube. These patients should be allowed to have "pleasure feedings." These are feedings of food and fluids in the consistencies and flavors that patients prefer. They generally eat and drink only small amounts. They may derive great comfort from being able to take that drink of cold water that they crave or to enjoy the taste of a favorite food.

If patients have no desire to eat or drink, they still need to have good mouth care. Ordinarily, the mouth is kept moist and rinsed by eating and drinking as well as by oral hygiene. If there is no oral intake, the lining of the mouth will become dry and crusted. This occurs even if the patient is receiving fluid through an IV or feeding tube. Mouth care includes the use of moistened swabs or special solutions to moisten the mouth and regular cleaning of the teeth or allowing sips of fluids or ice chips by mouth. Thus the suffering of a parched mouth is avoided.

Artificial Feeding and Hydration

A number of researchers have looked at the outcome of giving artificial feeding and hydration to terminal patients. This includes feeding by stomach tubes and hydration through the veins (intravenously). Intuitively it would seem that supplementing nutritional intake would prolong life. However, research shows that this artificial feeding actually *shortens* survival in many patients. Research has not found improved survival or better outcomes of treatment in terminal cancer patients who receive artificial feeding. On the other hand, artificial feeding may be appropriate in cancer patients who need support during treatment for a potentially curable disease. Also patients with cancer who are physically unable to take food and fluids by mouth, such as patients with blockages in the throat or upper intestine, may benefit from a feeding tube if their prognosis is months or years of remaining life. Sarah's distress about John's lack of intake near the end of life is common among family members and often results in increased stress levels. Nursing home staff members and hospice team members need to be able to educate patients and family members about the realities of artificial feeding at the end of life so that they can provide the most comfort to the patient.

Dementia patients lose their ability to swallow as their disease progresses. This usually occurs after the patient is bed-bound and unable to speak coherently. Providing a feeding tube at this stage of illness has not been shown to prolong survival, prevent aspiration pneumonia, reduce the risk of pressure sores or infections, improve function, or make patients more comfortable (Finucane, Christmas, and Travis 1999). The SUPPORT investigators reviewed the effect of tube feeding and intravenous feeding in a number of terminal conditions. They found improved survival with artificial feeding in coma patients but decreased survival in acute renal failure, chronic obstructive pulmonary disease, cirrhosis, acute respiratory failure, and multisystem failure with sepsis (Borum et al. 2000). Cases of

pure neurologic injury such as persistent vegetative state, where patients can survive for months or years on artificial feeding, are rare.

Even when patients and families understand that feeding tubes at the end of life are not going to extend life, they may still believe that providing fluids is useful to the person who is dying. Some family members may believe that dehydration will hasten death. In addition, many family members fear that their loved one will suffer more if they do not receive artificial fluids. There is no medical evidence that not providing artificial fluids causes a more painful death. In fact, Joanne Lynn points out that there are benefits to dehydration at the end of life (Lynn and Harrold 1999:133–34). Dehydration has an analgesic effect in some patients, leading to less need for pain medicine. Patients experience dehydration as sleepiness rather than discomfort. They are less likely to have lung congestion, cough, and vomiting near the end of life. As their amount of urine decreases, there is less need to move the patient for urinary care, and they have a lower incidence of urinary infections.

Some Americans have heard from their religious leaders and politicians that artificial feeding and hydration are a necessary part of patient care for those who cannot eat and drink normally. Nationally known cases such as those of Nancy Cruzan and Terri Schiavo have raised issues about judging quality of life and about respecting all humans regardless of their condition. It is true that we need to consider the values of the patient and family in making these decisions. It is also true that there should be a clear understanding of the goal of artificial feeding and whether this goal can be accomplished through giving food and fluids artificially. There should also be an open discussion of the potential risks associated with artificial feeding, including aspiration pneumonia (which occurs in about half of patients with disordered swallowing who receive tube feedings), swelling, congestive heart failure, nausea and vomiting, diarrhea, and infections. If the patient and family choose to pursue artificial hydration or nutrition because of their values, they should understand that a time will come in advanced illness when the patient's body simply cannot absorb the tube feeding or the feeding causes more complications than benefits. They should be prepared to discontinue it at that time.

State laws vary on artificial feeding and hydration. Some "living will" laws limit withholding artificial feeding and hydration if the patient has not specifically stated that they do not want this treatment. There have been attempts to pass laws that would take away the authority of the

person appointed as durable power of attorney for medical care to make a decision to withhold or withdraw artificial feeding. Providers should be familiar with the laws in their state and with the policies of the institution in which the patient is receiving care. Because of these legal concerns, some providers are reluctant to withhold artificial feeding and hydration if the patient is unable to make their own decision and the identity or authority of the surrogate decision maker is unclear.

It is often emotionally more difficult to stop artificial feeding and hydration than to have never started it. Legally, there is no difference between *not starting* a treatment and *stopping* a treatment that is not benefiting a patient. The AMA Code of Medical Ethics states: "There is no ethical distinction between withdrawing and withholding life-sustaining treatment" (AMA Council on Ethical and Judicial Affairs 1994). Some religious organizations and ethicists, however, do maintain that there is a difference between these two.

For some people, deciding to stop a treatment can pose unique emotional discomfort. Many people feel that the decision to stop the treatment is taking into human hands what should be in God's. Some people are reluctant to start artificial feeding or fluids for fear that they could never be stopped. This leads to a situation where patients who might benefit are not receiving the treatment. If there is uncertainty about whether a patient would benefit from artificial feeding or hydration, a time-limited trial can be helpful to answer the question. The treatment can be stopped if the patient has not improved within an agreed-upon time frame. A trial of a few days is enough to see if a patient will benefit from fluids. A trial of a few weeks should be sufficient to see if they will benefit from artificial feeding.

Shortness of Breath and Other Respiratory Symptoms

Importance and Incidence of Difficulty with Breathing

Shortness of breath, or dyspnea, is one of the most distressing and common symptoms experienced near the end of life. Dyspnea is defined as a subjective experience of uncomfortable breathing. Severe dyspnea is associated with a high level of anxiety and is sometimes described as being more agonizing than pain. Dyspnea occurs in up to 70 percent of patients

in the last six weeks of life and is more common than pain at this stage. It has a dramatic effect on both patient and family and is often a sign of poor prognosis.

Dyspnea is found in many end-stage conditions but is especially common in heart and lung disease. Patients with lung cancer have been found to have moderate to severe dyspnea in 50 to 60 percent of cases. Moderate to severe shortness of breath occurs in 19 to 55 percent of other cancers. Up to 76 percent of patients with chronic lung disease reported distressing breathlessness in the final year of life. Dyspnea is also the most common symptom of congestive heart failure.

Dyspnea limits patients' functional ability, at times even causing difficulty in having conversations or eating a meal. Patients with dyspnea are frequently dependent on others for care in activities such as bathing and dressing. Many become socially isolated because they don't have the energy to get out or to visit with friends. In addition to being weaker, they may lose their appetite and have memory loss because of their difficulty in breathing. Symptoms of depression, anger, anxiety, and loneliness can relate to the severity of the dyspnea. Patients with dyspnea often suffer from the fear of suffocating or dying. Their loved ones suffer the anxiety and fear along with them.

Treatments for Dyspnea

Many patients with dyspnea can find relief with treatments directed at the cause of the shortness of breath. For instance, patients with congestive heart failure benefit from diuresis to remove excess fluid in the lungs, and patients with asthma benefit from bronchodilators to relieve spasm in the airways. Other examples of disease-specific treatments for dyspnea are the use of nitroglycerine for angina, drainage of excess fluid around the lungs (pleural effusions), antibiotic treatment for pneumonia or bronchitis, oxygen for those who are low on oxygen, and many others.

If the cause of the dyspnea cannot be treated directly, patients can still obtain relief through oxygen, opioids, nonpharmacologic treatments, and relief of anxiety. The degree of shortness of breath experienced by patients often does not correlate with their oxygen levels. Oxygen has been widely used and has a strong placebo effect but is most effective in those who have low oxygen levels. Oxygen is usually provided through a nasal cannula

(tube in the nose). Some patients require high oxygen flows or even oxygen delivered under pressure through tight-fitting masks to obtain normal blood oxygen levels. Patients who need face masks to provide the oxygen often find that it limits their ability to eat, drink, and speak. The pressurized masks may also cause sores on the face.

When patients' dyspnea is not controlled with oxygen and medications for their underlying disease, opioids have been effective in giving relief, particularly near the end of life. Patients are generally given low doses of morphine or oxycodone at first. Several studies have shown that the use of opioids, starting with low doses and titrating to the patient's symptoms, does not cause significant respiratory suppression (Rocker et al. 2007).

The anxiety associated with dyspnea may respond to mild tranquilizers such as the benzodiazepines. These are often used along with opioids, but the opioids are more specific in treating the sensation of dyspnea in advanced disease.

Nonpharmacologic treatments can be helpful in relieving shortness of breath. One of the first steps is to reassure the patient and family since the tension in the room leads to increased symptoms for the patient. There may be a need to ask some people to leave the room if there are several crowding around the bed. The patient needs space in which to breathe. A view of the outdoors or air movement with a fan may give relief. If possible, the room should be kept cool, without chilling the patient. In humid regions, a dehumidifier or air conditioner can remove moisture from the air, making it easier for the patient to breathe. If the air is very dry, adding humidity may help. Some patients get relief by having their head elevated or by turning onto their side. Behavioral approaches such as visualization, hypnosis, or distraction will be effective in some patients.

Cough and Secretions

Frequent coughing episodes can cause dyspnea, pain, weakness, loss of appetite, insomnia, difficulty communicating, and social embarrassment. Cough occurs in 47 to 86 percent of lung cancer patients and is a distressing symptom in about half of chronic lung disease patients in their last year of life. Coughing may be caused by secretions or other sources of irritation in the airways. When possible, the specific cause should be treated. For nonspecific causes, opioids are the most effective cough suppressants.

Codeine is frequently used in cough syrups, but all of the opioids are effective in suppressing cough. Some patients need to have more effective coughs to clear their secretions. These patients may benefit from aerosol treatments or medications to loosen the secretions.

In the final few days of life, many patients develop congestion in their upper airways, often with an audible sound referred to as the "death rattle." In many cases, this sound occurs because the patient has become so weak and lethargic that they are no longer swallowing. Normally, the mouth produces about a quart of saliva a day. This accumulates in the back of the throat if the patient is not swallowing, particularly if they are lying on their back. In these cases, the patient's breathing can be noisy because the air is gurgling through these secretions. The air can still be moving well and the lungs can be fairly clear. The patient can be breathing comfortably with this condition (they are usually unresponsive at this stage), but it can be distressing for the family to listen to this sound as they sit by the bedside. There are several medications with anticholinergic action that can diminish the production of saliva. Suctioning is uncomfortable, is rarely able to reach the secretions, and may promote the secretion of more fluid. Suctioning is not generally recommended in these circumstances. Another way to relieve this noisy breathing is to roll the patient over onto his or her side without elevating the head so that the secretions tend to drain out of the mouth or into peripheral airways where they do not make as much noise. John's noisy breathing was a source of distress for Sarah and needed to be addressed appropriately.

Gastrointestinal Symptoms

Nausea and Vomiting

Nausea and vomiting are highly distressing symptoms that can interfere with quality of life. They occur in 40 to 70 percent of patients with advanced cancer and are common in liver and kidney diseases as well as AIDS. The causes include a variety of conditions, medications, and environmental stimuli. Patients who are experiencing severe nausea often become sensitized to odors in their environment. Smells that are usually pleasant may cause nausea. When patients are nauseated, the food placed before them should be attractively presented and in small amounts. Cool, fruity flavors and carbonated drinks may be more palatable than hot, greasy, or spicy foods or noncarbonated drinks.

Treatment of nausea and vomiting includes a search for specific revers- ible causes, such as medications, constipation, infections, and acid peptic disease. If the mechanism of the nausea can be identified, the medication is targeted at that cause. If the mechanism is not clear, haloperidol is often the most effective antiemetic. Haloperidol is less sedating than some other commonly used antiemetics. There are several brain pathways and neu- rotransmitters involved in nausea and vomiting, and cases that are difficult to treat often require a combination of medications.

Constipation

Constipation is another symptom that can cause a great deal of misery if not addressed. Dr. Cicely Saunders, founder of the modern hospice move- ment, reportedly once gave a lecture in which every other slide said, "Noth- ing matters more than the bowels." The majority of patients with advanced disease are less active and eating less, and most will have constipation. In assessing constipation, it is important to determine the patients' normal bowel patterns and whether they have needed laxatives in the past.

Constipation is nearly inevitable as a side effect of opioids and will re- quire treatment for as long as the patient needs the opioids. Treatment is with a stimulant laxative. A natural laxative called senna is often pre- scribed in combination with stool softeners. If this is not effective, osmotic laxatives such as milk of magnesia may be added or suppositories may be given. Patients should be encouraged to maintain adequate fluid intake. A fiber supplement or high fiber diet is not as effective for the constipation related to opioids and can cause impactions if the patient is not drinking adequate amounts of fluid. Even if the patient is eating little, the colon will continue to produce some feces, which are largely made up of bacteria and bowel secretions. These patients continue to need monitoring of their bowel status and laxative treatments as indicated.

Diarrhea is less common in the terminal population but is also distress- ing. It may be caused by medications or intestinal infections (particularly *Clostridium difficile*). A patient who has been constipated and then develops diarrhea should always be checked for a fecal impaction. When a hard stool blocks the lower colon, liquid feces may be forced past the impaction, giving the symptom of diarrhea. Removing the impaction and treating the constipation is the appropriate response in this situation.

Other Common Symptoms in Terminal Patients

Skin and Odor Problems: Effect on Patients

One of the difficult aspects of advanced disease for some patients is the impact of the disease and treatments on their appearance. Changes in appearance can make it difficult for the patients to feel that they are the same person. Hair loss, severe weight loss, changes in skin color, swelling, and visible tumors or medical devices mark them as changed. Some patients are in despair because of changes that they find unacceptable, such as a colostomy bag. Others have conditions that are disturbing to view, such as large facial ulcers caused by head and neck cancers, severe bedsores, or dead and blackened hands or feet caused by a loss of circulation. People with these types of deformities can become socially isolated because other people find it hard to be with them. Some patients choose to stay in dark rooms where no one can see them and to ban all mirrors from their rooms. Other patients have wounds or conditions that create disgusting odors, which also leads to isolation. The psychological effect of such conditions is as damaging as the physical symptoms.

DECUBITUS ULCERS

Decubitus ulcers, also known as pressure ulcers or bedsores, are not uncommon at the end of life. Patients are at risk because of immobility, poor healing, poor nutrition, older age, reduced circulation, and incontinence. The best treatment is prevention, which includes recognizing the risk, keeping the skin clean and dry, and checking the skin regularly for signs of damage. Patients should be turned or repositioned regularly. Some patients will need pain medications before turning or dressing changes. Some patients can heal their decubitus ulcers even with poor nutritional intake and bed-bound state, but the primary palliative goal is management of symptoms related to pressure ulcers.

UNPLEASANT ODORS

This problem can occur with draining fistulas (openings through the skin that leak feces or urine) or from skin wounds that are foul-smelling because of the presence of infection or dying tissue. Some patients and families may not notice the presence of the odor and do not need management of it. Others may be distressed and embarrassed by the odor. There are several ways to help manage odors. Simple measures include the use of a pan of charcoal briquettes (which absorb odor) or a pan of vinegar in the room, usually under the bed. Activated charcoal dressings can be applied to the wound. If the problem is infection in the wound, topical antibiotics may decrease drainage and odor. The use of masking scents, such as peppermint oil, may be helpful in the room. However, many products used to improve the scent in a room such as sprays or scented candles only provide a heavy new odor that mixes with the patient's body odor in an unpleasant way rather than eliminating it.

INFECTIONS

Infections such as pneumonia, urinary tract infections, and skin infections are not uncommon in terminal patients. When considering management of these infections, the goals of treatment should be considered. In America, a patient who has an infection is treated almost automatically with an antibiotic. However, studies have shown that the benefits of antibiotics may be much less in hospice patients than commonly believed. Antibiotics did not help to relieve symptoms or to prolong life in hospice patients with pneumonias or skin infections (cellulitis). The drugs were more effective in relieving symptoms in urinary tract infections but nonetheless did not prolong survival. (Reinbolt et al. 2005).

Even if antibiotics were found to prolong survival, this is not the goal of many terminal patients near the end of life. Their goal is often to control symptoms rather than to prolong life. Pneumonia used to be called "the old man's friend" because it was considered a blessing to someone dying from a lingering chronic illness. If the primary goal is comfort, symptoms can be controlled in most cases without antibiotics. If it was likely that a patient would benefit from antibiotics to alleviate symptoms, the treatment would usually be with oral rather than intravenous antibiotics.

WEAKNESS

One of the most common symptoms of advanced disease is weakness. This leads to loss of ability to participate in usual activities and to dependence on others for care. In almost all cases of terminal illness, patients will eventually need help and care from others. This occurs in the late stages of cancer, where patients may only require care for a few weeks at the end of life, but can be present for months or years in cases of neurologic disorders and heart and lung diseases. Especially in America, where being independent is almost a measure of our self-worth, this seems to be the hardest symptom for patients to accept. Unfortunately, there are few effective treatments to restore the patient's former level of strength, but they may be able to learn ways to maintain their function.

If the patient is to receive rehabilitation, the goals should be realistic. This would include maintaining comfort, learning to use energy-conserving measures so that he or she can participate in meaningful activities, and maintaining function. An occupational therapist may be helpful in teaching patients how to conserve their energy, and limited exercise programs may help them to maintain function to a limited degree.

Patients and their families need support in coping with the decreased level of function. Most patients find it difficult to accept care from others and worry about being a burden on their families. Accepting care seems especially hard for those who have defined themselves as caregivers. They might be able to reframe their understanding of the situation if they can reflect on how much they wanted to help those that they cared for. Those people gave them the gift of allowing care. They can give the same gift to those who want to care for them. They also may be helped to find sources of meaning in their lives other than doing tasks. Some people benefit from talking with a counselor or spiritual companion about the changes they are experiencing and how they choose to find meaning in these changes.

The Final Road to Death

The Common Road

Most patients nearing the end of life exhibit a common set of changes. These include decreased energy and increased weakness, decreased appetite and intake, more time spent sleeping, decreased urine output, and periods of confusion. Eventually, most patients reach a stage of being poorly responsive. It is difficult at this stage to know if they are totally unconscious, asleep, or awake. Some are still able to hear what is being said to them but are too weak to speak or even to open their eyes. One sign of this awareness might be a slight raising of the eyebrows or other change in facial expression when someone speaks to them. It is appropriate to remember that any patient who seems unresponsive may still be aware of what is being said in the room. Family members can still speak to the patient, comforting or giving messages that they feel are important. These patients may also be aware of touch, and gentle touch may be comforting to them.

From the patients' point of view at this stage, their primary experience seems to be sleepiness and weakness. Their bodies may feel heavy from the weakness. They may have difficulty finding a comfortable position or be unable to change their own position if uncomfortable. However, they sleep through much of this stage. It is often more uncomfortable for the family members who sit beside them day after day than it is for the patients. This is the stage when family members ask repeatedly, "How long can this go on?" The process may take days or even weeks, which seems like an eternity to those who are waiting for the end with each breath.

The Uncommon Road

A smaller number of patients experience increased agitation and restlessness as the end of life approaches rather than becoming sleepier. This symptom is not only distressing to patients; it is upsetting to family members and a significant cause of difficulty in managing the patient's care, whether in the patients home or in a facility. Terminal agitation is seen most commonly in patients with underlying dementia or brain lesions such as metastases from cancer. It also occurs in those who are emotionally or spiritually unprepared for death. It may occur in nearly half of all patients at some point in illness.

Terminal agitation may manifest as full-blown delirium, with symptoms of severe restlessness, combativeness, paranoia, frightening hallucinations, and angry outbursts. Some patients are too weak to get out of bed but remain extremely restless. They often are too confused to speak coherently and lack the cognitive capability to work through unresolved issues or their fear of dying. Many are too near the end of life to regain this capability. The goal of treatment in these cases is to relieve their agitation so that they can die more peacefully.

The first step in managing delirium is to assess the patient for causes that may be relieved. Uncontrolled pain can cause delirium, as can urinary retention, severe constipation, and a host of other physical discomforts. Medications are also a common cause. If the cause cannot be eliminated, treatment of terminal delirium may require the use of antipsychotics. Non-pharmacologic treatments that may be helpful include keeping the patient's environment quiet and gently lit. It might be necessary to limit exposure to people or items that seem to be upsetting. The patient's eyeglasses and hearing aids should be in place to help with their orientation. Providing familiar objects or calming music and having family members stay with the patient may be helpful. Some will benefit from spiritual rituals or readings that they find comforting, such as saying the rosary for a Catholic.

Palliative Sedation

Palliative sedation, sometimes called terminal sedation, is sedation to the point of unawareness that is done with the intention of relieving distressing symptoms that do not respond to other interventions. This may be done for delirium, severe anxiety, or uncontrollable pain. Although many patients need treatment for anxiety during their terminal illness, few need to be sedated to the point of unconsciousness. When utilized, palliative sedation is administered for twenty-four to forty-eight hours to relieve the symptoms, and then the sedation is decreased to see if the patient still requires it for symptom control. This procedure is controversial because patients cannot eat or drink during deep sedation. There is concern that the sedation might hasten death in some circumstances by stopping intake. However, use of this treatment has not been shown to decrease overall survival, and it is considered legally and ethically appropriate if the patient has severe suffering that cannot be controlled by other means. (Plonk and Arnold 2005) Any time that terminal sedation is being considered, there should be full and open discussion with the patient (if capable) and family about the risks and benefits, with the understanding that the goal is not to hasten death. Ideally, a specialist in palliative medicine will be involved in the management of such patients.

Emergencies Near the End of Life

There are some situations that may arise quickly in terminal patients and need aggressive intervention in order to relieve symptoms. A sudden increase in pain may signal the development of a new complication of illness such as a fracture or obstruction. Sudden onset of severe dyspnea can have numerous causes and should be evaluated to see if it is reversible. The management of pain and shortness of breath have been discussed.

Another emergency that may arise in terminal patients is seizures. Patients with brain injuries or metastases are at the highest risk for this complication. A single seizure will generally stop on its own within a few minutes. A seizure is not an emergency that requires a response within minutes, but the patient should be started on a medication to prevent further seizures if possible. Prolonged seizing that does not stop on its own requires more urgent treatment with benzodiazepines or anticonvulsants.

Severe hemorrhage is perhaps the most frightening emergency in terminal patients. Even a small amount of bright red blood looks like a large amount when it is spread on white sheets or a floor. Bleeding emergencies are rare but dramatic. Patients with tumors that are eroding into major blood vessels or those with bleeding disorders such as leukemia and end-stage liver disease are at highest risk. If major hemorrhage is a possibility, one strategy is to keep dark colored towels in the patient's room. Blood is much less dramatic and frightening when it is mopped up with dark towels. If the bleeding is from a surface wound, pressure is held on the wound. If the bleeding is massive, the patient will likely die within minutes.

Signs and Symptoms of Approaching Death

Common Physical Changes

As patients reach the last days of life, bodily changes occur that help caregivers and family members to recognize that the end is near. Not all patients will have all of these signs, and the signs may come and go, so they are not exact predictors of the time of death. However, they are helpful as markers of this stage of illness.

Patients are weak by this stage, usually bed-bound. They may have periods of lucidity or may be totally unable to respond even when awake. Their skin color may become grayer or sallow, and the skin may lose its turgor. They are taking in minimal amounts, perhaps a few sips of fluid or a few bites of soft food or nothing at all. They will need good mouth care with moistened swabs to prevent the discomfort of dry mouth. Their urine output decreases. Initially they produce smaller amounts of more concentrated urine, and the output may cease completely in the last hours of life.

The breathing pattern changes, becoming more irregular. Patients can have pauses in their breathing that last up to a minute. The family members at the bedside often fear that the patient has taken their last breath, only to see patient start breathing again. These pauses (called apnea) are not uncomfortable to the patient. Sarah was upset by this occurrence but was able to cope with the apneic spells when she understood that they were not causing suffering for John.

Patients also may lose their ability to swallow as they become weak and unresponsive. They may choke when they try to eat or drink or take medications. The death rattle, discussed above, may seem to family members to indicate that the patient is "drowning" but may be causing little distress for the patient. Using medications that dry the mouth can relieve the excessive secretions. It is also helpful to turn patients over onto their side so that some of the secretions drain out of the mouth.

Changes also occur in the circulatory system as the end of life approaches. The patient's blood pressure may drop, usually on the last day of life but occasionally for several days before the end. The heart rate may increase, perhaps as a response to the stresses the body is experiencing. The skin of the extremities may become cool as the blood is shunted to vital organs. These changes usually occur first on the feet, hands, and knees but may also affect the nose and ears. This shunting often causes purple-blue discoloration of these areas, called mottling. Mottling is usually a sign that death will occur within hours, but it can come and go for a few days at the end of life.

Rarely, a patient will have a final surge of energy and awareness near the end of life. This may allow them an opportunity to say last words to loved ones or to interact after a period of being unresponsive. Some families take this as a sign that the person is getting better, but it just may be a final rally before their death.

Glimpses of Mystery at the End of Life

It is common for dying people to appear to be seeing or talking to unseen others. If they are capable of saying what they are seeing, they often describe the presence of deceased loved ones or of angels. These visions are generally comforting and do not require treatment. They may occur anytime in the last several weeks of life but are increasingly common as death grows closer. Some patients reach up as if for unseen hands. Many families think of this as the presence of loved ones who are there to accompany the patients in their transitions to the next life. The true significance of these visions is unknown, but they are said to occur in up to 75 percent of dying patients.

Many families wonder what is keeping the patient from dying if the process is prolonged. They search for ways to help the person let go, such as ensuring that all close family members have visited and said their goodbyes. Although there are many anecdotal reports of patients who died just after a beloved family member arrived to say goodbye, there is little evidence that such events determine the timing of death. Other families who have heard that patients sometimes have a hard time letting go if their family members are in the room will leave the patient for a period of time to see if that will ease their dying. They are often disappointed to find that dying will happen on its own schedule, without being controlled by the actions of those surrounding the patient. Death has been likened to birth: we may be ready for it to come, but it comes at its own time. Sarah experienced this distress of waiting for the end. It generally does not appear to be a time of suffering for the patient if symptoms are controlled. The purpose of this time is not understood medically, but it may help family members let go of their attachment to the person. They do not want to lose their loved one, but they don't want to keep them in this state.

Some families wonder if the timing of death is affected by a patient's will to live. There is some evidence that patients who are dying of chronic illness may have influence over the timing of their deaths to some degree in terms of how willing they are to let go. However, many patients are ready to let go, but their bodies have not yet given out. It seems that the body can be ready when the mind is not, or the mind can be ready when the body is not. The bodily factors are probably more important in the timing of death than the mental readiness.

Care at the Time of Death

The moment when a patient dies is not an emergency, either at home or in a facility. Caregivers should be calm and quiet, shifting their attention to the family members who are with the patient or who need to be notified of the death. In most cases the death is expected, and family members will not be surprised to receive the notification if they are not present at the bedside. If death is unanticipated, the staff member who is notifying the family should determine whether it is safe to do so over the phone. In some cases, the family should simply be asked to come to the facility because of a change in the patient's condition. If a family member is notified of the death over the phone, it is appropriate to ask if he or she are alone and to determine whether someone else is needed to drive to the facility.

Many family members will want to spend time at the bedside of their deceased loved one. It is respectful to allow them as much time as they need for this. It is rare for them to want to stay with the body for more than a few hours. They should be allowed to grieve in their own way. There is a wide range of what is normal in expressing grief, even within one family.

Some families will want spiritual support or rituals practiced in the patient's room around the time of death. They may involve their own clergy or a chaplain from a hospice team or the facility. Some faith traditions have specific rituals related to care of the body, such as specific practices for washing or placing the body. If possible, the social worker should gather this information before the death so that the patient's religious traditions can be respected. In some cases, family members will want to be the ones to wash and prepare the body. In all circumstances, the privacy and dignity of the person who has just died should be honored. The body should be treated with respect.

Conclusion

Caring for terminal patients and their families is often challenging and sometimes emotionally draining for the professionals involved, who must include self-care as one of their skills. One way of doing self-care is to be well informed about end-of-life care. This gives increased confidence and comfort with the situations that are encountered. Family members of the patients will assume that all professionals who are involved in the patient's care will be knowledgeable about medical issues that arise. They will be asking questions about what to expect, the meaning of changes that they observe, and how much time is left before the death. Well-informed caregivers can do much to relieve the anxiety that patients and families are experiencing and to support them through the journey.

The rewards of this type of care are also profound. These patients are at a stage of life where they don't want to waste time with trivialities. Their conversations can be rich, focusing on the topics of deepest meaning. If they face their deaths with peace and grace, they give their caregivers spiritual comfort and strength to face their own mortality. Patients and families often form close bonds with their caregivers and don't hesitate to express their gratitude for the care and support they receive through terminal illness. Most professionals in health care choose their profession because they want to help people. Caring for those who are dying rewards them with the certainty that they have truly helped people at a time when they are the most vulnerable.

References

AMA Council on Ethical and Judicial Affairs, 1994. "Opinion 2.20: Withholding or Withdrawing Life-Sustaining Medical Treatment." *AMA Code of Medical Ethics.* http://www.ama-assn.org/ama1/pub/upload/mm/Code_of_Med_Eth /opinion/opinion220.html. Accessed February 13, 2009.

Bernabei, R., G. Gambassi, K. Lapane, F. Landi, C. Gatsonis, R. Dunlop, et al. 1998. "Management of Pain in Elderly Patients with Cancer." *Journal of the American Medical Association* 279:1877–82.

Borum, M. L., J. Lynn, Z. Zhong, K. Roth, A. F. Connors, N. A. Desbiens, et al. 2000. "The Effect of Nutritional Supplementation on Survival in Seriously Ill Hospitalized Adults: An Evaluation of the SUPPORT Data." *Journal of the American Geriatrics Society* 48:S33–S38.

Ferrell, B. A. 2004. "The Management of Pain in Long-Term Care." *Clinical Journal of Pain* 20:240–43.

Finucane, T. E., C. Christmas, and K. Travis. 1999. "Tube Feeding in Patients with Advanced Dementia: A Review of the Evidence." *Journal of the American Medical Association* 282:1365–70.

Langmore, S. E., M. S. Terpenning, A. Schork, Y. Chen, J. T. Murray, D. Lopatin, et al. 1998. "Predictors of Aspiration Pneumonia: How Important Is Dysphagia?" *Dysphagia* 13:69–81.

Lunney, J. R., J. Lynn, and C. Hogan. 2002. "Profiles of Older Medicare Decedents." *Journal of the American Geriatrics Society* 50:1102–12.

Lynn, J., and J. Harrold. 1999. *Handbook for Mortals.* New York: Oxford University Press.

Plonk, W. M., and R. A. Arnold. 2005. "Terminal Care: The Last Weeks of Life." *Journal of Palliative Medicine* 8:1042–54.

Reinbolt, R. E., A. M. Shenk, P. H. White, and R. M. Navari. 2005. "Symptomatic Treatment of Infections in Patients with Advanced Cancer Receiving Hospice Care." *Journal of Pain Symptom Management* 30:175–82.

Rocker, G. M., T. Sinuff, R. Horton, and P. Hernandez. 2007. "Advanced Chronic Obstructive Pulmonary Disease: Innovative Approaches to Palliation." *Journal of Palliative Medicine* 10:783–97.

SUPPORT Principal Investigators. 1995. "A Controlled Trial to Improve Care for Seriously Ill Hospitalized Patients." The Study to Understand Prognoses and Preferences for Outcomes and Risks of Treatment (SUPPORT). *Journal of the American Medical Association* 274:1591–98.

Identifying and Addressing the Psychosocial, Social, Spiritual, and Existential Issues Affecting Nursing Home Residents at the End of Life

JEAN C. MUNN

CASE STUDY

Mrs. Bench, a widowed eighty-eight-year-old resident has lived in Blue Valley Nursing Home for four years. Her main medical challenges have been related to her heart condition and her diabetes; she has mild cognitive impairment. Last week, during a follow-up doctor's appointment, Mrs. Bench found out she has breast cancer, and that the cancer has spread to other parts of her body. The physician tells Mrs. Bench (in the presence of her two daughters) that with chemotherapy there is a chance that Mrs. Bench could extend her life for months and that without the chemotherapy, she will likely have about four to six months to live. After a few moments of silence, Mrs. Bench tells the physician she is not inclined to have the chemotherapy. Both daughters softly protest. The older daughter asks Mrs. Bench to mull it over before she makes a final decision. The physician suggests that Mrs. Bench get back in touch with her over the next week with a decision.

When Mrs. Bench returns to the nursing home, her daughters ask the social worker to meet with Mrs. Bench to try and convince her to accept the chemotherapy. The social worker suggests that the two daughters, Mrs. Bench, and she meet to discuss what the doctor said and what the options are. After checking with Mrs. Bench, a meeting is scheduled for the following afternoon. During the meeting the two daughters plead with their mother to accept the chemotherapy. Mrs. Bench discloses she doesn't want to spend her last months feeling sick from chemotherapy and that she is ready to join her late husband "in heaven." The younger daughter leaves the room in tears. The older daughter says she will return tomorrow and states that she hopes her mom will reconsider the chemotherapy.

After the daughters leave, Mrs. Bench turns to the social worker and says, "Maybe I should agree to the chemotherapy, I don't want my daughters to think I am giving up."

Introduction

The purpose of this chapter is to discuss the social work role with individual residents and groups of residents in long-term care at the end of life. While it may seem obvious that the social work role in long-term care is directly associated with resident well-being, at the end of life or within the dying trajectory that role often becomes ambiguous as family needs and facility policies gain attention. Indeed, the current emphasis on the family as the unit of care can contribute to ambiguity and confusion. For example, in the case study above, the daughters' preferences may not be in keeping with the resident's best interest. Therefore, this chapter will focus on the social work roles as resident advocate, facilitator, educator, and therapist for residents who die in these settings.

I will review pertinent literature that discusses end-of-life care in a variety of settings. This information is important as there is less research on the end-of-life experience in long-term care than in other settings. Therefore, the preferences of community-dwelling patients will provide some insight into what residents in long-term care wish at the end of life. I will then look at existing research conducted in long-term care and follow that with a discussion of the social work role, stressing overarching themes of advocacy and assessment along with challenges and appropriate interventions. Five NASW standards: Empowerment and Advocacy, Assessment and Planning, Knowledge (combined with Continuing Education), Self-Awareness, and Intervention are integrated into the description as these are most critical to the social worker–resident relationship at the end of life.

Finally, I will provide some resources (information on training, a theoretical perspective, and a useful conceptual framework) to assist social workers in meeting these challenges and enhancing the well-being of residents. I conclude with some questions for reflection based on the case study.

Current Literature

As we begin to consider options for Mrs. Bench, we might look at research into the end-of-life experience of residents in long-term care. Existing research documents that long-term-care settings, specifically nursing homes, are sites of death for older adults (Mitchell et al. 2005); however, the quantity and scope of this research is limited. Therefore, it is helpful to look at research conducted in other sites of care, specifically hospitals and ambulatory clinics, to develop a context for caring for older adults at the end of life. Several of these studies have sought to determine what is important at the end of life. They have used qualitative, quantitative, and mixed methodologies. In addition, these studies are based on input from dying people, bereaved family members, experts in the field, and medical care providers.

One way to help residents, such as Mrs. Bench, who die in long-term care, is to consider what a good death is. Based on current research, a death is considered good if it includes peaceful acceptance and limited physical pain or other symptoms (Hanson, Henderson, and Menon, 2002) and if "person's preferences for dying and the moment of death agree with the observations of how the person actually died as reported by others" (Patrick, Engelberg, and Curtis 2001:721). Within the nursing home setting, three central components of good care related to end of life are individualized care, caregiver teamwork, and advance care planning. All included a physical element such as absence of pain (Singer, Martin, and Kelner 1999; Patrick, Engelberg, and Curtis 2001; Tong et al. 2003). Another set of studies sought to identify the attributes of a good death (Steinhauser et al. 2000; Steinhauser et al. 2001) and resulted in five domains: completion, relationship with the healthcare system, preparation, symptom impact, and affective social support.

Yet despite evidence that nursing homes are providing and will continue to provide end-of-life care to almost one-fourth of older adults (Facts on Dying 2004; Teno 2002), the focus on end-of-life care in nursing home settings has received less attention than acute-care settings or home health. Existing research in end-of-life care has focused on community-dwelling cancer patients whose death trajectory is predictable and who may remain cognitively intact until actively dying (Morris et al. 1986; Kayser-Jones 2002; O'Boyle and Waldron 1997). This is an important omission as many aspects of the dying experience (e.g., care philosophy, available services, relationships with caregivers as well as caregiver training and knowledge) are setting specific (Mezey et al. 2002). Furthermore, the long-term-care population is older and more likely to suffer from dementia and experience chronic illness for long periods before death. Notably, the long-term setting as a site of end of life care has been examined; the role of social work within this setting has not (Lacey 2005a, 2005b).

In order to address issues regarding the end-of-life experience specific to long-term care, the National Institute on Aging funded a comprehensive study, *End of Life in Nursing Homes and Assisted Living Facilities*, led by Dr. Sheryl Zimmerman. The chapter author was part of the investigative team. This project collected data for 792 resident deaths in a stratified, random sample of 199 resident-care/assisted-living facilities and 31 nursing homes across four states (Florida, Maryland, North Carolina, and New Jersey). Of the 792 decedents, 451 had interviews with family caregivers, and 677 had staff interviews. The purpose of the study was to describe experiences at the end of life and to compare the structure, process, and outcomes of end-of-life care (Donabedian 1966). Although the focus of this study was not social work, it has provided the most comprehensive description of the end-of-life experience in long-term care. One product of the study, a measure of the Quality of Dying in Long-Term Care, is discussed in the assessment section of this chapter.

Concurrent with the parent study, the same research team conducted a qualitative study of ten homogeneous focus groups drawn from a purposive sample of long-term-care residents (two groups; n = 11); family caregivers (two groups; n = 19); paraprofessional staff (three groups; n = 20); and licensed/registered staff (three groups; n = 15) from five nursing homes and eight residential-care/assisted-living communities in North Carolina. One especially notable finding was the lack of social work support reported by the four participant groups and the recommendation that social workers in long-term care become more involved with residents and families at the end of life (Munn et al. 2008), confirming other sources that indicated a need for social work involvement (Gwyther et al. 2005)

Therefore, the author obtained additional funding from the John A. Hartford Foundation and returned to the North Carolina facilities from which the earlier focus group participants were recruited and conducted three focus groups (n = 11) with social workers. Data from these groups indicated that social workers make a conscious effort to visit residents who are known to be dying. However, they largely perceive their role as obtaining and acknowledging advance directives and arranging for removal of resident property following death. They indicated a reliance on medical personnel, specifically nursing staff, to determine which residents are at the end of life and to inform social work staff if their involvement is needed. Some participants indicated a desire to become more involved and reported varying levels of involvement influenced by the type of facility (e.g., private vs. Medicare/Medicaid-certified), facility policies, and responsibilities associated with needs of other residents. Social workers also relied on hospice staff, facility chaplains, and counselors to provide emotional and psychosocial support to residents and families of dying residents (Munn and Adorno 2008).

The Social Work Role with Residents

As we consider the dilemma of Mrs. Bench, from the case study that begins this chapter, we also should consider the role of the social worker in her medical decision making. Indeed, the role of social work at the end of life is currently being acknowledged and defined. Two Social Work Summits on End-of-Life and Palliative Care have been held, in 2002 and 2005, in order to advance the state of the science and to "promote, enhance, and shape the future of social work practice, education, and research in end-of-life and palliative care" (Christ and Blacker 2005:9). These summits, sponsored in part by the Project on Death in America, the National Association of Social Workers, and the National Hospice and Palliative Care Organization, prioritized four areas: practice (aimed at defining scope and standards of practice); education (in BSW, MSW, and continuing-education programs); research (setting an agenda and funding sources); and policy (including capacity building) (Christ and Blacker 2005; Gwyther et al. 2005). Another product of the second summit is a list of competencies based on the assumption that "the patient and the family are the unit of care" (Gwyther et al. 2005:91). (Additional information regarding these significant meetings can be found at http://www.swlda.org.) The PDIA also has sponsored the development of the Social Work End-of-Life Educational Project, resulting in a currently used, advanced training module (Csikai and Chaitin 2006).

On a less specific level, but containing an end-of-life emphasis, the John A. Hartford Foundation has established a multifaceted Geriatric Social Work Initiative that supports education and training as well as career development of social work scholars in order to develop a cadre of leaders in gerontological social work and infuse gerontological content into curricula at established schools of social work (see gswi.org).

In 2004, the NASW published practice guidelines for end-of-life and palliative care that describe a minimum knowledge base that includes ten standards: ethics and values; knowledge; assessment; intervention and treatment planning; attitude/self-awareness; empowerment and advocacy; documentation; interdisciplinary team work; cultural competence; and continuing education. In addition, the *Journal of Social Work and End-of-Life and Palliative Care* is currently published by Taylor and Francis.

These efforts underscore the importance of social workers in providing care to dying people as social workers bring to these settings a unique set of skills and training, including identification of community financial and psychosocial resources, conducting a comprehensive assessment, a strengths-based perspective, a theoretical perspective that relates clients to their environments, and the ability to recognize crises and provide crisis management (U.S. Department of Health and Human Services 2006; Howe and Daratsos 2006) Indeed, end-of-life and palliative care represent a significant opportunity for social work involvement (Csikai and Chaitin 2006). Studies conducted in other settings as well as one in nursing homes indicate that social work involvement is important and improves end-of-life care (Cobbs 2001; Morrison et al. 2005) and patient outcomes (Reese et al. 2006). However, the role of social workers at the end of life in all settings is still being precisely defined (Christ and Sormanti 1999). Compton, Galaway, and Cournoyer (2005; cited in Heyman and Gutheil 2006:57) identified five roles for social workers with clients at the end of life: broker (linking clients and resources); facilitator; teacher (providing information); mediator (conflict resolution); and advocate. As a social worker assists Mrs. Bench, he or she may fill all these roles at one time or another. Lacey emphasizes that social workers inform residents (and families) of "their rights, roles, and obligations in medical decision-making" (2005a:35).

Notably, much of the existing literature on end-of-life and palliative care has come from medical disciplines such as nursing. This deficit is understandable (but not acceptable) as, until the last quarter of the twentieth century, dying was viewed as a purely medical event. During the first part of the twentieth century, this medical focus resulted in marked progress in addressing the medical problems of the general population (Teno et al. 2001). However, in 1949 the medical model was challenged by a whole-person concept (Sulmasy 2002). Later, Donabedian's work (1966) indicated that achieving health and satisfaction should be the ultimate indicator of quality of care. More recently, biopsychosocial and ecological models have been advanced (Engel 1977; White, Williams, and Greenburg 1996); these are patient-centered and consider psychological and social needs such as relationships. In 1990, the Institute of Medicine defined quality of care as the degree to which health services "increase the likelihood of the desired health outcomes and are consistent with the current professional knowledge" (IOM 2005:21). However, none of these models specifically addresses end-of-life care (Sulmasy, 2002).

Initially, concepts regarding end-of-life care (and, more specifically, palliative care) were also consistent with the medical model. As a result, the greatest improvements in end-of-life care have occurred in the areas of pain and symptom management (Ersek and Wilson 2003; Kayser-Jones 2002; Teno et al. 2001). However, more recent definitions of palliative care have expanded to include multiple domains and to use patient satisfaction as one of the criteria for evaluation. Historically, social workers have been associated with addressing psychosocial issues (Reese et al. 2006; Brandsen 2005); therefore, these changes bring social work to the forefront in providing optimal end-of-life care. Further social work practice and theoretical models such as the biopsychosocial framework, systems theory, and the ecological perspective are embraced by social workers and add to their understanding of death and other phenomena (Nakashima 2002). Social workers also address spiritual issues at the end of life as evidenced by the mandate from the Council on Social Work Education that spirituality be addressed in certified schools of social work. (Reese et al. 2006; Brandsen 2005). This focus is important at the end of life as spiritual beliefs influence the illness and dying trajectories and the search for meaning that comes with death (Dane and Moore 2005).

Therefore, the remainder of this chapter focuses on the roles of long-term-care social workers with residents who are at the end of life. While physical well-being or comfort is by definition a component end-of-life care, I will focus on nursing home residents' psychological, social, and spiritual needs; the assessment of those needs; and interventions to meet those needs, integrating the NASW practice guidelines. Furthermore, my emphasis remains on the interaction between the 41,000 long-term-care social workers (who report social work as their profession; have at least a bachelor's degree [which may or may not be in social work]; and are employed in one of four industries collectively described as long-term care [i.e., a home health agency, a nursing home, a residential-care/assisted-living facility, or community care for the aged], as derived from U.S. Department of Health and Human Services 2006) and the 1,000 older adults who die in nursing homes each day.

Advocacy

A simple, two-word definition of the social work role in nursing homes is "resident advocacy." It is within this role of advocacy that social workers may promote self-determination for residents while acting as liaisons for residents with family and the healthcare staff (Csikai and Bass 2000). The role of advocate often begins before a resident's admission to the facility, is formalized upon admission, and, for the two-thirds of nursing home residents who die in place (Hanson, Henderson, and Rodgman 1999), continues throughout the dying process and, in some circumstances, beyond the death itself. The NASW directive states that social workers involved in end-of-life or palliative care should "advocate for the needs, decisions, and rights of clients" and "ensure that people have equal access to resources to meet their biopsychosocial needs in palliative and end of life care."

One method of advocating for residents at the end of life is through advance directives. Ideally, advance directives that truly reflect resident preferences are completed while the resident is cognitively intact and in conjunction with the resident's medical doctor (Biola et al. 2007). However, as medical doctors and their extenders (i.e., physician assistants and nurse practitioners) are often unavailable to for conferences (Shield et al. 2005), the social worker may serve as the sole source of information regarding advance directives. Current literature documents social work involvement in assisting with advance directives, facilitating decision making, education, and explaining treatment options (Heyman and Gutheil 2006).

Indeed, a discussion of advance directives is required upon admission to the skilled nursing facility, and it is usually the purview of the social worker to conduct this discussion, which involves asking about existing documents such as a living will or healthcare power of attorney. Further, the social worker describes and explains two documents frequently invoked in nursing homes: a "do not resuscitate" order and an order indicating "do not hospitalize." Social workers have indicated that although they are necessary, these discussions can be problematic to conduct upon admission (Lacey 2006), and advance directives alone are not sufficient (Lacey 2005b). Rather, it is important, to view the discussion of advance directives and end-of-life planning as a process (Travis et al. 2002). As discussed in earlier chapters, nursing home residents often live for many years with varying trajectories of chronic disease and dying. A cursory discussion of advance directives at admission is not sufficient to reflect circumstances that occur within these trajectories nor anticipate the changes in ways that defuse crisis decision making (Travis et al. 2002). Therefore, social workers (as other medical personnel) must listen for empathic moments and be open to further end-of-life discussions with residents throughout their nursing home residence. Social workers can also elicit such discussions through values histories (Kane, Hamlin, and Hawkins 2005) or reminiscence and life review discussed below.

However, although self-determination and advocacy are core social work values, they are difficult to implement in settings in which residents have high levels of dementia or reliance on family and healthcare providers as sources of information relevant to medical decisions (Heyman and Gutheil 2006; Brandsden 2005). Even residents with no cognitive impairment often prefer to involve professional care providers and family members in making important healthcare decisions (Kane, Hamlin, and Hawkins 2005). In the case of cognitively impaired residents, this model ideally includes the principle of substituted judgment, in which surrogates make decisions based on resident preferences articulated when the resident was able to do so (Kapp 1999). With these issues in view, the shared decision-making model is discussed in chapter 7.

Quality of Life

On the other hand, paramount among social work responsibilities is the promotion of quality of life that emphasizes dignity, choice, and self-determination. Other definitions of quality of life are drawn from studies across settings and generally include physical, functional, emotional, social, and spiritual domains (Cella 1994). However, more general definitions (i.e., those not related to death and dying) exclude or deemphasize the social and spiritual domains (Stewart et al. 1999). In contrast to more general definitions of quality of life, current quality definitions in palliative-care and end-of-life literature have come to emphasize psychological, social, and spiritual aspects of support.

Nonetheless, although it is beyond the scope of social work services to manage pain, social workers can promote addressing physical needs by advocating for optimal pain management. The importance of social, spiritual, and psychological needs is not diminished, because these areas are difficult to address in the presence of excruciating pain or other physical symptoms such as shortness of breath, constipation, or insomnia, which are often associated with the dying experience. In some models of palliative care, the resolution of physical needs is imperative because resolution of these issues frees the dying person to attend to important spiritual needs such as making peace with God, forgiving others, and finding purpose and meaning at the end of life (Arnold et al. 2006; Dane and Moore 2005; Koenig 2002; Steinhauser et al. 2000). Research supports that social workers are involved spiritual practices with their clients, especially at the end of life (Dane and Moore 2005)

Another way to define the social work role is that of modeling and advocating respect for the dying. This respect is demonstrated by being fully emotionally present for the resident (Berzoff et al. 2006) and "placing the needs of the client at the focal point of any planning, intervention, starting where the client is at [sic], and handling confidential material responsibly" (Rice et al. 2000, as cited in Brandsen 2005:56). These definitions lead to an essential element in describing quality of life at the end of life, dignity.

DIGNITY

Within the larger context, dignity and self-worth are associated with usefulness to society (Johnson 1998). However, this definition marginalizes those in long-term care, especially those who are dying. Therefore, at the end of life, dignity requires redefinition. A biopsychosocial approach undergirds a revised concept of dignity for those who die in these settings as dignity embraces both physical well-being (absence of pain, cleanliness) and an affective aspect (feelings of worth and personhood) for these residents.

Munn and colleagues (2007) found that personhood comprises a significant facet of the quality of dying in nursing homes. In developing the Quality of Dying in Long-Term Care, a measure specific to the quality of dying in nursing homes and assisted-living/residential-care facilities, the psychometric examination suggests that maintaining one's dignity is deeply important. This importance is especially salient at the end of life as these residents have endured significant losses in health, cognitive awareness, relationships, and vitality. Furthermore, the QOD-LTC items constituting this factor represented tasks performed by facility staff such as providing compassionate physical touch, maintaining resident cleanliness, and providing a nurse or aide with whom the resident is comfortable as well as a doctor who knows the resident "as a whole person." This description suggests that a death with dignity involves an interactive process between the dying individual and facility staff and that staff are at least partially responsible for maintaining dignity throughout the dying process. Ideally, dignity is based upon communication with the dying person in a way that allows for his/her values and wishes to be acknowledged. Furthermore, staff, especially social workers, are critical in maintaining the dignity of cognitively impaired residents who are dying. As dignity is equated with human worth (Johnson 1998), maintaining the resident's dignity by keeping him/her clean, acknowledging his/her personhood, and providing physical touch affirms the worth of the dying person. Other studies indicate maintaining dignity may be as important as controlling pain (Back et al. 1996; Covinsky et al. 2003). In this context, death with dignity is the ultimate goal. Table 6.1 depicts an empirical approach to determining the meaning of dignity in a study by Chochinov and colleagues (2002) that defines dignity based on input from patients who are nearing death.

These researchers used semistructured interviews with fifty terminally ill patients (with advanced cancer diagnoses) recruited over a fifteen-month period. Using latent-content analysis and the constant comparative method, four research team members coded the data into three major categories of themes: illness-related concerns; dignity-conserving repertoire; and social-dignity inventory. Some subthemes are reminiscent of those from other research or scholarship. For example, the issue of control is one that has been identified as important from the earlier anthropological studies (Justice 1997). Also, mental clarity is a theme described earlier. Steinhauser

TABLE 6.1

Majority Dignity Categories, Themes, and Subthemes

ILLNESS-RELATED CONCERNS	DIGNITY-CONSERVING REPERTOIRE	SOCIAL-DIGNITY INVENTORY
Level of independence	Dignity-conserving perspectives	
Cognitive acuity	Continuity of self	Privacy boundaries
Functional capacity	Role preservation	Social support
	Generativity/legacy	Care tenor
	Maintenance of pride	Burden to others
	Hopefulness	Aftermath concerns
	Autonomy/control	
	Acceptance	
Symptom distress	Dignity-conserving practices	
Physical distress	Being "in the moment"	
Psychological distress	Maintaining normalcy	
Medical uncertainty	Resilience/fighting spirit	
Death anxiety	Seeking spiritual comfort	

Source: Adapted from Chochinov et al. 2002:436.

and colleagues (2000, 2001) described concerns about being a burden as important at the end of life.

HOPE

In addition to avoiding negative affective states such as anxiety and depression, there is a need to focus on positive emotions (Johnson 1998). Yalom (1980) notes that fear of death, making meaning, and the need for hope are central themes for people who are dying. Chochinov and colleagues also introduce a positive concept, hopefulness, that is often absent from discussions about the end of life. In a medicalized view of death, hope for survival is the only form of hopefulness, and when such hope is no longer realistic, there is no reason to hope at all. However, from a psychological point of view, the absence of hope is defined as depression, and the concern is that of suicidal ideation. However, when the dying person is considered holistically, there are other reasons for hopefulness that can be enhanced and supported. One model involves two types of hope at the end of life: curative (hope to recover) and palliative (hope for relief from pain and a peaceful death) (Perakylal 1991). In other models, hopefulness takes on many forms: hope for survival, for an afterlife, for salvation, or for a better life in a better place. In this context, hope is seen as "a person's positive orientation toward his or her personal future" (Sullivan 2003:393).

One component of hopefulness, trust, implies that the dying patient is dependent on others (Tulsky 2002). This trust requires that medical practitioners be both honest and hopeful. In fact, hopefulness may become the hope for a good death, one with dignity, and the presence of hopefulness may engender the realization of that hope. And although hope should not be seen simply as a reaction to the physical symptoms associated with death, it may be possible to "diversify hope" (Sullivan 2003:402) for the dying person by reducing physical symptoms in ways that allow for awareness at the time of death, promoting the access of family and friends into the setting of death, and allowing for life review and finishing unfinished business or reconciling broken relationships (Sullivan 2003). So hope in this context is not simply the patient's reaction to his/her prognosis; it is the maintenance of positive orientation to the patient's personal future. Without this positive orientation, in some form, the person's death becomes marked by despair (Erikson 1963), a bad death indeed.

Within Corr's task-based theoretical framework (1991–1992), all four domains contribute to the maintenance of dignity and hope. For example, Steinhauser and colleagues (2000, 2001) found that among four groups of respondents (seriously ill patients, bereaved family members, physicians, and other care providers [including social workers]), being kept clean was the primary concern at the end of life, which suggests that this one physical aspect of quality of care is paramount in promoting death with dignity. And although it is the long-term-care social worker's role to provide or obtain psychological, social, and spiritual support for residents, social workers may be called upon to advocate for residents who do not have family members and are too weak or cognitively impaired to advocate for cleanliness. It is not an overstatement to say that social work advocacy for dignity and hope at the end of life for residents of long-term care encompasses the essence of the social work role in working with residents at the end of life.

Assessment

Assessment is basis of social work practice (Gwyther et al. 2005) and is considered the hallmark of gerontological social work (Geron and Little 2003). Individualized assessment provides the basis for resident-specific intervention and treatment (Kovacs, Bellin, and Fauri 2006). There are multiple factors associated with end-of-life assessment articulated as competencies developed in the 2002 national Social Work Leadership Summit on Palliative and End-of-Life Care. These encompass assessment of "physical, functional, financial, social emotional, spiritual, and psychological resources, supports, and unmet needs" (Gwyther et al. 2005:97) as starting points. In addition, the assessment provides an opportunity for interaction between the nursing home social worker and resident, thus lessening resident feelings of isolation and helplessness (Altilio 2004). The NASW (2004) includes standards for assessment along with developing interventions and treatment planning

STANDARDIZED ASSESSMENT

Within the nursing home, social workers assess residents on a mandated schedule, using the Minimum Data Set and a standardized Resident Assessment Protocol for developing plans of care based on that assessment. Assessment skills are crucial as facility reimbursement from Medicaid and Medicare are based, in part, on the assessment. Version 3.0 of the MDS comprises a new measure to be implemented fall 2010 (see www.cms.gov). This version provides increased input from the resident in the assessment process and, consequently, greater interaction between staff and resident during the assessment process. Embedded within the MDS 3.0 are some scales or revisions of scales that were validated before use in the MDS. For example, in Section D: Mood, the Patient Health Questionnaire 9 (PHQ-9), a subscale of the Patient Health Questionnaire, is used to measure depression and the severity of depression. It is short (nine items), reducing respondent burden and administration time. The items relate to the prior two weeks with a four-point response scale (Not at all = 0; Several days =1; More than half the days = 2; Nearly every day = 3). Scores range from 0 to 27, with higher scores indicating higher levels of depression and established cut-points (minimal = 1–4; mild = 5–9; moderate = 10–14; moderately severe = 15–19; severe = 20–27). This measure has been validated on a large (n = 6,000) sample of ambulatory clinic patients and was found to have good psychometric properties (Cronbach's α = .89; test/retest = 0.84). The test developers measured construct validity using the SF-20 Quality of Life Scale. The PHQ-9 also demonstrates excellent sensitivity to identifying both the presence and severity of depression. Furthermore, validation studies indicate that this measure provides insight into change over time (Kroenke, Spitzer, and Williams 2001).

Another embedded (see Section C: Cognitive Patterns) measure is the Brief Interview for Mental Status. While less information is available regarding the validation of the BIMS, it has significant face validity and taps into cognitive processes assessed by other measures such as the Folstein Mini-Mental State Exam. For example, the BIMS tests short-term memory, temporal orientation, recall, and organized thinking. Again, the respondent burden is manageable. Within the MDS 3.0, two forms of the PHQ-9 and the BIMS are provided. The first, preferred version allows for direct administration to residents who can respond and a second observational version allows for use with residents who cannot answer directly. Both the PHQ-9 and the BIMS are stand-alone measures that can be administered individually at times other than the standardized assessment schedules.

The MDS 3.0 (see Section E: Behavior) contains items related to psychosis (e.g., the presence or absence of hallucinations or delusions) as well as multiple items assessing the presence and frequency (within a given time period) of physical and verbal behavioral symptoms. Risks to the resident or others and effects on the resident or others also are evaluated. Specific behaviors such as wandering and rejection of care are measured for presence, effect, and frequency. This section also measures if these behaviors have changed since the last assessment. These items do not constitute a validated scale but rather are an index of observable behavioral symptoms that can be related to resident well-being and safety.

SPECIALIZED ASSESSMENT

In addition to the measures proposed for inclusion in the MDS 3.0, nursing home social workers perform specialized assessments, often at the request of members of the interdisciplinary care team (e.g., nurses, physicians) or when the social worker wishes to confirm or disconfirm a change in status. At the end of life, these assessments need not be limited to cognitive or affective status, as issues of spirituality, social support, quality of care, and quality of dying become salient. Unfortunately, measures developed specifically for the long-term-care setting and end-of-life administration are infrequent; however, some measures standardized in other settings are suitable, either in their present forms or with some revisions. Obviously, revised measures must undergo additional validation; however, for clinical purposes they are useful in identifying areas important in developing plans of care or problem identification without the rigorous evaluations required for research measures.

READINESS FOR DEATH

Readiness for death has been associated with the quality of the dying experience (McCanse 1995). However, during the dying process, residents' sense of worth or personhood is particularly vulnerable (Moody et al. 2000), and some memories, thoughts, and values may not be disclosed for fear of being socially unacceptable (Byock 1996). As with other types of assessment, interactions with residents may bring forward thoughts, values, and concerns not acknowledged before the assessment process (Moody et al. 2000), consequently increasing the likelihood of healthy dying. One measure of readiness for death is the McCanse Readiness for Death Instrument (McCanse 1995) (see appendix). This twenty-six-item measure is based on a holistic conceptualization of readiness for death and has acceptable psychometric properties (Cronbach's $\alpha = .76$) with four conceptual domains of healthy dying: withdrawal from internal and external environment; decreased social interaction; increased death-acceptance behaviors; and admission of readiness to die. In addition, there is one global question; Moody and colleagues (2000) tested a revised version (i.e., using different response options) of this measure and found similar factors with a revised factor pattern based on items associated with each factor. The validation of both versions of the measure is somewhat limited by the small samples used in development. However, this measure is notable in discriminating between symptoms of depression in nonterminal populations as compared to healthy dying among those at the end of life. For example, participation in activities is seen as evidence of good mental health for most long-term-care residents (Dobbs et al. 2005); however, at the end of life, withdrawal from activities may be desirable as dying residents experience functional decline or focus on closure. Using a measure such as the MRDI acknowledges these differences for staff and family and promotes appropriate care planning.

Another assessment of readiness for death can be as simple as asking residents, "Are you at peace?" This approach derives from instrument development that has been conducted with seriously ill, community-dwelling patients (Steinhauser et al. 2000, 2001), as well as surrogate respondents for residents who die in long-term care (Munn et al. 2007). Steinhauser and colleagues (2006) systematically examined correlations between this simple probe and well-validated measures of quality of life and spiritual well-being (e.g., the Functional Assessment of Chronic Illness Therapy-Spiritual and the Established Population for Epidemiologic Studies of the Elderly social support subscale). Findings indicate that being at peace correlates well with the FACIT-SP; however, being at peace is discrete from having social support. Although designed as a tool for physicians, this probe easily translates into use by other medical professionals and seems especially appropriate for social work discussions with residents at any point on the dying trajectory. Ideally, resident responses lead to identifying areas of unmet needs (e.g., unfinished business, need for spiritual support); however, they also confirm resident readiness for death.

SPIRITUAL ASSESSMENT

Spirituality (i.e., searching for meaning and purpose; belief in a higher being [Steinhauser et al. 2006:104]) is important to older adults in general (Koenig 2002) and becomes more important to people as they become ill or approach death (Hermann 2006; Steinhauser et al. 2006). Yet validated measures of spiritual support or unmet need during the dying experience are difficult to find. None is identified within the social work literature; however, the nursing literature includes one measure, the Spiritual Needs Inventory (Herman 2006) that is specific to end of life. While not developed for use with long-term-care residents, most of the seventeen items apply to long-term-care residents who are cognitively intact. The measure comprises five subscales—outlook, inspiration, spiritual activities, religion, and community—and is based on Maslow's theories of motivation. Respondents are asked how often they need a given activity (e.g., laughing, reading a religious text, praying) to live life fully and then if the need is currently being met. Cronbach's alpha for the measure is good ($\alpha = 0.85$), and the measure is short enough to have minimal respondent burden. Within the clinical setting, this measure can contribute to identifying areas in which spiritual support can be enhanced as well as to creating empathic moments between the social worker and resident (see appendix).

SOCIAL SUPPORT

Social support (i.e., the quality of and nature of social ties) is associated with positive outcomes for older adults. Although there are validated measures of social support or support networks (structural aspects of social ties) for community-dwelling older adults, they are not specific to long-term care or end of life. People in nursing homes are particularly susceptible to isolation because they are removed from common sources of social support such as friends, family, and neighbors. Indeed, lack of social support is a risk factor for institutionalization, suggesting that social support was lacking before moving into the facility (Lubben and Gironda 2003). On the other hand, research confirms that family members often retain ties with residents after admission (Port et al. 2003), and some research suggests that isolated older adults reconfigure their social networks to include physicians and nursing home staff (Munn et al. 2008).

There is a well validated and frequently used measure of social connectedness, the Lubben Social Network Scale (Lubben and Gironda 2003), with three current versions: the twelve-item revised version (LSNS-R); an abbreviated six-item version (LSNS-6); and an eighteen-item expanded version (LSNS-18) (see appendix). These measures, especially the LSNS-6, may be helpful to screen for social isolation at admission. With some considerable revision (e.g., including resident and staff referents) the measures could be used in the long-term setting. However, at the end of life, informal assessment (e.g., discussions regarding individual preferences for social interaction and frequency and quality of visits) can be more appropriate.

QUALITY OF CARE

As with other areas of assessment in nursing homes, end-of-life quality-of-care measures have not been developed specific to this setting. However, there are scales designed to measure the quality of end-of-life care for people with dementia. As rates of dementia are high in nursing homes, estimated at 50 percent of the resident population (Burton et al. 2001; Magaziner et al. 1998; Magaziner, et al. 2000; Rhoades, Patter, and Krauss 1998), it is intuitive that these scales can be used in the nursing home setting. Volicer, Hurley, and Blasi (2001) developed a set of three scales applicable to measuring the quality of end-of-life care for people with dementia. For the purposes of this chapter, two measures related directly to resident care (as opposed to family satisfaction with care) and focusing on the patient's symptoms in the last ninety days before death, the Symptom Management at the End of Life in Dementia and the Comfort Assessment in Dying with Dementia, are described. The ten-item SM-EOLD measures two domains of symptom management, psychological symptoms and states (e.g., calm, depression, fear, anxiety) and physical (pain, shortness of breath, skin breakdown) with adequate psychometric properties (Cronbach's α = .78). The fourteen-item CAD-EOLD measures patient comfort through four subscales—physical distress, emotional distress, well-being, and dying symptoms—and the overall α = .85. Both scales are designed for research and are to be administered retrospectively to surrogate respondents. However, these observational scales lend themselves to prospective use for clinical purposes.

QUALITY OF DYING

Only one measure, the Quality of Dying in Long-Term Care has been developed specifically for long-term care (Munn et al. 2007). This measure includes two versions: the eleven-item QOD-LTC, appropriate for use with all residents, and the twenty-three-item QOD-LTC-C for use with residents who are cognitively intact. Each item begins with "How true is the following statement?" with a 5-point Likert-type response scale (1= not at all, 2 = a little bit, 3 = a moderate amount, 4 = quite a bit, 5 = completely). The QOD-LTC-C comprises five subscales: sense of purpose, closure, control, social connection, and preparatory tasks. Similarly, the QOD-LTC comprises three subscales: personhood, closure, and preparatory tasks. This measure, however, was created and validated for retrospective use with family and staff surrogates of residents who have died within the facility. Within those populations, the measure had good to adequate psychometric properties, and empirical literature supports these areas for assessment. In the absence of other measures, these measures can be revised for clinical purposes and be helpful in identifying areas of well-being as well as concern.

For example, the item "[Resident] was able to say important things to those close to [him/her]" could be revised to "Are you [or have you been] able to say important things to those close to you?" (Both measures and administrative details are available at www.eol.unc.edu). Although using revised measures that have not be validated for research is unwise, the absence of other measures specific to the long-term-care setting suggests that such use may be helpful for clinical purposes.

INFORMAL ASSESSMENT

However, not all assessment is formalized. Nursing home social workers, in daily contact with residents, also provide another set of eyes to identify residents' needs and changes in status, especially for those who are approaching the end of life. As such, nursing home social workers need to be aware of such signs and symptoms of imminent death as anxiety, restlessness, or symbolic communication (Gwyther et al. 2005). This informal assessment also takes the form of recognizing changes in resident status based upon knowledge of individual residents and resident preferences. Therefore, knowledge is another guideline important to the social work role in dealing with residents at the end of life.

Challenges

Residents with Dementia

Reported rates of dementia in nursing homes vary considerably; however, there is substantial support that approximately one-half of all nursing home residents have a diagnosis of dementia (Burton et al. 2001; Magaziner et al. 1998; Magaziner et al. 2000; Rhoades, Patter and Krauss 1998). These high rates are not surprising as dementia is a key factor in determining nursing home placement and nursing homes provide the majority of dementia care (Lacey 2006). Interacting with residents with advanced dementia poses special challenges in end-of-life care and decision making because their ability to communicate meaningfully about medical decisions and preferences frequently is significantly impaired. Unless resident preferences have been documented before the onset of dementia, medical decisions are made by surrogate decision makers and medical professionals. For persons with dementia, palliative care has been identified as the preferred model of end-of-life care, with limited hospitalizations and few intrusive interventions. However, nursing home social workers may become involved when there are confounding issues associated with withholding and withdrawing treatments (Lacey 2006). While the decision-making responsibility frequently falls to people other than the resident, social workers must advocate that these decisions are made in the spirit of substituted judgment (i.e., surrogates must make decisions based on resident preferences articulated when the resident was able to do so) (Kapp 1999) and in the context of personal choice rather than access to resources (Mackelprang and Mackelprang 2005). In addition, there are assessments and interventions that are helpful. Assessments specific to end-of-life care for residents with dementia are described in the previous section. Furthermore, although structured life review with specific questions is not recommended for residents with dementia, more amorphous types of reminiscence are appropriate and helpful in individual and group settings. One-on-one interactions confirm the personhood of the dying individual and promote dignity and worth (Johnson 1998) Social work empathy and active listening are meaningful to cognitively impaired residents, who continue to experience affective and emotional needs.

Resident Resistance

Care providers document hesitation of the part of patients (or, in long-term care, residents) to ask for psychological help from outsiders (Arnold et al. 2006). Indeed, clients' hesitation to discuss the end of life was found to be the most significant barrier to making end-of-life decisions (Heyman and Gutheil 2006). Social workers can address this hesitancy by "being present" and using sensitivity to incorporate end-of-life discussions at appropriate moments throughout the resident's stay (Baker 2005). Indeed, some studies of social work attitudes to advance-directive communication have identified seven stages in the process: initiation of the topic, disclosure of information, identification of surrogate decision maker, discussion of treatment options, elicitation of patient values, interaction with family members, and collaboration with other healthcare providers (Black 2005:27). Furthermore, confronting death can result in spiritual growth for the dying (Reese 2001). Therefore, viewing end-of-life planning as an ongoing process and creating opportunities for discussion is an important aspect of the social work role.

Social Workers' Personal Death Attitudes

In addition to challenges presented by resident attitudes, social workers' personal attitudes toward death and dying can influence their ability to initiate and maintain helpful interactions with residents regarding end-of-life issues (Black 2005). Standard 5 of the NASW standards for palliative care (2004) indicate that social workers need to be aware of their own values and beliefs and how these may influence their practice. Attitudes result from life experience as well as training (or lack of training), and end-of-life interactions with residents can bring forward other experiences with dying as well as beliefs and values (Csikai 1999). Indeed, long-term-care social workers attending focus groups on social work involvement at the end of life indicated experience as the most important element in their ability to work dying with residents (Munn and Adorno 2009). If unresolved or unacknowledged, personal beliefs and attitudes can result in avoiding or minimizing contact with dying residents, emotional withdrawal, and communicating false optimism (Black 2005) or approaching discussions of advance directives in an apologetic manner (Lacey 2005). However, current literature suggests that older social workers, those who attend church, and female social workers are more likely to discuss the end of life with their clients (Baker 2005). Not surprisingly, social workers who perceive themselves as competent and desire to work with older adults elicit patient preferences. On the other hand, there is evidence that professional care providers see themselves as experts and impose their own beliefs and values on clients (Kane, Hamlin, and Hawkins 2005). Therefore, social workers need to understand their own values and beliefs while establishing boundaries that prohibit the imposition of those beliefs.

Knowing Who Is Dying

One essential problem is determining who is appropriate for end-of-life care is determining who is dying (Fowler, Coppola, and Teno 1999; Hickman,

Tilden, and Tolle 2001; Patrick, Engelberg, and Curtis 2001; Teno and Coppola 1999) and at what point residents cease to be seriously ill and begin to die (Finucane 1999; George 2002; Grady 2005). Indeed, many residents of nursing homes suffer from multiple chronic illnesses and often spend years in the ambiguous dying trajectory (Bern-Klug 2004). These difficulties have led to well-documented underuse of hospice in long-term care or late hospice referrals (Welch et al. 2008). It is imperative, then, that social workers address end-life-issues as a longitudinal process that begins at admission and continues throughout the resident's stay. As noted above, preparation of advance directives is one clear task associated with nursing home social work (Brandsen 2005); however, simply completing advance directives at admission is not sufficient.

Interventions

Despite the challenges described above and the dearth of empirical literature, there are meaningful interventions for social workers and residents at the end of life. The NASW (2004) standards include a directive that social workers plan interventions that enhance the client's autonomy. These interventions serve as adaptive tasks in the Moos and Schaefor (1986) model and interventions to relieve distress and suffering are noted as the most desirable goals for social work (Csikai and Raymer 2005). Interventions with residents can include individual therapies (e.g., supportive counseling, problem-solving exercises, reminiscence and life review); serving as liaisons with family, professional care providers, and resources; spiritual exploration and reframing of hope; education on what to expect; and conflict resolution (Arnold et al. 2006; Gwyther et al. 2005;). Some optimal outcomes of interventions include enhanced communication, closure, and improved care. Research supports that dying people wish to discuss spiritual interventions and resolve unfinished business and may depend on professional staff to facilitate this resolution and that social work involvement in such interventions is useful (Reese and Raymer 2004). Forgiveness and saying good-bye are among the greatest concerns of those who are dying (Puchalski 1997). Therefore, for the purposes of this chapter, I will focus on interventions that address psychological and spiritual issues based on processes of reminiscence and life review with individual residents and groups of residents and on the involvement of outside agencies for mental health care and hospice.

Reminiscence

The term reminiscence refers to a general process that includes recalling (aloud or silently) a person's life events. This process may take place alone, with another individual, or within a group setting (Woods et al. 1992). Potential outcomes from reminiscence include: identity formation; increased meaning and coherence in life; a sense of mastery; and acceptance and reconciliation. These outcomes are achieved through telling and retelling one's own narrative, often in response to questions regarding one's values and experiences (Bohlmeijer et al. 2007). It is assumed that reminiscence occurs naturally with aging (Butler 1963) and increases the older person's ability to let go and accept death (Garland and Garland 2001). Thus reminiscence at the end of life can provide a sense of meaning and reconciliation. Indeed, some researchers suggest that reminiscence provides the impetus for anticipatory mourning, enhances reconciliation (Coleman et al. 1999), and serves as death preparation (Haight and Gibson 2005). Furthermore, identity formation, which is augmented by life review and reminiscence, culminates at the final stage of life, indicating an ability to meet death with ego integrity rather than despair (Erikson, Erikson, and Kivnick 1986). Furthermore, reminiscence is useful with residents who are cognitively impaired although, smaller increases in life satisfaction are found than with cognitively intact residents (Bohlmeijer et al. 2007).Therefore, reminiscence is appropriate for all older adults but may be particularly relevant at the end of life. On the other hand, studies of reminiscence have not found that results are uniformly positive. When reminiscence takes place without some reintegration or reframing, there is the potential for bitterness and negativity.

Life review, however, is a more structured form of reminiscence that reviews the entire life span, both positive and negative events, and, unlike reminiscence, includes an element of evaluation (Haight and Burnside 1993). Life review allows for the reframing of negative memories and a synthesis resulting in a meaningful life story for both the older adult and the social worker or counselor (Haight and Webster 1995). Notably, this reframing is especially important for people undergoing high levels of psychological stress. Life review may take place over multiple interviews, ranging from as few as three or four to as many as twenty-eight (Bohlmeijer et al. 2007) One-on-one interviews allow for the greatest individualization for each resident, and longer interventions are suggested for older adults (Knight 1988); however, even one session of life review at the end of life may be helpful.

The introduction of life review or reminiscence is appropriate at entry into a facility. As noted elsewhere, the transition into a nursing home is often considered a crisis and requires some of the same adaptive tasks that are helpful at the end of life (Oleson and Shadrick 1993). It is optimal, then, that nursing home social workers begin life review with residents when they are admitted to facility. This intervention assists with the significant transition to the nursing home setting and its concurrent losses and fosters a trusting relationship between social worker and resident. This relationship supports ongoing conversations about end-of-life preferences and changing dimensions of resident needs and preferences. An additional benefit of life review with residents is the establishment of a resident's personal life history leading to an enhanced sense of personhood for the resident and an acknowledgement of personhood by staff, specifically the social worker. This sense of personhood has been identified as an important component in the quality of dying (Munn et al. 2007); the acknowledgement of personhood (including dignity) can lead to a higher quality of life and consequent higher quality of death. The usefulness of this intervention to a resident at the end of life has been well documented (Baker 2005) as "a means to recognize his or her purpose, value and meaning and also to facilitate feelings related to guilt, remorse and forgiveness" (Dane and Moore 2005:67).

There are spiritual practices such as guided imagery, prayer, and yoga that can encourage life review (Dane and Moore 2005). However, a more pragmatic framework for conducting the life review is the Haight Life Review and Experiencing Form (see appendix) (Haight and Webster 1995). This series of questions allows the social worker to guide the life review and encourage reframing and evaluation. Conducting the life review also provides the opportunity to strengthen the relationship between the social worker and resident. This trust, established over time, is essential in the relationship between the social worker and resident.

Another method of conducting life review is using a life-history grid (see appendix). The life-history grid provides an opportunity to organize and present data related to multiple areas and periods of a resident's life. Further, the use of life-history grids allows social workers to incorporate data from a variety of sources and demonstrate patterns that occur and reoccur over time (Sheafor, Horejsi, and Horejsi 1997). The life-history grid is based on principles of placing one's life in the contexts of individual, social, and historical time (Elder 1999) over the subject's full life trajectory. Residents are able to review their lives while remembering significant world events as well as personal and family memories. The life-history grid depends in part on the memory of dates and places; therefore, it is less helpful for residents with cognitive impairment.

Groups

Reminiscence and life review can be conducted with groups of nursing home residents and social workers can decide, with the resident, if group or individual interactions are preferred. Although a complete discussion of group formation and leadership is beyond the scope of this chapter (see Toseland 1990; and Haight and Gibson 2005), some suggestions for group conduct with nursing home residents is appropriate.

BENEFITS OF GROUPS

Research supports positive outcomes associated with group attendance in which older adults find opportunities for validation, taking on meaningful roles within the group, learning from others and obtaining information, and problem solving. Indeed, group attendance is particularly helpful for residents who are socially isolated and have interpersonal problems. Furthermore, groups are sources of support for nursing home residents who are likely to be physically removed from other sources of support such as family and community-dwelling friends. The supportive nature of groups also has the capacity to create bonds between residents that transcend the group meeting. However, residents for whom there are physical barriers or who suffer from some mental-health problems may benefit from smaller groups or individual life review (Toseland 1990). Groups need not include only older adults at the end of life as life review is beneficial to others.

SOCIAL WORKER PREPARATION

In order to conduct groups with older adults, social workers need to sensitize themselves to current issues of older adults, such as experiences with loss; recognize their strengths; and understand that there is great variability in physical and cognitive function (Toseland 1990). In facilitating reminiscence groups, social workers need to become aware of the historical context of earlier life stages (Haight and Gibson 2005). One source of information is Gibson's (2004) timeline of the 1990s that includes public, social, and historical events. Social workers can also gather props and triggers from those eras. In a more general sense, social workers need to review their own skills at group leadership and seek additional education if needed.

GROUP PLANNING AND COMPOSITION

When composing resident groups, social workers need to recognize some differences that affect group dynamics. For example, as age has a significant impact on both historical context and physical function, social workers can consider conducting groups of the oldest (eighty-five years older) separately from those in their sixties or seventies. However, other issues such as energy level, hearing difficulties, cognitive status, and personal backgrounds can also contribute to the group dynamic. So without resorting to stereotypes or rigid rules, it is helpful to consider commonalities among residents when developing groups of older adults (Toseland 1990). Ideally, the social worker can meet individually with group members to gather background information and establish rapport with members. The social worker can also explain, in general, what to expect and can answer questions. Reminiscence groups are typically composed of ten to twelve members and meet weekly for eight to twelve sessions. Effective group meetings usually last two hours and are opportunities for residents to enjoy refreshments as well socialize informally; however, variations from this model are frequent (Haight and Webster 1995).

GROUP CONDUCT

Social workers by default become group leaders as they are responsible for the composition of the group. However, residents in nursing homes have a variety of backgrounds, and leaders arise within the community. Ideally, residents take on as much leadership within the group as possible. Using a reciprocal leadership style is one manner of encouraging resident autonomy. This model is based on mutual aid among group members, and in it members are partners in developing the group aims and conducting group meetings. As this leadership model is recommended for groups of older adults making stressful transitions, it is particularly appropriate for those adjusting to nursing home life and facing the end of life. Within this type of group, members can freely share feelings and thoughts that otherwise might remain hidden (Toseland 1990).

Reminiscence groups are likely to fall into the larger classification of support groups. Support groups are characterized as involving high levels of interaction among group members and emotional self-disclosure. Therefore, group members need to listen with empathy to one another and to share coping strategies. Older adults are likely to respond empathetically, and they become sources of wisdom, enhancing a sense of meaning essential to healthy dying. Typically, leaders emerge; however, all members can become part of the leadership process. It is important, however, for social workers to foster a safe, warm, and cohesive environment in which the group members are able to trust one another and the social worker as well. In order to facilitate trust, the social worker can skillfully point out areas of importance and reinforce sharing by members. In addition, social workers can praise supportive comments and use collective pronouns ("us" and "we") when describing group functions. Also, social workers need to intervene if one group member tends to dominate or if group members engage in side conversations. Finally, beginning and ending rituals increases group cohesion (Toseland 1990).

However, reminiscence groups, unlike other support groups, are designed with the specific purpose of evoking the life experience of the members and are structured around those experiences. Optimally, the social worker will develop a theme for the first meeting, and group members will establish consequent themes. Some possible frameworks include a chronological approach, beginning with childhood and ending in old age, or themes such as friends, toys, school, or family. These structures seldom are absolute, and groups should be able to pursue tangential themes if they emerge. However, in every case, members are encouraged to elicit emotions associated with the themes and events (Haight and Webster 1995). Some experts (see Capuzzi and Gross 1998) suggest beginning with happy memories in the earlier sessions, delaying negative topics until trust and cohesion have been developed within the group. Balancing open-ended topics with specific topics is another way to optimize group dynamics (Haight and Webster 1995).

Props and triggers can be used to elicit memories. Triggers can stimulate visual, auditory, tactile, olfactory, or taste sensations. For example, music is a powerful stimulant and can evoke memories associated with personally significant times, places, and people. Objects that evoke memories can be passed around, creating interaction among group members. Objects can be supplied by the social worker or group members can bring objects that have meaning to them. Some facilities create reminiscence rooms furnished and decorated in styles of the past. These are especially helpful if they also provide a quiet area in which staff, families, and residents can reminisce. It is important, however, that props and triggers are appropriate for the ages, cultures, genders and geography of group members (Haight and Webster 1995).

GROUPS OF RESIDENTS WITH DEMENTIA

With some modifications, reminiscence groups can be conducted with residents with dementia. Groups should be smaller, ideally two to four members. Group sessions need to be shorter and nonverbal participation enhanced by sensory stimuli. The goal of these groups can be providing stimuli and reminding members of who they are in terms of lifelong occupations or identities. There should be ample time for group formation, and the social worker can provide unconditional warmth and reassurance. Groups should also be flexible and adjusted based on energy levels, variations in group participation, and personalities. As with all groups, residents who are aggressive, hyperactive, or socially inappropriate are more likely to benefit from individual interactions (Haight and Webster 1995).

Case Management

One overlooked, but important role of social workers is connecting dying residents with outside resources or sources of care, that is case management. NASW (2004) defines social work case management as

a method of providing services whereby a professional social worker assesses the needs of the client and the client's family, when appropriate,

and arranges, coordinates, monitors, evaluates, and advocates for a package of multiple services to meet the specific client's complex needs. . . .
Services provided under the rubric of social work case management practice may be located in a single agency or may be spread across numerous
agencies or organizations.

It is intuitive that despite the multiple missions of nursing homes and
the dedication of nursing home social workers, all resident needs cannot
be met within one facility. There are various community agencies and resources to which long-term-care social workers can link residents. For example, there is great heterogeneity of spiritual and religious beliefs among
older adults. It is unlikely that one social worker can provide appropriate
spiritual support to residents of all faiths. Rather, social workers can facilitate obtaining spiritual support from the group of the resident's choice.
Furthermore, residents who require mental-health services for depression
can benefit from community mental-health services, or social workers can
facilitate meetings with Medicare and Medicaid professionals, financial ad-
visors, attorneys, and family members. Another potential third-party provider for residents at the end of life is hospice.

Although much has been written regarding the barriers to hospice use
in nursing homes, recent data indicate a significant increase, although
rates vary across states and geographic areas (Welch et al. 2008). Hospice
is often considered optimal end-of-life care as it provides expert oversight
in pain relief, a trained multidisciplinary team (including nurses, volunteers, chaplains, music therapists, bereavement counselors, and physicians
in additional to social workers), and a focus on spirituality (Dobbs et al.
2006). Research has shown that nursing home residents receiving hospice
are less likely to be hospitalized, are more likely to receive alternative pain
treatments, and receive more attention to personal hygiene (Munn et al.
2006) compared to non-hospice residents at the end of life. Nursing home
residents receiving hospice are also more likely to have advance directives.
Finally, studies note that residents with hospice receive more attention to
and spiritual and emotional needs (Miller et al. 2002; Parker-Oliver et al.
2003). Family members, nursing staff, and paraprofessional caregivers all
report positive effects of hospice involvement at the end of life in nursing
homes and assisted-living facilities. Furthermore, residents in long-term
care report that hospice helps them to understand the dying process and,
after preparing for death, experience a higher quality of life before dying

(Munn et al. 2008). Therefore, referrals to hospice serve as one intervention that social workers can provide in order to improve the dying experience in long-term care. After referral, social workers can serve as liaisons between the hospice and facility staffs.

Resources

Training

Although two NASW standards (Knowledge and Continuing Education) relate to social work training, there is little empirical data available on nursing home social work training, skills, or involvement at the end of life (Lacey 2005b). However, current literature does document the lack of end-of-life content in social work curricula and the absence of faculty trained to teach end-of-life content (Walsh-Burke and Csikai 2005). For example, B. Kramer (2003) found that only 3.35 percent of the content of social work textbooks is related to the end of life. Social work courses tend to include only small amounts of end-of-life content, usually within a foundation course such as Human Behavior in the Social Environment or sometimes within a graduate level course on death, dying, and bereavement. Furthermore, even if social workers receive classroom training, they are less likely to have received clinical supervision related to the end of life (Berzoff et al. 2006). Thus, even when courses specific to death, dying, and bereavement are offered, they are seen as inadequate preparation for work in the field (Christ and Sormanti 1999). For long-term-care social workers, this omission is exacerbated by the lack of gerontological content in social work curricula. Yet social work competencies developed at the Social Work Leadership Summit on Palliative and End-of-Life Care acknowledge that gerontological social workers must provide services to clients with chronic illness as well as end-of-life issues (Gwyther et al. 2005). Furthermore, although discussions of advance directives are mandated in nursing homes, professionals have limited knowledge (Kane, Hamlin, and Hawkins 2005) of even these minimal competencies. Some other areas found to be deficient in social work curriculum include culture-, gender-, and age-appropriate end-of-life assessments; training in working with diverse families; knowledge of physical symptoms; and healthcare policy (Kramer 2003).

However, social workers report obtaining specialized end-of-life training outside the standard BSW and MSW curricula. One small study found that these programs included both written and programmatic formats, were held outside of the social worker's agency, and were not associated with schools or universities (e.g., at the Association of Oncology Social Worker's annual meeting). The participants found this training to be somewhat satisfactory, stating that it was not sufficiently advanced for their needs; however, hospice social workers reported more practice-site training (Christ and Sormanti 1999). Some distance-learning courses exist. For example, the NASW offers Understanding End-of-Life Care: The Social Worker's Role and the Association of Oncology Social Workers provides a specialized course for oncology social workers (Walsh-Burke and Csikai 2005).

One model continuing education program associated the Smith College School for Social Work currently conducts a post-master's program on end-of-life care for social workers (Berzoff et al. 2006). This innovative program uses a relational approach presented over two summers with intervening field experiences. Social workers who attended the program indicated that supervision supported their exploration of challenging issues associated with the end of life. Also, an outcome of the Project on Death in American has been the development of the Social Work End-of-Life Educational Project, resulting in a currently used, advanced training module (Csikai and Chaitin 2006). These initiatives are helpful but may fail to accommodate the severely constrained resources of long-term-care social workers who have the lowest salaries within the profession. Also, staff social work services are not reimbursable in long-term care; therefore, employers are unlikely to pay for training (U.S. Department of Health and Human Services 2006).

Theories of Dying

In the absence of a large body of empirical research, another way to help is to look at theories of dying for guidance as these theories can provide linkages and constructs for examining the dying resident's experience. There are several theoretical approaches to understanding the dying process, such as task-based theories (Corr 1991–1992; Kalish 1979) and the living dying interval (Engle 1998; Engle, Fox-Hill, and Graney 1998). Social work, as a profession, focuses on theories that can be empirically verified (Turner

1995). Therefore, the more applied, task-based theory developed by Richard Kalish (1979) and modified by Corr (1991–1992) is applicable by social workers in long-term care for several reasons.

These task-based theories (in contrast to stage-based theories of Kubler-Ross [1969] and Buckman [1993]) recognize the importance of human agency: dying people participate in and make decisions about the individual dying process, which relates to the social work value of self-determination for clients. In addition, Kalish (1979) recognizes the social context of dying and the collaborative nature of performing the tasks associated with dying akin to the person-in-environment approach that social work promotes. Furthermore, these features of task-based theory are especially salient in long-term care as it is the nature and mission of long-term care that caregivers perform supportive tasks for physically and cognitively impaired residents.

On the other hand, an examination of eight tasks indicates that dying is a multifaceted process, a theme reflected in contemporary literature (Cella 1994; Steinhauser et al. 2000, 2001; Sulmasy 2002; Teno 1999). The eight tasks are:

1. Contemplating arranging affairs
2. Dealing with loss
3. Arranging for future care needs
4. Planning the future
5. Anticipating pain, discomfort, and functional decline
6. Coping effectively with the death encounter
7. Deciding to slow down or speed up the process
8. Dealing with the psychosocial problems that beset the dying individual

For example, task 4 (planning the future) indicates that even in the terminal state, one has reason to hope for a better outcome. Also, in the long-term-care setting, residents often have assumed the sick role (task 8) upon admission; yet there may be hesitancy or ambiguity to assuming the dying role (Bern-Klug 2004). For example, the resistance to hospice enrollment by residents or their families (Schockett et al. 2005) illustrates such hesitancy to move from the sick to dying role. In our case study, it is Mrs. Bench's daughters who hesitate to have their mother assume this role.

TABLE 6.2

Corr's Task-Based Theory of Dying

AREA	TASK
Physical	To satisfy *bodily needs* and *minimize physical distress,* in ways that are consistent with other values
Psychological	To maximize *psychological* security, autonomy, and richness in living
Social	To sustain and enhance those *interpersonal attachments* significant to the person concerned and to address the *social implications* of dying
Spiritual	To identify, develop, or reaffirm sources of *spiritual* energy and in so doing, foster *hope*

Source: Adapted from Corr 1991–1992.

Corr's (1991–1992) modification of Kalish's work seems a bit simplistic. Although still a multifaceted definition of the dying process (see table 6.2), there is more complexity in later work than these four categories describe. However, notably, Corr does retain an interactive or dynamic component, which is important to understanding death. For example, the physical tasks of satisfying bodily needs and minimizing physical distress are well documented as components of a good death (Koenig 2002; Teno 1999); however, Corr notes that these tasks take place within a value system that varies from person to person, reflecting the value of autonomy over beneficence, another core value of social work. Further, similar to a strengths-based perspective, each component of Corr's typology provides a positive aspect in that each area has a potentially positive outcome.

Conceptual Framework

Using an existing conceptual model can assist in understanding the situation of Mrs. Bench, presented in the case study. Moos and Schaefer (1986) developed a model for understanding life crises and trajectories that is particularly appropriate for the nursing home setting, as it can be used to examine two important events: admission to long-term care and the point at which the resident is known to be dying. Both events are transitions

GENERAL DETERMINANTS OF OUTCOME ↔ RESOLUTIONS PHASE ↔ ULTIMATE OUTCOME

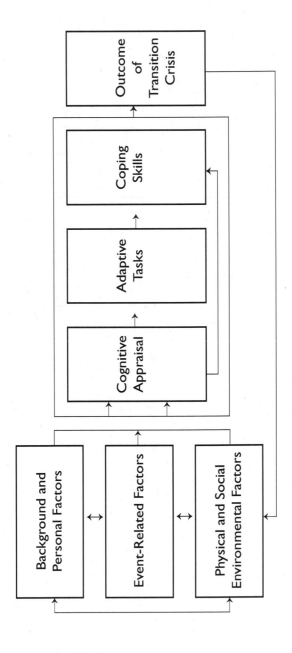

Figure 6.1   Adapted from: Moos & Schaefer (1986) as presented in Oleson & Shadick (1993, p. 480) Application of Moos and Schaefer's (1986) model to nursing care of elderly persons relocating to a nursing home.   *Source:* National Consensus Project for Quality Palliative Care. (2004:3)

that can be perceived as crises (Oleson and Shadrick 1993). Regarding our case study, Mrs. Bench, seems to be in the cognitive-appraisal stage of this model. Furthermore, the model illustrates where the applied profession of social work can be helpful in facilitating adaptive tasks, thereby enhancing the client's coping skills.

The model is also appropriate for use with task-based theories as tasks are part of the model itself and Kalish's (1979) eight tasks are commensurate with the adaptive tasks in the conceptual model. Also, both model and theory place the dying resident in a social context. Further, this model represents an opportunity for social work intervention (see figure 6.1). As related to the end of life in long-term care, the first segment of the model, general determinants of outcome, represents individual, family, and facility-level factors that influence one another and are specific to the resident. For example, personal factors such as cognitive status, ethnic background, and social support influence the resident's entry into the long-term-care system (Vourlekis and Simon 2006) as well as the experience of dying (Howe and Daratsos 2006).

Other Resources

In addition to theoretical and conceptual models, expert panels have provided guidance for end-of-life care. Again, while not developed specifically to long-term care in general or nursing homes in particular, these frameworks indicate the expectations of high-quality end-of-life care across settings. The National Quality Framework includes eight domains:

1. Structure and process of care
2. Physical aspects of care
3. Psychosocial and psychiatric aspects of care
4. Social aspects of care
5. Spiritual, religious, and existential aspects of care
6. Cultural aspects of care
7. Care of the imminently dying patient
8. Ethical and legal aspects of care

The National Consensus Project Guidelines for Quality Palliative Care are framed within these domains. Within those eight domains, four (points

3 through 6) are considered the purview of social workers in the nursing home. Indeed, social work traditionally has contributed to these areas of care and can continue to contribute with additional research and evidence-based practice. Thus, social workers can access these multidisciplinary studies to increase their understanding of the needs of dying residents while supporting the need for more research specific to social work in nursing homes.

Conclusion

So, where does this leave Mrs. Bench?
    Questions for consideration:

1. How might Mrs. Bench's social worker fulfill each of the following roles: broker (linking clients and resources); facilitator; teacher (providing information); mediator (conflict resolution); and advocate?

2. Which interventions seem most appropriate for Mrs. Bench?

3. Using a task-based theory of dying, with which tasks could the social worker assist Mrs. Bench?

4. As noted above, Mrs. Bench appears to be in the cognitive-appraisal component of the Moos and Shaefor conceptual framework. How might the social worker assist in this task as well as move her into initiating some adaptive tasks?

5. Would you refer Mrs. Bench to hospice? What are your reasons for doing so or not doing so?

References

Altilio, T. 2004. "Pain and Symptom Management: An Essential Role for Social Workers." In *Living with Dying: A Comprehensive Resource for Healthcare Practitioners*, ed. J. Berzoff and P. Silverman, 380–408. New York: Columbia University Press.

Arnold, E. M., K. A. Artin, D. Griffith, J. L. Person, and K. Graham. 2006. "Unmet Needs at the End of Life: Perceptions of Hospice Social Workers." *Journal of Social Work in End-of-Life and Palliative Care* 2 (4): 61–83.

Back, A. L., J. I. Wallace, H. E. Starks, et al. 1996. "Physician-Assisted Suicide and Euthanasia in Washington State: Patient Requests and Physician Responses." *Journal of the American Medical Association* 275:919–25.

Baker, M. 2005. "Facilitating Forgiveness and Peaceful Closure: The Therapeutic Value of Psychosocial Intervention in End-of-Life Care." *Journal of Social Work in End-of-Life and Palliative Care* 1 (4): 83–96.

Bern-Klug, M. 2004. "The Ambiguous Dying Syndrome." *Health and Social Work* 29:55–65.

Berzoff, J., et al. 2006. "Clinical Social Work Education in Palliative and End-of-Life Care: Relational Approaches for Advanced Practitioners." *Journal of Social Work in End-of-Life and Palliative Care* 2 (1): 45–63.

Biola, H., P. D. Sloane, C. S. Williams, T. P. Daaleman, S. W. Williams, and S. Zimmerman. 2007. "Physician Communication with Family Caregivers of Long-Term Care Residents at the End of Life." *Journal of the American Geriatrics Society* 55 (6): 846–56.

Black, K. 2005. "Social Workers' Personal Death Attitudes, Experiences, and Advance Directive Communication Behavior." *Journal of Social Work in End-of-Life and Palliative Care* 1 (3): 21–33.

Bohlmeijer, E., M. Roemer, P. Cuijpers, and F. Smit. 2007. "The Effects of Reminiscence on Psychological Well-Being in Older Adults: A Meta-Analysis." *Aging and Mental Health* 11 (3): 291–300.

Brandsen, C. K. 2005. "Social Work and End-of-Life Care: Reviewing the Past and Moving Forward." *Journal of Social Work in End-of-Life and Palliative Care* 1 (2): 45–70.

Buckman, R. 1993. "Communication in Palliative Care: A Practical Guide." In *Oxford Textbook of Palliative Medicine*, ed. D. Doyle, G. Hanks, and N. MacDonald, 141–58. Oxford: Oxford Medical Publications.

Burton, L. C., P. S. German, A. L. Gruber-Baldini, J. R. Hebel, S. I. Zimmerman, and J. Magaziner. 2001. "Medical Care for Nursing Home Residents: Differences by Dementia Status." *Journal of the American Geriatrics Society* 49:142–47.

Butler, R. 1963. "Life Review: An Interpretation of Reminiscence in the Aged." *Psychiatry* 26:65–76.

Byock, I. R. 1996. "The Nature of Suffering and the Nature of Opportunity at the End of Life." *Clinical Geriatric Medicine* 12 (2): 237–52.

Capuzzi, D., and D. R. Gross. 1998. *Introduction to Group Counseling*. Denver, Colo.: Love.

Cella, D. F. 1994. "Quality of Life: Concepts and Definition." *Journal of Pain and Symptom Management* 9 (3): 186–92.

Chochinov, H. M., T. Hack, S. McClement, et al. 2002. "Dignity in the Terminally Ill: A Developing Empirical Model." *Social Science and Medicine* 54: 433–43.

Christ, G., and S. Blacker. 2005. "Series Introduction: The Profession of Social Work in End-of-Life and Palliative Care." *Journal of Palliative Medicine* 8 (2): 415–17.

Christ, G. H., and M. Sormanti. 1999. "Advancing Social Work Practice in End-of-Life Care." *Social Work in Health Care* 30 (2): 81–99.

Cobbs, E. L. 2001 "Improving the Quality of End-of-Life Care: How?" *Journal of the American Geriatrics Society* 49 (6): 833–34.

Coleman E. A., L. C. Grothaus, N. Sandhu, and E. H. Wagner. 1999. "Chronic Care Clinics: A Randomized Controlled Trial of a New Model of Primary Care to Frail Older Adults." *Journal of the American Geriatrics Society* 47:775–83.

Corr, C. A. 1991–1992. "A Task-Based Approach to Coping with Dying." *Omega* 24 (2): 81–92.

Covinsky, K., C. Eng, L. Lui, et al. 2003. "The Last Two Years of Life: Functional Trajectories of Frail Older People." *Journal of the American Geriatrics Society* 51:492–98.

Csikai, E. 1999. "The Role of Values and Experience in Determining Social Workers' Attitudes Toward Euthanasia and Assisted Suicide." *Social Work in Health Care* 30 (1): 75–95.

Csikai, E. L., and K. Bass. 2000. "Health Care Social Workers' Views of Ethical Issues, Practice, and Policy in End-of-Life Care." *Social Work in Health Care* 32 (2): 1–22.

Csikai, E. L., and Chaitin, E. 2006. *Ethics in End-of-Life Decisions in Social Work Practice.* Chicago: Lyceum.

Csikai, E. L., and Raymer, M. 2005. "Social Workers' Educational Needs in End-of-Life Care." *Social Work in Health Care* 41 (1): 53–73.

Dane, B., and R. Moore. 2005. "Social Workers' Use of Spiritual Practices in Palliative Care." *Journal of Social Work in End-of-Life and Palliative Care* 1 (4): 63–82.

Dobbs, D. J., L. Hanson, S. Zimmerman, C. S. Williams, and J. Munn. 2006. "Hospice Attitudes Among Assisted Living and Nursing Home Administrators, and the Long-Term Care Hospice Attitudes Scale." *Journal of Palliative Medicine* 9 (6): 1388–400.

Dobbs, D., J. C. Munn, S. Zimmerman, M. Boustani, C. Williams, P. Sloane, J. Preisser, P. Reed, and C. Port. 2005. "Risk Factors Related to Activity Involvement in Long-Term Care." *Gerontologist* 45 (Special Issue I): 81–86.

Donabedian, A. 1966. "Evaluating the Quality of Medical Care." *Milbank Memorial Fund Quarterly* 44:166–96.

Elder, G. H. 1999. *Children of the Great Depression*. Twenty-fifth anniversary ed. Boulder, Colo.: Westview Books.

Engel, G. L. 1977. "The Need for a New Medical Model: A Challenge for Biomedicine." *Science* 196 (4286): 129–36.

Engle, V. F. 1998. "Care of the Living, Care of the Dying: Reconceptualizing Nursing Home Care." *Journal of the American Geriatrics Society* 46:1172–74.

Engle, V. F., E. Fox-Hill, and M. J. Graney. 1998. "The Experience of Living-Dying in a Nursing Home: Self-Reports of Black and White Older Adults." *Journal of the American Geriatrics Society* 46 (9): 1091–96.

Erikson, E. 1963. *Childhood and Society*. New York: Norton.

Erikson, E. H., J. M. Erikson, and H. Q. Kivnick. 1986. *Vital Involvement in Old Age*. New York: Norton.

Ersek, M., and S. Wilson. 2003. "The Challenges and Opportunities in Providing End-of-Life Care in Nursing Homes." *Journal of Palliative Medicine* 6 (1): 45–57.

Facts on Dying. 2005. "Policy Relevant Data on Care at the End of Life." www.chcr.brown.edu/dying/factsondying.htm. Accessed September 22, 2005.

Finucane, T. E. 1999. "How Gravely Ill Becomes Dying: A Key to End-of-Life Care." *Journal of the American Medical Association* 282 (17): 1670–72.

Fowler, F. J., K. M. Coppola, and J. Teno. 1999. "Methodological Challenges for Measuring Quality of Care at the End of Life." *Journal of Pain and Symptom Management* 17 (2): 114–19.

Garland, J., and C. Garland. 2001. *Life Review in Health and Social Care: A Practitioner's Guide*. Philadelphia: Brunner-Routledge.

George, L. 2002. "Research Design in End-of-Life Research." *Gerontologist* 42 (Special Issue III): 86–103.

Geron, S. M., and F. C. Little. 2003. "Standardized Geriatric Assessment in Social Work Practice with Older Adults." In *Social Work and Health Care in an Aging Society*, ed. B. Berkman and L. Harootyan, 268–96. New York: Springer.

Gibson, F. 2004. *A Past in the Present: Using Reminiscence in Health and Social Care*. Baltimore, Md.: Health Professions Press.

Grady, P. A. 2005. "Introduction: Papers from the National Institutes of Health State-of-the-Science Conference on Improving End-of-Life Care." *Journal of Palliative Medicine* 8 (Supplement I): S1–S3.

Gwyther, L., et al. 2005. "Social Work Competencies in Palliative and End-of-Life Care." *Journal of Social Work in End-of-Life and Palliative Care* 1 (1): 87–120.

Haight, B. K., and I. Burnside. 1993. "Reminiscence and Life Review: Explaining the Differences." *Archives of Psychiatric Nursing* 7:91–98.

Haight, B. K, and F. Gibson. 2005. *Burnside's Working with Older Adults: Group Process and Techniques*. Sudbury, Mass.: Jones and Bartlett.

Haight, B. K., and J. D. Webster. 1995. *Art and Science of Reminiscing: Theory, Research, Methods, and Applications.* New York: Springer.

Hanson, L.C., M. Henderson, and M. Menon. 2002. "As Individual as Death Itself: A Focus Group Study of Nursing Home Death." *Journal of Palliative Medicine* 5 (1):117–25.

Hanson, L. C., M. Henderson, and E. Rodgman. 1999. "Where Will We Die? A National Study of Nursing Home Death." *Journal of the American Geriatrics Society* 47:S22.

Herman, C. P. 2006. "Development and Testing of the Spiritual Needs Inventory for Patients Near the End of Life." *Oncology Nursing Forum* 33 (4): 737–44.

Heyman, J., and I. A. Gutheil. 2006. "Social Work Involvement in End of Life Planning." *Journal of Gerontological Social Work* 47 (3/4): 47–61.

Hickman, S. E., V. P. Tilden, and S. W. Tolle. 2001. "Family Reports of Dying Patients' Distress: The Adaptation of a Research Tool to Assess Global Symptom Distress During the Last Week of Life." *Journal of Pain and Symptom Management* 22 (1): 565–74.

Howe, J. L., and L. Daratsos. 2006. "Context of Palliative and End-of-Life Care and Role of Social Work Practice." In *Handbook of Social Work in Health and Aging*, ed. B. Berkman, 315–23. New York: Oxford University Press.

Institute of Medicine. 2005. "Measuring the Quality of Health Care." http://www.nap.edu/html/quality/report.html. Accessed October 15, 2005.

Johnson, P. R. S. 1998. "An Analysis of Dignity." *Theoretical Medicine and Bioethics* 19:337–52.

Justice, C. 1997. *Dying and the Good Death: The Pilgrimage to Die in India's Holy City.* Albany: State University of New York Press.

Kalish, R. A. 1979. "The Onset of the Dying Process." In *Death, Dying, and Transcending*, ed. R. A. Kalish, 5–17. Farmingdale, N.Y.: Baywood.

Kane, M., E. R. Hamlin, and W. E. Hawkins. 2005. "Perceptions of Preparedness to Assist Elders with End-of-Life Care Preferences." *Journal of Social Work in End-of-Life and Palliative Care* 1 (1): 49–69.

Kapp, M. B. 1999. *Geriatrics and the Law.* New York: Springer.

Kayser-Jones, J. 2002. "The Experience of Dying: An Ethnographic Nursing Home Study." *Gerontologist* 42 (Special Issue III): 11–19.

Knight, B. G. 1988. "Factors Influencing Therapist-Related Change in Older Adults." *Journal of Gerontology* 43:111–12.

Koenig, H. G. 2002. "A Commentary: The Role of Religion and Spirituality at the End of Life." *Gerontologist* 42 (Special Issue III): 20–23.

Kovacs, P. J., M. H. Bellin, and D. Fauri. 2006. "Family-Centered Care: A Resource for Social Work in End-of-Life and Palliative Care." *Journal of Social Work in End-of-Life and Palliative Care* 2 (1): 13–27.

Kramer, B. 2005. "Challenges to Providing End-of-Life Care to Low-Income Elders: Lessons Learned from a Model Program for Vulnerable Older Adults." *Gerontologist* 45 (5): 651–60.

Kroenke, K., R. L. Spitzer, and J. B. W. Williams. 2001. "The PHQ-9: Validity of a Brief Depression Severity Measure." *Journal of General Internal Medicine* 16:606–13.

Kubler-Ross, E. 1969. *On Death and Dying*. New York: Macmillan.

Lacey, D. 2005a. "Nursing Home Social Worker Skills and End-of-Life Planning." *Social Work in Health Care* 40 (4): 19–40.

Lacey, D. 2005b. "Educational Needs of Hospice Social Workers: Spiritual Assessment and Interventions with Diverse Populations." *American Journal of Hospice and Palliative Medicine* 22:269–76.

Lacey, D. 2006. "End-of-Life Decision Making for Nursing Home Residents: A Survey of Nursing Home Social Services Staff." *Health and Social Work* 31 (3): 189–99.

Lubben, J., and M. Gironda. 2003. "Centrality of Social Ties to the Health and Well-Being of Older Adults." In *Social Work and Health Care in an Aging Society*, ed. B. Berkman and L. Harootyan, 319–50. New York: Springer.

McCanse, R. P. 1995. "The McCanse Readiness for Death Instrument (MRDI): A Reliable and Valid Measure for Hospice Care." *The Hospice Journal* 10 (1): 15–26.

Mackelprang, R. W., and R. E. Mackelprang. 2005. "Historical and Contemporary Issues in End-of-Life Decisions: Implications for Social Work." *Social Work* 50 (4): 315–24.

Magaziner, J., P. German, S. I. Zimmerman, R. Hebel, L. Burton, A. L. Gruber-Baldini, et al. 2000. "The Prevalence of Dementia in a Statewide Sample of New Nursing Home Admissions Ages Sixty-five and Older: Diagnosis by Expert Panel." *Gerontologist* 40 (6): 663–72.

Magaziner, J., S. I. Zimmerman, K. M. Fox, and B. J. Burns. 1998. "Dementia in United States Nursing Homes: Descriptive Epidemiology and Implications for Long-Term Residential Care." *Aging and Mental Health* 2 (1): 28–35.

Mezey, M., N. N. Dubler, E. Mitty, and A. A. Brody. 2002. "What Impact Do Setting and Transitions Have on the Quality of Life at the End of Life and the Quality of the Dying Process?" *Gerontologist* 42 (Special Issue III): 54–67.

Miller S. C., V. Mor, N. Wu, P. Gozalo, and K. Lapane. 2002. "Does Receipt of Hospice Care in Nursing Homes Improve the Management of Pain at the End of Life?" *Journal of the American Geriatrics Society* 50:507–15.

Mitchell, S. L., J. M. Teno, S. C. Miller, and V. Mor. 2005. "A National Study of the Location of Death for Older Persons with Dementia." *Journal of the American Geriatrics Society* 53:299–305.

182

Psychosocial, Social, Spiritual, and Existential Issues

Moody, L. E., T. Beckie, C. Long, A. Edmonds, and S. Andrews. 2000. "Assessing Readiness for Death in Hospice Elders and Older Adults." *The Hospice Journal* 15 (2): 49–65.

Moos, R. H., and J. A. Schaefer. 1986. *Coping with Life Crises: An Integrated Approach.* New York: Plenum Press.

Morris, J. N., V. Mor, R. J. Goldberg, S. Sherwood, D. S. Greer, and J. Hiris. 1986. "The Effect of Treatment Setting and Patient Characteristics on Pain in Terminal Cancer Patients: A Report from the National Hospice Study." *Journal of Chronic Disease* 39 (1): 27–35.

Morrison, R., E. Chichin, J. Carter, O. Burack, M. Lantz, and D. Meier. 2005. "The Effect of a Social Work Intervention to Enhance Advance Care Planning Documentation in the Nursing Home." *Journal of the American Geriatrics Society* 53:290–94.

Munn, J., and G. Adorno. 2008. "By Invitation Only: Social Work Involvement at the End of Life in Long-Term Care." *Journal of Social Work in End-of-Life and Palliative Care* 4 (4): 333–57.

Munn, J., D. Dobbs, A. Meier, C. Williams, H. Biola, and S. Zimmerman. 2008. "The End-of-Life Experience in Long-Term Care: Five Themes Identified from Focus Groups with Residents, Family Members, and Staff." *Gerontologist* 48 (4): 485–94.

Munn, J. C., L. C. Hanson, S. Zimmerman, P. D. Sloane, and C. M. Mitchell. 2006. "Is Hospice Associated with Improved End-of-Life Care in Nursing Homes and Assisted Living Facilities?" *Journal of the American Geriatrics Society* 54 (3): 490–95.

Munn, J., S. Zimmerman, L. Hanson, C. Williams, P. Sloane, K. Steinhauser, E. C. Clipp, and J. Tulsky. 2007. "Measuring the Quality of Dying in Long-Term Care." *Journal of the American Geriatrics Society* 55:1371–79.

NASW. 2004. "NASW Standards for Case Management." http://www.socialworkers.org/practice/standards/sw_case_mgmt.asp#def. Accessed August, 31, 2008.

Nakashima, Mitsuko. 2002. "A Qualitative Inquiry Into the Psychosocial and Spiritual Well-Being of Older Adults at the End of Life." Ph.D. diss., University of Kansas

O'Boyle, C. A., and D. Waldron. 1997. "Quality of Life Issues in Palliative Medicine." *Journal of Neurology* 244 (Supplement IV): S18–S25.

Oleson, M., and K. G. Shadick. 1993. "Application of Moos and Schaefer's 1986 Model to Nursing Care of Elderly Persons Relocating to a Nursing Home." *Journal of Advanced Nursing* 18:479–85.

Parker-Oliver, D., D. Porock, S. Zweig, M. Rantz, and G. F. Petroski. 2003. "Hospice and Nonhospice Nursing Home Residents." *Journal of Palliative Medicine* 6:69–75.

Patrick, D. L., R. A. Engelberg, and J. R. Curtis. 2001. "Evaluating the Quality of Death and Dying." *Journal of Pain and Symptom Management* 22 (3): 717–26.

Perakyla, A. 1991. "Hope Work in the Care of Seriously Ill Patients." *Qualitative Health Research* 1 (4): 407–33.

Port, C. L., A. L. Gruber-Baldini, L. Burton, M. Baumgarten, J. R. Hebel, S. Zimmerman, et al. 2003. "Resident Contact with Family and Friends Following Nursing Home Admission." *Gerontologist* 41:589–96.

Pulchalski, C. M. 1997. "Spirituality in Health: The Role of Spirituality in Critical Care." *Critical Care Clinics* 20:487–504.

Reese, D. 2001. "Addressing Spirituality in Hospice: Current Practices and a Proposed Role for Transpersonal Social Work." *Social Thought: Journal of Religion in the Social Sciences* 20 (1/2): 135–61.

Reese, D. J., and M. Raymer. 2004. "Relationships Between Social Work Involvement and Hospice Outcomes: Results of the National Hospice Social Work Survey." *Social Work* 49 (3): 415–22.

Reese, D. J., M. Raymer, S. F. Orloff, S. Gerbino, R. Valade, S. Dawson, et al. 2006. "The Social Work Assessment Tool (SWAT)." *Journal of Social Work in End-of-Life and Palliative Care* 2 (1): 65–95.

Rhoades, J., D. E. B. Potter, and N. Krauss. 1998. *Nursing Homes: Structure and Selected Characteristics.* AHCPR Publication No. 98-0006, MEP Research Findings No. 4. Rockville, Md: Agency for Healthcare Quality Research.

Schockett, E. R., J. Teno, S. C. Miller, and B. Stuart. 2005. "Late Referral to Hospice and Bereaved Family Member Perception of Quality of End-of-Life Care." *Journal of Pain and Symptom Management* 30 (5): 400–408.

Sheafor, B. W., C. R. Horejsi, and G. A. Horejsi. 1997. *Techniques and Guidelines for Social Work Practice.* Boston: Allyn and Bacon.

Shield, R. R., R. Wetle, J. Teno, S. C. Miller, and L. Welch. 2005. "Physicians 'Missing in Action': Family Perspectives on Physician and Staffing Problems in the End-of-Life Care in the Nursing Home." *Journal of the American Geriatrics Society* 53:1651–57.

Singer, P. A., D. K. Martin, and M. Kelner. 1999. "Quality End-of-Life Care: Patients' Perspectives." *Journal of the American Medical Association* 281: 163–68.

Steinhauser, K. E., H. B. Bosworth, E. C. Clipp, M. McNeilly, N. A. Christakis, J. Parker, et al. 2002. "Initial Assessment of a New Instrument to Measure Quality of Life at the End of Life." *Journal of Palliative Medicine* 5 (6): 829–41.

Steinhauser, K. E., N. A. Christakis, E. C. Clipp, M. McNeilly, S. Grambow, J. Parker, et al. 2001. "Preparing for End of Life: Preferences of Patients, Families, Physicians, and Other Care Providers." *Journal of Pain and Symptom Management* 22 (3): 727–37.

Steinhauser, K. E., N. A. Christakis, E. C. Clipp, M. McNeilly, L. McIntyre, and
J. A. Tulsky. 2000. "Factors Considered Important at End of Life by Patients,
Family Physicians, and Other Care Providers." *Journal of the American Medical
Association* 284 (19): 2476–82.

Steinhauser, K. E., C. I. Vols, E. C. Clipp, H. B. Bosworth, N. E. Christakis, and
J. A. Tulsky. 2006. "Are You at Peace? One Item to Probe Spiritual Support at
the End of Life." *Annals of Internal Medicine* 166 (1): 101–5.

Stewart, A. L., J. Teno, D. Patrick, and J. Lynn. 1999. "The Concept of Quality
of Life of Dying Persons in the Context of Health Care." *Journal of Pain and
Symptom Management* 17 (2): 93–108.

Sullivan, M. D. 2003. "Hope and Hopelessness at the End of Life." *American
Journal of Geriatric Psychiatry* 11 (4): 393–405.

Sulmasy, D. P. 2002. "A Biopsychosocial-Spiritual Model for the Care of Patients
at the End of Life." *Gerontologist* 42 (Special Issue III): 24–33.

Teno, J. 1999. "Putting Patient and Family Voice Back Into Measuring Quality of
Care for the Dying." *The Hospice Journal* 14 (3/4): 167–76.

Teno, J. M. 2002. "Now Is the Time to Embrace Nursing Homes as a Place of
Care for Dying." *Innovations in End-of-Life Care* 4 (2). http://www.edc.org/
lastacts. Accessed March 4, 2004.

Teno, J., and K. M. Coppola. 1999. "For Every Numerator, You Need a
Denominator: A Simple Statement but Key to Measuring the Quality of Care
in Dying." *Journal of Pain and Symptom Management* 17 (2): 109–13.

Teno, J. M., S. Weitzen, T. Wetle, and V. Mor. 2001. "Persistent Pain in Nursing
Home Residents." *Journal of the American Medical Association* 285 (7):788.

Tong, E., S. A. McGraw, E. Dobihal, R. Baggish, E. Cherlin, and E. H. Bradley.
2003. "What Is a Good Death? Minority and Non-minority Perspectives."
Journal of Palliative Care 19 (3): 168–75.

Toseland, R. 1990. *Group Work with Older Adults*. New York: New York University
Press.

Travis, S. S., M. Bernard, S. Dixon, W. J. McAuley, G. Loving, and L. McClanahan.
2002. "Obstacles to Palliation and End-of-Life Care in a Long-Term Care
Facility." *Gerontologist* 42 (3): 342–49.

Tulsky, J. A. 2002. "Hope and Hubris." *Journal of Palliative Medicine* 5 (3): 339–41.

Turner, F. J. 1995. "Social Work Practice: Theoretical Base." In *Encyclopedia of
Social Work*, ed. R. L. Edwards, 2258–65. New York: NASW

U.S. Department of Health and Human Services. 2006. *The Supply and Demand
of Professional Social Workers Providing Long-Term Care Services*. Report to
Congress. Washington, D.C.: Assistant Secretary of Planning and Evaluation,
Office of Aging, Disability, snd Long-Term Care Policy.

Volicer, L., A. C. Hurley, and Z. V. Blasi. 2001. "Scales for Evaluation of End-of-Life Care in Dementia." *Alzheimer Disease and Associated Disorders* 15 (4): 194–200.

Vourlekis, B., and K. Simons. 2006. "Nursing Homes." In *Handbook of Social Work in Health and Aging*, ed. B. Berkman, 601–13. New York: Oxford University Press.

Walsh-Burke, K., and Csikai, E. L. 2005. "Professional Social Work Education in End-of-Life Care: Contributions of the Project on Death in America's Social Work Leadership Development Program." *Journal of Social Work in End-of-Life and Palliative Care* 1 (2): 11–26.

Welch, L. C., S. C. Miller, E. W. Martin, and A. Nanda. 2008. "Referral and Timing of Referral to Hospice Care in Nursing Homes: The Significant Role of Staff Members." *Gerontologist* 48 (4): 477–84.

White, K. L, T. F. Williams, and B. G. Greenberg. 1996. "The Ecology of Medical Care." *Bulletin of the New York Academy of Medicine* 73:187–212.

Yalom, I. D. 1980. *Existential Psychotherapy*. New York: Basic Books.

7

Identifying and Addressing Family Members' Psychosocial, Spiritual, and Existential Issues Related to Having a Loved One Living and Dying in a Nursing Home

PATRICIA J. KOLB

For many families, it is extremely difficult to place a relative in a nursing home, and family members and residents experience many challenges. Stereotypes abound regarding families heartlessly sending older relatives to nursing homes and abandoning them, but reality repeatedly discredits these stereotypes. Nursing home placement is frequently a decision of last resort that is made only when family and community resources are inadequate for an older relative to remain at home safely (Kolb 2003). Other responsibilities and demands on time, money, and energy of informal caregivers, as well as gaps in formal care systems in the community, often combine to make community-based support systems inadequate to sustain an older relative safely outside of a nursing home in spite of relatives' best efforts.

The resulting nursing home placement is often distressing for residents and relatives. Relatives may experience many psychological and emotional reactions, including grief, depression, guilt, and regret, during the admission and adjustment processes. Family members' cultural expectations about multigenerational roles and responsibilities when a relative becomes chronically ill and older influence their reactions to placement. Reactions become more complex when relatives learn that the nursing home resident is terminally ill. Social workers must recognize that the involvement of relatives and close friends can bring important strengths to difficult situations because of the support that they can provide to the resident. Individuals who have long-term relationships with the resident can also provide information about earlier family experiences with health problems and decision making, as well as coping skills that have been developed by the resident and relatives.

Mr. Song

The experiences of Mr. Song, a nursing home resident, and his family provide examples of a son's distressed reactions to his father's chronic illness that were based on challenging realities and strong cultural beliefs:

Mr. Song is a seventy-four-year-old Korean, Catholic, married man who was admitted to a nursing home with diagnoses of depressive disorder and esophageal cancer. He received intensive radiation therapy and recovered completely. Two years later he was again sent to the hospital for diagnostic tests, as blood was discovered in his stools. The test indicated that he had colon cancer. His physician told his wife and son about his new onset of cancer and recommended chemotherapy or surgery as viable treatments. The physician asked the son how his father should be approached with this news, and even asked the son to be a translator to discuss treatment options. But the son strongly insisted that his father not be informed about the new onset of cancer, stating, 'We want to keep my father as comfortable as possible until he dies. He suffered from severe pain and side effects due to radiation therapy when he had esophageal cancer. We don't want him to go through another invasive treatment, such as chemotherapy or surgery.' Although the physician approached the family several times, they reacted in the same way and even demanded that the physician not discuss anything with the father. The physician believed, however, that the family members were not acting fairly by keeping the information from Mr. Song about his current medical condition. Because it was Mr. Song's life, the physician believed that the decision should be solely Mr. Song's and not his relatives'.

(Park and Kang 2007:178–79)

In the example of Mr. Song and his son, the social worker provided support to Mr. Song and his son through psychoeducation provided to the son, advocacy provided for Mr. Song, and serving as a culture mediator with the interdisciplinary staff. The social worker needed to be culturally sensitive in order to understand the cultural aspects of the son's attitudes and behavior and culturally competent in working with Mr. Song and his son and as a culture mediator who would help interdisciplinary staff understand the family members within their cultural context.

The social worker is generally the primary point of contact with nursing home staff for the family. Social workers need to work with residents, relatives, and staff to identify, assess, and address impediments and conflicts in family involvement. Park and Kang's example illustrates a situation in which the social worker needed to be involved with a chronically ill resident and his relative regarding end-of-life issues and the need for cultural competence in this work. It is apparent that conflicts can occur between nursing home staff from different backgrounds who believe in residents' autonomy in decision making and families whose cultures differ and who do not share a belief in residents' sole autonomy. Cultural beliefs of loved ones, the dying person, or healthcare providers, in addition to psychological factors including diagnosable depression or anxiety, can preclude communication about death (Neimeyer and Werth 2005).

Park and Kang recommend that social workers and healthcare providers respect relatives' and residents' different beliefs and values and suggest that service providers may need to consider a compromise in a situation of this kind. They recommend that Mr. Song's social worker clarify and explain the culturally influenced "family-centered" choices and wishes of Mr. Song's son to the interdisciplinary team and educate the family about the benefits of telling Mr. Song the truth and the importance of respecting Mr. Song's autonomy (2007:179). Kwak and Hanley's (2005) review of findings from thirty-two empirical research studies about end-of-life decision making among racially and ethnically diverse groups indicated that family-centered decision making was more often a preference among Asians and Hispanics.

"Family"

It seems apparent that Mr. Song, his wife, and his son are "family" and that Mr. Song's residence in a nursing home and chronic, terminal illness would place exceptional demands and stresses on the members of this family. As social workers, we know that contemporary social work in the United States defines "family" more broadly, having moved away as a profession from the traditional definition of family as limited to an entity with two biological parents and family ties based on blood, marriage, or adoption. Current social work practice and policy is guided by the definition of "family" adopted in 1981 by the National Association of Social Workers: "a grouping that consists of two or more individuals who define themselves as a family and who over time assume those obligations to one another that are generally considered an essential component of family systems" (NASW 1982:10). Nursing home placement and chronic and terminal illnesses create great strains on people living in diverse family configurations.

The inclusive NASW definition includes families formed by lesbian, gay, bisexual, and transgender individuals. LGBT people are often caregivers for members of their families of origin, as well as to same-sex partners or close friends belonging to their families of choice (Cantor, Brennan, and Shippy 2004). Social workers need to understand that members of these families often experience discriminatory treatment by healthcare providers and disenfranchised grief when a loved one suffers from a chronic terminal illness and dies (Walter 2003). Social workers should demonstrate empathy and advocacy in situations made even more difficult by disenfranchisement.

The trend toward an increasing number of nontraditional families in the United States is directly related to demographic changes that include an increase in the number of single-parent households that resulted from higher divorce rates and increasing numbers of never-married, single-parent households. Furthermore, unmarried heterosexual partners may also experience disenfranchised grief if the importance of the relationship to the partners is not understood by others (Walter 2003).

In addition to social workers' acceptance of a broad definition of "family," it is essential for social workers to acknowledge the importance in many families of more traditional conceptualizations of family, as the example of Mr. Song and his son illustrates, and understand the origins of these beliefs that influence the values and behavior of many older adults and their families. In fact, according to McGoldrick, Giordano, and Garcia-Preto (2005:11–12), "Cultural meanings may persist many generations after migration and after people have ceased to be aware of their heritage. Indeed, the suppression of their cultural history may lead to cultural patterns they themselves fail to appreciate. They may perceive their behavior as resulting purely from intrapsychic or familial factors when, in fact, it derives from hidden cultural history." Culturally influenced attitudes about chronic illness and death contribute to relatives' emotional reactions. Behaviors may be misinterpreted by interdisciplinary team members and therefore require intervention by social workers as culture mediators (Fandetti and Goldmeier 1988).

Retention of traditional cultural values is influenced by a family's migration history, including the reasons for migration or immigration and whether a large proportion of a family, community, or nation have migrated or immigrated and settled together (McGoldrick, Giordano, and Garcia-Preto 2005:19). The maintenance of cultural traits tends to be intensified in groups where emigration was experienced under the threat of cultural annihilation, as has occurred among African Americans, Cubans, Jews, Native Americans, and Poles, and is also intensified when individuals have immigrated as part of a larger group (McGoldrick, Giordano, and Garcia-Preto 2005:19). Movement into a nursing home from a tight-knit family and ethnic community can exacerbate feelings of grief and isolation for residents and their relatives burdened with the challenges of coping with chronic illness and healthcare systems constructed on the medical model. Adaptation to a healthcare setting in which providers may not understand the language, traditions, and values of residents and family members presents additional challenges.

Roles of Nursing Home Social Workers in Practice with Families

Social workers are often the first point of contact for nursing home residents and relatives. Their roles in nursing homes often include making admission arrangements, preadmission and postadmission assessment of service needs, making financial arrangements, and addressing psychosocial needs. Family caregivers may experience high levels of depression, anger, and anxiety for many years after placing their relative in a nursing home even when they are not confronted with terminal illness, and social workers have a major role in assessment, planning, and interventions related to these reactions (Richardson and Barusch 2006; Zarit and Whitlatch 1992). Social workers and other members of the nursing home staff may be able to directly address many of the relatives' concerns, but it may also be necessary to refer relatives to service providers outside of the nursing home because of demands on the social worker's time or the specific needs of relatives. These providers may be case managers, therapists, attorneys, clergy, and others.

Social workers provide support and education to residents and their families. In their discussion of family services provided by nursing home social workers, Gleason-Wynn and Fonville (1993:34) write:

> When a resident is admitted to a nursing home, a family is also being "admitted". Their needs, wishes, and desires must be heard, and the myths and understandings of nursing home placement and elder care have to be addressed and resolved. It is important that staff recognize and deal with the disruption and distress that takes place within a family when a loved one is institutionalized. Family members are dealing with an imperfect solution, the deterioration of a loved one, and their own feelings of failure to provide care. A change in environment and disruption in family relationships represent a family crisis that has a great deal of grief and loss. This is often exhibited in the family's guilt-ridden behavior, and in feelings of abandonment and despair in the resident.

Practice approaches used by social workers to provide support to families include counseling and case management, family psychoeducational and support groups, and support for family-council development and participation. Social workers also train interdisciplinary staff about residents' and family members' psychosocial needs and cultural preferences (Cuadrado 2007; Gleason-Wynn and Fonville 1993; Kolb 2007; Wong 2007). They collaborate with interdisciplinary staff in improving communication between families and nursing home staff through partnership programs such as the Partners in Caregiving program in New York State (Robison and Pillemer 2005) and support family involvement in nursing home culture change (Gilbert and Bridges 2003). As active participants in the nursing home's interdisciplinary care-planning meetings, social workers provide advocacy, assistance with interpretation and understanding of medical interventions and care plans, and community and facility resource information to residents and their relatives (Beaulieu 2002).

Many communication skills, such as active and empathic listening, that social workers use in their work with older adults diagnosed with a life-threatening illness are also important in work with relatives. Information and referral services are often needed following diagnosis of a life-threatening illness. Individual and group psychoeducation can be effective when family members need information and support in understanding the diagnosis and potential effects of the illness on their relative's life (Richardson and Barusch 2006).

Consistency of Care Giving by Relatives and Friends After Nursing Home Admission

There is great variation in the involvement of family and friends with residents following nursing home admission, and frequency of contact may vary substantially over time. Port (2004:774–75) found that family members with "transportation problems, poor relationships with facility staff, and a smaller number of family and friends who visit were significantly related to lower visit frequency" of relatives of residents with dementia in a nursing home. Gaugler and colleagues' (2000) study of 185 primary caregivers of cognitively impaired elderly nursing home residents found that postplacement involvement was affected by long-lasting effects of preplacement stress. Their most significant finding was that there were fewer visits from family caregivers whose relative in the nursing home had exhibited severe problematic behavior such as aggression or wandering before placement. These were also the residents with the most severe behavior problems in early institutionalization, and Gaugler et al. suggested that caregivers who had coped with challenging behavior before admission may visit less because they prefer to avoid these situations.

In many families, relatives, friends, and the resident have strong emotional reactions to placement, and admission has followed extensive efforts to keep the person at home. This is especially true in families that have retained traditional expectations for family roles and responsibilities when a member becomes old. In Kolb's study (2003), relatives and friends who remained involved with nursing home residents after admission generally assumed three types of responsibilities with the hope of ensuring the best quality of life for the residents. They served as sponsor (the primary contact person listed in the resident's chart), monitored care provided by staff, and provided assistance of a personal nature. Similarly, Bern-Klug and Forbes-Thompson (2008:46) found in their research that family members perceived their responsibilities to be serving as "overseers of care," as well as "representatives of the resident's perspective and history" and "keepers of family connections."

As a sponsor, responsibilities may include completion of paperwork, decision making about financial arrangements, and serving as the primary contact for administration and nursing home service providers (Brody 1990; Dobrof 1977; Kolb 2003). In families in which the resident is terminally ill, additional consultations and support may be required from the social worker pertaining to medical and emotional crises and end-of-life decision making by relatives, particularly as the resident's health deteriorates. Sponsors interviewed in Kolb's (2003) study attended interdisciplinary team meetings and regularly interacted with nursing home staff about issues that range from medical treatments and emergencies to residents' depression and roommate concerns. Sponsors also participate in end-of-life planning and decision making, as indicated in the example of Mr. Song and his family.

Relatives monitor staff assistance to the resident that includes bathing, feeding, toileting, medications, and general care (Kolb 2003). Many respondents in Bern-Klug and Forbes-Thompson's study (2008:46) assumed responsibility for overseeing the resident's basic care, including monitoring staff attentiveness to changes in health status, resident cleanliness, timeliness of bedding and clothing changes, assistance in repositioning, respectful treatment of the resident, and adequacy of time spent in care tasks.

Kolb (2003:122) found that tasks of a more personal nature assumed by relatives and friends included "visiting, bringing ethnic foods and other food, feeding, managing finances, closing residents' homes after admission, serving as interpreters, providing emotional support, providing clothing, and washing residents' laundry at home."

Motivation for Care Giving

Kolb (2000, 2003) identified several factors that motivated caregivers to remain involved with residents after their admission to a nursing home. These included:

1. Acceptance of care giving as a responsibility in life
2. Filial piety

3. Mutuality
4. Care giving resulting from long-term intergenerational family discussion and decision making

For some people, acceptance of care giving as a responsibility is related to the relative's cultural or religious beliefs. Davis (2007:23) notes that

the long tradition of a culture of caring persists within the African American community, and it is based not only on blood ties but on a different sense of community. It may result from vestiges of ties that existed in African villages or may have been reflected in the slave quarters of the plantation when it became obvious that slaves could not count on the master's benevolence in times of need. The family support system has been critical to the survival of the black community, and African Americans often rely heavily on family members as a primary source of support. . . . These cultural values are passed on to each successive generation.

Filial piety, or filial obligation or responsibility, is frequently cited as a motivation for providing assistance to older adults, especially in Asian and Latino cultures (Connell and Gibson 1997; Finley, Roberts, and Banahan 1988; Garcia-Preto 2005; Kolb 2000, 2003; Park and Kang 2007; Selig, Tomlinson, and Hickey 1991; Shibusawa 2007; Wong 2007). Nevertheless, intergenerational and geographical differences influence care-giving practices in many Japanese American families, and there are variations in filial piety among Latino subgroups (Richardson and Barusch 2006; Shibusawa 2007). According to Shibusawa (2007:141)

in traditional Japanese culture the primary responsibility of caring for frail elders belongs to adult children. Filial obligation is based on Confucian norms, which dictate familiar roles and responsibilities according to gender, generation, and birth order (Johnson, 1993). Respect for one's parents is also reinforced by Shintoism, the indigenous religion of Japan, which maintains that when elderly parents die they become spirits and protect the family.

An additional motivator for informal care for nursing home residents is mutuality. In Kolb's (2000, 2003) study, this motivator was reflected primarily by daughters of African American and Afro-Caribbean residents.

This care-giving motivator suggests that "both mothers and daughters learn to take care of their relationships and attend to each other's well-being and development" (Kolb 2003:126). It is frequently observed that strong bonds of attachment and open communication exist in many African American families and enable ongoing exchange of support (Davis 2007).

Care giving may also continue after a family member moves to a nursing home because intergenerational discussion and decision making has existed throughout the lifetime of the caregiver. This is consistent with the "tight-knit helping" intergenerational relationship described by Silverstein, Lawton, and Bengtson (1994), in which there are high levels of opportunity for meaningful interaction, a high level of emotional closeness and consensus, and high levels of helping behavior.

Relatives' Psychological Reactions

Caregivers often experience depression, loneliness, social isolation, difficulty sleeping, role stress and role conflict, and disrupted family relationships, with the greatest stress experienced by caregivers whose relatives have dementia or other serious mental impairments (Richardson and Barusch 2006:204). Variations in type of illness and caregiver coping strategies contribute to differences in effects of care-giving responsibilities on individuals.

In her analysis of data from an ethnographic study in which forty-four relatives of nursing home residents were interviewed, Bern-Klug (2008) found that while relatives may experience relief that the resident is in a physically safe place, emotions like guilt and sadness can also be present. Relatives may also experience " 'competing concerns' which are examples of possible role strain and 'psychological pressures.' The latter include (1) it's hard to see the loved one in the present condition, and (2) guilt about the placement" (Bern-Klug 2008:41). These findings, in addition to Bern-Klug's (2008:41) findings about role support and role stress, suggest a need for role reinforcement by staff, that is, assistance to relatives in "meeting their own role expectations as family caregivers." Examples of role reinforcement include going to the emergency room to meet the resident, accompanying a family member on a visit to the resident, allowing the relative to describe family care-giving experiences, and helping the relative to disperse the resident's household items (Bern-Klug 2008).

Richardson and Barusch (2006:206–7) recommend their ABCDEF practice guide as an effective tool that can supplement care-giving assessment tools such as the Caregiver Burden Interview, used to assess more specific problems in different areas of functioning. The ABCDEF guide includes assessment of clients' (A) actions, (B) biological/health functioning, (C) cognitive status, (D) demographic indicators, (E) environmental influences, and (F) feelings. While this guide was developed with care giving for community residing elders in mind, it is also relevant to assessment of needs of family caregivers for nursing home residents and encourages us to view the resident and family caregivers from a holistic view as a family system.

Richardson and Barusch (2006:207) explain this assessment process as follows:

> The actions (A) assessment focuses on the behaviors and activities of care recipients and caregivers alike. In some cases, a functional assessment, which focuses on the antecedents and consequences of an action, will help reveal the motives and circumstances behind care recipients' behavior problems. Assessing the biological status (B) or health of caregivers and care recipients is important. . . . The cognitive (C) assessment covers family members' coping approaches, and demographic (D) factors shed light on a family's cultural context. When evaluating the client's environment (E), their living arrangements and the physical design of their residence are important considerations. In addition, the social worker should evaluate family interactions and other family systems as well as clients' informal and formal systems. The feelings (F) of the care recipient and his caregivers reveal a family's overall functioning and well-being.

While other members of the interdisciplinary team have primary responsibility for certain aspects of the resident's assessment and care, nursing home social workers need to know the results of all assessments in order to provide social work services from a holistic perspective.

Many issues arise in nursing homes that require social workers to provide information and support and facilitate family communication. These include newly diagnosed medical conditions, treatment decisions, pain management, advance directives, do not hospitalize orders, room changes, roommate issues, hospice enrollment, and caregiver stress and anticipatory grief. Some caregivers of older adults with Alzheimer's disease and

other diseases in which functioning gradually disappears experience anticipatory grief over extended periods of time. This is "a sense of withdrawal
and disengagement from the dying person before the person actually dies"
in which grieving occurs repeatedly as the older adult loses functional abilities (McInnis-Dittrich 2005:358). Although anticipatory grief may occur,
relatives often experience additional grieving when the resident dies.

Richardson and Barusch (2006) point out that social workers' communication skills are used to help older adults understand and cope with
new diagnoses. Social work with families also requires application of these
skills. Coping skills are taught and information and referral services provided. Social workers can identify questions that family members may have
about treatment options and arrange for necessary information to be made
available, as well as providing answers to questions.

Interventions for caregivers of older adults with chronic impairments
also include support groups, stress-management techniques, and psychoeducational and educational approaches (Hooyman and Kramer 2006;
McInnis-Dittrich 2005; Richardson and Barusch 2006). Employed as a
nursing home social worker, McBee (2008) successfully developed an innovative approach that integrates complementary and alternative medicine
approaches into social work practice with nursing home residents, relatives, and staff. McBee's approach, "Mindfulness-Based Elder Care" (2008:
xxi), demonstrates that mindfulness practices focusing on abilities of frail
elders, their families, and professional caregivers "provide paths to the in-
ner strengths and resources we all possess."

McBee (2008:123) explains her use of "Mindfulness-Based Elder Care"
with caregivers:

In caregiver groups, the variety of techniques taught includes deep
breathing, visualization, gentle yoga, and mindfulness. Participants
practice the skills in the group and between sessions, with the help of
instructions on a CD provided. Each week a new practice is taught or reviewed. After the first session, each group begins with a few moments of
silent sitting. This time becomes longer each week. A discussion of skills
from the previous weeks follows, with time provided for any thoughts
or concerns about them and any questions. The discussion focuses on
learning to look at events differently and how the participants can use
what they learned in their daily lives. Following the discussion, a new
technique is presented or reviewed and practiced. The group ends with

another period of silent sitting. At the conclusion, the next week's home-work is discussed, handouts reinforcing the practice are distributed, and practice suggestions are offered. The caregiver group is very experiential and personal, evoking powerful responses from the participants.

Social Work Addressing End-of-Life Experiences in Families

During the twentieth century, dramatic advances were made in develop-ment of medical interventions that "may be used to attempt to 'rescue' a seriously ill or dying person from death. Our line of defense against death runs the gamut from ventilators and organ transplantation to dialysis and open-heart surgery" (Bern-Klug, Gessert, and Forbes 2001:40). The avail-ability of these options to prolong life in the face of severe chronic ill-nesses results in challenging decisions to be made by people with chronic illnesses and their families and need for information and support from social workers and other healthcare professionals. Bern-Klug, Gessert, and Forbes (2001:41) point out that "at the beginning of the 21st century, dying is acknowledged or recognized only under very limited circumstances." Nei-meyer and Werth (2005) emphasize the importance of psychosocial issues in the quality of life of individuals approaching death and their loved ones.

While family members may avoid talking with professionals about end-of-life care or wishes regarding life-sustaining interventions, Richardson and Barusch point out that relatives "feel more in control when they know what to expect and are able to know what to expect as the disease worsens." They add that "social workers can help these families by anticipating family members' confusion about progressive illness and by initiating talks about the future" (2006:242). Bern-Klug, Gessert, and Forbes (2001:43–44) point out that

social workers in hospital, hospice, nursing home, and assisted-living settings can assist families in visualizing the dying and death of a loved one in the broadest and most meaningful terms. . . . Skills in values clari-fication, emotional assessment, crisis intervention, goal setting, decision making, active listening, bereavement counseling, advocacy, and inter-personal communication can be helpful in working with clients and fam-ilies. The process should include a discussion of what constitutes peace of mind for the person who is dying and for the family.

Inadequate end-of-life care for residents can occur (Wetle et al. 2005), and nursing home social workers play an important role in addressing residents' and relatives' need for improved end-of-life care. Social work advocacy with other healthcare providers on behalf of the dying person and family members can help ensure sensitivity and understanding of family needs (McInnis-Dittrich 2005).

Families and other professionals may ask social workers for assistance regarding psychosocial issues and holistic care (Richardson and Barusch 2006:238). Social workers can encourage families to participate in advance care planning and understand that social support, community resources, and financial help may be needed (Bern-Klug, Gessert, and Forbes 2001:46). Furthermore, Bern-Klug and Forbes-Thompson (2008:50) emphasize that "staff needs to be constantly reminded of how emotionally difficult it can be for family members to have a loved one living and dying in a nursing home."

The *Clinical Practice Guidelines for Quality Palliative Care* (National Consensus Project 2004) provide important guidelines for social work with relatives of patients needing palliative care, in addition to guidelines applicable to work with patients. This is apparent in the stated goals of the guidelines:

1. Pain and symptom control, psychosocial distress, spiritual issues and practical needs are addressed with patient and *family* throughout the continuum of care.

2. Patients and *families* obtain the information that they need in an ongoing and understanding manner, in order to grasp their condition and treatment options. Their values and goals are elicited over time; the benefits and burdens of treatment are regularly reassessed; and the decision-making process about the care plan is sensitive to changes in the patient's condition.

3. Genuine coordination of care across settings is ensured through regular and high-quality communication between providers at times of transition or changing needs, and through effective continuity of care that utilizes the techniques of case management.

4. Both patient and *family* are prepared for the dying process and for death, when it is anticipated. Hospice options are explored, opportunities for personal growth are enhanced and bereavement support is available for the family.

(National Consensus Project 2004:1; italics added)

Both a philosophy and a structured system for delivering care, the goals of palliative care are "enhancing quality of life for patient and family, optimizing function, helping with decision-making and providing opportunities for personal growth" (National Consensus Project 2004:2).

The domains of a high quality of palliative care are consistent with professional principles of family care for relatives of chronically ill and dying nursing home residents that are described in social work literature, and the National Consensus Project provides excellent practice guidelines that are appropriate for social workers. The palliative-care domains include the structure and processes of palliative care; physical aspects of care; psychological and psychiatric aspects of care; a grief and bereavement program for patients and families; interdisciplinary assessment and care planning for meeting social needs of patients and families; assessment and responses to spiritual and existential dimensions; assessment and responses to culture-specific patient and family needs; recognition and provision of care to patients and relatives pertaining to signs and symptoms of impending death; and addressing ethical and legal aspects of care (National Consensus Project 2004:7–20). For example, the structure and process guidelines include the following (8–11):

Guideline 1.1 The plan of care is based on a comprehensive interdisciplinary assessment of the patient and family. . . .

Guideline 1.2 The care plan is based on the identified and expressed values, goals and needs of patient and family, and is developed with professional guidance and support for decision-making.

Guideline 1.3. An interdisciplinary team provides services to the patient and family, consistent with the care plan.

Guideline 1.4 The interdisciplinary team may include appropriately trained and supervised volunteers.

Guideline 1.5 Support for education and training is available to the interdisciplinary team.

Guideline 1.6 The palliative care program is committed to quality improvement in clinical and management practices.

Guideline 1.7 The palliative care program recognizes the emotional impact on the palliative care team of providing care to patients with life-threatening illnesses and their families.

Guideline 1.8 Palliative care programs should have a relationship with one or more hospices and other community resources in order to ensure continuity of the highest-quality palliative care across the illness trajectory.

Guideline 1.9 The physical environment in which care is provided should meet the preferences, needs and circumstances of the patient and family to the extent possible.

Social Work with Families in End-of-Life Planning

Social work practice with families includes discussion of end-of-life decisions, including advance directives. Advance directives, including living wills, healthcare proxies, and burial plans, need to be discussed with family members in addition to residents. Social workers need to help family members understand that advance directives often allow them to assume greater control over the care of the resident than would otherwise be allowed. When advance directives already exist, they are often misunderstood and misinterpreted, and relatives may disagree with preferences written in the documents (Richardson and Barusch 2006). Social workers should review advance directives with the resident and relatives, be available to assume the role of mediator in family discussions, and help connect families with a counselor, if necessary.

Sometimes problems arise because of lack of staff compliance with advance directives. Richardson and Barusch (2006:242) note that

advance directives are sometimes inaccessible because they are located in a different state or are locked away in someone's office. Health care professionals are often unsure how to proceed if family members disagree with each other. Despite these limitations, social workers will increasingly become involved in assisting older people and their families to plan in advance for end-of-life care.

Knowledge and preferences regarding advance directives are influenced by cultural beliefs (Kwak and Hanley 2005), and it is important for social workers to understand the ways that cultural beliefs influence attitudes and behavior within families about end-of-life planning. For example, among American Indians it is normal to avoid talking directly about death, and social workers can provide opportunities for discussion about advance directives but should "honor the elder and the family's wishes if they choose not to do so" (Day 2007:61). Cuadrado (2008:243) notes that among Puerto Ricans, "families may not feel comfortable talking to the resident about health care proxies or living wills, for fear that speaking of the possibility of illness, incapacity, or death might hurt the feelings of the resident or cause these events to materialize." Cuadrado (2007:243) adds that in her work as a nursing home social worker, "when death was imminent, relatives were less likely to select life-prolonging measures, believing that existence in the spiritual realm is peaceful and pain free."

Wong (2007) identified relevant attitudes and behavior of Chinese American nursing home residents and their relatives. Explaining end-of-life planning and advance directives for social workers providing services to Chinese American nursing home residents and their families, Wong writes:

> In working with Chinese American residents and their relatives, social workers may experience difficulties in their efforts to address ethical decision making and end-of-life planning concerning advance directives, care in the end stage of life, and funeral arrangements. A traditional Chinese belief is that a sick person should be protected from additional emotional suffering that might result from knowing that they are dying. Traditionally children usually did not discuss funeral arrangements with their parents before a parent's death. To talk about dying, resuscitation, and hospice care and funeral arrangements when a relative's health is still stable would be considered disrespectful or a curse. When residents reach a medical crisis, relatives may still feel guilty if they make a critical decision that implies giving up hope and preparing for their relative's death.
>
> A health care proxy is considered acceptable by some Chinese American families, and an adult child is often assigned this role. . . . Opting for a "Do Not Resuscitate Order" (DNR) is a difficult decision, as children may feel that they are helping to cut short the life of their parents, which would result in feelings of guilt. When a resident suffers from a great deal of pain or reaches the end of life, relatives of Chinese American residents consider palliative or hospice care to be appropriate.
>
> (Wong 2007:99–100)

Cultural competence in work with families regarding end-of-life decision making, including discussion of advance directives, requires knowledge of within-group differences as well as similarities in attitudes and behaviors. For example, Matsumura and colleagues (2002) reported that in a study comparing attitudes about end-of-life care of Japanese-speaking

Japanese Americans and English-speaking Japanese Americans, the latter were more likely to prefer autonomy in decision making and disclosure of a terminal prognosis and were more positive about advance care planning and avoidance of life-sustaining equipment. However, participants belonging to both groups preferred that decisions be made by family or friends as a group compared to one individual. Shibusawa (2007:155) advises that it is "important . . . for nursing home staff to be sensitive to Japanese American elders who may not be as forthcoming in articulating their wishes regarding end-of-life care."

Likewise, Solis-Longoria (2007) wrote that among Mexican Americans the level of acculturation and income and the ages of family members can influence discussion of advance directives. Religious and cultural values such as fatalism also influence the views of some Mexican Americans about advance directives. Solis-Longoria (2007:208) adds that

resuscitation wishes may . . . be a difficult topic to explore, as some elders and their families may feel that only God has the right to make this decision. Mexican American elders may prefer to have cardiopulmonary resuscitation (CPR) initiated and be considered to have full-code status. Another cultural belief is that a terminal diagnosis or certain treatment options may not be discussed with elders so that they can maintain a positive attitude and continue to have hope.

The Deathbed Phase

Richardson and Barusch (2006:240) discuss the "deathbed phase" as the phase in the dying process that "revolves around the actual death and the ways that people experience it." Older adults and their relatives and friends are likely to experience a great deal of stress at this time regardless of whether they have done everything possible to prepare for this phase. Describing the experiences of family members with a relative dying from Alzheimer's disease, Nuland (1993:105) writes:

All along the way, family members have been experiencing feelings of ambivalence, helplessness, and crisis. They fear what they are seeing, as well as what they have yet to see. No matter how often they are reminded, many people persist in believing they are permitting conscious suffering. And yet, it is always so hard to let go. Such legal instruments as living wills and durable power of attorney may function as so-called advance directives, but all too often they do not exist; a grieving wife or husband, or children already struggling with family problems of their own, are adrift in a sea of conflicting emotions. The difficulty of deciding is compounded by the difficulty of living with what has been decided.

Discussing multiple roles of social workers during this phase, Richardson and Barusch (2006:240) indicate that social workers "educate others about death and its characteristics, inform families about managing symptoms and expressing care, identify the needs of dying people and their family members, and facilitate communication within families. Social workers must also work with others to raise social awareness about what constitutes a comfortable death, or a 'good death.'" In addition, Bern-Klug, Ekerdt, and Wilkinson (1999) recommend that social workers provide information to dying people and their families about local funeral and burial options and costs and serve as community advocates informing people about their rights.

It is also important in this phase for social workers to be sensitive to cultural attitudes and practices and address these competently. For families who experience nursing home placement as culturally stigmatizing, death in a nursing home may come with a double burden because of the cultural stigma of nursing home placement. Kolb and Hofstein (2007:132) note that when a relative dies in a nursing home, many Italian American families "find it difficult to explain to other relatives how they 'let it happen' and face the community that knows about the relative dying while a nursing home resident."

Talamantes, Gomez, and Braun (2000) suggest that death rituals honor the person and provide supportive opportunities for families. There are cultural differences in death rituals, and social workers need to know and understand the rituals practiced by residents' relatives and friends. For example, Solis-Longoria (2007) notes that often Mexican American relatives and friends offer support to the elder in the dying process through a vigil and that burning candles provide constant remembrance of a person who has died.

According to Richardson and Barusch (2006:243), "most families base their decisions to bury or cremate a deceased loved one on tradition and religious preferences, and many people remain uninformed about burial options. Norms about final arrangements are sometimes unclear and vary across families, religious, socioeconomic status, and ethnic and cultural backgrounds."

Other rituals following death reflect religious and cultural differences. While there are variations in practice, in the Jewish faith traditional mourning after death involves seven days of shiva in which family and friends experience deep mourning, visits to the family and assistance in meal preparation and other domestic activities are provided, and there is a formal mourning period of diminished entertainment and social activities for one year following the death (McInnis-Dittrich 2005).

Cuadrado (2008:244) describes the traditional Puerto Rican ritual following death, *el novenario*, and the benefits of this custom from a social work perspective:

These are nine evenings following burial when relatives, neighbors, and friends gather to pray and talk about the loved one, and become, quite naturally, a short-term bereavement group. It is also a transitional period to life without the deceased. The practice generally continues on the island, but, given the hectic lives of the younger generation in the states, it has been slowly declining here.

The traditional need to gather following a loss is an important part of healing. The social worker in the nursing home should consider that the death of a resident not only affects the family but also staff and other residents for whom the departed may have been a friend. Gathering all of them together for prayer, a memorial service, or discussion may be helpful.

Conclusion

Social workers have essential roles in supporting the well-being of relatives of nursing home residents, and the needs of relatives increase as the resident nears the end of life. Relatives may react to a relative's placement with grief, depression, guilt, anger, and regret. Family caregivers may experience high levels of loneliness, social isolation, difficulty sleeping, role stress and role conflict, disrupted family relationships, and anxiety for many years after placing their relative in a nursing home even when they are not confronted with terminal illness.

Contrary to stereotypes, many family members maintain frequent contact with their relative in the nursing home. They may serve as sponsor, monitor/oversee basic care by staff, and provide assistance of a more personal nature such as bringing food, including ethnic foods, to the resident, serving as interpreters, managing finances, and providing clothing. Relatives may also serve as representatives of the resident's perspective and history, as well as keepers of family connections.

Nursing home social work with relatives includes assessment, support and education, counseling, case management, end-of-life planning, and assistance with decision making and family psychoeducational and support groups so that it will be less difficult for the family caregiver to do this work. Social workers support family participation in nursing home culture change. Services addressing the concerns of relatives also include work with interdisciplinary staff to train staff about residents' and relatives' psychosocial needs and cultural preferences and collaboration with staff to improve communication between families and nursing home staff. Social workers also serve as advocates for residents and their families and provide them with community and facility resource information. They assist with interpretation and understanding of medical interventions and care plans, encourage family participation in care-planning meetings, and address impediments and conflicts in family involvement.

In assisting relatives, social workers must understand the effects of cultural expectations and traditions regarding family roles in old age, sexual orientation, family dynamics, and experiences of relatives with the resident before and after placement, including preplacement stress for caregivers and residents. They need to respect relatives' and residents' beliefs and values, including those that are different from beliefs and values of the social worker. Relatives who are diverse ethnically and racially and in sexual orientation may be misunderstood by staff, and this requires that social workers be culture mediators.

Relatives of terminally ill residents nearing the end of life may need more consultations with social workers about medical and emotional crises and end-of-life decision making, and social workers have a major role in assessment, planning, and interventions related to relatives' experiences. Grief for the dying person may be disenfranchised grief that is not supported by society and requires understanding and support from the social worker. Cultural beliefs and psychological characteristics of residents, relatives, and staff can preclude effective communication about death, and social workers need to understand the reasons for this and serve as culture mediators to help interdisciplinary staff understand the individual and family dynamics under the particular circumstances.

An extensive range of social work assistance is provided to relatives of a dying nursing home resident. This includes services provided directly to family members including, but not limited to, support and active listening, crisis intervention, work with relatives pertaining to goal setting and decision making, facilitating communication within families, clarifying advance directives and responding to relatives' questions and concerns so that misunderstandings and misinterpretations can be minimized, providing information about end-of-life care, preparing the patient and family for the dying process and death, and bereavement counseling.

Assistance to the family and the dying resident also requires work with other health care providers at the nursing home. This includes advocacy on behalf of the dying person and family members to help ensure sensitivity and understanding of family needs, constantly reminding staff about the emotional challenges inherent in having a loved one living and dying in a nursing home, working with staff to ensure coordination and continuity of care, including palliative care, and serving as culture mediator with multidisciplinary staff regarding advance directives. Social workers must also work with others to raise social awareness about what constitutes a comfortable death and to support and understand the importance of cultural and religious death rituals.

References

Beaulieu, E. M. 2002. *A Guide for Nursing Home Social Workers*. New York: Springer.

Bern-Klug, M. 2008. "The Emotional Context Facing Nursing Home Residents' Families: A Call for Role Reinforcement Strategies from Nursing Homes and the Community." *Journal of the American Medical Directors Association* 9 (1): 36–44.

Bern-Klug, M., D. J. Ekerdt, and D. S. Wilkinson. 1999. "What Families Know About Funeral-Related Costs: Implications for Social Work Practice." *Health and Social Work* 24 (2): 128–37.

Bern-Klug, M., and S. Forbes-Thompson. 2008. "Family Members' Responsibilities to Nursing Home Residents: 'She Is the Only Mother I Got.'" *Journal of Gerontological Nursing* 34 (2): 43–52.

Bern-Klug, M., C. Gessert, and S. Forbes. 2001. "The Need to Revise Assumptions About the End of Life: Implications for Social Work Practice." *Health and Social Work* 26 (1): 38–47.

Brody, E. 1990. *Women in the Middle: Their Parent-Care Years.* New York: Springer.

Cantor, M. H., M. Brennan, and R. A. Shippy. 2004. *Caregiving Among Older Lesbian, Gay, Bisexual, and Transgender New Yorkers.* New York: The National Gay and Lesbian Task Force Policy Institute.

Connell, C., and G. Gibson. 1997. "Racial, Ethnic, and Cultural Differences in Dementia Caregiving: Review and Analysis." *Gerontologist* 37 (3): 355–64.

Cuadrado, M. 2007. "Puerto Rican Elders." In *Social Work Practice with Ethnically and Racially Diverse Nursing Home Residents and Their Families,* ed. P. Kolb, 219–52. New York: Columbia University Press.

Davis, M. 2007. "African American Elders." In *Social Work Practice with Ethnically and Racially Diverse Nursing Home Residents and Their Families,* ed. P. Kolb, 7–40. New York: Columbia University Press.

Day, P. 2007. "American Indian Elders." In *Social Work Practice with Ethnically and Racially Diverse Nursing Home Residents and Their Families,* ed. P. Kolb, 41–71. New York: Columbia University Press.

Dobrof, R. 1977. "Part I: Guide to Practice." In *Maintenance of Family Ties of Long-term Care Patients: Theory and Guide to Practice,* ed. R. Dobrof and E. Litwak, 1–79. DHEW Publication no. (ADM) 77-400. Washington, D.C.: U.S. Government Printing Office.

Fandetti, D., and J. Goldmeier. 1988. "Social Workers as Culture Mediators in Health Care Settings." *Health and Social Work* 13 (Summer): 171–79.

Finley, N., M. Roberts, and B. Banahan. 1988. "Motivators and Inhibitors of Attitudes of Filial Obligation Toward Aging Parents." *Gerontologist* 28 (1): 73–83.

Garcia-Preto, N. 2005. "Latino Families: An Overview." In *Ethnicity and Family Therapy,* ed. M. McGoldrick, J. Giordano, and N. Garcia-Preto, 153–65. New York: The Guilford Press.

Gaugler, J., S. A. Leitsch, S. H. Zarit, L. I. Pearlin. 2000. "Caregiver Involvement Following Institutionalization: Effects of Preplacement Stress." *Research on Aging* 22 (4): 337–59.

Gilbert, C., and G. Bridges. 2003. "Center for Nursing and Rehabilitation— Culture Change in an Urban Environment." In *Culture Change in Long-Term Care,* ed. A. S. Weiner and J. L. Ronch, 233–43. New York: The Haworth Social Work Practice Press.

Gleason-Wynn, P., and K. Fonville. 1993. *Social Work Practice in the Nursing Home Setting: A Primer for Social Workers.* LaGrange, Tex.: M and H.

Hooyman, N., and B. Kramer. 2006. *Living Through Loss: Interventions Across the Life Span.* New York: Columbia University Press.

Kolb, P. 2000. "Continuing to Care: Black and Latina Daughters' Assistance to Their Mothers in Nursing Homes." *Affilia* 15 (4): 502–25.

Kolb, P. 2003. *Caring for Our Elders: Multicultural Experiences with Nursing Home Placement*. New York: Columbia University Press.

Kolb, P. 2007. Introduction to *Social Work Practice with Ethnically and Racially Diverse Nursing Home Residents and Their Families*, ed. P. Kolb, 1–6. New York: Columbia University Press.

Kolb, P., and R. Hofstein. 2007. "Italian American Elders." In *Social Work Practice with Ethnically and Racially Diverse Nursing Home Residents and Their Families*, ed. P. Kolb, 106–35. New York: Columbia University Press.

Kwak, J., and W. E. Hanley. 2005. "Current Research Findings on End-of-Life Decision Making Among Racially or Ethnically Diverse Groups." *Gerontologist* 45 (5): 634–41.

Matsumura, S., et al 2002. "Acculturation and Attitudes Toward End-of-Life Care: A Cross-Cultural Survey of Japanese Americans and Japanese." *Journal of General Internal Medicine* 17: 531–39.

McBee, L. 2008. *Mindfulness-Based Elder Care: A CAM Model for Frail Elders and Their Caregivers*. New York: Springer.

McGoldrick, M., G. Giordano, and N. Garcia-Preto, eds. 2005. *Ethnicity and Family Therapy*. New York: The Guilford Press.

McInnis-Dittrich, K. 2005. *Social Work with Elders: A Biopsychosocial Approach to Assessment and Intervention*. Boston: Allyn and Bacon.

National Association of Social Workers. 1982. "Changes in NASW Family Policy." *NASW News* 27 (2): 10.

National Consensus Project for Quality Palliative Care. 2004. *Clinical Practice Guidelines for Quality Palliative Care*. Pittsburgh, Penn.: National Consensus Project for Quality Palliative Care.

Neimeyer, R. A., and J. L. Werth. 2005. "The Psychology of Death." In *The Cambridge Handbook of Age and Ageing*, ed. M. L. Johnson, 387–393. Cambridge: Cambridge University Press.

Nuland, S. B. 1993. *How We Die: Reflections on Life's Final Chapter*. New York: Vintage.

Park, S., and S. Kang. 2007. "Korean American Elders." In *Social Work Practice with Ethnically and Racially Diverse Nursing Home Residents and Their Families*, ed. P. Kolb, 162–90. New York: Columbia University Press.

Port, C. L. 2004. "Identifying Changeable Barriers to Family Involvement in the Nursing Home for Cognitively Impaired Residents." *Gerontologist* 44 (6): 770–78.

Richardson, V. E., and A. S. Barusch. 2006. *Gerontological Practice for the Twenty-first Century*. New York: Columbia University Press.

Robison, J., and K. A. Pillemer. 2005. "Partners in Caregiving: Cooperative Communication Between Families and Nursing Homes." In *Promoting Family Involvement in Long-Term Care Settings*, ed. J. E. Gaugler, 201–24. Baltimore, Md.: Health Professions Press.

Selig, S., T. Tomlinson, and T. Hickey. 1991. "Ethical Dimensions of Intergenerational Reciprocity: Implications for Practice." *Gerontologist* 31 (5): 624–30.

Shibusawa, T. 2007. "Japanese American Elders." In *Social Work Practice with Ethnically and Racially Diverse Nursing Home Residents and Their Families*, ed. P. Kolb, 136–61. New York: Columbia University Press.

Silverstein, M., L. Lawton, and V. Bengtson. 1994. "Types of Relations Between Parents and Adult Children." In *Intergenerational Linkages: Hidden Connections in American Society*, ed. V. Bengtson and L. Harootyan, 43–76. New York: Springer.

Solis-Longoria, Y. 2007. "Mexican American Elders." In *Social Work Practice with Ethnically and Racially Diverse Nursing Home Residents and Their Families*, ed. P. Kolb, 191–218. New York: Columbia University Press.

Talamantes, M. A., C. Gomez, and K. Braun. 2000. "Advance Directives and End-of-Life Care: The Hispanic Perspective." In *Cultural Issues in End-of-Life Decision Making*, ed. K. L. Braun, J. H. Pietsch, and P. L. Blanchette, 83–99. Thousand Oaks, Calif.: Sage.

Walter, C. A. 2003. *Loss of a Life Partner: Narratives of the Bereaved.* New York: Columbia University Press.

Wetle, T., R. Shield, J. Teno, S. Miller, L. Welch. 2005. "Family Perspectives on End-of-Life Care in Nursing Homes." *Gerontologist* 45 (5): 642–50.

Wong, R. 2007. "Chinese American Elders." In *Social Work Practice with Ethnically and Racially Diverse Nursing Home Residents and Their Families*, ed. P. Kolb, 72–105. New York: Columbia University Press.

Zarit, S. H., and C. J. Whitlatch. 1992. "Institutional Placement: Phases of Transition." *Gerontologist* 32:665–72.

8

Identifying and Addressing Ethical Issues in Advanced Chronic Illness and at the End of Life

CHARLES E. GESSERT AND DON F. REYNOLDS

CASE STUDY

Throughout her life, Mrs. F was reserved and modest. She disliked displays of affection and felt that her sexual relationships with her husband were "dirty." She avoided health care, did not have a physician, and would not discuss her health or healthcare preferences with her family.

Mrs. F's family noticed that she began showing signs of forgetfulness at age seventy-four. Over the next six years, she experienced increasing memory loss, confusion and disorientation. Though Mrs. F's family attempted to care for her at home, eventually—following extended acrimony within the family—a judge appointed Mrs. F's daughter and granddaughter to serve as her guardians, and she was admitted to a nursing home. Although the court gave Mrs. F's guardians broad authority to make healthcare decisions for her, no one prepared them to exercise that authority effectively. The guardians and the nursing home never discussed their expectations with each other.

Upon admission, Mrs. F's cognitive impairment was advanced, and she could not participate in major care decisions. She had not made a verbal or written advance directive. Without instructions from Mrs. F, her guardians searched their memories for "clues" that would help them advocate for her care in the nursing home.

Mrs. F's fastidious personal modesty meant that she hated to have anyone see her undressed. Accordingly, she was embarrassed by her semipublic nudity when she was being cleaned after incontinence. She was uncomfortable with physical intimacy and hated being "kissed on" by her husband during his visits to the nursing home.

Mrs. F's guardians also drew on their knowledge of her earlier fears and beliefs. Mrs. F had not liked riding in an automobile when her husband was driving—he was a terrible driver—and her guardians could see her terror when he took her out riding to Sunday brunch. Her lifetime pattern of avoiding health care informed her guardians about hospitalization decisions.

During Mrs. F's years in the nursing home, her guardians often felt frustrated by the staff's failure to respond to their requests. The guardians felt that the staff did not respect Mrs. F's modesty and that they failed to protect her from unwanted physical contact with her husband and from the automobile excursions that she feared. These failures occurred despite the guardians' clear legal status as surrogate decision makers.

After four years in the nursing home, at age eighty-four, Mrs. F was chronically confused and no longer verbal. She developed chronic obstructive bronchitis and had two episodes of pneumonia. Mrs. F's physician and daughter agreed to a do-not-hospitalize, do-not-attempt-resuscitation order, but the order never reached Mrs. F's chart. When the physician retired, his order was not passed along to his successor.

Mrs. F was subsequently treated for another pneumonia, this time with IV fluids and antibiotics. Her new physician said he would hospitalize Mrs. F if her condition deteriorated. Mrs. F's daughter requested a consultation by a physician-ethicist. The facility's administrator, director of nursing, and director of social work services participated in the consultation. They agreed to request do-not-hospitalize and do-not-attempt-resuscitation orders, to forego any escalation of treatment, and to provide comfort measures and engage hospice as needed. Following the consultation, Mrs. F declined rapidly. Her daughter requested hospice, but a week passed before it was ordered. Mrs. F died an uncomfortable death less than three hours after the hospice began providing palliative care. The delay in implementing hospice care for Mrs. F deprived the guardians and the nursing home staff of an opportunity to witness the peaceful passing of a mother, grandmother, and long-time resident.

Thinking About Ethics

Common Problems

Some of the ethical problems encountered in nursing home practice are rooted in the life and family of the resident before admission to the nursing home.

- In the case of Mrs. F, discord within the family, which led to a contested guardianship hearing, was longstanding. Mrs. F also had an aversion to discussing her own mortality; in consequence, she did not complete an advance directive or discuss her care preferences with her family.

Other problems arise in the course of the care that is provided (or not provided) during residence in the nursing home; these include disagreements among family members—or between families and staff—regarding day-to-day care.

- Mrs. F's guardians requested that her longstanding sensitivity to modesty and privacy be integrated into her care but found that the nursing home was not responsive.

Still other problems are rooted in institutional or societal policies; they are problems for all residents of a particular nursing home or for all nursing homes in general.

- In Mrs. F's nursing home, hospice care was not routine, nor were advance care planning sessions that involved the surrogate decision makers. Such routine institutional policies would have diminished or averted many of the problems confronted by Mrs. F and her guardians.

In fact, most of the problems that arose in the care of Mrs. F had multiple roots and might have been addressed or averted through interventions before or during her nursing home residence.

Of course, the ethical issues that arise in nursing homes are not limited to those illustrated by Mrs. F's case. For example, some nursing home residents do not have cognitive impairment at the time of admission but slowly lose their capacity to guide their own affairs. In such cases, the nursing home and the family are faced with responsibility for "progressive surrogacy" (High and Rowles 1995), the gradual shift of decision making from the resident to family and other caregivers. Such care raises questions regarding residents' competence (to make legally binding decisions) and capacity (to address the decision at hand). The range of ethical issues that arise in nursing homes is broad and differs substantially from that encountered in acute care and research. The ethics of nursing home care is an emerging field within bioethics (Carter 2002; Fleming 2007; Hayley et al. 1996; Moody 1992).

This chapter examines the principles and concepts used in the analysis and resolution of ethical issues in nursing homes. We focus on end-of-life-care issues in the elderly and use the terms "elderly" and "resident" interchangeably. We focus on issues of autonomy in the context of dependency, providing care in the context of progressive cognitive impairment, elders' preferences regarding decision making and medical interventions, and the roles of families in ethical issues in nursing homes. The chapter concludes with an overview of the roles that social workers may have in preventing, assessing, and resolving ethical issues for both the individual resident and the nursing home as a whole.

Introduction to Ethical Principles and Concepts

Several similar terms are used in discussing ethical issues: "ethics," "bioethics," "medical ethics," and "clinical ethics." The broadest of these terms, ethics, refers to the study of the nature of morality and especially of the moral choices that people make in relating to one another. Bioethics examines moral choices in health care, addressing both theoretical problems and issues that arise in the care of individual patients. The terms "medical ethics" and "clinical ethics" refer to "applied bioethics": the identification, analysis and resolution of moral issues—what is right and wrong—that arise in the care of patients. Medical ethics focuses on moral choices in the practice of medicine; clinical ethics considers the full range of moral choices that arise in the care of patients. Nursing home ethics may be considered a branch of clinical ethics, with the important distinction that the nursing home is both the resident's home and a place where the resident receives health care. Therefore the concerns of nursing home ethics transcend the boundaries of clinical care, encompassing moral choices that affect the daily lives of the residents. Because so many nursing home residents are elderly, moral choices associated with aging and end-of-life care are a principal focus of nursing home ethics.

When is a resident care issue an "ethical" problem? Resident care issues are ethical problems when they require moral reasoning: weighing what is right and wrong. Unlike many of the clinical questions that arise in the care of nursing home residents, ethical questions cannot be answered solely by obtaining better information or better technology. Ethical issues address the question of what we ought to do from a values or morality perspective, not a technical or efficacy perspective. Anyone involved in the care of a resident—family members, nursing home staff, physicians—may ask ethical questions, often phrased as "What is the right thing to do?" Asking ethical questions does not require special expertise.

Principles

The basic principles of contemporary American bioethics were delineated in two publications: *The Belmont Report* (National Commission for the Protection of Human Subjects of Biomedical and Behavioral Research 1979), which focused on the protection of human subjects in research, and *Principles of Biomedical Ethics* (Beauchamp and Childress 1989). Over the past generation, these principles have remained the central concepts in bioethical teaching, discussion and clinical care. They include autonomy, beneficence, non-maleficence, and justice.

AUTONOMY

"Autonomy" literally means self-rule. Respect for self-determination is deeply rooted in American history and imagination (Collopy, Boyle, and Jennings 1991). We are "a culture that celebrates the individual" (Dubler and Nimmons 1992:94; Gessert 2008). In clinical practice, the principle of autonomy means that competent adult patients can determine what healthcare services they do or do not want to receive. The exercise of autonomy hinges on the person's full understanding of the potential risks and benefits of proposed treatments or research. The process of informed consent is used to assure that patients approve of the clinical care that they receive.

The principle of autonomy is central to American bioethics; the concept has been examined, analyzed, and debated extensively in bioethics literature (DuBose, Hamel, and O'Connell 1994; Pellegrino and Thomasma 1988; Schneider 1998). In social work, respect for autonomy is reflected in the principle of "client self-determination" (Luptak 2004; National Association of Social Workers 2006; Osman and Perlin 1994), which has been one of the central tenets of social work ethics for the last half-century (Reamer 1998).

BENEFICENCE

The principle of beneficence is the obligation to do good for the patient; it suggests acts of "mercy, kindness, and charity" (Beauchamp and Childress 1989). Beneficence may be seen as providing balance or counterpoint for the principle of autonomy. It usually becomes the dominant ethical principle when it is not possible to know a person's preferences, as is frequently the case when caring for institutionalized elders with cognitive impairment.

Beneficence may be considered the primary ethical principle of the helping professions. "The belief that there is an obligation to provide benefits is an unchallenged assumption in biomedicine: Promoting the welfare of patients—not merely avoiding harm—is the goal of health care" (Beauchamp and Childress 1989:194). The principle of beneficence inspires and defines much of social work, especially in instances where the social worker provides support for vulnerable individuals: "social assistance for extremely dependent patients provides a clear case of societal action based on the obligation of beneficence" (Beauchamp and Childress 1989:195).

NON-MALEFICENCE

In the words of the Hippocratic Oath, the principle of non-maleficence is the obligation to "abstain from whatever is deleterious and mischievous." It is often associated with the maxim *Primum non nocere*: "First, do no harm." Non-maleficence complements the principle of beneficence and may provide important guidance when addressing issues that arise frequently in nursing homes, such as the distinction between killing and letting die, the difference between withholding and withdrawing life-sustaining treatments, and the obligations of surrogate decision makers for cognitively impaired residents (Beauchamp and Childress 1989).

JUSTICE

The principle of justice addresses issues of fairness. In bioethics, it is most commonly invoked to address questions of distributive justice, that is, the appropriate distribution of scarce resources such as time, effort, expertise, and funding. Concerns about justice cannot be resolved solely by examining the welfare or best interests of the individual; in this regard, justice differs from autonomy, beneficence, and non-maleficence. Justice encompasses the wider effects of decisions on others, including both those who are intimately involved—such as informal and formal caregivers—and society at large. Justice is important to such questions as the appropriate use of aggressive medical care near the end of life and the allocation of staff time among nursing home residents. Elderly nursing home residents may raise questions of justice within their own families, either claiming a right to family resources after a lifetime of supporting other family members or, conversely, resisting the depletion of family resources in paying for their care late in life.

Extending Autonomy

The rights of autonomous people—adults of sound mind—to determine their own health care are seldom challenged. "The central figure of the standard bioethical analysis is the competent adult, ill enough to seek medical assistance and to that extent vulnerable, but still essentially at the height of his or her powers" (Collopy, Boyle, and Jennings 1991:8). Competent adults may decline any medical intervention, including treatments that may be life saving. Autonomous people have extensive rights in determining both the care that they are to receive currently and care they will receive at a future time when they are not able to participate in care decisions (Dworkin 1986). In 1990, the federal Patient Self Determination Act (42 U.S.C. 1395 cc [a]) clarified the rights of adults to refuse medical treatments that they did not want and the responsibilities of institutions that accept Medicare or Medicaid reimbursement to inquire about and recognize advance directives. Adults of all ages are now encouraged to plan ahead, in effect to extend their autonomy beyond the period of time when they are "adults of sound mind" to a future time when they are incapacitated.

ADVANCE DIRECTIVES

Written advance directives range from formal documents that are provided or promoted by state governments to informal statements written by hand. Advance directives may address any or all of three broad areas: the individual's preferences regarding the use of specific medical interventions, the identification of one or more surrogate decision makers, and statements of the individual's values and goals. Preferences for medical care are documented in "instructional" advance directives; these instructions often focus on the use of cardiopulmonary resuscitation, feeding tubes, and ventilators, especially during terminal illness (Abbo, Sobotka, and Meltzer 2008). Surrogate decision makers may be designated formally by the completion of a durable power of attorney for healthcare; in many jurisdictions the DPAHC must be signed, dated, and witnessed to be legally binding. However, in the absence of a legally executed DPAHC, institutions and other care providers may recognize less formal written or verbal guidance regarding preferences for surrogate decision makers. Statements of values and goals—often organized as answers to a series of questions, such as the Five Wishes (see www.agingwithdignity.org)—may be included as an addendum to an instructional advance directive or placed in a less structured document, such as letter to one's family.

The federal Patient Self-Determination Act of 1990 requires that inpatient facilities such as hospitals and nursing homes ask about advance directives at the time of admission. The development of advance directives is now a recognized part of good health care, particularly for older adults, and an important facet of social work in nursing homes (Lacey 2006; Osman and Perlin 1994).

SURROGACY

Surrogate or proxy decision makers are called upon to assist in care decisions when the patient or resident loses the capacity to make decisions on her own. A surrogate may be a family member, a friend or other person who knows the resident well, or a guardian appointed by a court, who might not have personal knowledge of the resident. Surrogates may be temporary or permanent, formal (legally established) or informal. For example, a hospital may turn to family members for assistance in making critical care decisions in an emergency, even though the patient has not named a specific surrogate. The formal designation of a surrogate decision maker using a DPAHC is recommended in advance care planning. The right to name one's preferred surrogate decision maker is recognized as integral to personal autonomy in health care, and the authority of such surrogates is generally recognized by both families and institutions. Most states have laws to guide the selection of an appropriate informal surrogate in the absence of a DPAHC or a court-appointed guardianship. Some of these laws provide a process by which interested people act together to identify a surrogate; others provide a prioritized list of interested people who may serve as a surrogate. The American Bar Association provides information on default surrogate-consent statutes by state online at http://www.abanet.org/aging/legislativeupdates/pdfs/Famcon_Chart.pdf.

Surrogates often have major roles in decision making near the end of life, especially in the presence of cognitive impairment. However, the role of the surrogate is likely to develop gradually, step by step, as the capacity of the resident wanes. This "progressive surrogacy" (High and Rowles 1995) is a recognized facet of care giving, and in most families it begins long before nursing home admission. Many elders who cannot make complex decisions can still guide the appointment of an agent, someone they trust. For many elders, confidence in the goodwill of the surrogate is of primary importance, as "incompetent patients may well prefer decisions to be made by a relative who loves them even if the decision may differ from their own" (Cohen et al. 2005:1218; also see High 1988:50).

SUBSTITUTED JUDGMENT

What should a surrogate decision maker use to guide decisions? Should decisions reflect what the resident would decide if she was able to make her own decisions? Or should the decision be guided by what the surrogate determines is best for the resident, regardless of her wishes?

The substituted-judgment standard calls on the surrogate to make decisions guided by what the resident herself would decide if she was able. The exercise of substituted judgment hinges on the surrogate's understanding of the resident's healthcare values, goals, and preferences. Surrogates may draw upon written directives, prior conversations, or knowledge of the resident's lifestyle in exercising substituted judgment (Elliott, Gessert, and Peden-McAlpine 2007). The substituted-judgment standard is rooted in respect for the resident's autonomy and is an outgrowth of the conviction that "when patients lose their decision-making capacity, they ought not thereby forfeit all of their autonomy" (Sulmasy and Sugarman 2001:13).

Substituted judgment should involve more than simply honoring previously expressed preferences for care. When surrogates are asked to exercise substituted judgment, they are not just being asked to recall what the elders wanted in the past but to imagine what the elders would want in light of all that has transpired, including the circumstances that created the resident's dependency on others for decision making (Kuczewski 2004). Surrogates are called upon to consider residents' values and life stories in making decisions.

BEST INTERESTS

The best-interests standard calls upon surrogates to make decisions on the basis of what is considered to be best for the resident. Surrogates turn to the best-interests standard when it is not possible to know what the resident would have wanted. Residents may leave no instructions—written or verbal—to guide their health care, or their known preferences may not be applicable to the situation at hand. When this occurs, substituted judgment cannot be used, and the surrogate is obliged to make decisions on the basis of what is best for the resident (Drane and Coulehan 1995; Sullivan 2002). The use of the best-interests standard is common in nursing homes, since even under the best of circumstances it is difficult for residents to anticipate how future illnesses will unfold and therefore difficult for them to provide surrogates with specific requests or guidance.

In some instances, the best-interests standard may also be used to override the expressed wishes of a resident. For example, an elder might complete an advance directive requesting resuscitation if her heart stops. However, later when she has advanced cognitive impairment, she might have a cardiac arrest and a resuscitation that leaves her with several broken ribs. A surrogate decision maker might then determine that future cardiopulmonary resuscitation would cause harm without commensurate benefit and that her status should be "do not resuscitate." Such a decision would be based on an assessment of the resident's best interests.

Many elders recognize that they cannot anticipate all of the issues and circumstances that might arise and are comfortable having their surrogate decision makers use their own judgment about what care is warranted.

Such elders are tacitly—or overtly—accepting the limits of their own autonomy, and turning to the judgment and beneficence of their surrogates for care decisions.

From Theory to Practice:
Applying Ethical Principles and Concepts

Problems

As illustrated by the case of Mrs. F, many real-world ethical problems encountered in nursing homes do not fit neatly within the framework of familiar ethical principles. In fact, while anyone can ask ethical questions, the use of ethical principles and concepts in solving clinical problems often requires experience and skill. These principles and concepts provide a starting point for ethical thinking and analysis, but only a starting point. In fact, ethical principles are not intended to be applied as laws: "the principles . . . are only prima facie binding. None can be considered absolute. . . . principles and rules have to be weighed and balanced in situations of decision" (Childress 1994:79).

When weighing the merits of various care options, ethical principles may sometimes appear to be in conflict with one another. An elderly resident may have an advance directive that states that she "never" wants to be placed on a ventilator, but she may experience distressing air hunger (dyspnea) near the end of life. Should autonomy or beneficence be used to guide her care? In some instances, advance directives seem to create a tension between the "then person" (who completed the advance directive when competent) and the "now person" (who has dementia and needs care) (Nelson 1994a). As Ronald Dworkin asks, "Does a competent person's right to autonomy include . . . the power to dictate that life-prolonging treatments be denied him later, even if he, when demented, pleads for it?" (Dworkin 1986:4). This may easily be seen as a winner-take-all battle between autonomy and beneficence.

Some of the problems with ethical principles and concepts arise when we expect more practical help from them in clinical decision making than they can actually provide. To appreciate why this is so, we must first understand what these ethical principles and concepts are—and what they are not.

About Ethical Principles

The ethical principles and concepts that are familiar in American bioethics were conceived and nurtured in the world of acute care. They are based on an idealized interaction between physician and patient, a relationship that has boundaries and is somewhat insulated from concerns such as the needs of family, community, or society. In this model of autonomy, the patient provides or withholds consent for a surgical procedure or for participation in a study, acting as a free agent. The differences between autonomy in the acute-care setting, focused on decisions that are discrete in time and place, and autonomy in the family home or nursing home setting, which applies to ongoing conditions of daily living, as well as healthcare decisions, is well recognized (Carter 2002; Collopy, Boyle, and Jennings 1991; Fleming 2007; Hayley et al. 1996; Kuczewski 1999; Moody 1992)

The NASW Code of Ethics endorses "the right of clients to self-determination" in "selecting among care options" (National Association of Social Workers 2008). In acute-care settings, the application of this right is clear. A course of action must be selected, and in most instances a limited number of discrete options can be identified. The patient or surrogate can then exercise her right "to choose among all care options." Conversely, care options in the nursing home are more diffuse. They may be envisioned as continuously branching paths, with day-to-day care affected by the shifting priorities and preferences of residents, family members, and staff, as well as by institutional priorities and goals. Ultimately, nursing home care—and therefore nursing home ethics—is more about day-to-day issues such as dining, bathing, toileting, and treating chronic healthcare conditions than it is about major healthcare options such as the resident's resuscitation status (Collopy, Boyle, and Jennings 1991; Kane and Caplan 1990).

EVERYDAY ETHICS

In a family home, each family member is expected to behave in a manner that is consistent with the welfare of the entire family. The family constitutes an "intimate community" that the individual must accommodate, to some degree, in exchange for the security and nurturance of home. In the nursing home, the resident is part of another intimate community, albeit one that may not be of his or her own choosing. Thus, nursing home residents' autonomy may be constrained at several levels. First, residents' autonomy may be limited by the physical or cognitive impairments that made nursing home admission necessary. Second, nursing home residents are part of an intimate community; the needs and welfare of the rest of the community affect each resident's autonomy.

In the nursing home setting, as in the family home, decisions about basic day-to-day activities are commonplace, while decisions about major clinical options, such as choosing between specific courses of medical care, arise less frequently. Accordingly, consideration of autonomy in the nursing home should start with an examination of residents' roles in directing everyday mundane activities. Care must be exercised to protect the autonomy of dependent (and therefore vulnerable) residents. The ethical issues in the nursing home are the ethics of everyday matters, the ethics of the mundane (Caplan 1990, 1992; Collopy 1990; Kane et al. 1997; Moody 1992; Powers 2001): "The nursing home . . . presents a diffuse, ongoing, incremental flow of acceptance and refusal, acquiescence and noncooperation, negotiation and trial" (Collopy, Boyle, and Jennings 1991:9).

CULTURE AND ETHICS

Ethical principles and concepts are abstractions—like beauty or truth—that transcend cultural boundaries. However, specific ethical principles are given different weight or priority from community to community and from culture to culture. For example, Western and especially Euro-American culture gives high priority to personal autonomy. Respect for the right to self-determination in health care is rarely challenged. Other cultural traditions—both in the United States and internationally—emphasize the centrality of family or community welfare in decisions and give the family or community precedence over the rights of the individual. Nursing home residents and their families often reflect cultural traditions and assumptions in many ways, such as in preferences to guide their own care or to defer to their family in decision making.

Experience with the Extension of Autonomy

Although societal efforts to preserve and extend autonomy—advance directives, for example—are widespread, their effects have been uneven. Simply put, they do not always work.

ADVANCE DIRECTIVES

Elders, especially those with anticipated or progressive dependency, are now routinely encouraged to complete advance directives. The use of advance directives has increased, as has research documenting their limitations (Dresser 1994; Fagerlin and Schneider 2004; Goodman, Tarnoff, and Slotman 1998; Hardin and Yusufaly 2004; Reilly, Teasdale, and McCullough 1994; Teno 2004; Teno et al. 1997; Tonelli 1996; Watts 1992; Welie 2001). Even today, less than one in three adults has completed an advance directive (Ackerman 1997; Dresser 1994; Fagerlin and Schneider 2004; Holley et al. 1997), despite the official encouragement of their use implicit in the federal Patient Self-Determination Act (Mezey et al. 1997). When advance directives have been completed, they sometimes have a negligible effect on medical care (Goodman, Tarnoff, and Slotman 1998; Hanson et al. 1994; Hardin and Yusufaly 2004; Teno et al. 1997). And when advance directives do affect care, their power may still be less than anticipated: one study found that while advance directives were associated with decreased hospitalizations and expenses, they had no effect on family satisfaction with care or site of death (Molloy et al. 2000). Most of the criticism of advance directives applies specifically to "instructional directives," which are intended to guide or direct specific care decisions (Fagerlin and Schneider 2004; Tonelli 1996). Advance directives that identify surrogate decision makers, such as the durable power of attorney, have been found to be more useful (Dresser 1994; Fagerlin and Schneider 2004) and have been recommended by national healthcare and gerontology organizations, including the National Association of Social Workers.

There are several reasons why advance directives—particularly "instructional directives"—have not lived up to initial expectations. They have not been as widely accepted by patients as initially hoped: many people fail to complete them. Some patients find it difficult to describe their specific care preferences, both because their preferences vary from one clinical scenario to the next (Reilly, Teasdale, and McCullough 1994) and because future clinical scenarios are difficult to imagine. Others may want their families to make decisions because they prefer to have the interests of the family predominate. However, advance directives are not designed and are not sufficient to address "the important concerns of family members of dying patients" (Teno 2004:159). While many advance directives do focus on end-of-life care decisions (Ackerman 1997), this may have the unanticipated effect of limiting their usefulness as the approach of death is often difficult to anticipate, and "when living wills are applied to cases with uncertain prognoses, they can promote confusion, not autonomy " (Watts 1992:533).

SURROGACY AND SUBSTITUTED JUDGMENT

One of the principal arguments for advance directives—especially "instructional directives" or living wills—is that such documents support the exercise of substituted judgment. However, the accuracy of surrogates' decisions has been studied extensively (Ditto et al. 2001; Fagerlin et al. 2001; Hare, Pratt, and Nelson 1992; Houts et al. 2002; Layde et al. 1995; Meeker and Jezewski 2005; Pruchno et al. 2006; Seckler et al. 1991; Shalowitz, Garrett-Mayer, and Wendler 2006; Sulmasy et al. 1998). With or without living wills, the degree of alignment with the elder's wishes is generally poor (Cohen et al. 2005; Cook et al. 2001; Hardwig 1993; Layde et al. 1995; Suhl et al. 1994), often no better than what would be expected from chance alone (Gerety et al. 1993; Miura et al. 2006; Phipps et al. 2003; Suhl et al. 1994; Uhlmann, Pearlman, and Cain 1988). A review of sixteen studies concluded that overall, prior discussion of preferences does not improve accuracy (Shalowitz, Garrett-Mayer, and Wendler 2006), although one study did conclude that prior conversation was helpful (Sulmasy et al. 1998). Accuracy may improve when families are instructed to use substituted judgment instead of best interests in their decision making (Meeker and Jezewski 2005; Tomlinson et al. 1990)

Given the extensive evidence of problems with substituted judgment, it is not surprising that surrogacy in general and substituted judgment in particular have been extensively critiqued (Baergen 1995; Bailey 2002; Bramstedt 2003; Drane and Coulehan 1995; Kuczewski 2004; Vig et al. 2006; Welie 2001). One study found that surrogates' predictions of patients' preferences more closely resembled the surrogate's own treatment preferences than those of the patient (Fagerlin et al. 2001). Clearly, the characteristics of the surrogate may have an effect on substituted judgment decisions (Hardwig 1993; Pruchno et al. 2005, 2006; Sulmasy et al. 1998). Perhaps the strongest argument in favor of substituted judgment is that this is what residents want; we should understand substituted judgment as encompassing the will of the patient to have the judgment of the surrogate prevail (Veatch 2000). In this light, the surrogate's accuracy becomes less important. Surrogates should be assured that they are empowered, from the outset, to honor the autonomy of the resident insofar as possible, and that they may also incorporate the best interests of the resident and the family in decisions without betraying their roles as trusted advocates. This is, in fact, what we find that families do in practice (Elliott, Gessert, and Peden-McAlpine 2007)

Combining and Blending in Clinical Practice

At the bedside and in the nursing home, ethical principles are blended and combined. Transitions are gradual (Elliott, Gessert, and Peden-McAlpine 2007). When residents are able to speak competently for themselves, we rely upon autonomy. With advancing impairment, the voice of the resident is joined by the voice of the surrogate; the surrogate often serves to reinforce and defend the autonomy of the resident. Gradually, however, the surrogate's voice predominates. Many surrogates strive to use substituted judgment, especially initially, so as to extend the autonomy of the resident. However, substituted judgment can only go so far, and in practice surrogates use a blend of substituted judgment (autonomy) and best interests (beneficence) in making decisions. As the resident's impairment progresses, surrogates often find that they are obliged to make many decisions solely on the basis of the best interests of the resident. This change is largely unavoidable, as clinical issues late in life are difficult to anticipate ahead of time and accordingly the preferences of the resident may be unknown and unknowable. In many instances, families may use best interests to a greater degree than substituted judgment (Hirschman, Kapo, and Karlawish 2006), which helps to explain the "poor correlation" between the care options selected by patients and surrogates. When surrogates do blend substituted judgment and best interests (Kuczewski 2004; Meeker 2004), they should do so without qualms, guilt, or self-deprecation.

Ethics in the Nursing Home

What Is Autonomy in the Nursing Home?

The institutionalization of an elder often signals that his or her autonomy is diminished (Mattimore et al. 1997; Moody 1992). In many cases nursing home admission is justified as being in the best interests of the elder rather than honoring the autonomy of the elder. Accordingly, the use of autonomy as our dominant ethical principle in the care of institutionalized elders is often difficult and sometimes paradoxical (Agich 1990; Hickman 2004). Autonomy in long-term care settings is always constrained, either in regard to physical autonomy of movement and activity, in terms of self-determination in matters of daily living and health care, or, often, both (Agich 1990; Collopy, Boyle, and Jennings 1991; Collopy 1988, 1990; Hofland 1988, 1994; Hofland and David 1990; Jameton 1988; Moody 1988; Pullman 1999). Major challenges for nursing home residents include living with dependency, living in a residential community, and living with cognitive impairment.

LIVING WITH DEPENDENCY

In acute care settings such as hospitals and clinics, it is generally assumed that patients are free to exercise personal autonomy in their decisions. Infringements of autonomy caused by disability or dependency are assumed to be temporary and minimal and are generally justified by the prospect of return to full autonomy. However, in nursing homes, almost all residents are dependent on others (Collopy, Boyle, and Jennings 1991), often with permanent and progressive impairment. Nursing home residents "exhibit various kinds of dependencies and not the independence so prized by the traditional view of autonomy that stresses values of independence and rational free choice" (Agich 1990:12). Full acceptance that dependency in old age is natural and expected is needed so that we can find a balanced "creative use of dependency" that respects the elder's self (Collopy, Boyle, and Jennings 1991:13).

Clearly, dependency is a normal, expected part of the human experience: "dependency has a positive and proper place in the scheme of human life" (Collopy, Boyle, and Jennings, 1991:20). At the beginning of life, dependency is universal and unequivocal. In our aging society, more and more people are surviving well into their eighties, nineties, and beyond and experiencing a return to a degree of dependency in old age, and our culture's acceptance and accommodation of dependency late in life is improving. The fact is that if we are lucky enough to live a long life—if we do not die "prematurely" while vigorous—we should expect to experience a degree of dependency late in life. The domains that we control diminish as we near the end of life (Sullivan 2002). If fact, our mortality may serve as an object lesson in humility, teaching us that there are some things that we cannot control or subject to our autonomous wishes.

LIVING IN A RESIDENTIAL COMMUNITY

Dependency leads to intimate interaction with others, either in the family, in an institution, or in the community at large. Dependent elders need and usually are parts of communities, and their autonomy is constrained by the needs and welfare of those communities. In a residential facility such as a nursing home, residents' autonomy resembles that seen in a family home: "in . . . decisions about lifestyle and day-to-day living, [the patient] must share center stage with others. . . . the ethical principle of 'autonomy' gives way to 'accommodation'" (Dubler and Nimmons 1992:217).

Of course, the community that the elder enters upon admission to a nursing home differs from the "community" of a family home in many respects. The nursing home is usually a community of strangers. In the nursing home, the resident's autonomy—in regard to privacy, control over schedule, personal preferences, and day-to-day life—is constricted in much the same way that it is in a family home, but with important differences. In the nursing home, the incursions upon the elder's autonomy are less likely to be flexible, negotiable, or subject to exceptions. Nursing home staffing problems, such as high turnover rates and absenteeism, may compound the problem: staff may have limited time—or limited interest—in negotiating with individual residents. Living in a nursing home may mean sharing a room, losing control of one's personal possessions, and suffering routine violations of personal modesty and privacy, none of which were part of life before institutionalization.

LIVING WITH COGNITIVE IMPAIRMENT

Cognitive impairment may be both a cause and a consequence of admission to a nursing home, as institutionalization "can have an adverse effect on competency" (Caplan 1992). Many social workers—especially those working in nursing homes—become familiar with clients with cognitive impairment (Goldstein and Tye 1987; Gwyther 1998) and with the effects of cognitive impairment on autonomy (Moody 1992).

For many nursing home residents, especially those with Alzheimer's disease, cognitive impairment is slowly progressive (Jecker 1990; Moody 1992). A nontechnical (commonsense) approach to determining decisional capacity is often appropriate (Collopy, Boyle, and Jennings 1991); decision-making capacity should be determined on a decision-by-decision basis. Ethicists tend to focus on " 'decision-specific capacity': does this patient have enough ability at this time, given these circumstances, to make this decision?" (Dubler and Nimmons 1992:120–21). In one study, 92 percent of mild-to-moderate Alzheimer's patients indicated that they would participate in decisions, and most family members agreed (Hirschman et al. 2005). A degree of self-determination clearly may be maintained in the context of dementia (Dworkin 1986), but care providers must be careful to assure that the impaired elder has an adequate understanding of the decision at hand (Jefferson et al. 2008).

Nursing home residents who have irreversible and progressive cognitive impairment are often eligible for hospice benefits. However, they tend to be underrepresented in hospice programs. Physicians may be reluctant— or unable—to determine when residents are eligible for hospice, and many families do not consider advanced cognitive impairment to be a terminal condition (Gessert, Forbes, and Bern-Klug 2001; Lamberg, Person, and Kiely 2005). While aggressive medical interventions are sometimes withheld in patients with dementia (Hanson et al. 1994), this is not enough. Nursing homes should work with residents, families, and staff to plan for the progression of cognitive impairment and to develop care plans that emphasize palliative care. Application for hospice benefits when residents become eligible should become more routine.

The elder with dementia may be seen as having a special claim on our protection, in much the same way that the dependent infant has a special claim. This claim is based on our respect for personal dignity and our interest in preserving dignity throughout the course of life (Kuczewski 1999); it is not primarily based on autonomy rights.

What Do Elders Want?

Whenever possible, ethical decision making in the nursing home should be guided by what elders want. In two broad areas—desire for self-determination and desire for curative care—institutionalized elders' preferences differ from those that are familiar in acute care settings.

WHO SHOULD GUIDE CARE?

Some elders may prefer to have family members involved in care decisions so that the welfare of the family can be considered (Puchalski et al. 2000; Sehgal et al. 1992). Many elders find decision making burdensome, especially in the context of fatigue and impairment, and prefer to have others—family members or professionals—shoulder the responsibility for difficult decisions (Bradley, Zia, and Hamilton 1996; Nolan et al. 2005; Puchalski et al. 2000; Sehgal et al. 1992; Sulmasy et al. 2007; Terry et al. 1999). Some elders do not feel that end-of-life decisions are in their hands in any event (Kelner 1995). In a study of decision-making scenarios, elders preferred those that incorporated best-interests judgments either as the sole standard or, more commonly, in combination with substituted judgment (Moore et al. 2003). Another study found that some elders complete advance directives principally to decrease the impact of decision-making burdens on their families (Seymour et al. 2004). The preferences of nursing home residents for who will make care decisions should be assessed on a case-by-case basis.

WHAT CARE IS PREFERRED?

Most people tend to favor medical interventions when the burden is smaller, the benefit is greater, and a good outcome is more likely (Fried and Bradley 2003; Fried et al. 2002; Houts et al. 2002; Kelner 1995). However, poorer health and worse prognoses are associated with lower desire for medical interventions (Gerety et al. 1993); elders want fewer and less aggressive interventions as prognosis worsens (Mezey et al. 1996; Michelson et al. 1991; Monturo and Strumpf 2007; Murphy et al. 1994; Murphy and Santilli 1998; Phillips et al. 1996; Reilly, Teasdale, and McCullough 1994; Suhl et al. 1994). Treatment preferences in dementia follow much the same pattern (Dworkin 1986; Gjerdingen et al. 1999; Gwyther 1997; Nolan et al. 2005). When considering the care that they would want if they developed dementia, elders tend to emphasize their social goals rather than their desire for curative care (Gwyther 1997), and many are comfortable deferring to others' judgments regarding care (Nolan et al. 2005). Desire for aggressive medical treatment in dementia decreases as severity increases (Gjerdingen et al. 1999). Elders' preferences tend to vary from one scenario to another (Reilly, Teasdale, and McCullough 1994), which helps to explain why advance directives are sometimes difficult for elders to complete and for surrogates to implement. Elders may have less aversion to forgoing treatment than their family members do because of the lower death anxiety of elders.

Families and Surrogacy

Families' roles in the care of nursing home residents range from daily involvement in physical care and close partnership with staff to distant or absent roles and families who regard nursing home staff as adversaries. Working with families is central to social work: "sometimes families function as a kind of extended client, to the point that the resident's interests and preferences are submerged by the family's wishes" (Collopy, Boyle, and Jennings 1991).

The involvement of family means that a spectrum of needs, priorities, and agendas are likely to influence care decisions. The autonomy of the elder is affected by the needs of the family, both before and after nursing home admission. In some instances, honoring the autonomy of elders means deferring to their wishes to have the priorities of the family come first. This creates the complex and perhaps ironic situation where, in order to "ensure that the interests of the patient, and not the interests of the caregivers or the caregiving institution, come first," (Collopy, Boyle, and Jennings 1991) nursing home staff may be called upon to urge families to make decisions that reflect their own best interests, so as to honor the wishes of the elder.

ROLES

Families are central to decision making on behalf of impaired elders (Levin et al. 1999; Levine and Zuckerman 1999; Lewis et al. 2000; Nelson 1995; Puchalski et al. 2000) both because of the gradual, incremental nature of their "progressive surrogacy" (High and Rowles 1995) and because they are most likely to have the necessary "biographical expertise" (Bowers 1988) to make personal decisions. The retention of decision-making authority within the family is broadly embraced by society: "the dependencies of frailty, like those of childhood, are best sheltered and supported in the 'close' of the family" (Collopy, Boyle, and Jennings 1991). Most families want to be involved and to accept responsibility (Meeker and Jezewski 2005); they embrace their roles as advocates for their elders (Kellett 1999; Meeker 2004; Nelson 1994b)

Family decision-making responsibilities generally increase as residents' impairment progresses. Family involvement in decision making often serves to extend the elder's autonomy (Jecker 1990; Kuczewski 1996; Levine and Zuckerman 1999). However, the principal justification for family involvement in decision making is that it is what elders want: "many patients are content or even anxious to delegate decisions to their families, often because they care less what decisions are made than that they are made by people they trust" (Fagerlin and Schneider 2004). Families may be envisioned as a source of meaning, as a key to the elder's core identity (Levine and Zuckerman 1999; Nelson 1994b; Nelson 1995)

Most elders do not want to be institutionalized (Mattimore et al. 1997), and institutionalization is often the option of last resort. Institutionalization has been found to be associated with a range of factors, including family conflict, length of care giving, low family efficiency, and family need for socioemotional support (Fisher and Lieberman 1999; Freedman 1996; Freedman et al. 1994; Gaugler et al. 2000; Gaugler, Zarit, and Pearlin 1999; Nielsen et al. 1996). Of course, some residents are integral members of large, close families that continue to be concerned about and involved with ongoing care throughout the nursing home residency, while others may be the sole surviving members of their families or may be distant—emotionally or geographically—from their closest relatives.

PRESSURES ON THE FAMILY

Many families find significant meaning in their roles in providing ongoing care for relatives after nursing home admission (Elliott, Gessert, and Peden-McAlpine 2007; Kellett 1998); some also find their roles to be stressful and emotionally charged (Bern-Klug 2008). For social workers, in most instances "the client" includes both the resident and the family.

The emotional climate for families of nursing home residents is complex. The nursing home admission may engender a sense of relief, both because of the additional care their elder will receive and because he or she will be in a safe environment (Bern-Klug 2008). However, many families may also experience self-reproach and guilt if they feel that they have failed to meet their own or their elder's expectations for care in the family home. Many families feel a strong sense of duty to their elders (Nelson 1998), and such families may delay admission as long as possible and then feel that they have "abandoned" their relatives to institutional care (Bern-Klug 2008; Collopy, Boyle, and Jennings 1991; Drysdale, Nelson, and Wineman 1993).

Many families find decision making on behalf of their relatives stressful (Bern-Klug 2008; Elliott, Gessert, and Peden-McAlpine 2007; Forbes, Bern-Klug, and Gessert 2000; Hansen, Archbold, and Stewart 2004; Meeker 2004; Powell 1999; Pratt et al. 1987; Terry et al. 1999). The stress may arise from or be exacerbated by several factors, including the difficulty of knowing or imagining what the elder would want, lack of familiarity with end-of-life care, and lack of support from other family members and professional staff (Bern-Klug 2008). Conflict in care-giving families is widely recognized (Bern-Klug 2008; Gwyther 1995; Nelson 1998; Semple 1992), and decision-making responsibilities may aggravate dysfunctional relationships within the family. Underlying fault lines within the family, long-standing disagreements, or old grievances may be brought to light by the pressures of care-giving responsibilities.

Good communication between professional staff and families may alleviate some of the decision-making pressures on families. In nursing homes, families and staff are often "witnesses" rather than actors; they may have little control over the progression of residents' impairment, especially as death approaches. However, in communicating with families about residents' changing conditions—especially when impairment is progressing—professional staff may ask for or inadvertently create the sense that "decisions" are needed when there is little to decide. Those who are inexperienced with end-of-life care—including most families—may be alarmed by the deterioration of the residents' health and may feel that the nursing home staff should "do something." With this susceptibility in mind, when nursing home staff inform families about changes in residents' conditions, they should be careful to acknowledge the clinical course that is expected in light of the elders' diagnoses. In this way, it may be possible to avoid confronting families with the sense that they need to take action when no action will benefit the resident. For example, cardiopulmonary resuscitation is rarely successful following unwitnessed cardiac arrests of nursing home residents. Asking families if they want their relatives to be resuscitated under such circumstances may be misleading. Acknowledging the limited role that families and staff have in controlling some clinical outcomes may diminish attendant anxiety and guilt. Conversely, families may be uncomfortable with their care-giving responsibilities (Montello and Lantos 2002) if they feel that their decisions are hastening or contributing to the death of their relative (Bern-Klug 2008; Forbes, Bern-Klug, and Gessert 2000).

As death approaches, families may agonize over the progression of symptoms that are routine to those more familiar with death. Younger family members tend to be more uneasy with the approach of death than the elders themselves (de Vries, Bluck, and Birren, 1993), and family members may project their own values and fears onto the elder. For some, the most disturbing aspect of death is not personal mortality but the loss of someone they are close to: "death, for many people, is neither an abstract, generalized thought, nor concern for personal demise; rather, it is the actual or threatened loss of a significant person" (Kastenbaum and Costa 1977:243; quoted in de Vries, Bluck, and Birren 1993:371;). Among elders, death anxiety may be yet lower in those who are satisfied with their lives, such as those who have completed satisfactory life reviews (Fishman 1992).

Admission to a nursing home is often precipitated by the exhaustion of family care-giving resources, as much or more than by the increasing dependency of the elder. Many relatives of nursing home residents are dealing with multiple issues outside of the nursing home (Bern-Klug 2008), including health, family, and financial crises. In fact, nursing home staff should not assume that all families are solely or even primarily concerned about the resident's welfare. Family members may be weighing other considerations, including their own financial interests or those of other members of the family. Such financial considerations may provide incentives for sustaining or withholding care.

In light of these pressures, it is not surprising that many families struggle with the difficult judgments that they are called to make on behalf of their relatives. Indeed, work with families is often the principal venue for the identification and resolution of ethical issues in the nursing home.

"Preventive Ethics" in the Nursing Home

In most nursing homes, social workers have two broad roles: working with individual residents and their families, and working to improve the institutional environment. In both of these roles, social workers have opportunities to avert ethical problems before they arise; they can practice "preventive ethics" (McCullough et al. 1995).

Building Relationships with Residents and Families

Nursing home social workers should encourage residents and families to view their nursing home experiences holistically, with an eye to anticipating and preventing situations that lead to ethical problems. Two characteristics of nursing home life are particularly important in this regard. First, for many elders, the nursing home is their final home. Even if the resident is not severely impaired at admission, in time disability and dependency are likely to increase. Residents, families, and staff should plan for progressive impairment. Second, progressive impairment—physical and especially cognitive—leads to increasing reliance on surrogate decision makers. Accordingly, surrogates should be identified early and should be involved in care-planning discussions throughout the elder's stay in the nursing home, starting at the time of admission, even if their input in care decisions is not vital initially.

The routine involvement of surrogates in care decisions is one of the keys to avoiding ethical problems. Regular, respectful communication fosters trust and helps to identify small issues before they become big issues. Ongoing involvement of the family after admission may also contribute to the family's resolution of feelings and ambivalence regarding nursing home placement (Kellett 1998). Families tend to assess quality of care in terms of the "social and emotional" care provided to their relatives (Duncan and Morgan 1994) and to value good communication with staff. Most important, when family members or other surrogates are involved in care, they remain abreast of changes in the resident's condition and changes in the goals of care. Family members who have not been regularly involved may react with dismay when suddenly confronted with end-of-life decisions. The "daughter from California Syndrome" described by Molloy and colleagues—in which a family member appears and disrupts care management by demanding inappropriate aggressive care—illustrates the importance of routine communication with families (Molloy et al. 1991).

Surrogates should be encouraged to participate in staff care conferences, either in person or by telephone. Surrogates should be asked to discuss goals of care, thereby providing the staff with an opportunity to monitor surrogates' decision-making processes (Kuczewski 1999). The frequency and level of family engagement is important; lower levels of "daily contact" with relatives and family have been found to be associated with less documentation of planning, such as do-not-resuscitate orders (Mark et al. 1995). Care conferences may also be used to engage families in individualizing residents' day-to-day routines wherever possible, which may significantly improve residents' quality of life.

In many nursing homes, social workers have key roles in advance care planning (Lacey 2006; Morrison et al. 2005; Osman and Perlin 1994). The development of written advance directives is an important product of advance care planning (Schonwetter et al. 1996; Seymour et al. 2004), but the completion of an advance directive does not signal that the planning is "done." In many instances, residents' conditions progress in ways that were not anticipated, and advance directives must be reexamined and reinterpreted. In all cases, advance care planning should be seen as an ongoing process that is revisited regularly. The nursing home team may choose to devote a portion of care conferences with surrogates to reviewing plans and to thinking ahead, exploring "what if" scenarios to identify the preferred balance between rehabilitative and palliative goals in light of advancing impairment. For example, in residents with progressive dementia, questions about artificial nutrition and hydration (Pasman et al. 2004) are common, as are questions about how aggressively to treat infections like pneumonia (Schwaber and Carmeli 2008). Discussion of such issues will help to prepare surrogates to be effective advocates for the resident when they discuss these matters with the physician.

Interactions between residents' families and nursing home staff intensify as death approaches. While most people who work or live in nursing homes are familiar with death (Munn et al. 2008), many families would benefit from help navigating their journey through the dying experience (Remsen 1993; Reynolds et al. 2002). Focus groups of family caregivers found that "few family members expressed a sense of normalcy regarding dying in long-term care" (Munn et al. 2008).

Family members may feel the need to "do something," but may not be aware that medical interventions that benefit younger, more robust individuals—such as hospitalizations, ICU admissions, feeding tubes, ventilators, and cardiopulmonary resuscitation—generally are not beneficial near the end of life and may be burdensome. In fact, aggressive care should be limited or stopped altogether for many residents as death approaches. Family members often need help in envisioning opportunities for care giving within the context of the resident's palliative-care plan.

Families should be encouraged to reexamine the goals of care with staff as the resident declines, emphasizing that a good death is generally characterized by "comfort, dignity, and closure" (Munn et al. 2008). Experienced staff may be able to direct families' attention to the death of the person rather than the death of the body: "The emotional process of dying is almost wholly nonmedical, pertaining to incorporeal concerns. It is fundamentally a story about a person" (Kiernan 2006). Families should be assisted in directing their energy to aspects of care that they can affect, such as assuring the presence of the family at the bedside, good communication within the family, and attention to the known wishes of the resident. Families should be provided with privacy and invited to conduct services or rituals of their choosing and to attend to the aesthetics of care: family presence, silence, comfort, and dignity.

The family's need for support does not end with the death of the resident. Families often benefit from discussing the death. Such conversations are likely to help the family process the death and integrate it into their lives and to provide valuable feedback on the support that they received. The social worker should offer to connect families with bereavement resources.

Changing the Culture of the Nursing Home

Work with individual residents and families should be complemented by efforts to assure that institutional policies support the practice of "preventive ethics." In fact, the degree to which the nursing home embraces preventive ethics goes a long way toward determining whether ethical dilemmas are commonplace or unusual and whether the nursing home social worker's role is frustrating or gratifying. Building and supporting a preventive-ethics culture in a nursing home often starts with an assessment of the ethics resources available in the area; such resources vary widely from location to location. Every state has a long-term-care ombudsman program that can direct the social worker to long-term-care-ethics resources. Larger hospitals are likely to have ethics committees, which also can be a valuable resource. Pioneer Network (www.pioneernetwork.net) is a national organization that can refer the social worker to informal state or regional networks that are committed to long-term-care ethics. University- and community-based ethics organizations and initiatives may also be a resource. Embracing preventive ethics means making a commitment to providing services that meet the needs of residents and families in a way that anticipates and prevents ethical conflict. Key principles of preventive ethics—such as the ongoing involvement of families in advance care planning—are easiest to implement if they are understood to be integral to the institution's care culture. When fully integrated into the nursing home, the commitment to preventive ethics is reflected in the institution's mission, marketing, personnel policies and day-to-day work with clients, and it will affect both internal policies and external relationships.

In many institutions, the implementation of a preventive-ethics approach hinges on attitudes toward dying and death. Acknowledging that death is an integral and expected part of the human experience opens the door to engaging in more meaningful advanced care planning with residents and families and thereby anticipating and preventing many conflicts. Accepting that death is part of the nursing home experience may also lead to the development of new services. The nursing home may find that it needs to strengthen its capacity to deliver palliative care (Hanson and Ersek 2006; Reynolds et al. 2002; Zerzan, Stearns, and Hanson 2000) perhaps with the assistance of an established palliative care team. The circumstances under which cardiopulmonary resuscitation will be initiated should be reviewed (Ditillo 2002; Gordon 1994, 1995; Murphy 1988; Silverman 1992; Tresch and Thakur 1998; Zweig 1997), as an unwitnessed cardiopulmonary arrest of an elder with advancing chronic illness should not automatically be considered an indication for resuscitation (Finucane 1995). Residents and families should be fully informed about palliative-care and resuscitation policies and options at the time of admission and at family care conferences.

The interface between the nursing home and the hospital deserves special attention as this is where the hard work of building a cogent and ethically sound advance care plan can get derailed. Nursing home staff should not assume that goals of care established in the nursing home will be recognized or honored in the hospital unless an understanding between the institutions has been established. The nursing home should strive to develop policies that limit hospitalizations, whenever possible, for common conditions such as pneumonia and for routine end-of-life care (Fried, Gillick, and Lipsitz 1995; Ouslander, Weinberg, and Phillips 2000) and to develop partnerships with local hospitals to honor established goals of care when hospitalizations are necessary.

Nursing homes should assure that residents have timely access to hospice services, either by developing an internal service or an external relationship with a hospice care provider (Buckingham 1983; Gozalo and Miller 2007; Keay and Schonwetter 2000; Miller 2004; Miller, Gozalo, and Mor 2001; Miller and Mor 2004; Miller et al. 1998; Parker-Oliver and Bickel 2002; Parker-Oliver et al. 2003; Zerzan, Stearns, and Hanson 2000). The development of hospice programs in nursing homes has been found to improve end-of-life experience for all residents, not just those enrolled in hospice (Miller, Gozalo, and Mor 2001). Staff should be trained to recognize terminal decline so as to facilitate timely referral to hospice (Welch et al. 2008).

Of course, not all ethical problems can be anticipated and prevented. Nursing homes should assure that staff have access to ethics consultations when needed. Ethics consultation resources can be either internal (Fleming 2007) or external and may involve staff training, the development of ethics committees (Hogstel et al. 2004), or conducting regular ethics rounds (Libow et al. 1992).

Conclusion: The Nursing Home Opportunity

The nursing home presents a rich environment for the social worker to improve end-of-life care and to do so in an ethically sound and satisfying manner. Social workers in nursing homes should strive to develop expertise and comfort—through experience—in assessing and resolving the ethical problems that arise routinely in nursing homes. The key is to appreciate that many familiar bioethical tools were developed in and work best in acute care settings, where they may be applied to specific events and decisions. These tools must be reconceived or adapted for use in the residential setting, where basic issues of day-to-day life are likely to loom larger than major care decisions. In this context, the autonomy of residents may be understood to be restricted but all the more precious because of its fragility and attenuation. Social workers are challenged to work with residents, families, and nursing home administrators to protect, preserve, and extend resident autonomy insofar as possible and to work with the family in promoting the best interests of the resident thereafter, including dignified end-of-life care.

References

Abbo, E. D., S. Sobotka, and D. O. Meltzer. 2008. "Patient Preferences in Instructional Advance Directives." *Journal of Palliative Medicine* 11 (4): 555–62.

Ackerman, T. F. 1997. "Forsaking the Spirit for the Letter of Law: Advance Directives in Nursing Homes." *Journal of the American Geriatrics Society* 45 (1): 114–16.

Agich, G. J. 1990. "Reassessing Autonomy in Long-Term Care." *Hastings Center Report* 20 (6): 12–17.

Baergen, R. 1995. "Revising the Substituted Judgment Standard." *Journal of Clinical Ethics* 6 (1): 30–38.

Bailey, S. 2002. "Decision Making in Health Care: Limitations of the Substituted Judgement Principle." *Nursing Ethics* 9 (5): 483–93.

Beauchamp, T. L., and J. F. Childress. 1989. *Principles of Biomedical Ethics*. 3rd ed. New York: Oxford University Press.

Bern-Klug, M. 2008. "The Emotional Context Facing Nursing Home Residents' Families: A Call for Role Reinforcement Strategies from Nursing Homes and the Community." *Journal of the American Medical Directors Association* 9 (1):36–44.

Bowers, B. J. 1988. "Family Perceptions of Care in a Nursing Home." *Gerontologist* 28 (3): 361–68.

Bradley, J. G., M. J. Zia, and N. Hamilton. 1996. "Patient Preferences for Control in Medical Decision Making: A Scenario-Based Approach." *Family Medicine* 28 (7): 496–501.

Bramstedt, K. A. 2003. "Questioning the Decision-Making Capacity of Surrogates." *Internal Medicine Journal* 33 (5–6):257–59.

Buckingham, R. W. 1983. "Hospice in a Long-Term Care Facility: An Innovative Pattern of Care." *Journal of Long Term Care Administration* 11 (1): 10–14.

Caplan, A. L. 1990. "The Morality of the Mundane: Ethical Issues Arising in the Daily Lives of Nursing Home Residents." In *Everyday Ethics: Resolving Dilemmas in Nursing Home Life*, ed. R. A. Kane and A. L. Caplan, 37–50. New York: Springer.

Caplan, A. L. 1992. *If I Were A Rich Man Could I Buy a Pancreas? And Other Essays on the Ethics of Health Care*. Bloomington: Indiana University Press.

Carter, M. W. 2002. "Advancing an Ethical Framework for Long-Term Care. *Journal of Aging Studies* 16 (1):57–71.

Childress, J. F. 1994. "Principles-Oriented Bioethics: An Analysis and Assessment from Within." In *A Matter of Principles? Ferment in U.S. Bioethics*, ed. E. R. DuBose, R. Hamel and L. J. O'Connell, 72–98. Valley Forge, Penn.: Trinity Press International.

Cohen, S., C. Sprung, P. Sjokvist, A. Lippert, B. Ricou, and M. Baras, et al. 2005. "Communication of End-of-Life Decisions in European Intensive Care Units." *Intensive Care Medicine* 31 (9): 1215–21.

Collopy, B. J. 1988. "Autonomy in Long Term Care: Some Crucial Distinctions. *Gerontologist* 28 (Suppl.): 10–17.

Collopy, B. J. 1990. "Ethical Dimensions of Autonomy in Long-Term Care." *Generations* 14 (Suppl.): 9–12.

Collopy, B., P. Boyle, and B. Jennings. 1991. "New Directions in Nursing Home Ethics." *Hastings Center Report* 21 (Suppl. 2): 1–15.

Cook, D. J., G. Guyatt, G. Rocker, P. Sjokvist, B. Weaver, P. Dodek, et al. 2001. "Cardiopulmonary Resuscitation Directives on Admission to Intensive Care Unit: An International Observational Study." *Lancet* 358 (9297):1941–45.

De Vries, B., S. Bluck, and J. E. Birren. 1993. "The Understanding of Death and Dying in a Life-Span Perspective." *Gerontologist* 33 (3): 366–72.

Ditillo, B. 2002. "Should There Be a Choice for Cardiopulmonary Resuscitation When Death Is Expected? Revisiting an Old Idea Whose Time Is Yet to Come." *Journal of Palliative Medicine* 5 (1): 107–16.

Ditto, P. H., J. H. Danks, J. H., W. D. Smucker, J. Bookwala, K. M. Coppola, R. Dresser, et al. 2001. "Advance Directives as Acts of Communication: A Randomized Controlled Trial." *Archives of Internal Medicine* 161 (3): 421–30.

Drane, J. F., and J. L. Coulehan. 1995. "The Best-Interest Standard: Surrogate Decision Making and Quality of Life. *Journal of Clinical Ethics* 6 (1): 20–29.

Dresser, R. 1994. "Confronting the 'Near Irrelevance' of Advance Directives." *Journal of Clinical Ethics* 5 (1): 55–56.

Drysdale, A. E., C. F. Nelson, and N. M. Wineman. 1993. "Families Need Help Too: Group Treatment for Families of Nursing Home Residents." *Clinical Nurse Specialist* 7 (3): 130–34.

Dubler, N., and D. Nimmons. 1992. *Ethics on Call: A Medical Ethicist Shows How to Take Charge of Life-and-Death Choices.* New York: Harmony Books.

DuBose, E. R., R. Hamel, and L. J. O'Connell, eds. 1994. *A Matter of Principles: Ferment in U.S. Bioethics.* Valley Forge, Penn.: Trinity Press International.

Duncan, M. T., and D. L. Morgan. 1994. "Sharing the Caring: Family Caregivers' Views of Their Relationships with Nursing Home Staff." *Gerontologist* 34 (2): 235–44.

Dworkin, R. 1986. "Autonomy and the Demented Self." *Milbank Quarterly* 64 (Suppl. 2): 4–16.

Elliott, B. A., C. E. Gessert, and C. Peden-McAlpine. 2007. "Decision Making on Behalf of Elders with Advanced Cognitive Impairment: Family Transitions." *Alzheimer Disease and Associated Disorders* 21 (1): 49–54.

Fagerlin, A., P. H. Ditto, J. H. Danks, and R. M. Houts. 2001. "Projection in Surrogate Decisions About Life-Sustaining Medical Treatments." *Health Psychology* 20 (3): 166–75.

Fagerlin, A., and C. E. Schneider. 2004. "Enough: The Failure of the Living Will." *Hastings Center Report* 34 (2): 30–42.

Finucane, T. E. 1995. "Attempted Resuscitation in Nursing Homes: So How Should We Presume?" *Journal of the American Geriatrics Society* 43 (5):587–88.

Fisher, L., and M. A. Lieberman. 1999. "A Longitudinal Study of Predictors of Nursing Home Placement for Patients with Dementia: The Contribution of Family Characteristics." *Gerontologist* 39 (6): 677–86.

Fishman, S. 1992. "Relationships Among an Older Adult's Life Review, Ego Integrity, and Death Anxiety." *International Psychogeriatrics* 4 (Suppl. 2): 267–77.

Fleming, D. A. 2007. "Responding to Ethical Dilemma in Nursing Homes: Do We Always Need an 'Ethicist'?" *HEC Forum* 19 (3): 245–59.

Forbes, S., M. Bern-Klug, and C. Gessert. 2000. "End-of-Life Decision Making for Nursing Home Residents with Dementia." *Journal of Nursing Scholarship* 32 (3): 251–58.

Freedman, V. A. 1996. "Family Structure and the Risk of Nursing Home Admission." *Journal of Gerontology: Social Sciences* 51B (2): S61–S69.

Freedman, V. A., L. F. Berkman, S. R. Rapp, and A. M. Ostfeld. 1994. "Family Networks: Predictors of Nursing Home Entry." *American Journal of Public Health* 84 (5): 843–45.

Fried, T. R., and E. H. Bradley. 2003. "What Matters to Seriously Ill Older Persons Making End-of-Life Treatment Decisions? A Qualitative Study." *Journal of Palliative Medicine* 6 (2): 237–44.

Fried, T. R., E. H. Bradley, V. R. Towle, and H. Allore. 2002. "Understanding the Treatment Preferences of Seriously Ill Patients." *New England Journal of Medicine* 346 (14): 1061–66.

Fried, T. R., M. R. Gillick, and L. A. Lipsitz. 1995. "Whether to Transfer? Factors Associated with Hospitalization and Outcome of Elderly Long-Term Care Patients with Pneumonia." *Journal of General Internal Medicine* 10 (5):246–50.

Gaugler, J. E., A. B. Edwards, E. E. Femia, S. H. Zarit, M.-A. P. Stephens, A. Townsend, et al. 2000. "Predictors of Institutionalization of Cognitively Impaired Elders: Family Help and the Timing of Placement." *Journal of Gerontology: Psychological Sciences* 55B (4): P247–P255.

Gaugler, J. E., S. H. Zarit, and L. I. Pearlin. 1999. "Caregiving and Institutionalization: Perceptions of Family Conflict and Socioemotional Support." *International Journal of Aging and Human Development* 49 (1): 1–25.

Gerety, M. B., L. K. Chiodo, D. N. Kanten, M. R. Tuley, and J. E. Cornell. 1993. "Medical Treatment Preferences of Nursing Home Residents: Relationship to Function and Concordance with Surrogate Decision-Makers." *Journal of the American Geriatrics Society* 41 (9): 953–60.

Gessert, C. E. 2008. "The Problem with Autonomy." *Minnesota Medicine* 91 (4): 40–42.

Gessert, C. E., S. Forbes, and M. Bern-Klug. 2001. "Planning End-of-Life Care for Patients with Dementia: Roles of Families and Health Professionals." *Omega* 42 (4): 273–91.

Gjerdingen, D. K., J. A. Neff, M. Wang, and K. Chaloner. 1999. "Older Persons' Opinions About Life-Sustaining Procedures in the Face of Dementia." *Archives of Family Medicine* 8 (5):421–25.

Goldstein, R., and S. Tye. 1987. "Social Work Management of the Alzheimer's Patient: Who Needs What Support?" *Mount Sinai Journal of Medicine* 51 (1): 86–92.

Goodman, M. D., M. Tarnoff, and G. J. Slotman. 1998. "Effect of Advance Directives on the Management of Elderly Critically Ill Patients." *Critical Care Medicine* 26 (4): 701–4.

Gordon, M. 1994. "Cardiopulmonary Resuscitation in the Elderly Long-Term Care Population: Time to Reconsider." *Annals of the Royal College of Physicians and Surgeons of Canada* 27 (1): 81–83.

Gordon, M. 1995. "Should We Provide Cardiopulmonary Resuscitation to Elderly Patients in Long-Term Care?" *Cardiology in the Elderly* 3 (1):53–57.

Gozalo, P. L., and S. C. Miller. 2007. "Hospice Enrollment and Evaluation of Its Causal Effect on Hospitalization of Dying Nursing Home Patients." *Health Services Research* 42 (2): 587–610.

Gwyther, L. P. 1995. "When 'the Family' Is Not One Voice: Conflict in Caregiving Families." *Journal of Case Management* 4 (4): 150–55.

Gwyther, L. P. 1997. "The Perspective of the Person with Alzheimer Disease: Which Outcomes Matter in Early to Middle Stages of Dementia?" *Alzheimer Disease and Associated Disorders* 11 (Suppl. 6): 18–24.

Gwyther, L. P. 1998. "Social Issues of the Alzheimer's Patient and Family." *American Journal of Medicine* 104 (4A): 17S–21S.

Hansen, L., P. G. Archbold, and B. J. Stewart. 2004. "Role Strain and Ease in Decision-Making to Withdraw or Withhold Life Support for Elderly Relatives." *Journal of Nursing Scholarship* 36 (3): 233–38.

Hanson, L. C., M. Danis, E. Mutran, and N. L. Keenan. 1994. "Impact of Patient Incompetence on Decisions to Use or Withhold Life-Sustaining Treatment." *American Journal of Medicine* 97 (3): 235–41.

Hanson, L. C., and M. Ersek. 2006. "Meeting Palliative Care Needs in Post-Acute Care Settings: 'To Help Them Live Until They Die.'" *Journal of the American Medical Association* 295 (6): 681–86.

Hardin, S. B., and Y. A. Yusufaly. 2004. "Difficult End-of-Life Treatment Decisions: Do Other Factors Trump Advance Directives?" *Archives of Internal Medicine* 164 (14):1531–33.

Hardwig, J. 1993. "The Problem of Proxies with Interests of Their Own: Toward a Better Theory of Proxy Decisions." *Journal of Clinical Ethics* 4 (1): 20–27.

Hare, J., C. Pratt, and C. Nelson. 1992. "Agreement Between Patients and Their Self-Selected Surrogates on Difficult Medical Decisions." *Archives of Internal Medicine* 152 (5):1049–54.

Hayley, D. C., C. K. Cassel, L. Snyder, and M. A. Rudberg. 1996. "Ethical and Legal Issues in Nursing Home Care." *Archives of Internal Medicine* 156: 249–56.

Hickman, S. E. 2004. "Honoring Resident Autonomy in Long-Term Care: Special Considerations." *Journal of Psychosocial Nursing* 42 (1): 12–16.

High, D. M. 1988. "All in the Family: Extended Autonomy and Expectations in Surrogate Health Care Decision-Making." *Gerontologist* 28 (Suppl.): 46–51.

High, D. M., and Rowles, G. D. 1995. "Nursing Home Residents, Families, and Decision Making: Toward an Understanding of Progressive Surrogacy." *Journal of Aging Studies* 9 (2): 101–17.

Hirschman, K. B., C. M. Joyce, B. D. James, S. X. Xie, and J. H. T. Karlawish. 2005. "Do Alzheimer's Disease Patients Want to Participate in a Treatment Decision, and Would Their Caregivers Let Them?" *Gerontologist* 45 (3): 381–88.

Hirschman, K. B., J. M. Kapo, and J. H. T. Karlawish. 2006. "Why Doesn't a Family Member of a Person with Advanced Dementia Use a Substituted Judgment When Making a Decision for That Person?" *American Journal of Geriatric Psychiatry* 14 (8): 659–67.

Hofland, B. F. 1988. "Autonomy in Long Term Care: Background Issues and a Programmatic Response." *Gerontologist* 28 (Suppl.): 3–9.

Hofland, B. F. 1994. "When Capacity Fades and Autonomy Is Constricted: A Client-Centered Approach to Residential Care." *Generations* 18 (4): 31–35.

Hofland, B. F., and D. David. 1990. "Autonomy and Long-Term-Care Practice: Conclusions and Next Steps." *Generations* 14 (Suppl.): 91–94.

Hogstel, M. O., L. C. Curry, C. A. Walker, and P. B. Burns. 2004. "Ethics Committees in Long-Term Care Facilities." *Geriatric Nursing* 25 (6): 364–69.

Holley, J. L., L. Stackiewicz, C. Dacko, and R. Rault. 1997. "Factors Influencing Dialysis Patients' Completion of Advance Directives." *American Journal of Kidney Disease* 30 (3): 356–60.

Houts, R. M., W. D. Smucker, J. A. Jacobson, P. H. Ditto, and J. H. Danks. 2002. "Predicting Elderly Outpatients' Life-Sustaining Treatment Preferences Over Time: The Majority Rules." *Medical Decision Making* 22 (1):39–52.

Jameton, A. 1988. "In the Borderlands of Autonomy: Responsibility in Long Term Care Facilities." *Gerontologist* 28 (Suppl.): 18–23.

Jecker, N. S. 1990. "The Role of Intimate Others in Medical Decision Making." *Gerontologist* 30 (1): 65–71.

Jefferson, A. L.,S. Lambe, D. J. Moser, L. K. Byerly, A. Ozonoff, and J. H. Karlawish. 2008. "Decisional Capacity for Research Participation in Individuals with Mild Cognitive Impairment." *Journal of the American Geriatrics Society* 56 (7): 1236–43.

Kane, R. A., and A. L. Caplan, eds. 1990. *Everyday Ethics: Resolving Dilemmas in Nursing Home Life*. New York: Springer.

Kane, R. A., A. L. Caplan, E. K. Urv-Wong, I. C. Freeman, M. A. Aroskar, and M. Finch. 1997. "Everyday Matters in the Lives of Nursing Home Residents: Wish for and Perception of Choice and Control." *Journal of the American Geriatrics Society* 45 (9): 1086–93.

Kastenbaum, R., and P. Costa. 1977. "Psychological Perspectives on Death." *Annual Review of Psychology* 28:225–49.

Keay, T. J., and R. S. Schonwetter. 2000. "The Case for Hospice Care in Long-Term Care Environments." *Clinics in Geriatric Medicine* 16 (2): 211–23.

Kellett, U. M. 1998. "Meaning-Making for Family Carers in Nursing Homes." *International Journal of Nurse Practitioners* 4 (2): 113–19.

Kellett, U. M. 1999. "Searching for New Possibilities to Care: A Qualitative Analysis of Family Caring Involvement in Nursing Homes." *Nursing Inquiry* 6 (1): 9–16.

Kelner, M. 1995. "Activists and Delegators: Elderly Patients' Preferences About Control at the End of Life." *Social Science and Medicine* 41 (4): 537–45.

Kiernan, S. P. 2006. *Last Rights: Rescuing the End of Life from the Medical System*. New York: St. Martin's Press.

Kuczewski, M. G. 1996. "Reconceiving the Family: The Process of Consent in Medical Decisionmaking." *Hastings Center Report* 26 (2): 30–37.

Kuczewski, M. G. 1999. "Ethics in Long-Term Care: Are the Principles Different?" *Theoretical Medicine* 20:15–29.

Kuczewski, M. 2004. "From Informed Consent to Substituted Judgment: Decision-Making at the End-of-Life." *HEC Forum* 16 (1): 27–37.

Lacey, D. 2006. "End-of-Life Decision-Making for Nursing Home Residents with Dementia: A Survey of Nursing Home Social Services Staff." *Health and Social Work* 31(3): 189–99.

Lamberg, J. L., C. J. Person, D. K. Kiely, et al. 2005. "Decisions to Hospitalize Nursing Home Residents Dying with Advanced Dementia." *Journal of the American Geriatrics Society* 53 (8): 1396–1401.

Layde, P. M., C. A. Beam, S. K. Broste, A. F. Connors, N. Desbiens, J. Lynn, et al. 1995. "Surrogates' Predictions of Seriously Ill Patients' Resuscitation Preferences." *Archives of Family Medicine* 4:518–23.

Levin, J. R., N. S. Wenger, J. G. Ouslander, G. Zellman, J. F. Schnelle, J. L. Buchanaan, et al. 1999. "Life-Sustaining Treatment Decisions for Nursing Home Residents: Who Discusses, Who Decides, and What Is Decided?" *Journal of the American Geriatrics Society* 47 (1): 82–87.

Levine, C., and C. Zuckerman. 1999. "The Trouble with Families: Toward an Ethic of Accommodation." *Annals of Internal Medicine* 130 (2): 148–52.

Lewis, M., K. Hepburn, S. Narayan, R. M. Lally, S. Corcoran-Perry, M. Maddox, et al. 2000. "Decision-Making by Family Caregivers of Elders Experiencing Dementia." *American Journal of Alzheimer's Disease and Other Dementias* 15 (6): 361–66.

Libow, L. S., E. Olson, R. R. Neufeld, T. Martico-Greenfield, H. Meyers, N. Gordon, et al. 1992. "Ethics Rounds at the Nursing Home: An Alternative to an Ethics Committee." *Journal of the American Geriatrics Society* 40 (1): 95–97.

Luptak, M. 2004. "Social Work and End-of-Life Care for Older People: A Historical Perspective." *Health and Social Work* 29 (1): 7–15.

Mark, D. H., J. Bahr, E. H. Duthie, and D. D. Tresch. 1995. "Characteristics of Residents with Do-Not-Resuscitate Orders in Nursing Homes." *Archives of Family Medicine* 4 (5): 463–67.

Mattimore, T. J., N. S. Wenger, N. A. Desbiens, J. M. Teno, M. B. Hamel, H. Liu, et al. 1997. "Surrogate and Physician Understanding of Patients' Preferences for Living Permanently in a Nursing Home." *Journal of the American Geriatrics Society* 45 (7): 818–24.

McCullough, L. B., N. L. Wilson, J. A. Rhymes, and T. A. Teasdale. 1995. "Managing the Conceptual and Ethical Dimensions of Long-Term Care Decision Making: A Preventive Ethics Approach." In *Long-term Care Decisions: Ethical and Conceptual Dimensions*, ed. L. B. McCullough and N. L. Wilson, 221–40. Baltimore, Md.: Johns Hopkins University Press.

Meeker, M. A. 2004. "Family Surrogate Decision Making at the End of Life: Seeing Them Through with Care and Respect." *Qualitative Health Research* 14 (2): 204–25.

Meeker, M. A., and M. A. Jezewski. 2005. "Family Decision Making at End of Life." *Palliative and Supportive Care* 3 (2):131–42.

Mezey, M., M. Kluger, G. Maislin, and M. Mittelman. 1996. "Life-Sustaining Treatment Decisions by Spouses of Patients with Alzheimer's Disease." *Journal of the American Geriatrics Society* 44 (2): 144–50.

Mezey, M., E. Mitty, M. Rappaport, and G. Ramsey. 1997. "Implementation of the Patient Self-Determination Act (PSDA) in Nursing Homes in New York City." *Journal of the American Geriatrics Society* 45 (1): 43–49.

Michelson, C., M. Mulvihill, M.-A. Hsu, and E. Olson. 1991. "Eliciting Medical Care Preferences from Nursing Home Residents." *Gerontologist* 31 (3): 358–63.

Miller, S. C. 2004. "Hospice Care in Nursing Homes: Is Site of Care Associated with Visit Volume?" *Journal of the American Geriatrics Society* 52 (8): 1331–36.

Miller, S. C., P. Gozalo, and V. Mor. 2001. "Hospice Enrollment and Hospitalization of Dying Nursing Home Patients." *American Journal of Medicine* 111:38–44.

Miller, S. C., and V. Mor. 2004. "The Opportunity for Collaborative Care Provision: The Presence of Nursing Home/Hospice Collaborations in the U.S." *Journal of Pain and Symptom Management* 28 (6): 537–47.

Miller, S. C., V. Mor, K. Coppola, J. Teno, L. Laliberte, and A. C. Petrisek. 1998. "The Medicare Hospice Benefit's Influence on Dying in Nursing Homes." *Journal of Palliative Medicine* 1 (4): 367–76.

Miura, Y., A. Asai, M. Matsushima, S. Nagata, M. Onishi, T. Shimbo, et al. 2006. "Families' and Physicians' Predictions of Dialysis Patients' Preferences Regarding Life-Sustaining Treatment in Japan." *American Journal of Kidney Diseases* 47:122–30.

Molloy, D. W., R. M. Clarnette, E. A. Braun, M. R. Eisemann, and B. Sneiderman. 1991. "Decision Making in the Incompetent Elderly: 'The Daughter from California Syndrome.'" *Journal of the American Geriatric Society* 39 (4): 396–99.

Molloy, D. W., G. H. Guyatt, R. Russo, R. Goeree, B. J. O'Brien, M. Bedard, et al. 2000. "Systematic Implementation of an Advance Directive Program in Nursing Homes." *Journal of the American Medical Association* 283(11): 1437–44.

Montello, M., and J. Lantos. 2002. "The Karamazov Complex: Dostoevsky and DNR Orders." *Perspectives in Biology and Medicine* 45 (2):190–99.

Monturo, C. A., and N. E. Strumpf. 2007. "Advance Directives at End-of-Life: Nursing Home Resident Preferences for Artificial Nutrition." *Journal of the American Medical Directors Association* 8 (4):224–28.

Moody, H. R. 1988. "From Informed Consent to Negotiated Consent." *Gerontologist* 28 (Suppl.): 64–70.

Moody, H. R. 1992. *Ethics in an Aging Society.* Baltimore, Md.: Johns Hopkins University Press.

Moore, C. D., J. Sparr, S. Sherman, and L. Avery, L. 2003. "Surrogate Decision-Making: Judgment Standard Preferences of Older Adults." *Social Work in Health Care* 37 (2): 1–16.

Morrison, R. S., E. Chichin, J. Carter, O. Burack, M. Lantz, and D. E. Meier. 2005. "The Effect of a Social Work Intervention to Enhance Advance Care Planning Documentation in the Nursing Home." *Journal of the American Geriatrics Society* 53 (2): 290–94.

Munn, J. C., D. Dobbs, A. Meier, C. S. Williams, H. Biola, and S. Zimmerman. 2008. "The End-of-Life Experience in Long-Term Care: Five Themes Identified from Focus Groups with Residents, Family Members, and Staff." *Gerontologist* 48 (4): 485–94.

Murphy, D. J. 1988. "Do-Not-Resuscitate Orders: Time for Reappraisal in Long-Term-Care Institutions." *Journal of the American Medical Association* 260 (14): 2098–2101.

Murphy, D. J., D. Burrows, S. Santilli, A. W. Kemp, S. Tenner, B. Kreling, et al. 1994. "The Influence of the Probability of Survival on Patients' Preferences Regarding Cardiopulmonary Resuscitation." *New England Journal of Medicine* 330 (8): 545–49.

Murphy, D. J., and S. Santilli. 1998. "Elderly Patients' Preferences for Long-Term Life Support." *Archives of Family Medicine* 7 (5): 484–88.

National Association of Social Workers. 2006. *Social Work Speaks: National Association of Social Workers Policy Statements, 2006–2009.* 7th ed. Washington, D.C.: NASW Press.

National Association of Social Workers. 2008. "Code of Ethics." http://www.socialworkers.org/pubs/code/code.asp.

National Commission for the Protection of Human Subjects of Biomedical and Behavioral Research. 1979. *The Belmont Report: Ethical Principles and Guidelines for the Protection of Human Subjects of Research.* Available from http://ohsr.od.nih.gov/guidelines/belmont.html.

Nelson, J. L. 1994a. "Dementia and Advance Decision Making: Who's Choosing for Whom?" *Alzheimer Disease and Associated Disorders* 8 (1): 3–7.

Nelson, J. L. 1994b. "Families and Futility." *Journal of the American Geriatrics Society* 42 (8): 879–82.

Nelson, J. L. 1995. "Critical Interests and Sources of Familial Decision-Making Authority for Incapacitated Patients." *Journal of Law, Medicine, and Ethics* 23:143–48.

Nelson, J. L. 1998. "Reasons and Feelings, Duty and Dementia." *Journal of Clinical Ethics* 9 (1): 58–65.

Nielsen, J., C. Henderson, M. Cox, S. Williams, and P. Green. 1996. "Characteristics of Caregivers and Factors Contributing to Institutionalization." *Geriatric Nursing* 17 (3): 124–27.

Nolan, M. T., M. Hughes, D. P. Narendra, J. R. Sood, P. B. Terry, A. B. Astrow, et al. 2005. "When Patients Lack Capacity: The Roles That Patients with

Terminal Diagnoses Would Choose for Their Physicians and Loved Ones in Making Medical Decisions." *Journal of Pain and Symptom Management* 30 (4): 342–53.

Osman, H., and T. M. Perlin. 1994. "Patient Self-Determination and the Artificial Prolongation of Life Support." *Health and Social Work* 19 (4): 245–52.

Ouslander, J. G., A. D. Weinberg, and V. Phillips. 2000. "Inappropriate Hospitalization of Nursing Facility Residents: A Symptom of a Sick System of Care for Frail Older People." *Journal of the American Geriatrics Society* 48 (2): 230–31.

Parker-Oliver, D., and D. Bickel. 2002. "Nursing Home Experience with Hospice." *Journal of the American Medical Directors Association* 3 (2): 46–50.

Parker-Oliver, D., D. Porock, S. Zweig, M. Rantz, and G. F. Petroski. 2003. "Hospice and Nonhospice Nursing Home Residents." *Journal of Palliative Medicine* 6 (1): 69–75.

Pasman, H. R. W., B. D. Onwuteaka-Philipsen, M. E. Ooms, P. T. van Wigcheren, G. van der Wal, and M. W. Ribbe. 2004. "Forgoing Artificial Nutrition and Hydration in Nursing Home Patients with Dementia: Patients, Decision Making, and Participants." *Alzheimer Disease and Associated Disorders* 18 (3): 154–62.

Pellegrino, E. D., and D. C. Thomasma. 1988. *For the Patient's Good: The Restoration of Beneficence in Health Care.* New York: Oxford University Press.

Phillips, R. S., N. S. Wenger, J. Teno, R. K. Oye, S. Youngner, R. Califf, et al. 1996. "Choices of Seriously Ill Patients About Cardiopulmonary Resuscitation: Correlates and Outcomes." *American Journal of Medicine* 100 (2): 128–37.

Phipps, E., G. True, D. Harris, U. Chong, W. Tester, S. I. Chavin, et al. 2003. "Approaching the End of Life: Attitudes, Preferences, and Behaviors of African-American and White Patients and Their Family Caregivers." *Journal of Clinical Oncology* 21 (3): 549–54.

Powell, T. 1999. "Extubating Mrs. K: Psychological Aspects of Surrogate Decision Making." *Journal of Law, Medicine, and Ethics* 27 (1):81–86.

Powers, B. A. 2001. "Ethnographic Analysis of Everyday Ethics in the Care of Nursing Home Residents with Dementia." *Nursing Research* 50 (6): 332–39.

Pratt, C., W. Schmall, S. Wright, and J. Hare. 1987. "The Forgotten Client: Family Caregivers to Institutionalized Dementia Patients." In *Aging, Health, and Family: Long-Term Care*, ed. T. H. Brubaker, 197–213. Newbury Park, Calif.: Sage.

Pruchno, R. A., E. P. Lemay, L. Feild, and N. G. Levinsky. 2005. "Spouse as Health Care Proxy for Dialysis Patients: Whose Preferences Matter?" *Gerontologist* 45 (6): 812–19.

Pruchno, R. A., E. P. Lemay, L. Feild, and N. G. Levinsky. 2006. "Predictors of Patient Treatment Preferences and Spouse Substituted Judgments: The Case of Dialysis Continuation." *Medical Decision Making* 26 (2):112–21.

Puchalski, C. M., Z. Zhong, M. M. Jacobs, E. Fox, J. Lynn, J. Harrold, et al. 2000. "Patients Who Want Their Family and Physician to Make Resuscitation Decisions for Them: Observations from Support and Help. Study to Understand Prognoses and Preferences for Outcomes and Risks of Treatment. Hospitalized Elderly Longitudinal Project." *Journal of the American Geriatrics Society* 48 (5 Suppl.): S84–90.

Pullman, D. 1999. "The Ethics of Autonomy and Dignity in Long-Term Care." *Canadian Journal on Aging* 18 (1): 26–46.

Reamer, F. G. 1998. "The Evolution of Social Work Ethics." *Social Work* 43 (6): 488–500.

Reilly, R. B., T. A. Teasdale, and L. B. McCullough. 1994. "Projecting Patients' Preferences from Living Wills: An Invalid Strategy for Management of Dementia with Life-Threatening Illness." *Journal of the American Geriatrics Society* 42 (9): 997–1003.

Remsen, M. F. 1993. "The Role of the Nursing Home Social Worker in Terminal Care." *Journal of Gerontological Social Work* 19 (3/4): 193–205.

Reynolds, K., M. Henderson, A. Schulman, and L. C. Hanson. 2002. "Needs of the Dying in Nursing Homes." *Journal of Palliative Medicine* 5 (6): 895–901.

Schneider, C. E. 1998. *The Practice of Autonomy: Patients, Doctors, and Medical Decisions.* New York: Oxford University Press.

Schonwetter, R. S., R. M. Walker, M. Solomon, A. Indurkhya, and B. E. Robinson. 1996. "Life Values, Resuscitation Preferences, and the Applicability of Living Wills in an Older Population." *Journal of the American Geriatrics Society* 44 (8): 954–58.

Schwaber, M. J., and Y. Carmeli. 2008. "Antibiotic Therapy in the Demented Elderly Population: Redefining the Ethical Dilemma." *Archives of Internal Medicine* 168 (4): 349–50.

Seckler, A. B., D. E. Meier, M. Mulvihill, and B. E. C. Paris. 1991. "Substituted Judgment: How Accurate Are Proxy Predictions?" *Annals of Internal Medicine* 115 (2): 92–98.

Sehgal, A., A. Galbraith, M. Chesney, P. Schoenfeld, G. Charles, and B. Lo. 1992. "How Strictly Do Dialysis Patients Want Their Advance Directives Followed?" *Journal of the American Medical Association* 267 (1): 59–63.

Semple, S. J. 1992. "Conflict in Alzheimer's Caregiving Families: Its Dimensions and Consequences." *Gerontologist* 32 (5): 648–55.

Seymour, J., M. Gott, G. Bellamy, S. H. Ahmedzai, and D. Clark. 2004. "Planning for the End of Life: The Views of Older People About Advance Care Statements." *Social Science and Medicine* 59 (1):57–68.

Shalowitz, D. I., E. Garrett-Mayer, and D. Wendler. 2006. "The Accuracy of Surrogate Decision Makers: A Systematic Review." *Archives of Internal Medicine* 166 (5):493–97.

Silverman, H. J. 1992. "Deciding When Not to Discuss or Provide Cardio-pulmonary Resuscitation." *Journal of Critical Care* 7 (2): 129–35.

Suhl, J., P. Simons, T. Reedy, and T. Garrick. 1994. "Myth of Substituted Judgment: Surrogate Decision Making Regarding Life Support Is Unreliable." *Archives of Internal Medicine* 154 (1):90–96.

Sullivan, M. D. 2002. "The Illusion of Patient Choice in End-of-Life Decisions." *American Journal of Geriatrics Psychiatry* 10 (4): 365–72.

Sulmasy, D. P., M. T. Hughes, R. E. Thompson, A. B. Astrow, P. B. Terry, J. Kub, J., et al. 2007. "How Would Terminally Ill Patients Have Others Make Decisions for Them in the Event of Decisional Incapacity? A Longitudinal Study." *Journal of the American Geriatrics Society* 55 (12): 1981–88.

Sulmasy, D. P., and J. Sugarman. 2001. "The Many Methods of Medical Ethics (or, Thirteen Ways of Looking at a Blackbird)." In *Methods in medical ethics*, ed. J. Sugarman and D. P. Sulmasy, 3–18. Washington, D.C.: Georgetown University Press.

Sulmasy, D. P., P. B. Terry, C. S. Weisman, D. J. Miller, R. Y. Stallings, M. A. Vettese, et al. 1998. "The Accuracy of Substituted Judgments in Patients with Terminal Diagnoses." *Annals of Internal Medicine* 128 (8):621–29.

Teno, J. M. 2004. "Advance Directives: Time to Move On." *Annals of Internal Medicine* 141 (2): 159–60.

Teno, J. M., S. Licks, J. Lynn, N. Wenger, A. F. Connors Jr., R. S. Phillips, et al. 1997. "Do Advance Directives Provide Instructions That Direct Care? Support Investigators Study to Understand Prognoses and Preferences for Outcomes and Risks of Treatment." *Journal of the American Geriatrics Society* 45 (4): 508–12.

Terry, P. B., M. Vettese, J. Song, J. Forman, K. B. Haller, D. J. Miller, et al. 1999. "End-of-Life Decision Making: When Patients and Surrogates Disagree." *Journal of Clinical Ethics* 10 (4): 286–93.

Tomlinson, T., K. Howe, M. Notman, and D. Rossmiller. 1990. "An Empirical Study of Proxy Consent for Elderly Persons." *Gerontologist* 30 (1): 54–64.

Tonelli, M. R. 1996. "Pulling the Plug on Living Wills: A Critical Analysis of Advance Directives." *Chest* 110 (3):816–22.

Tresch, D. D., and R. K. Thakur. 1998. "Cardiopulmonary Resuscitation in the Elderly: Beneficial or an Exercise in Futility?" *Emergency Medicine Clinics of North America* 16 (3): 649–63.

Uhlmann, R. F., R. A. Pearlman, and K. C. Cain. 1988. "Physicians' and Spouses' Predictions of Elderly Patients' Resuscitation Preferences." *Journal of Gerontology: Medical Sciences* 43 (5): M115–M121.

Veatch, R. M. 2000. "Re: 'End-of-Life Decision Making'" (letter). *Journal of Clinical Ethics* 11 (3): 284.

Vig, E. K., J. S. Taylor, H. Starks, E. K. Hopley, and K. Fryer-Edwards. 2006. "Beyond Substituted Judgment: How Surrogates Navigate End-of-Life Decision-Making." *Journal of the American Geriatrics Society* 54(11): 1688–93.

Watts, D. T. 1992. "The Family's Will or the Living Will: Patient Self-Determination in Doubt." *Journal of the American Geriatrics Society* 40 (5): 533–34.

Welch, L. C., S. C. Miller, E. W. Martin, and A. Nanda. 2008. "Referral and Timing of Referral to Hospice Care in Nursing Homes: The Significant Role of Staff Members." *Gerontologist* 48 (4): 477–84.

Welie, J. V. M. 2001. "Living Wills and Substituted Judgments: A Critical Analysis." *Medicine, Health Care, and Philosophy* 4 (2):169–83.

Zerzan, J., S. Stearns, and L. Hanson. 2000. "Access to Palliative Care and Hospice in Nursing Homes." *Journal of the American Medical Association* 284 (19): 2489–94.

Zweig, S. 1997. "Cardiopulmonary Resuscitation and Do-Not-Resuscitate Orders in the Nursing Home." *Archives of Family Medicine* 6 (5):424–29.

Final Discharge Planning

Rituals Related to the Death of a Nursing Home Resident

PEGGY SHARR AND MERCEDES BERN-KLUG

A RESIDENT'S GRIEF

I was in the nursing home to collect data for an ethnographic study. As I walked down the long hall, I noticed Barry sitting in his wheelchair in the doorway to his room. Our eyes met and I greeted him. He stretched his arm out toward me and said, "Here, I want you to read this," as he handed me a newspaper turned to the obituary section. "It's Evan. He died." I read the death notice. When I finished, Barry said, "He wasn't feeling well last week and they sent him to the hospital on Wednesday or Thursday. I saw him the night before he left. Then he got there and died. Now he is gone." Barry's voice had tapered to almost a whisper, as he shook his head in disbelief, then he continued, "I am sad. He was my buddy. I'm gonna miss him." The activity director had given Barry a copy of the paper so he could see the obituary. I asked Barry if there would be a service at the nursing home for Evan. Barry replied, "No, they don't do that here. I can't get out to go to the . . . I have known him for such a long time. We used to go to the same restaurant. Then I see him again when I get in here, and now he is gone." I asked Barry if he would like it if we said a few solemn words on behalf of Evan. He agreed immediately and put his hands together in prayer. I led the prayer and Barry concluded with, "Amen, Lord. Amen." Tears were streaming down his face, "I'm gonna miss him. I'm gonna miss my old buddy. Thank you." I handed him back the paper and offered to find a pair of scissors so he could cut the obituary, to which Barry replied, "I'm not going to cut it. I'm going to keep the whole page as it is."

(M. Bern-Klug's unpublished field notes [names changed])

The death of a loved one, and dealing with the grief that follows, is one of the greatest challenges human beings face. All cultures acknowledge death through some kind of rite of passage to allow the bereaved to make sense of the passing of a loved one and to begin the grieving process. Death is a common reality for nursing home staff and residents. The aim of this chapter is to demonstrate the value of conducting culturally competent rituals in the nursing home that honor the deaths of residents. First, we will describe what a rite of passage is and how it relates to death—specifically the death of a nursing home resident. We will then explore grief rituals and how they fit into the rite of passage process.

We also explore cultural competency and its importance in the rituals. We offer recommendations for helping nursing home staff plan rituals that fit the religions and cultures of residents and families. It is imperative to consider the uniqueness of each resident and to tailor each memorial service if needed. We conclude the first half of the chapter by sharing examples of rituals and memorial services submitted by practicing nursing home social workers. The second part of the chapter is about funeral rituals that take place away from the nursing home. This information is provided to encourage social workers to build familiarity with local funeral-related options and costs, in order to be able to share this information with residents and families.

Throughout the chapter we refer to "nursing home staff" as our audience because when it comes to grief rituals, any number of staff could be involved—nurses, activities directors, chaplains, nurse's aides, and so on. However, in most cases it will be the activities director or the social worker who will be responsible for overseeing the ritual or memorial service.

Rites of Passage and Grief Rituals

The American Heritage Dictionary defines "rite of passage" as a "ritual or ceremony signifying an event in a person's life indicative of a transition from one stage to another, as from adolescence to adulthood." When we think of rite of passage, we typically think of moving from puberty into adulthood, giving birth to a child, or matrimony. Yet, aside from birth, death is the one transition that everyone will surely experience. Because the experience of death can be so difficult, observing it as a rite of passage may be particularly comforting for some.

Van Gennep ([1908] 1960) proposed in his book, *Rites of Passage*, that a rite of passage includes three phases: separation of the individuals from their preceding social state; a period of transition in which they are neither one thing nor the other; and a reintegration phase in which, through various rites of incorporation, they are absorbed into their new social state. When applied to the nursing home, the first stage would be when a resident is placed in the nursing home, which separates the resident from their previous social state—living independently. Loved ones now interact with the resident in the nursing home rather than an independent living situation. In the second stage, the resident is actively dying—during this phase the resident neither is actively participating in life nor has died. Loved ones, staff, and residents experience the anticipation of the resident's passing. In the third stage, the resident has died, moving into a new state—death—and the surviving loved ones, staff, and residents are in a new social situation, living life without the resident.

Rituals mark the rite of passage. Rituals symbolize change and can provide comfort that change is typical. Rando (1985) defines ritual as a specific behavior or activity that gives symbolic expression to certain feelings and thoughts, individually or as a group. Rituals are also cultural devices that facilitate the preservation of social order and provide ways to comprehend the complex and contradictory aspects of human existence within a given societal context (Romanoff and Terenzio 1998). "For rituals frequently portray unknown and unknowable conditions, ideals, or imaginings—and make them tangible and present, despite the fact that they [may be] ineffable and invisible" (Moore and Myerhoff 1977:18).

Moore and Myerhoff (1977:7–8) outline the components of rituals as follows:

- Repetition, either of occasion, content, or form, or any combination of these.
- Acting: not a spontaneous activity but rather a self-conscious act usually not only saying or thinking something but also doing something.
- "Special" behavior or stylization: actions or symbols are extraordinary, or ordinary ones are used in an unusual way that calls attention to them and sets them apart from other mundane uses.
- Order: an organized event, both of persons and cultural elements, having a beginning and an end and therefore bound to order.
- Evocative presentational style or staging: collective rituals intended to produce an attentive state of mind, and often an even greater commitment of some kind. Ceremony commonly does this through manipulations of symbols and stimuli.
- The "collective dimension": A collective ritual has a social meaning. Its very occurrence contains a social message.

According to these authors, all of these formal properties make ritual an ideal vehicle for conveying messages in an authentic manner. Grief rituals are specific symbolic acts related directly to a death. These rituals can be instrumental in restoring a sense of normalcy, and *can play an important role in the bereavement process by providing predictability and familiarity at a time when one feels circumstances are beyond human control* (Castle and Phillips 2003). Nursing home staff and the resident's family, friends, and peers may all be affected by the death of the resident. Therefore grief rituals can facilitate the natural process of grieving and offer a way for the survivors to honor the life of the deceased. These rituals are intended to honor not only the deceased loved one but also one's relationship to the loved one (Castle and Phillips 2003). According to Hunter (2007–2008), grief rituals embody not one but two rites of passage: one is the passage of the deceased individual from the world of the living to the world of the dead, and the other is the passage of bereavement for those left behind, which redefines one's role in life without the deceased individual. Achterberg (1992:158) wrote:

Rituals for healing have the purpose of giving credence and significance to life's transitions; they provide maps of form and guidance for behavior during perilous times when bodies, minds, and spirits are broken. The acts of ritual allow people to share their common experiences and to give visible support to one another. The symbols and events of healing ritual cement the healer/healee bonds and engender faith and hope that the passage into the place of wholeness, harmony, or relief of suffering will be achieved.

Grief rituals include the use of symbolic elements, objects as well as actions. In the case of grief ritual, symbolic objects meaningful to the bereaved, such as photos and mementos of the deceased, may play an important role. Nonphysical symbols such as music and prayer can also play an important role (Castle and Phillips 2003). Other symbolic acts may include yearly remembrance celebrations, including creating an altar or planting a tree in honor of the deceased, establishing a memorial fund, or publishing the loved one's poems. These actions, or rituals, acknowledge that although the relationship with the deceased has changed, it does endure after death (Castle and Phillips 2003). These types of rituals help structure a way to recall the lost loved one and to make some statement about the mourner's feelings.

Performing and participating in grief rituals is one way of finding meaning in death. For those affected by a death in a nursing home, connecting them can be therapeutic. Staff and residents are provided a way to say goodbye by "sending off" the resident with dignity and honor. Death is not hidden or secretive. Instead, death is acknowledged openly, and the life of the person who died is celebrated.

Rando (1985) states that there are many unconscious consequences of ritual, and the participants themselves frequently may not be able to explain some of the effects of the ritual upon them. Castle and Phillips (2003) found, from their study of the effects of grief rituals on the bereaved, that the most important aspects for successful grief ritual are that the activity be personally meaningful for the participants and that they feel safe in expressing their feelings. Other important aspects include being able to reminisce about the deceased; including others in the ritual; being able to maintain emotional bonds with the deceased; maintaining a sense of control through making decisions; having clearly defined time limits to the ritual; and a sense of "specialness" or sacredness in performing the ritual (Castle and Phillips 2003:62).

The resident's treatment by staff during the time leading up to and immediately following the death can mean the difference between family and friends feeling validated or alienated. According to Achterberg (1992), one of the most important aspects of rituals, particularly critical during times of mourning, is to reduce the sense of alienation. One way of avoiding alienation and helping to ensure validation is to adopt culturally competent policies regarding death and grief.

Cultural Competency and Grief Rituals

Grief rituals have been performed around the world for thousands of years. Hayden (1987) states that humans have been performing rituals for over 100,000 years, noting that rituals serve an important survival function by helping to maintain important social bonds. Individuals and their families commonly turn to cultural values, and religious or spiritual beliefs and practices, when faced with death. When considering this with a nursing home resident, staff's sensitivity to cultural diversity, beliefs, and practices are particularly important. The National Center for Cultural Competency defines cultural competence as having a defined set of values and principles and demonstrating behaviors, attitudes, policies and structures that enable one to work effectively cross-culturally; having the capacity to value diversity, conduct self-assessment, manage the dynamics of difference, acquire and institutionalize cultural knowledge, and adapt to diversity and the cultural contexts of the communities served; incorporating the above in all aspects of policymaking, administration, practice, and service delivery; and involving consumers, key stakeholders, and communities. Since culture is a primary factor in how individuals view and handle death, the importance of adopting culturally competent practices in the nursing home is crucial.

While funeral ceremonies appear to be a universal social experience across cultures, the content of services vary. For example, many cultures share memories and have conversations about the deceased. On the other hand, Muslims believe that they should not talk but rather weep to release their sorrow (Irish, Lundquist, and Nelson 1993:142). In contrast, weeping or crying among Americans of British ancestry is not as common (McGoldrick and Walsh 1991). To them, not crying may be seen as a sign of strength, of holding themselves together for others who may need them.

According to Hardy-Bougere (2008:67), misunderstandings can easily occur when healthcare providers and consumers come from diverse cultures with conflicting beliefs. Rosenblatt (1993) advises the use of active curiosity and genuine interest to understand the experience of death and grief the way that people in different cultures understand them. Rosenblatt further recommends that we should not presume to teach anyone to feel grief—everyone feels and experiences grief in a unique way. We cannot assume that because one does not cry or weep he or she is not sorrowful. And if a person "falls apart," one should not assume that he or she is not being strong. Nursing home staff members must be sensitive to the varying reactions in the way surviving loved ones handle the death of the resident. Even when one has had numerous experiences with a certain population, it is unreasonable to assume that other members of that same population will react in the same manner. "Helping a family deal with a loss often means showing respect for their particular cultural heritage and encouraging them to actively determine how they will commemorate the death of the loved relative" (McGoldrick et al. 1986:30).

Religious and Cultural Diversity in Rituals and the Grieving Process

Among the many influences that shape human behavior, religious, cultural, and ethnic context are among the most powerful. Individuals often rely upon spirituality or religion to seek comfort and create meaning during times of loss (Collins and Doolittle 2006). However, an individual's need to create meaning cannot be deciphered only from a religious or spiritual perspective—culture, ethnicity, and individual preferences are central elements as well. To avoid imposing majority values and assumptions on residents and their loved ones, it is important that nursing home staff respond to wishes in a sensitive and professional manner. Some knowledge about various religious beliefs and cultural and ethnic diversity can help staff members understand the range in meaning related to dying and death.

Religion

The 2007 report from the Pew Forum on Religion and Public Life documents that most Americans (85 percent) report they are religiously affiliated. Eighty-two percent of Americans are Christian, three percent are followers of Islam, and two percent are Jewish. Among Christians, there are twice as many people who report being Protestant as report being Roman

Catholic. Protestants constitute 53 percent of Americans. But it is important to remember that a nursing home staff will likely encounter other belief systems, including atheism, Hinduism, Buddhism, agnosticism, Wicca, and Native American religious practices, to name a few. The importance of this variation cannot be taken lightly.

Buddhism, for example, assigns equal importance to life and death (Yeung 1995). Buddhism also teaches that death is a "doorway into another type of existence where our evolution continues" (Longaker 1997:27). According to Yeung, reincarnation (the belief that one is reborn into a new form after death), is the biggest cultural difference between Western and Eastern thought. This difference, along with others, could greatly affect the memorial and funeral practices of the surviving loved ones.

Among many followers of Buddhism, great care is taken in protecting the soul. A ritual called the "passing ceremony" may be performed after death, but if this ceremony cannot take place right away, a white cloth is thrown over the body to prevent the escape of the soul (Habenstein and Lamers 1974:78). In some sects, family members and friends gather around and chant the name of the Buddha. The goal of this ritual is to get the dying individual to chant as well, which if done sincerely will bring the dying person into the most "connection with the Buddha—to assure salvation or a rebirth" (Yeung 1995:79). Because facilities may not allow or be comfortable with this ritual of chanting, Buddhists sometimes feel they must leave the facility to die at home; however, a private room may be all that is needed.

In Americanized Buddhism, meditation (a practice in some sects called *sukhavati*) is common. Therefore, it is not unusual for friends and family to meditate together while gathered around their dying or deceased loved one. In traditional Buddhism, expressing grief (crying and weeping) is thought to "hold the dead person back on [his or her] journey." However, in the United States, many Buddhists believe that grief actually helps facilitate the "journey" (Goss and Klass 2006:86), though this journey is that of the survivors through their grief, not of the dead into the next life (Goss and Klass 2006).

There are two main groups of Christians in the Unites States—Catholics and Protestants. Both share a similar belief that "heaven is the final destination in God's presence." However, the understanding of that afterlife may vary (Wood and Rowatt 2006:21). Christianity teaches that humans are created in the image of God and are saved by Jesus Christ. Further, eternal life with God exists for those who believe in, and follow "Jesus' word" (Wood and Rowatt 2006:20). Prayer and the reading from the Bible are central to both Catholics and Protestants. Christianity focuses on grace and acceptance from Jesus Christ; therefore, the focus at a funeral or memorial service may be on the resurrection and the promise of life after death "in Christ" (Wood and Rowatt 2006:20).

Christian church attendance in the United States has declined since the 1950s. Nonetheless, Christians generally continue to seek out a clergyperson to help with the funeral ritual (Wood and Rowatt 2006). Having an ordained priest hear the confessions of a dying person remains one of the chief rituals for Catholics (Davies 1994; Wood and Rowatt 2006). Along with the confession, the priest may anoint the dying person on the forehead and hands with olive oil (Barrack 2008). Most Protestants, on the other hand, believe that they have direct access to God and need not have assistance from a clergyperson. Like Catholics, most Protestants desire prayer at the time of death. Some Protestants may want to confess sins, but this act does not have to be performed by an ordained minister (Wood and Rowatt 2006). Grief rituals among Christians often involve giving gifts, sending flowers, memorial funds, planting a tree, placing a cross, and myriad private family rituals. For many Catholics, candles are a key element of grief rituals (Wood and Rowatt 2006:22).

Judaism teaches that the sacredness of a human being does not end with death; therefore, the laws and customs that surround death and mourning are set forth "to promote dignity of the human spirit" (Bukaitz 2007:3). Judaism teaches that people are created in the image of God, so the body must not be altered in any way and must be buried as quickly as possible—usually within twenty-four hours (Levine 1997). By having the burial quickly, the mourning process is not delayed. Immediately following the death, care of the deceased takes precedence over care of the mourners. The primary focus is on preparing for the deceased's final resting place. However, once the family returns home from the funeral, the focus shifts to the mourners' needs (Bukaitz 2007).

In mourning, Jewish tradition typically involves, in addition to prayer, a number of other rituals, including covering mirrors; tearing a piece of clothing; wearing a black ribbon, which is called *k'riah*; burning a candle or oil lamp night and day for a full week (Bukaitz 2007); hanging a wreath on the front door (York 2000:142); and *s'udat havra-ah* (the meal of consolation), in which loved ones bring and serve food to the mourners (Bukaitz 2007).

The chief principle in Islam is the belief that there is only one god, Allah. The holy book of Islam is the Koran (Qu'ran), "which is believed to be the word of God to the Prophet Mohammad" (Braun, Pietsch, and Blanchette 2000:202). Muslims believe that God sent many prophets, including Abraham, Moses, and Jesus Christ. However, they believe that Mohammad was the most recent and greatest (Braun, Pietsch, and Blanchette 2000:203).

Islam teaches that weeping rather than talking among one another will facilitate the release of sorrow. There is generally tea, sugar, and syrup available at the ceremony for mourners, who may become faint during their grieving (Irish, Lundquist, and Nelson 1993). Many Muslims believe that at the time of the death, the more prayers that are given for the deceased, "the easier the departed one's life will be in the afterworld" (Irish, Lundquist, and Nelson 1993:142).

In the dying person's last moments, a close relative will be by his or her side, praying and reading from the Koran. As soon as the loved one has passed, the following rituals are commonly performed: turning of the body to face toward Mecca (Islam's holiest city); having someone sit next to the body and read the Koran; closing the mouth, eyes, and covering the face; straightening both legs and stretching the hands to the side; announcing the death immediately; and hastening to bathe the body three times (in water with leaves of the plum tree, camphorized water, and pure water, if available); and finally covering the body with white cotton (Irish, Lundquist, and Nelson 1993:141–42). According to Irish, Lundquist, and Nelson, many Muslims in the United States have been trained in these rituals, including the bathing practice. Thus it would not be uncommon to encounter a Muslim nursing home resident, or a non-Muslim resident with Muslim family members, who would wish to perform some or all of these rituals.

Culture and Ethnicity

Culture refers to the common behaviors and experiences in the context and setting in which one lives. Ethnicity, on the other hand, refers to common ancestry through which values and customs are shared (Nichols 2009). It's important to consider that residents and their family members could be affected by multiple cultural or ethnic influences.

For example, because of family influence, social class, socioeconomic status, religious beliefs, region, political influences, immigration history, and other factors, the black population in the United States is a heterogeneous group. These influences could greatly effect the expression of grief and the preferences in grief rituals. As an example, in the South, there are generally no prohibitions regarding openly expressing extreme grief. It is common for family and friends to sing spiritual songs about the pain and suffering of the life of the deceased and the joy of her reunion with lost loves ones. However, other groups, such as black Catholics or northern Unitarians, may not express their emotions as openly (Irish, Lundquist, and Nelson 1993).

Latinos are also a heterogeneous group. Mexican Americans and Puerto Ricans are two of the largest Latino populations in the United States. However, a nursing home staff may encounter individuals from Cuba, Costa Rica, Honduras, Guatemala, Peru, or Argentina, just to name a few places. Catholicism is common among many Latino groups, but not universal—some Latinos could also identify as Jehovah's Witness, Baptist, Episcopalian, or Jewish or as no religion at all. Emotional responses are generally more open among Latino Catholics than among other U.S. Catholics (Irish, Lundquist, and Nelson 1993:76; and Buckley 1991:15). And Latinos commonly place great importance on family, especially when a death occurs. Family members often come from miles around even if they have not seen the deceased in years (Irish, Lundquist, and Nelson 1993). Death, among many Latinos, is seen as a "passage." Thus, Latinos often celebrate the life rather than mourning the death of the departed (Buckley 1991:15).

Because of the diversity of religious practices among Asians and Asian Americans (for example, Confucianism, Buddhism, and Christianity), how loved ones respond and care for their deceased may vary greatly. For example, some Chinese folk religions teach that the spirit of one who dies outside the home will roam aimlessly after death and may cause trouble. As a result, these believers may prefer to leave the hospital or nursing home facility to return home to die (Martinson 1998). Some Koreans view death as one of the five blessings (longevity, wealth, health, and virtue are the other four); therefore, a peaceful death may be viewed as the result of a blessed life (Martinson 1998). The desire for a peaceful death may make hospice care particularly attractive. Family involvement in the care of the dying is usually desired. As a result, family members may travel long distances to provide care for their loved one who is dying (Martinson 1998). Many Vietnamese believe that the soul leaves the body the moment of death, and crying out or showing emotions could prevent the soul from being reborn (Brawn and Nichols 1997).

While it is important to continue learning about end-of-life beliefs and practices of different groups, it's imperative not to assume that just because a resident or family belongs to a certain ethnic or religious group he or she ascribes to a particular belief system. Moreover, it is equally important to remember that there are many people who do not affiliate with any religion at all and who do not want to have the religious beliefs of others imposed on them. The mere presence of a Bible on the nightstand may offend a person who does not consider it a sacred book.

Nonreligious people may indeed choose to have a memorial service or rituals performed. However, it is important to ask what type of service would be meaningful or appropriate. In fact, it is necessary to check with every family about what sort of a ritual (if any) they would like to be part of in the nursing home. The social worker (or other designated staff member) might share a generic overview of what they typically provide regarding a facility ritual, and then ask the family if they would like to take part in the ritual and, if so, what changes they may want to make.

Nursing home staff who have an understanding of diversity among residents and are appreciative to other cultural attitudes and practices will be better equipped to help the residents and their loved ones through the planning process before death and the implementation of the memorial service in the nursing home after the death, if that is desired.

Grief Rituals in the Nursing Home

Death is common in nursing homes; therefore, staff and residents are regularly faced with the question of how to address death. Residents are admitted to nursing homes, in many cases, to live out the last years, months, even weeks of their lives. The staff may become an important part of the lives of some long-time residents. As nursing home residents observe how staff members handle death, they begin to contemplate how they and their loved ones will be treated when their time comes. Also, because of the level of closeness that nursing home residents and staff experience, honoring the deaths of residents in a sensitive and individual manner can, in addition to easing the minds of residents, provide closure for staff.

Nursing home staff may also experience bereavement. Therefore, honoring the passing of nursing home residents with a rite of passage is one way to attend to staff members' grief. Chapter 10 discusses the potential negative consequences, such as burnout, for nursing home staff member who may not have the opportunity to properly address their grief. Having staff acknowledge the passing of a resident with rituals is one way to help facilitate closure and alleviate the stress of unresolved grief.

The nursing home is a place that has been providing grief rituals for residents and their loved ones for decades. Grief rituals in nursing homes can help to reconfirm social ties and remind the bereaved that they are not alone, even in mourning. Nursing home staff members can offer support through acknowledgment and acceptance, thereby facilitating interaction with and reintegration into the social group (Rando 1985).

The level of involvement in the ritual process varies markedly from nursing home to nursing home. Some put great effort into observing their deceased. For example, Julie Berndt, a nursing home chaplain, describes her nursing home's rituals in detail in "When Death Comes in a Nursing Home: A Ritual to Say Goodbye" (2004a). First, a chime is rung three times over the intercom, followed by saying the deceased's name in order to alert the staff and residents that someone has passed and that a bedside service is about to begin. Family, friends, residents, and staff are given the opportunity to attend the bedside service. Once everyone has arrived, the chaplain leads a bedside prayer. Everyone is given the opportunity to share thoughts, feelings, and memories about the passing resident. An embroidered cloth, favorite quilt, or flag is placed over the gurney. Everyone is invited to follow along in a departure procession as the body is taken out of the nursing home.

The nursing home, according to Berndt (2004a), previously had no specific ritual and would hurry the process of getting the body out and a new resident in. The staff finally recognized that residents and staff needed more—they were actually performing their own rituals to honor their friends and fellow residents. In time, this nursing home developed these carefully planned rite-of-passage rituals.

Other nursing homes may have simpler versions; for example, one nursing home reported placing a dove on the door during active dying and then placing a white ribbon in the hall after the passing. One common ritual in nursing homes is to announce the death over the intercom, followed by staff and residents taking a moment of silence. Whether the grief ritual is simple or elaborate, considering the needs of the family members and being sensitive to cultural differences is crucial. Moreover, regardless of the nursing home's commonly practiced grief rituals, nursing home staff members need to be cognizant that family members may not want what is offered but instead prefer to facilitate their own grief rituals. It is important for nursing home staff to abandon their predispositions about what residents and families need or want. Asking is one of the best and most honorable ways to discover wishes and to help create a meaningful rite of passage for the resident and their loved ones.

Staff should not be in a rush to get on with business; time may be the element that the family needs the most. Staff should also acknowledge the death, not try to hide it or minimize it. Fellow residents and staff will surely notice the resident's absence and wonder what happened. Validation is the first step in allowing staff and residents to begin to heal from the loss. On the other hand, not acknowledging the death may send the message that the person's existence was insignificant to the group. "When it is impossible to carry out traditional rituals that have great meaning and serve to comfort the bereaved, the stress of bereavement is amplified" (Eisenbruch 1984)

As we discussed previously, asking the resident and family members during the planning process is a valuable way to learn about their desires. To better understand what to ask and when, it might be helpful to conceptualize the expectations of attending to the death of the resident. The phases can be broken down into steps, much like Van Gennep's ([1908] 1960) rites of passage discussed at the beginning of the chapter:

1. *Planning:* Before the active-dying phase of a resident, staff should discuss how the resident's active dying and death should be attended to. This is the time to explore things like religion and culture. Encourage the resident to be specific. Social workers can begin by giving a simple explanation of the grief ritual that is typically offered at the nursing home and then ask if it should be changed in any way. Put the resident's wishes in writing and add them to the resident's chart.

2. *Active dying:* During the active-dying phase, staff should refer to the resident's chart for specific instructions from the resident or family. Accommodations should be made, if needed, to help loved ones practice their rituals. Staff members should be cognizant of other staff members and residents who may be concerned about the dying resident.

3. *After death:* After the death, loved ones should be given the time they need with the decedent. Care should be taken to not alter the

body or the room in ways that might interfere with the beliefs and practices of the family. Accommodations should be made, if needed, to help loved ones practice their rituals. The death should not be hidden, unless that is the wish of the resident or family. Steps should be taken to acknowledge staff and residents' grief.

One way that nursing home staff can become more knowledgeable about cultural and ethnic differences is for the nursing home to conduct in-service trainings for its staff. To prepare for an in-service training, contact members of the community that are knowledgeable about specific religious, ethnic, or cultural groups, such as a local rabbi, priest, or minister or local community leaders who have close ties to diverse groups. In-service trainings should be given regularly.

While this chapter has suggested that honoring a nursing home resident's death with a rite of passage is a good idea, this does not mean that all residents and families will want such a rite. Rituals should be a resource and should never be imposed. As we've discussed, residents and family members should be the ones to decide if, when, where, and how the rituals would be employed.

Accounts of Rituals Used in Nursing Homes

In the summer of 2008 we sent an e-mail message to the one hundred members of the newly established national nursing home social worker listserv (sponsored by the University of Iowa School of Social Work http://www.uiowa.edu/~socialwk/NursingHomeResource/AboutOurListServ.html) telling members about this chapter and asking them to submit examples of how the nursing home marks the death of residents. Many listserv members replied. We selected examples of what nursing homes are doing, and then contacted the people who submitted the information, specifically asking for permission to include their entries (and names) in this book. The following quotations are examples of what listserv members shared.

Since all our residents come in the front door with dignity, I believe they should all leave the same way (figuratively). We found this beautiful poem called The Little Ship. We had it laminated and attach it to the door of the resident when he/she passes away. It stays there until the funeral occurs. We also play a hymn over the PA at passing. I post a little ship with the resident's name by the time clock for the staff. Death prefers no certain shift, so it is important to keep our staff informed. We send a Christmas card the year of passing—holidays are especially difficult. We also send a card on the first anniversary of death to family.

(Lynne Oliver, LCSW, Apostolic Christian Skylines, Peoria, Illinois)

At the Solon Nursing Care Center we offer food and drink to families while their loved one is passing on. We also offer that they can stay as long as they want and spend the night if they so desire. Quite a few families do make that choice to stay with their loved one through the night.

Once someone has died, we post a memorial sign by the front door and the Social Services office notifying residents, staff, and the family. We post their obituary by the Social Service memorial sign; put a white silk rose and a poem on their bed, if the family wants they can take the rose and poem with them. We ask for families to bring in a picture of their loved one, and we then have it engraved onto a square stone, usually a 4X4 granite stone that we then give to the family. We send a single white rose to the visitation and service, but if they don't have a service, we send the flower to the family's home. At their dining table, we put a vase with a white silk rose as a sign of remembrance. The vase at the table and flower on their bed remains until after services. We leave it up to each family to pack up the room unless they tell us otherwise. Annually we do a memorial service for all our residents. Hospice helps us with the annual service; we light candles, say prayers and read each person's name. If their family is present they come up and accept a white rose, if no family is present either a peer or staff will accept it on their behalf. Both staff and residents have done some online condolences on our wireless laptop computer. A memorial service is held the last Tuesday of the month at 6:30 for residents and families for the person's who have died that month, also anyone else that the group wants to commemorate. A resident and staff member lead the service.

(Carly Bessman, social service director, and Angi Anderson, public relations and marketing, Solon Nursing Care Center, Solon, Iowa)

At the Manilla Manor we have a Comfort Basket that we bring to the resident's room when families are sitting with a dying resident. The basket contains snacks, a coin purse with money to purchase pop from the pop machine. It also has a deck of cards, wood search books, magazines and books for children and adults about dying. We offer coffee, juices and homemade cookies, and free meals. After the resident has passed away, the body is draped with a white bedspread, and the staff and other residents form an honor guard (staff and residents stand along the hallway) as the resident's body is taken down the hall and out of the building. A sympathy card is put out by Social Services on a round table with a tablecloth with flowers. A bible is given to the family from the staff and resident and it is taken to the funeral home prior to the service to be displayed. A memorial services is conducted at the facility and family members are invited.

One of the neatest things that we do is we create a memory book where each resident who dies has a page—or two if needed—and there is a picture of the resident and then the page is left blank for staff to write whatever they wish. Some write goodbyes, some write memories, some write feelings, etc. This book is kept for the whole year and is there for reminiscing and for writing in whenever anyone has the need. What a great way to honor people we have had the privilege to serve. Also many times the staff cannot attend the scheduled family services so this is their way of having their time to say goodbye.

(Jean Gibbons, Manilla Manor, Manilla, Iowa)

At Dimondale Nursing Care Facility (NexCare), as the Director of Social Work, we have implemented training to each social worker on end of life—many of them have not experienced death in their immediate family. During morning activities, we announce the name/s of those who have passed away, along with directly going to residents that had developed a bond with their friend/family member/s. Next, we post announcements of a passing at time clocks because it's also important to support staff that provided care for our resident/family member/s, and offer counseling for staff and residents as needed. Many of our residents develop a bond with their peers, and once they become aware of a death, they may decline in their mood and sometimes their behavior. Monitoring is in place for those residents—we monitor for 14 days or as needed. Many times we provide Cognitive Behavioral Therapy, Aromatherapy, music therapy, pet therapy, or counseling as methods of helping them deal with death. If the mood is severe, we have a contract with a psychological service that comes to our facility and assess the resident. And finally, a social worker that was assigned to that unit where the resident resided sends a card to the family along with a general card that is sent from our facility. It is an honor to have provided excellent care to residents, their families, and our team at Dimondale.

(Albendia Sherrod, Dimondale Nursing Care Facility,
Dimondale, Michigan)

We do a variety of things to honor a [resident's] life. We base our actions on resident and family requests. We post a notice on the bulletin boards throughout our community. Administration emails a notice to staff. Families and residents may choose to have a memorial service at our community open to family, staff, residents, and friends. We plan with the residents and or family to create a memorial that is consistent with resident wishes. A resident-run group sends out a card to the family. A photo, the obituary, a flower, and a journal are set out in the lobby for staff and residents to share memories. The journal is mailed to the family. Social work staff facilitates a semi-annual remembrance ceremony. Staff is encouraged to share stories and remember the residents who have passed away during the past 6 months. A ribbon is tied on a wreath for each individual. Residents facilitate a semi-annual remembrance ceremony to honor residents that have passed away during the last 6 months.

(Sara Kellogg. LMSW, social service coordinator,
Oaknoll Retirement Residence)

At one of the nursing homes we work with, they put a laminated dove on the door when someone is actively dying, and when they die, they put a white ribbon on the door. Then they also put a little "flyer" on the bulletin board saying the person's name [and] that they died.

(Carrie A. Heithoff, Carroll, Iowa)

I work as a hospice SW at a SNF and I have started a "caring circle" to provide support for the staff after the death of a resident. Sometimes residents and family members attend also. We gather in a circle or around a table and remember the patient. Usually in the stories about the patient, I hear about the extra mile the staff went to provide quality of life for this patient and I talk about it to let them know what a difference they make to residents and I also talk about how this is not a job that we can do with a closed heart. I typically end the session by reading the Lord's Prayer and encouraging others to join me. (I provide copies of it). Then a moment of silence is given in memory of the patient. I encourage people to sing, and cite the example of one group that spontaneously started singing amazing grace.

(Marcy Rosen Bernstein, social worker, Continuum Hospice Care, Bronx)

At Country View Manor we understand each person grieves in his or her own way and our responses to families and friends have to be adjusted according to their personalities and their coping mechanisms. Staff members offer their sympathies and, if appropriate, fond memories about the deceased, as opportunities present themselves. We are in a small rural area and interactions occur as frequently at the grocery store or local café as they do here at the nursing home. Some families are so well known to us and bonded with the staff that they appreciate responses of affection such as holding hands, or even hugs. Others prefer to leave quietly, and we respect that preference as well. With a resident's passing, the bed is made and the housekeeping staff place a rose, a Bible, and a special verse on the bed. The facility sends the Willow Tree "Angel of Remembrance", a candle, and a decorative sprig (for example, a few pieces of artificial eucalyptus with a bow tied around it) for the visitation and funeral service, as well as a poem written specifically about that resident by our Activities Director. These poems have been read as part of the service at several of the funerals. At Christmas we send a special card and the poem "Christmas with Jesus" to the family. Residents are informed during the daily devotions about the passing of a resident. The residents who have passed away are also named during Resident Council and sympathy is again extended to the family in a public way via the monthly newsletter. As the social worker, I am available to offer additional support to families, residents and staff as needed through one on ones, or referrals to more in-depth counseling if needed.

(Cathy Vande Hoef, Country View Manor)

At Good Samaritan, we hold a bedside memorial service shortly after death with family present if they are able. We even wait for the family to arrive if needed for the service. We also place a crème colored quilt on the bed with a long stemmed silk rose and a copy of the poem "I'm Free". Families are welcomed to take the rose and the poem if they wish. We usually leave the quilt, rose and poem on the bed for 2–3 days or until the personal possessions are removed. We also send a plant to the family either to the funeral home or the family's home. We have a memorial service each quarter for family, residents, friends and staff of the residents of those who have passed away. We invite a local minister to give a short homily during the service. We have staff members read their obituary and share memories with those present. At the closing of the service, we give the family member a candle and the laminated copy of the obituary as a memento of their loved ones. Family members appreciate the service and the closure it brings to all of us. During the Christmas Season, we have a Giving Tree to remember our residents and others associated with our facility that have passed away. Family members and staff may purchase a special ornament with the name of their loved one on a tag to hang on the tree. The proceeds from the sale of these ornaments are used for special projects such as a dove room, purchasing quilts, roses, etc. Families and staff appreciate this opportunity to honor their loved one during the Holiday Season.

(Jane Kumberski, Good Samaritan, Van Buren, Iowa)

At the Iowa Veterans Home, we have a Hospice and Palliative Care Committee that provides a variety of services to residents at their end of life. When a resident passes away, we have a "Service of Farewell" that the staff conducts to recognize, one final time, the service that our veteran provided to his/her country. The service consists of a short prayer or saying that is done when the resident leaves the home the final time. When they enter the facility, the residents choose which prayer or saying they wish to have used, along with what type of covering to use when their body is removed. The Chaplains also conduct a quarterly "Memorial Service", in our Chapel, to recognize the residents that have passed away in the previous quarter. Family, friends and staff are all invited to the service and families are urged to bring pictures or other mementos celebrating the resident's life. The Chaplains also [send] out supportive information about the grieving process, one month after the death and then once prior to the holidays. In addition, our facility publishes an obituary notice that is displayed throughout the buildings, so that other residents, and staff, can be aware that the individual has passed away.

(Randall Inhelder, Iowa Veterans Home, Marshalltown, Iowa)

Rituals Outside of the Nursing Home

A funerary rite of passage is another type of grief ritual. Helping families find funeral and burial information is yet another way to help ease the minds of residents and families during a difficult time. In the United States, common funerary rites of passage include preparation or disposition of the body, the visitation or wake, and the funeral service. According to Rando (1985), the funeral functions as a ritual that marks the transition between life and death; it provides an occasion and location for confirming the reality of death and offers the opportunity for attendees to express their feelings of grief within a supportive social situation; and provides for disposition of the body or remains.

The death of a loved can be difficult in and of itself. Therefore, making final arrangement decisions can contribute to the stress survivors already face. The following section discusses some ways in which nursing home social workers can connect residents and families with funeral and burial resources.

Planning for the Funeral and Burial

Helping residents and family members gain familiarity with final-arrangement (funeral and burial) options can be considered part of discharge planning. Because death happens so frequently in nursing homes, social workers familiar with local funeral and burial options can be of great service to residents and families. Some residents may have their final arrangements decided and paid for before nursing home admission, while others leave the final-arrangement decisions to the survivors. There are at least ten issues that need to be addressed related to final arrangements, including what will happen to the body, where will the remains be kept, what type of ceremony will acknowledge the death, what merchandise will be needed, how will the merchandise be obtained (funeral home, Internet, homemade), what professional services will be needed, how will the services be obtained, how and when will expenses be paid, how should the deceased resident be memorialized, and who will make these decisions and when (Bern-Klug 2004). Social workers, although not expected to become experts in funeral options and costs, should be able to connect residents and families with local resources. This can be done through informational meetings, collecting local information and having it available at the nursing home, and having final-arrangement information posted on the nursing home's Web site.

The nursing home social worker can organize an information session and invite panelists to discuss local options. Consider inviting at least two of the following: a funeral director, a clergy member, a volunteer from the local Funeral Consumers Society (see list of chapters throughout the country at www.funerals.org), and a hospice social worker. Panelists can share their expertise with the nursing home community and respond to questions. Such a meeting could occur at least twice per year. Social workers should invite different panel members from different funeral homes and hospices to build their familiarity with local specialists and to show that the nursing home is not favoring one organization over another. Family members may appreciate receiving this information in a group setting where they can learn from other people's questions. Social workers could distribute additional resources as needed. A list of activities and decisions related to death is included in the appendix. Sharing this list with families ahead of time can help people prepare for final arrangements.

Other ways social workers can help survivors is to collect local information and place it in a three-ring binder that is kept in the nursing home library, sitting room, chapel, or social-services office. The binder should include the "General Price List" (explained later) of at least three local funeral homes, cemeteries, body-donation options, contact information of religious leaders, and reference materials. The Federal Trade Commission and AARP have consumer-oriented pamphlets with basic information about funeral planning that families may find useful.

By providing the information to the resident and family, the social worker signals that it is safe to discuss these issues ahead of time. When there are so many decisions to be made, a number of factors may increase stress levels: the emotional state that many people are in right after the death of a loved one; the amount of money that can be spent quickly; the finality of the decisions made; the sheer number of decisions to be made in a short time; uncertainty about the purpose of a funeral service—is it to honor the person who died or to unite the survivors?—decision maker inexperience; and etiquette uncertainty (not knowing what is OK to ask without reflecting poorly on the family) (Bern-Klug, Ekerdt, and Wilkinson 1999). A note of reminder: not all people will want to make final arrangement decisions ahead of time because of personal or cultural reasons. Families have the right to make final arrangement decisions after the death, if they so choose. Residents who have no surviving family members may present a challenge to the nursing home if final arrangement plans are not spelled out in advance of the death. The remainder of this section provides some general information about final arrangements.

WHAT WILL HAPPEN TO THE BODY?

The options available for final disposition will vary based on the geographic area and on local custom. For example, some rural areas may lack a nearby crematorium, thus making cremation less likely. Body donation options vary from locale to locale. While many medical and dental schools continue to have a body donation or "willed body" program, not all do. Some require that the paperwork be completed before the death, and some have restrictions as to the type of bodies (cause of death, age, etc.) that the program can accept. While most body-donation programs neither pay for nor charge for donated bodies, in some cases the survivors are responsible for the cost of transporting the body. Many donation programs offer to return the cremated remains to the survivors after a year or two or to bury the remains with other donated bodies in a local cemetery, complete with a final dedication ceremony to which survivors are typically invited. Social workers should keep up to date on local body-donation options and costs. Some families will choose this option because it is meaningful to contribute to education and science; others may select the option as a method of keeping costs low. It is often possible to have a service with the body present before it is donated if the family members desire, but arrangements should be discussed with the body-donation program and funeral director. Body-donation programs generally do not accept bodies that have been fully embalmed.

WHAT TYPE OF CEREMONY TO ACKNOWLEDGE THE DEATH?

When the official ceremony takes place at a mosque, synagogue, church, funeral home, or other location, the social worker should let the nursing home community—including residents—know about the service (if it is a public ceremony). It is also important for the nursing home to send some type of acknowledgment of the death to the family. Most nursing homes are short-staffed so it is uncommon for staff to attend funeral services during work hours. While staff members may choose to attend a viewing or funeral on their own time, the nursing home leadership should be clear that this is not expected. Boundary issues are discussed in chapter 10. Social work, activities staff, or volunteers under the direction of staff members should be available to assist residents and staff who want to send an acknowledgement. Many funeral homes now have online condolences that are accessible through their Web sites.

How death is communicated and acknowledged in a nursing home reflects the culture of the nursing home and the extent to which the nursing home views death as a normal part of life. Even when there will be a ceremony away from the nursing home, it is important to offer some sort of a ritual acknowledging the death at the nursing home. In addition, especially for residents who had lived in the nursing home for months or years, a memorial service a few days after the death would send an important message. Family, staff, and fellow residents who were closest to the resident who died may wish to help plan the service by selecting music or readings or by saying something about the resident at the service. Hosting a memorial service on-site sends the message to surviving residents that the passing of a member of the nursing home community will be acknowledged. Edith Keller (age ninety-three) said it well: "I know that how you remember and take care of my neighbors is how you will remember and take care of me" (Berndt 2004b). Some nursing homes print the names of decedents in their newsletter or host an periodic memorial service honoring those who have died.

Learning About Local Funeral Home Options and Prices

The Federal Trade Commission's (www.ftc.gov), "Funeral Rule" requires all funeral homes in the United States to provide a written copy of options and prices to anyone who asks for it in person during business hours. The price and option information is called "The General Price List" and must list the price of sixteen items. Information in the table in the appendix underscores the range in prices in just one city. The Funeral Consumers Alliance (www.funerals.org) documents similar ranges in other cities throughout the country. Because so few families know that they have a right to a written price list, many do not "shop." Nursing home social workers who keep copies of local funeral homes' GPLs on hand can save families time and stress. Social workers should ask funeral homes to send them a copy every time the GPL is updated. Some family-friendly funeral homes include the GPL on their Web sites. If family members have questions about items or prices on the GPL, they should follow up with the funeral home. Disputes over funeral home purchases should be directed to the state attorney general's office. In addition to the funeral home costs, there may be cemetery costs, which can include the cost of the space, opening and closing the grave, a grave marker, setting the marker, and perpetual care of the grounds.

Help with Final Expenses

The average total cost of funeral and burial in 2009 is around $8,500. Data from a 1996 study documented that the "average" price can be misleading because the possible range in prices is so large. The 1996 Kansas City study documented total final arrangement costs from under $200 to over $15,000 (Bern-Klug, DeViney, and Ekerdt 2000). Many families do not realize the broad range in possible costs. Encourage families to talk with the funeral director about options that would add meaning to their arrangements and fit their budget.

There are three government benefit programs that may provide a small amount of money to help with final arrangement costs: Social Security, the Veterans Administration, and Medicaid. (States and counties sometimes have funds to assist low-income people with final arrangements; check with the local social-service agency). Having basic and local details about these benefits would be a service to residents and families.

As of fall 2008, the Social Security Administration provides a one-time $255 "death burial benefit" to a survivor who was receiving benefits based on the decedent's work record. To see if they qualify, survivors should contact Social Security at their toll-free number, (800) 772-1213, or refer to the Web site, www.ssa.gov.

People who were honorably discharged from the U.S. military may be eligible for benefits through the Veteran Burial Benefits program (www.cem.va.gov/burial.htm or toll-free (800) 827-1000). Benefits include a burial flag and a grave marker. Also, there are more than 120 national cemeteries located throughout the country where veterans (and in some cases survivors) can be buried, on a space-available basis.

Title 19 of the Social Security Act, also known as Medicaid, is a joint federal/state program. Prepayment of final arrangements cost (up to a state-specified limit—perhaps $1,000 or $2,000) is an "allowable" expense for people who are in the process of spending down their assets in order to qualify for Medicaid assistance with nursing home costs. While some families prepay a funeral home, consumer organizations like the AARP and the Funeral Consumers Alliance advise families to preplan but not prepay. Instead, families have the option of opening a "payable upon death" bank account and placing the final arrangement money there, or asking their state Medicaid office about other options.

Despite being able to prepay and still qualify for Medicaid, many family members will face additional costs after the death of the resident. Information in the appendix provides examples of ways that final arrangement costs can be minimized.

Social workers can ensure that there is a core set of final arrangement materials on-site to help staff, residents, and family members think through their options. A popular book by Earnest Morgan (in its thirteenth edition), *Dealing Creatively with Death: A Manual of Death Education and Simple Burial*, published by Barclay House, is a good investment. Other resources are available through the Funeral Consumers Alliance. The summer 2004 issue the journal of American Society on Aging, *Generations* was devoted to funeral and memorial practices and contains articles about dealing with family conflicts, helping families make final-arrangement decisions, cyberspace memorials, and funeral ceremonies in nursing homes. Issues can be purchased through www.asaaging.org.

In summary, nursing home staff members need not become experts in final arrangements, but they should be able to connect residents and family members with people who are, and with information that can facilitate a meaningful recognition of the end of a loved one's life. Honoring the death of a resident's life is part of caring for that individual.

References

Achterberg, J. 1992. "Ritual: The Foundation for Transpersonal Medicine." *Revision* 14 (3)" 158–65.
Barrack, M. K. "Sacrament of Anointing the Sick and Dying." Second Exodus. http://www.secondexodus.com/html/catholicdefinitions/anointing.htm. Accessed September 25, 2008.

Berndt, J. 2004a. "When Death Comes in a Nursing Home: A Ritual to Say Goodbye." *Generations, Funerals, and Memorial Practices* 24 (2): 53–54.

Berndt, J. 2004b. *The Sanctity of Life and the Sacredness of Death: A Journey of Putting Pioneer Values Into Practice.* Rochester, N.Y.: Pioneer Network.

Bern-Klug, M. 2004. "The Decision Labyrinth: Helping Families Find Their Way Through Funeral Options." *Generations: Journal of the American Society on Aging* (Summer): 31–36.

Bern-Klug, M., S. DeViney, and D. J. Ekerdt. 2000. "Variations in Funeral-Related Costs of Older Adults and the Role of Preneed Funeral Contracts and Type of Disposition." *Omega: Journal of Death and Dying* 41 (1): 23–38.

Bern-Klug, M., D. J. Ekerdt, and D. S. Wilkinson. 1999. "What Families Know About Funeral-Related Costs: Implications for Social Workers." *Health and Social Work* 2 (2): 128–37.

Braun, K., J. Pietsch, and P. Blanchette. 2000. *Cultural Issues in End-of-Life Decision Making.* Thousand Oaks, Calif.: Sage.

Brawn, K. L., and R. Nichols. 1997. "Death and Dying in Four Asian American Cultures: A Descriptive Study." *Death Studies* 21:327–59.

Buckley, F. J. 1991. "Popular Religiosity and Sacramentality: Learning from Hispanics a Deeper Sense of Symbol, Ritual, and Sacrament." *The Living Light* 27 (351): 4–15.

Bukaitz, F. M., 2007. "Jewish Customs and Traditions on the Journey Through Mourning a Loved One." Privately published.

Castle, J., and W. Phillips. 2003. "Grief Rituals: Aspects That Facilitate Adjustment to Bereavement." *Journal of Loss and Trauma* 8:41–71

Collins, W. L., and A. Doolittle. 2006. "Personal Reflections of Funeral Rituals and Spirituality in a Kentucky African American Family." *Death Studies* 30:957–69.

Davies, D. 1994. "Christianity." In *Rites of passage*, ed. J. Holm and J. Bowker, 41–65. London: Printer Publisher.

Eisenbruch, M. 1984. "Cross-cultural Aspects of Bereavement II: Ethnic and Cultural Variations in the Development of Bereavement Practices." *Culture, Medicine, and Psychiatry* 8 (4): 315–47.

Goss, R. E., and D. Klass. 2006. "Buddhism and Death." In *Death and Religion in a Changing World*, ed. Kathleen Garces-Foley, 69–92. Armonk, N.Y.: M. E. Sharpe.

Habenstein, R., and W. Lamers. 1974. *Funeral Customs the World Over.* Milwaukee, Wis.: Bulfin.

Hardy-Bougere, M. 2008. "Cultural Manifestations of Grief and Bereavement: A Clinical Perspective." *Journal of Cultural Diversity* 15 (2): 66–69

Hayden, B. 1987. "Alliances and Ritual Ecstasy: Human Response to Resource Stress." *Journal for the Scientific Study of Religion* 26 (1): 81–91.

Hunter, J. 2007–2008. "Bereavement: An Incomplete Rite of Passage." *OMEGA* 56 (2): 153–73

Irish, D. P., K. F. Lundquist, and V. J. Nelson, eds. 1993. *Ethnic Variations in Dying, Death, and Grief: Diversity in Universality*. Washington, D.C.: Taylor and Francis.

Levine, E. 1997. "Jewish Views and Customs on Death." In *Death and Bereavement Across Cultures*, ed. C. M. Parkes, P. Laungani, and B. Young, 98–130. London: Routledge.

Longaker, C., 1997. *Facing Death and Finding Hope*. New York: Doubleday.

Martinson, I. 1998. "Funeral Rituals in Taiwan and Korea." *Oncology Nursing Forum* 25 (10): 1456–760.

McGoldrick, M., and F. Walsh. 1991. *Living Beyond Loss: Death in the Family*. |New York: Norton

McGoldrick, M., P. Hines, E. Lee, and N. Garcia Preto. 1986. "Mourning Rituals: How Culture Shapes the Experience of Loss." *Networker* (Nov./Dec.): 28–36.

Moore, S.F., and B. G. Myerhoff, eds. 1977. *Secular Ritual*. Amsterdam: Van Gorcum.

Nichols, M. P. 2009. *The Essentials of Family Therapy*. 4th ed. Boston: Pearson Education.

Rando, T. A. 1985. "Creating Therapeutic Rituals in the Psychotherapy of the Bereaved." *Psychotherapy* 22:236–40.

Romanoff, B. D., and M. Terenzio. 1998. "Rituals and the Grieving Process." *Death Studies* 22:697–712.

Rosenblatt, P., 1993. "Ethnic Variations in Dying, Death, and Grief: Diversity in Universality." In *Ethnic Variations in Dying, Death, and Grief: Diversity in Universality*, ed. D. P. Irish, K. F. Lundquist, and V. J. Nelson, 13–19. Washington, D.C.: Taylor and Francis.

Van Gennep, A. [1908] 1960. *The Rites of Passage*. Trans. M. Vizedom and G. Cafee. Chicago: University of Chicago Press.

Wood, C. A., and G. W. Rowatt. 2006. "Contemporary Grief Rituals for Christians in North America." *International Journal of Health Promotion and Education* 44 (1): 19–23.

Yeung, W. 1995. *A Cross-Cultural Look at Death, Dying, and Religion*. Chicago: Nelson-Hall.

York, S., 2000. *Remembering Well: Rituals for Celebrating Life and Mourning Death*. San Francisco: Jossey-Bass.

Grief, Self-Care, and Staff-Care

Repeated Loss in the Nursing Home Environment

SARA SANDERS AND PATTI ANEWALT

THE CASE OF INGRID

Ingrid was a twenty-nine-year-old social-services director at a 120-bed nursing home in an urban area of the Northwest. The facility had a strong reputation in the community and had a waiting list for new residents. With an undergraduate degree in social work, Ingrid knew from an early age that she wanted to work with older adults, and nursing home social work had been a primary interest. The nursing home where Ingrid was employed was part of a larger chain of facilities within a four-county area. Ingrid had worked in the nursing home for less than one year (she had previously been employed at the Area Agency on Aging) so she looked to the other, more experienced social-service directors for support and guidance.

For the first six month in her position, Ingrid came to work feeling excited about another day at the facility. She enjoyed meeting with residents and families and prided herself on going "above and beyond" to support residents as they approached the end of their lives. She provided comprehensive information during care planning about the psychosocial needs of the residents, which was appreciated by both the families and the larger interdisciplinary team. During the seventh month of her employment, four residents died at the facility within a two-week period. Ingrid had worked with all four residents since their admission to the facility, and they had had family systems that were particularly receptive to Ingrid's assistance. As each resident died, a new resident was contacted and admitted to the facility within twenty-four hours. This was the standard protocol at this facility given the long waiting list for admissions. The nursing home staff rarely took time to address their feelings of grief associated with deceased residents because of the preparations required for the next admission. Ingrid was expected to be instrumental in the admission process, despite the grief she was experiencing.

By the end of her first year of employment at the nursing home, Ingrid's excitement and passion for her work had diminished. She spent less time with residents and families and provided less psychosocial insight at case planning sessions. During a monthly meeting with her social-service counterparts from other facilities, Ingrid indicated that she was considering leaving the nursing home setting for another area of social work. She described herself as becoming less interested in working with older adults and thought that working with younger individuals might be less depressing and bring her more satisfaction.

Previous chapters have established that nursing homes are a prominent location of end-of-life care for older adults in the United States (Lopez 2007). In this chapter, we will focus on the effects that working in a nursing home with dying residents can have on the staff. Nursing home staff members encounter the deaths of multiple residents every year. Each death, to a varying degree, affects their emotional and psychological well-being. Some staff members will view their work with dying individuals as a privilege, a final gift that they can give to beloved residents, such as Ingrid at the onset of this chapter. However, others will become overwhelmed by the experience of caring for multiple dying residents, thereby creating grief overload and symptoms of compassion fatigue and burnout, similar to what was occurring in Ingrid by the end of the case study. For staff who do not address their grief, the experience of being surrounded by death can have adverse personal and professional consequences.

This chapter will provide a summary of how working in a nursing home can affect the emotional and psychological well-being of the social worker and other staff. Specifically, the topics of grief, burnout, and compassion fatigue and their effects on long-term-care staff will be explored. We will then examine how the nursing home setting and the residents' physical and social condition contributes to these emotional and psychological reactions for staff. Finally, we will address the necessity of self-care among nursing home staff and how social workers can be instrumental in creating an environment of psychological and emotional wellness in the nursing home environment.

Grief, Burnout, and Compassion Fatigue

Overview of Terms

Death in a nursing home setting is common. Consequently, coping with death requires all nursing home staff to have an understanding of grief, mourning, bereavement, and the implications of these concepts on the larger social system. *Loss* occurs whenever one cannot have someone or something they value. Loss is best understood in the context of a separation from a person, object, status, or relationship (Corr, Nabe, and Corr 2003). For Ingrid, loss was experienced each time a resident's condition deteriorated and when death occurred. With each initial loss, secondary losses can also occur. For Ingrid, secondary losses included predictability in one's role and normalcy during one's day.

The terms "bereavement" and "grief" are often used interchangeably; however, there are important differences between the two. *Bereavement* is usually understood from the perspective of what happens *to* an individual as a result of experiencing a loss; it is a *state of being* in response to the loss. Attig (1996:32) describes death and bereavement as "choiceless events" that result in feelings of helplessness and lack of control. In the case of Ingrid, her bereavement process was characterized by feeling alone and isolated in her emotional pain. Experiencing the death of four residents within a week's time left Ingrid with a sense of compassion fatigue. This eventually led to burnout in her role as social service director. Ingrid's earlier sense of anticipation of each workday was eventually replaced with disillusionment and a sense of burnout. Figley (2002:3) describes the compassion fatigue of professional helpers as secondary traumatic stress as a result of caring for others. Rothschild and Rand (2006:14) suggest compassion fatigue is the broad description, saving the term "burnout" for more acute situations.

In contrast to bereavement, *grief* is the innate, natural reaction one has to a loss. The ways in which a person reacts to a loss is as unique as the individual. Personality, previous experience with loss, culture, environment, and perceived sense of support are a few of the many variables that influence how a person reacts to loss. In the case of Ingrid, her grief was evidenced by her withdrawal from the residents at the nursing home and her becoming less engaged in the care processes related to residents and families. Grief is a universal experience. The severity of the grief reactions is more intense when the feelings of investment with what is lost are higher.

Mourning refers to the expression of grief, which can only occur when one feels permission to engage in this emotional release. Mourning is how a person intertwines the loss into daily life (DeSpelder and Strickland 2005). If there are simultaneous stressors occurring at the time of the loss, or if the environment is not conducive to supporting the bereaved person, a person might grieve but not mourn. In other words, they may experience grief reactions but not be able to integrate these reactions and the loss experience into daily life. Ingrid did not feel she had permission to express her grief over the death of the residents, and, in time, this compromised her ability to focus on the needs of the other residents. These unexpressed reactions to her grief may also have long-term effects that she will carry forward. This could affect her ability to function in future jobs as well as her current position. Another important aspect of mourning is the coping patterns that are needed to assist in navigating a person through the loss experience. Part of the process of mourning is adjusting to the loss. This process is an essential component of one's grief experience but can be difficult given that this involves not only adjusting to loss but recognizing the pain associated with the loss and integrating the significance of the loss into one's life.

The Adjustment Process

For fellow residents, families, and nursing home staff, grieving and mourning the death of a resident takes time. The process involves adjusting from what *was* to what *is* and what *will be*, given what has changed. It is common for those experiencing a significant loss, perhaps of a family member or close friend, to feel alone as they yearn for what was familiar and feel anxious about what the future may hold. Although everyone's grief and mourning is unique, bereaved individuals often seek the affirmation that they are "normal" and not alone as they navigate through their own grief journey. This reassurance and acknowledgment can have a significant and positive effect on bereaved individuals as they feel supported rather than alone on their grief journey. Eventually, most bereaved individuals reach a place where they are able to focus less on what was lost and more on the aspects of their lives that are still intact and available.

According to Worden (2009), mourning is an active rather than a passive process of adjustment. He suggests there are four tasks that should occur during mourning:

- To accept the reality of the loss
- To process the pain of grief
- To adjust to a world without the deceased
- To find an enduring connection with the deceased while embarking on a new life

By engaging in these four processes, the bereaved individual eventually transitions from experiencing intense emotions that can leave one feeling out of control, to slowly focusing less on what has been lost in the past and more on the future.

In addition to Worden, many others have examined how bereavement adjustment occurs. Attig (1996) describes bereavement as a time of transition from feeling helpless in response to a significant loss to taking an active approach in coping and relearning one's world. Klass (1999) explains how parents of deceased children transform the pain from their loss as they discover ways to maintain a spiritual connection with their child. Neimeyer (2003) suggests meaning reconstruction is the key component of a bereaved individual's grief experience.

Unique Types of Grief Seen in the Nursing Home Setting

Disenfranchised grief is experienced by some residents and staff members in many nursing homes. Doka (2002) defines disenfranchised grief as a loss that is not socially sanctioned, leaving the bereaved individual feeling alone and unsupported in his or her grief. Moss and Moss (2002) argue that expressions of grief are often minimized in the nursing home, which then reinforces disenfranchised grief. The message that nursing home residents have "lived a full life" and it was "their time to go" often accompanies their death. This belief pattern conveys the unspoken message to staff and family members that they should not be affected by the death. As mentioned earlier, it is not uncommon for the deceased resident's bed to be filled by a new resident the same day as the death. Ingrid and most likely other staff in the case referenced earlier experienced grief with each resident's death yet found it difficult to mourn as the focus quickly moved on to new admissions.

Pauline Boss (1999) coined the term "ambiguous loss" to help define those losses that create confusion about one's status and relationship with regard to the person who died. Examples of ambiguous loss are found in the nursing home setting. Staff, especially the direct-care nursing staff, are asked to provide intimate care in a family-like fashion to residents; however, the boundaries of their relationship and role with residents is often not clear. Staff are sent the message to care and develop a close relationship with residents and also to be unaffected by any intense grief reactions when the resident dies. This mixed message creates ambiguity and can complicate grief reactions as staff members struggle to decipher what is appropriate and not appropriate to feel and express.

Effects of Grief

Regardless of which theoretical approach is used to understand the grief experience, all models reference the depths of pain that can affect an individual emotionally, psychologically, spiritually, cognitively, physically, and behaviorally. *Emotional* responses to grief can include fear, anger, anxiety, deep sadness, and depression. Socially appropriate responses vary by culture; however, these reactions are the most socially acceptable responses to grief, given that most adults expect to feel some emotional reaction following the death of someone close. *Psychological* reactions can include many things, such as feeling the deceased's presence; visual, auditory, or olfactory sensations; and momentarily forgetting the person is deceased. These reactions can be overwhelming for the individual. Many bereaved people are fearful of sharing these reactions as they believe others will think they are "going crazy." Some adults do not realize that these types of psychological reactions are common. However, the psychological reactions can develop into a more complicated grief experience for some individuals if they continue living life as if their loved one has not died, such as setting the place for the deceased at meals or laying out the deceased's clothes for each day.

These reactions may require more intense professional assistance. From a *spirituality* standpoint, many will question what they previously believed in a quest to find meaning in the death and the events surrounding the death. Significant loss is often accompanied by a struggle with some of the existential questions about the meaning of life and how the world operates. Neimeyer (2003) has published extensively about how bereaved individuals strive to rework their understanding of life and derive meaning in life after significant losses. The spiritual effect of grief can be frightening for individuals. It is important to reassure people that these reactions and questions are normal.

From a *cognitive* perspective, most bereaved feel distracted and unable to focus and have questions as they seek to understand the reality that someone has died. These reactions most frequently occur immediately following a loss. *Physically*, bereaved individuals may have difficulty sleeping or eating and may feel weak. They may experience physiological symptoms of pain. Others report various illnesses or a compromised immune system. *Behaviorally*, some people find it difficult to sit still after the death of a loved one. They feel the need to stay busy all the time. Others lack the initiative to accomplish what used to be normal, everyday activities. Although bereaved individuals are affected to some degree in most of these ways (emotionally, spiritually, cognitively, physically, and behaviorally), the actual experience for each person is as unique as the individual.

Compassion Fatigue and Burnout

Staff members in nursing homes need to be mindful that because their primary focus is on the needs of others, they are particularly susceptible to compassion fatigue (Leon, Altholz, and Dziegielewski 1999; Figley 1999). Compassion involves an awareness of others distress and pain and a desire to relief this discomfort from their lives. Fatigue can be characterized as stress, exhaustion, or tiredness as a result of some form of physical or emotional work. Compassion fatigue results from "too much caring and too little self caring" (Ochberg 2008). This is evidenced by tiredness and emotional depletion. As the level of care intensifies near the end of life, nursing home staff can find it more challenging to maintain a professional relationship, as opposed to a personal relationship, with both residents and family members. When individuals are truly present to others struggling with significant pain and grief, they can not help but be affected. What they are feeling in response to the pending loss can be overwhelming. The importance of finding ways to offset this cannot be overemphasized. As Moss and Moss (2002) suggest, nursing home staff must be supported in exploring ways to find balance between being present and emotionally available to the residents they provide care for, while still being aware of and find ways to express the grief they experience when a resident dies. As nursing home staff continually focus on the needs of residents, families, and coworkers, particularly when a resident is facing death, some level of compassion fatigue is likely to occur. Attentively listening to others who are in pain may result in the listener also experiencing some pain. Being present to others' pain can initiate one's own feelings of helplessness. While medications often improve physical pain, emotional pain is different. No one can give a grieving person what they really want, which is to not have the loss they are experiencing. In addition to feeling helpless, listening and being a supportive presence to others can stimulate the listener's own grief issues.

Left unaddressed, compassion fatigue can lead to burnout, a state of complete exhaustion as a result of being involved in emotionally challenging situations over a period of time (Pines and Arnson, cited by Figley 1999). Burnout is measured by the level of emotional exhaustion, depersonalization, and reduced personal accomplishment (Maslach, Jackson, and Leiter 1996). Figley (2002:19) describes the cause of burnout as "frustration, powerlessness and the inability to achieve work goals." While there have been several studies documenting the potentially negative effects of compassion fatigue and burnout when working with the elderly and terminally ill (Anderson and Gaugler 2007; Bakker et al. 2005; Leon, Atholz, and Dziegielewski 1999), more research is needed on the effects of compassion fatigue on nursing home staff. This will provide insight into the consequences of unrecognized and unresolved issues of grief and loss.

Factors Associated with Grief in the Nursing Home Staff

Regardless of the quality of the facility or staff, grief and loss issues are prominent in long-term-care settings. Moving into a nursing home requires residents to adjust to a new environment, develop new relationships, and face limited autonomy and control over their daily routines. Additionally, the reasons for moving into a nursing home usually involve changes in physical abilities, the death of a spouse, or the inability to continue living alone. As residents living with chronic illnesses transition toward a more palliative approach near the end of life, their expectations about this last chapter of life may change as well, resulting in additional losses. It is important to remember that the majority of older adults do not actively seek nursing home placement. Thus, the transition to a nursing home is accompanied by many negative emotions for most people.

Working with residents during this final phase of life can be rewarding for staff. Staff have the opportunity to develop close relationships with older adults who are in a time of need. They also have the opportunity to walk residents through a time of transition, helping to enhance their quality of life. Additionally, staff often develop meaningful relationships with many families. Nurses aides often use family-related terms to describe their relationships with the residents they care for (Fisher and Wallhagen 2008). The development of strong relationships with residents and families can be self-gratifying for staff. While these positive elements of working in a long-term-care setting exist for staff, it can also be difficult for staff to observe residents as they experience many losses, physical decline, and approaching death.

In 2006, Strom-Gottfried and Mowbray challenged the field of social work to consider the question, "Who heals the helper?" They argued that working within certain organizations or social-service settings and with certain populations of clients exacerbates grief reactions. While the nursing home setting was not specifically identified in their work, several conditions place nursing home social workers and other nursing home staff at particular risk for intense grief reactions and possible burnout. Three areas of nursing homes will be examined as factors associated with staff grief and burnout: The nursing home environment, the residents' physical and cognitive health status, and the resident's social condition.

The Nursing Home Environment

Stigma

Regardless of setting, working with dying individuals can be physically, psychologically, and emotionally difficult. While the tasks of providing end-of-life care are similar for professionals in hospitals, hospices, or nursing homes, the nursing home environment is unique and can have a significant effect on the grief experienced by staff. Unfortunately, the phrase "nursing home" evokes negative connotations for many people. Old and young alike characterize nursing homes as a place where people go to die or as Forbes (2001) indicated, "heaven's waiting room." Staff are constantly fighting the notion that nursing homes provide substandard care, with media reports of nursing home violations and residents receiving poor care fueling the stigma associated with these settings. Additionally, nursing homes have not received the same positive accolades and community praise as hospice programs for providing high-quality care to the frail and dying. These factors can be demoralizing for staff as they strive to provide quality care to vulnerable individuals.

The stigma associated with long-term care isolates staff from being able to express their reactions associated with the death of residents. The notion of "what would you expect . . . you work in a nursing home" sends the message that strong grief reactions are not normal and should be suppressed. The organizational structure of nursing homes unintentionally supports this stigma by not recognizing the effect of death on staff and that the residents have unique care needs as they approach death, which require specialized staff care (Schell and Kayser-Jones 2007). This can lead to poor staff self-care, as well as poor resident care.

Multiple Workload Demands

The workload demands on all staff members in nursing homes are high, including the continual need to address the care of residents, answering call buttons and other alarms, managing residents with difficult behaviors, and charting to ensure compliance with regulations. Additionally, staff members are expected to develop a familial environment for residents, filling the roles of family or friends for residents in increase their quality of life and overall well-being (Kelley et al. 1999). It has been suggested that residents should set the tone for relationships with staff; however, staff members realize that different residents need particular relationships, such as "therapeutic" relationships, "personal friendships," or "friendly" relationships (McGilton and Boscart 2007:2155). Such strategies as sharing mutual interests, learning about one another's families, and sharing stories from the past can assist in creating close, meaningful staff-resident relationships

(McGilton and Boscart 2007). While fostering a familial environment within facilities may be beneficial for residents, it can have emotional consequences for staff as they try to balance the stress of daily workloads and the added stress of feeling responsible for having a close relationship with the residents. Also, the expectation that staff become emotionally close to residents does not take into consideration the emotional wear and tear that this can have on staff as the resident approaches death. This can create confusion between one's personal role and needs and one's professional role and responsibilities. The more the staff person shares with residents about their personal lives, the greater the potential for developing blurred personal and professional boundaries. These blurred roles affect not only the staff members but also residents and their families.

Another aspect of workload stress is the responsibilities of the staff preceding and following the death of a resident. Research has found that not all nursing home staff members are comfortable providing care for dying individuals or postmortem care (Schell and Kayser-Jones 2007). While this type of care may be a grief outlet for some staff as it assists with closure in the relationship with the resident, for other staff it can provoke fear and stress. This issue is complicated by poor staffing patterns and lack of training and support, which can affect the care that people receive while they are dying and also postmortem. The work of hospice professionals can assist in decreasing this workload stress. If they are involved in the care of the dying patient, they can be a source of education and support both before and after the death of the resident.

The high workload of nursing homes, coupled with minimal pay, lack of education and training of some staff, emotional and psychological stress, and working with a majority of residents who are cognitively impaired and sometimes aggressive, can reduce job satisfaction (Brodaty, Draper, and Low 2003; Novak and Chappell 1996; Rodney 2000), which ultimately contributes to staff turnover. Research has found that 50 percent of nursing home staff members do not have enough time to complete their work-related tasks and fear losing their jobs should organizational change within the nursing home occur (Brodaty, Draper, and Low 2003). Additionally, over one-third of nursing home staff feel that the psychological stress of their work is not adequately addressed (Brodaty, Draper, and Low 2003). Outlets for processing the emotions associated with one's work in the nursing home are not always available so staff hold onto their psychological stress and grief, exacerbating the likelihood of burnout in the future.

Death of Residents

As discussed in chapter 1, over 20 percent of people each year die in nursing homes (Happ et al. 1999), and this does not account for the number of nursing home residents who die at the hospital or en route to the hospital (Lopez 2007). Witnessing death on a daily basis can be emotionally difficult for staff members, especially for those who are not comfortable or familiar with the dying process and how to work with dying residents and their families, much less manage their own emotional reactions (Wadensten et al. 2007). Early work by Kubler-Ross (1969) and Worden (2009) found that over 90 percent of professionals caring for terminally ill patients struggled in some way. The research confirmed the effects that patients' terminal illnesses can have on caregivers (Worden 2009). Many nursing home staffs need more education on death and dying (Jenull and Brunner 2008), which will help them professionally and personally. Hospices are the ideal resource for this type of training.

Even when staff members establish appropriate boundaries with residents, stress related to the dying process and the subsequent deaths of residents can affect their professional and personal lives. The stress is increased when staff members have developed enmeshed relationships with residents in an attempt to address their own unmet needs or as a result of their efforts to create a familial environment. Feelings of grief and loss are further heightened when relationships with residents and families have transitioned from a professional to personal level. This can create challenges for staff members as they try to remain invested in the care of other residents.

Finally, because of the frequency of residents' deaths and the need to "fill the empty bed," staff members often do not have the opportunity to engage in any form of grief work before being "back on the job" with another resident and family. This can leave staff "emotionally exhausted and drained of energy in their daily work" (Evers, Tomic, and Brouwers 2001:440).

Resident Physical Condition

COGNITIVE IMPAIRMENT

Witnessing the physical and in some cases cognitive decline of residents can be emotionally challenging and can contribute to burnout and grief in family and staff members. As explained in chapter 1, nursing homes provide care to individuals of advanced age with multiple chronic health conditions. Compounding the physical decline, over 50 percent of nursing home residents have Alzheimer's disease or another form of dementia (National Alzheimer's Association 2007). This creates challenges for staff members as they strive to develop meaningful relationships with the residents while also managing behavioral issues associated with memory impairment. Feeling stressed and at times defeated by their perceived inability to help these residents can result in staff members' becoming demoralized and disillusioned with their jobs.

DETERMINING TERMINAL STATUS

Another issue that accompanies care of older individuals with advanced chronic diseases is the challenge of determining when a person clearly reaches a terminal state (Bern-Klug 2004). Some residents will have a slow steady decline, allowing staff to say good-bye and emotionally prepare for their deaths. Other residents will experience sudden death, possibly leaving staff yearning for closure in those relationships. Staff can experience interruptions and changes in the care they provide to dying residents. In some cases, residents are transferred to the hospital and die there. In other cases, residents remain in the nursing home and begin to receive services from an outside hospice agency. Regardless of the plan for end-of-life care, nursing home staff members remain both physically and emotionally involved in providing the majority of daily care to the dying resident. Watching this decline and providing end-of-life care at the facility can be rewarding for a staff but can also create intense grief reactions, particularly when staff members are caring for a dying resident whom they have known and felt close to for a considerable period of time.

Resident Social Condition

Residents come to nursing homes facing many psychosocial transitions. Some psychosocial issues, such as a history of family conflict or lifelong mental-health conditions, may have been present before nursing home placement. Other psychosocial issues are directly associated with the long-term-care environment and the residents' physical or cognitive decline.

Nursing home staff members naturally become confidants for the residents as they seek to reconcile past issues and current psychosocial stress and prepare for the final chapters of their lives. Residents whose families do not visit as often as they would like often view the staff as "family." In some cases, nursing home members staff may also become the target for a resident's anger and frustration, particularly when the resident realizes that some of these issues will never be resolved and that he or she is unable to regain a previous sense of normalcy. Residents' treating staff with projected frustration and anger can also contribute to staff grief and burnout.

MULTIPLE LOSSES

One of the most significant issues facing nursing home residents is the multiple losses they face as a result of their physical and cognitive condition and placement in a nursing home. These losses, such as the resident's home, possessions, spousal or other relationships, daily routines, independence, and pets, are common among nursing home residents and often trigger increased thoughts of mortality. Many nursing homes take steps to reduce the preventable losses, but losses occur in all facilities. There is wide variation among facilities about the types of possessions can be brought to the facility and the amount of control residents have over their daily routine. Addressing the grief associated with these losses can be difficult for staff members who may not have adequate training in working with individuals who are thinking about their own dying process and the end of their lives (Lopez 2007; Wadensten et al. 2007). Many residents also have unresolved grief issues from the past that manifest during nursing home placement, increasing their feelings of powerlessness, hopelessness, and a total loss of autonomy. Accentuating these feelings of loss is the fact that most residents do not want to be in a nursing home. Research has reported that even the residents who agree that nursing home placement is necessary view the nursing home environment negatively within three months of admission and often report that they have lost their ability to communicate their concerns to staff (Iwasiw et al. 2003). This results in additional loss as residents try to maintain a sense of identity, purpose, and control in their lives (Huppert et al. 2000).

Staff members are affected by how the residents respond to these losses. First, the residents may be more thoughtful about death and want to talk about it with others (Lopez 2007). This may be difficult for staff members, particularly if they are not comfortable with death and their own mortality. Staff may also be trying to create an atmosphere of happiness and joy and might view talk about death as depressing and sad. Staff may also begin to resent residents who project their feelings onto them or respond to their grief by giving up, becoming depressed, lashing out in anger, or withdrawing. These responses can leave staff feeling helpless or unappreciated, which can adversely affect staff morale and overall response to the job.

STATUS OF RESIDENTS' FAMILIES

Nursing home staff members provide care not only for the residents but also for their extended family systems, many of which have been engaged in long-term care giving for years before placement. As the resident's death approaches, staff members are faced with losing the relationship with the resident and, in some cases, the relationship that was developed with the family system.

Long-term care giving can create feelings of ambiguous loss for families as they try to determine the status of their relationship with the resident. Boss (1999) suggests that questions may arise regarding the relationship for caregivers of individuals who are physically present but psychological absent; these questions might resemble, "Am I still a wife even though this person does not recognize me?" As residents with cognitive impairments, in particular, approach the end stages of disease and death, research has found that the grief of families increases (Meuser and Marwit 2001; Sanders and Adams 2005). Thus, staff members are interacting with family members who may have unresolved grief associated with the cognitive decline of the residents. This has the potential to place staff at greater risk for burnout and compassion fatigue as they try to emotionally care for the families while also addressing their own grief.

Another issue that can compound the grief and burnout of nursing home staff is working with residents with absent families; these families may be not actively involved in care, may reside out of state, or may have already emotionally and psychologically disconnected from the resident. Sanders and colleagues (in press) found that some caregivers of individuals with end-stage dementia in nursing homes had emotionally disengaged from the patient and were simply waiting for the death to make the loss of the resident complete. In these cases, it would not be unusual for the staff to compensate for the lack of visits from family and form even closer bonds with these residents in an attempt to provide them with the feeling of having family support. It would be expected in these situations that staff members may feel more intense grief reactions as they lose a "family member" and then experience anger and resentment at the actual family members, who may become suddenly involved as death approaches. Additionally, families that are having trouble accepting the prognosis of the resident create challenges in staff interactions, which leads to increased feelings of stress (Jenull and Brunner 2008).

INTIMACY OF CARE

A significant loss for residents is associated with their inability to provide care for themselves. While nursing home staff may think little about the need to bathe, dress, or toilet a resident, for residents, this symbolizes a loss of autonomy and personhood. Residents respond to this in a variety of ways, but some may resist any form of assistance and react with aggression, particularly individuals who are cognitively impaired and possibly misinterpret the staff intentions. While the reactions of these residents may evoke stress for the staff, residents' response to personal care represents one last way for them to maintain some dignity and control over their changing lives. It also represents a grief response associated with their current condition.

CULTURAL ISSUES AMONG STAFF

While the majority of nursing home residents are white, the majority of the staff members are African American, members of a first-generation immigrant group, or another minority (Berdes and Eckert 2001). Cultural norms related to care giving, bereavement, and dependency can vary by ethnicity. Residents may have had limited exposure to individuals of other racial or cultural groups, thus creating the potential for communication challenges. Residents may deliberately or inadvertently make racist or discriminatory comments about and to staff (Berdes and Eckert 2001).

The current cohort of nursing home residents have lived for a majority of their lives during a period of racial and ethnic tension in the United States or their country of origin. As a result, cultural differences between them and the staff may become additional sources of stress and grief for staff as they try to provide care. Some staff members, because of their cultural norms, may have been socialized to revere older adults, and they might subsequently seek out close relationships with residents. The residents may not be open to the formation of these relationships, resulting in social distance between staff and residents (Grau and Wellin 1992). Additionally, the staff may be subjected to racial slurs, with one study finding that over 25 percent of nursing home staff members experienced this while providing care to residents (Ramirez, Teresi, and Holmes 2006). Working under these conditions can create occupational stress, leading to burnout if not appropriately addressed with staff.

Creating a Healthy Environment:
The Role of the Nursing Home Social Worker

The issues outlined in this chapter can create grief and stress for nursing home staff members, especially when they are not educationally and emotionally prepared. Because of the constant demands placed on nursing home staff members, many do not recognize the cumulative emotional effects that these issues have on them. It is not until staff members are experiencing compassion fatigue and burnout that they realize that they have unintentionally ignored the importance of self-care. It is the responsibility of the facility administration and directors to recognize the need to promote a philosophy of self-care throughout the facility. It is the responsibility of the individual staff member to take advantage of resources offered and make self-care an integral part of professional practice. This chapter concludes with a discussion on how the social worker can be a key player in helping to create a healthy work environment within the nursing home.

Working with dying residents has been labeled an occupational stressor for nursing home staff (Jenull and Brunner 2008). The combination of a heavy workload and the emotional stress of being with dying individuals can lead to unresolved grief, compassion fatigue, and ultimately burnout, which can contribute to social workers leaving the field. As suggested by Jenull and Brunner (2008) greater attention is needed at the organizational level to address the emotional and educational needs of staff members working with dying individuals. This is imperative given the pressure put on staff to provide high-quality care to the growing numbers of older adults who require nursing home care.

Nursing home social workers have the opportunity to play a critical role in working with other staff members and residents to ensure that feelings of grief and loss are addressed. Doing so contributes to a healthy atmosphere. Understanding the factors associated with the nursing home environment and the residents' physical and social condition is the first step needed for the nursing home leadership to create an environment and culture of "compassion wellness" (Berger 2005). While it is impossible to eliminate grief and loss and the factors associated with compassion fatigue and burnout from nursing homes, strategies need to be implemented to reduce the harmful effects that they can have on staff.

Social workers possess many skills that make them natural champions for promoting self-care and compassion wellness in nursing homes. Most important, social workers, through the content received in courses such as Human Behavior and the Social Environment, have a working knowledge of contemporary grief theories and the effects of death on individuals and the workplace environment. This provides them with insight into why staff, residents, and families respond the way that they do to the multiple losses that are constantly occurring within the nursing home environment.

Second, grounded in systems theory, social workers possess the awareness of how stress and change can affect the overall functioning of the larger nursing home environment. They recognize the dynamics that can exist among residents, families, and staff and how these dynamics can affect the provision of daily care. Additionally, social workers recognize the holistic needs of residents from the time of admission through death and have the opportunity to help residents examine unmet needs and challenges to their overall health. Finding ways to explain micro- and macrosystemic dynamics and normalize these changes and then reduce stressors that originate within the environment are natural functions of social workers. In order to be effective at this, social workers need the resources, job description, and support from administration to assume these responsibilities.

Social workers also are also highly trained in interpersonal and communication skills. These skills are essential to the development of relationships with staff to assist them in addressing their own feelings of grief. Similarly, social workers can help identify staff members who are struggling with feelings of grief and then connect these individuals with the resources to obtain additional assistance, if necessary.

Staff members who struggle with the dying and death of a resident can also benefit from finding ways to commemorate and integrate the death into their daily life. In some instances, this may entail the social worker using macropractice skills to promote organizational change to better support the needs of grieving staff members. In other situations, social workers may use micropractice skills, such as crisis intervention and other problem-solving strategies, to help staff who are experiencing strong feelings of loss. Because unaddressed grief and loss can create emotional crises, it is essential that both macro- and microlevel responses from the social worker be considered. People can become angry, forlorn, bitter, hopeless, and out of control as a result of grief. Crisis-intervention skills may be necessary to assist people who are on the verge of an emotional crisis and in need of immediate intervention, particularly when death is unexpected.

The social worker can play a crucial role by helping nursing home residents understand what they are experiencing and supporting the residents through the adjustment process. With this support, the goal for grieving residents is to eventually discover what can still bring meaning to their lives in the nursing home setting. Most nursing home residents are more familiar and comfortable with the more stoic approach to bereavement from years past. For this reason, they can benefit from the sensitivity and coaching of the social worker on alternative ways to cope with significant loss, including the death of a roommate.

In the process of serving other nursing home staff, residents, and family members, social workers should not overlook the effects of grief and loss on their own lives. This is what contributed to the stress experienced by Ingrid in the case presented at the beginning of this chapter. Coming from a strengths perspective, social workers who practice self-awareness and self-care and maintain clear professional boundaries serve as models for other nursing home staff. Social workers can set the example on how to care for oneself so one can be most effective in caring for others.

Self-Care Strategies for Nursing Homes

DEFINING REALISTIC EXPECTATIONS

Part of creating an environment of compassion wellness is establishing realistic expectations for the care of the residents. Rather than expect that staff members can ensure that all residents have a "good death," a more realistic expectation is that the staff would work toward creating a positive experience in the nursing home for each resident. This experience would be dictated by the resident and how he or she defines what is needed at the end of life. For some residents, this may be increased emotional support, but for others it may be time alone for self-reflection or a desire to continue a lifelong pattern of being more introverted. Helping staff identify a more realistic expectation in the care of the residents can be empowering. It can help alleviate feelings of guilt and defeat when residents reject staffs' desire to help. Being clear about one's role can help the social worker and other staff maintain a healthy, balanced involvement with nursing home residents.

DEVELOPING CLEAR BOUNDARIES

Across the nursing home business, there is no consensus on what it means to have clear professional boundaries. This topic has a great deal of ambiguity because one must consider boundaries within the context of culture, spirituality, and professional practice. Adding to this ambiguity, nursing homes combine healthcare and the desire to create a homelike environment for people as they reach the end of their lives.

However, as paid staff, individuals who work in nursing homes have set job descriptions and responsibilities. Unlike personal relationships, staff involvement at the nursing home is limited to the hours worked. Although it may "feel" personal as relationships with residents develop over time, it is not the same as the (unpaid) relationships staff members have with family or friends outside of work. For many nursing home staff members, being a caring, compassionate presence for others who experience significant loss taps into the essence of their choice of profession. The key is to recognize that they can be supportive and present to others' pain yet still be clear about their role and what they have to offer. This must be coupled with an intentional effort to be continually aware of the times when they become personally affected while striving to be professionally effective.

The idea of developing clear boundaries ties in with expectations. Staff must be reflective and closely examine how they are feeling as they provide care to residents. In doing so, they may realize their expectations are based on the development of personal and unhealthy relationships instead of professional relationships. Unhealthy relationships begin to develop when staff members start to focus on what *they* want or need from a relationship instead of focusing on what the resident needs. These relationships develop over time and can be rather insidious. Often the staff members are unaware of how they are turning to the residents to meet or address unmet needs in their personal lives. Unhealthy professional relationships with residents can lead to poor decision making around resident care, a lack of self-care, and even negative effects on relationships with other staff members and families. Being aware that a relationship has become unhealthy is critical for ensuring quality resident care.

Particularly given the homelike environment of the nursing home setting, staff must be vigilant and continually strive to differentiate between their personal and professional investment in a resident's situation. This is emphasized by Sheets (2000), who explains how blurred boundaries can compromise patient safety and also contribute to compassion fatigue and burnout, as seen in the case of Ingrid. Ideally, social workers and other nursing home staff should review, on a daily basis, which residents or situations may be influencing their own emotions. As caring individuals in a helping profession they cannot avoid being affected by those they care for. Yet they must intentionally respond to their personal needs, separate from the care they provide. Often vulnerable and fragile, residents and family members facing end of life and loss need professionals they can turn to and lean on for support. Staff members' needs should not be addressed with those entrusted in their care.

PROMOTING A WORK-LIFE BALANCE

Social workers can be strong advocates for a healthy work-life balance, which refers to the balance between daily work responsibilities and other important areas of people's lives, such as friends, families, hobbies, rest, and relaxation. There are many ways that nursing home staff can slip into an unhealthy work-life balance, particularly when beloved residents are dying. Some staff members who have been highly involved with the care of a resident for a long time might want to remain involved when the patient is dying, even if they are not scheduled to work. They may consider coming in during off times to see the resident, interact with the family, and assist in providing care. Others may call the facility to learn the status of a dying resident or ask to be contacted at home if the resident's condition worsens. While some would argue that these behaviors are a sign of care, compassion, and dedication to the residents, families, and facility, one could also argue that this sets a precedent within facilities of not promoting a healthy work-life balance and encouraging poor professional boundaries. What is considered care and compassion versus unhealthy professional boundaries varies greatly among facilities and staff. Social workers can take a leadership role in helping staff work through these perspectives by facilitating a discussion around the following questions: Am I engaging in this course of action for myself, or am I doing this because this is what is needed by the resident and family? Is my course of action what the resident and family would desire? Will my actions positively or negatively affect the grief of the family following the death of the resident?

Staff need opportunities for downtime. There is always plenty of work to be done in nursing homes, and additional help is always needed. However, this forces one to consider the question, "Who will take care of the residents if the staff are not taking care of themselves?" Staff should be encouraged to maintain a healthy work-life balance, and other opportunities for closure with dying residents need to be created rather than depending on staff use of their personal time. Social workers and nursing home leaders should discourage staff involvement in care when they are not scheduled to work. This is one clear strategy for creating a healthy work environment and promoting a good work-life balance.

CREATING OPPORTUNITIES FOR GROUP REMEMBERING

It is "best practice" for nursing home leaders to have a plan for how to offer grief support to residents and staff. This plan should be included in the organizational policy and procedure manual and implemented by the social worker at the time of a resident's death. This supports a culture within the nursing home that embraces the value of an active, compassion-wellness approach. Staff will more likely practice self-care and wellness at the personal level if it is promoted at the organizational level and by peers who are well respected and viewed as experts on the topic of grief. Figley (1996) emphasizes the importance of caregivers applying the "heal thyself" motto to offset the potential for compassion fatigue when working with the bereaved.

Sometimes it can be helpful to access other professionals such as a chaplain, a hospice social worker, or an employee assistance counselor to help staff process their feelings of loss related to the death of a resident. This can be particularly useful if several deaths have occurred within a short period of time, as described in the example at the outset of this chapter. Being active in this manner can help reduce unaddressed stress and compassion fatigue. Although not well substantiated yet with research, it would make sense that this would have a noticeable and positive effect on both overall morale and staff turnover.

When nursing home CNAs receive the opportunity to acknowledge their grief and obtain support, research confirms they cope better (Anderson and Gaugler 2007). Unfortunately, this study also found that most nursing homes offer few if any opportunities for grief expression, such as a memorial service. An active approach is clearly preferable, given that there is a direct relationship between addressing grief and reducing CNA burnout (Anderson 2008). This validates the importance of providing staff members with opportunities to recognize and acknowledge their grief. Ideas for establishing rituals related to dying and death can be found in chapter 9. When staff intentionally recognize, separate out, and express rather than suppress their grief, they are better able to stay energized and be present with residents and family members.

EDUCATIONAL OPPORTUNITIES

Another component of self-care and wellness is education about grief and loss. Information and support can provide strategies for staff to address the feelings provoked by the deaths of residents. Social workers are in a good position to provide this education to staff, given their awareness of human behavior and the need for developing strong coping skills to reduce burnout. Social workers may consider providing in-service staff trainings about:

- Overview of grief and loss within a nursing home setting
- Personal and professional boundary setting with residents, families, and other staff
- Self-care and coping strategies

Sample outlines for these educational programs can be found in the appendix.

SELF-CARE ACTIVITIES WITHIN THE NURSING HOME

Nursing homes that support preventive and supportive staff interventions create environments that encourage self-care. Being aware of when and how one is becoming too emotionally invested in a situation takes continual effort on the part of staff members. Some days this is easier to do than others. At the end of every day, it is important for staff to identify what they can do to "give back" to themselves after spending so much time caring for others. As social workers identify what personal rituals they can practice that help them keep their level of involvement healthy and balanced, they serve as a model for other staff members. Self-care activities that can be encouraged within the nursing home setting include:

- Helping staff identify what they can and cannot control about their jobs and resident reactions; this can be a group process and conducted during an in-service
- Providing opportunities for team building through potlucks, social events, or structured activities; these work best away from the nursing facility
- Developing peer-mentoring programs for staff
- Promoting the idea among staff that mistakes are opportunities for growth
- Identifying ways to remember and learn from residents who have died by asking the question, "How did interaction with this resident shape you and your views of life?"
- Providing opportunities for all staff to attend workshops and educational events outside the nursing home setting to better understand the elderly, end-of-life care, communication, and relationships
- Promoting wellness activities within the facility, such as healthy eating, exercise, and other stress-management techniques
- Providing incentives for staff who engage in self-care behaviors
- Identifying for staff forms of self expression that might be helpful, such as keeping a journal, poetry, gardening, music, art, crafts, and hobbies
- Encouraging mental-health days and the value of taking vacations
- Using humor to decrease stress; consider a humor bulletin board in the staff lounge

SELF-ASSESSMENT SUGGESTIONS

One of the most important ways to prevent compassion fatigue and burnout is to continually reflect on how one is affected by the day-to-day stressors of the nursing home environment. Each time a resident dies, it is important to carve out some time to discern how one is affected by that death. As part of this reflection, consider the following three questions: What will I take from this experience, or from knowing this person? What will I leave behind or let go of? How have I been changed by this person or this experience?

Self-assessment questionnaires are another helpful way to objectively assess how one is coping. B. Stamm's (2009) Professional Quality of Life Scale, Compassion Satisfaction and Fatigue Subscales—Revision IV (ProQOL R-V) can be found in the appendix, as can Ayala Malach Pines's (2005) Burnout Measure Short Version (BMS). Particularly during more stressful times, such as when there have been a few deaths within a short period of time in the nursing home, completing a self-assessment inventory is an objective, helpful way to monitor one's stress level and ability to cope. Feedback or concern expressed by one's peers or family members is another way staff may recognize dangers.

Conclusions

Self-awareness, finding ways and carving out times to mourn losses, and periodically monitoring one's level of compassion fatigue and burnout are important tasks for social workers in the nursing home environment. It's not a matter of *if* but of *when* nursing home residents and staff will be affected by losses and death. When social workers are familiar with contemporary grief theories and the psychosocial issues that arise from the nursing home environment, residents' physical condition, and the social condition of nursing homes, they can use these as tools to understand, support, and affirm the normalcy of what nursing home residents and staff experience as they grieve and mourn. For the bereaved, whether a resident or another staff member, it can be difficult to see past the pain of the loss. Drawing from these models provides the social worker with a context for understanding, recognizing, and supporting change and progress along the grief journey. A social worker's training and ability to listen helps the grieving person sort through the context of the loss and foster a sense of resiliency and hope. By providing this opportunity to grieve and mourn, over time social workers are helping the bereaved realize a sense of accomplishment and renewed meaning as they discover what they need to cope with their loss.

References

Anderson, K. 2008. "Grief Experiences of CNA's Relationships with Burnout and Turnover." *Journal of Gerontological Nursing, 34* (1), 42–49. (p. 47)

Anderson, K., and J. Gaugler. 2007. "The Grief Experiences of Certified Nursing Assistants: Personal Growth and Complicated Grief." *Omega* 54 (4): 301–18.

Attig, T. 1996. *How We Grieve*. New York: Oxford University Press.

Bakker, A., P. LeBlanc, and W. Schaufeli. 2005. "Burnout Contagion Among Intensive Care Nurses." *Journal of Advanced Nursing* 51 (3): 276–87.

Berdes, C., and J. M. Eckert. 2001. "Race Relations and Caregiving Relationships: A Qualitative Examination of Perspectives from Residents and Nurse's Aides in Three Nursing Homes." *Research on Aging* 23:109–26.

Berger, J. 2005. "Compassion Wellness." NHPCO AudioWeb Conference, December 8, 2005.

Bern-Klug, M. 2004. "The Ambiguous Dying Syndrome." *Health and Social Work* 29:55–65.

Boss, P. 1999. *Ambiguous Loss: Learning to Live with Unresolved Grief*. Cambridge, Mass.: Harvard University Press.

Brodaty, H., B. Draper, and L. F. Low. 2003. "Nursing Home Staff Attitudes Towards Residents with Dementia: Strain and Satisfaction with Work." *Journal of Advanced Nursing* 44:583–90.

Corr, C., C. Nabe, and D. Corr. 2003. *Death and Dying, Life and Living*. 4th ed. Pacific Grove, Calif.: Brooks/Cole.

DeSpelder, L., and A. Strickland. 2005. *The Last Dance: Encountering Death and Dying*. 7th ed. New York: McGraw-Hill.

Doka, K. 2002. *Disenfranchised Grief: New Directions, Challenges, and Strategies for Practice*. 3rd ed. Champaign, Ill.: Research Press.

Evers, W., W. Tomic, and A. Brouwers. 2001. "Effects of Aggressive Behavior and Perceived Self-Efficacy on Burnout Among Staff of Homes for the Elderly." *Issues in Mental Health Nursing* 22:439–54.

Figley, C. 1996. "Traumatic Death: Treatment Implications." In *Living with Grief After Sudden Loss*, ed. K. Doka, 91–102. Bristol, Penn.: Taylor and Francis.

Figley, C. 1999. "Compassion Fatigue: Toward a New Understanding of the Costs of Caring." In *Secondary Traumatic Stress: Self-Care Issues for Clinicians, Researchers, and Educators*, ed. B. Stamm, 3–28. 2nd ed. Baltimore, Md.: Sidran Institute and Press.

Figley, C., ed. 2002. *Treating Compassion Fatigue*. New York: Brunner-Routledge.

Fisher, L., and M. Wallhagen. 2008. "Day-to-Day Care: The Interplay of CNA's Views of Residents and Nursing Home Environments." *Journal of Gerontological Nursing* 34 (11): 26–33.

Forbes, D. A. 2001. "This Is Heaven's Waiting Room." *Journal of Gerontological Nursing* 27:37–45.

Grau, L., and E. Wellin. 1992. "The Organizational Culture of Nursing Homes: Influences of Responses to External Regulatory Controls." *Qualitative Health Research* 2:42–60.

Happ, M. B., E. Capetzuti, N. Strumpf, et al. 1999. "Advanced Care Planning and End-of-Life Care for Nursing Home Residents." *Gerontologist* 39:60–69.

Huppert, F. A., C. Brayne, C. Jagger, and D. Metz. 2000. "Longitudinal Studies on Ageing: A Key Role in the Evidence Base for Improving Health and Quality of Life in Older Adults." *Age and Aging* 29:485–86.

Iwasiw, C., D. Goldenberg, N. Bol, and E. MacMaster. 2003. "Resident and Family Perspectives: The First Year in a Long-Term Care Facility." *Journal of Gerontological Nursing* 29:45–54.

Jenull, B., and E. Brunner. 2008. "Death and Dying in Nursing Homes: A Burden for the Staff?" *Journal of Applied Gerontology* 27:166–80.

Kelley, L. S., E. Swanson, M. L. Maas, and T. Tripp-Reimer. 1999. "Family Visitation on Special Care Units." *Journal of Gerontological Nursing* 25:14–21.

Klass, D. 1999. *The Spiritual Lives of Bereaved Parents.* Philadelphia: Taylor and Francis.

Kubler-Ross, E. 1969. *On Death and Dying.* New York: MacMillann.

Leon, A., J. Altholz, and S. Dziegielewski. 1999. "Compassion Fatigue: Considerations for Working with the Elderly." *Journal of Gerontological Social Work* 32 (1): 43–62.

Lopez, R. P. 2007. "Suffering and Dying Nursing Home Residents: Nurses' Perception of the Role of Family Members." *Journal of Hospice and Palliative Nursing* 9:141–49.

Maslach, C., S. Jackson, and M. Leiter. 1996. *Maslach Burnout Inventory Manual.* 3rd ed. Palo Alto, Calif.: Consulting Psychologists Press.

McGilton, K. S., and V. M. Boscart. 2007. "Close Care Provider-Resident Relationships in Long-Term Care Environments." *Journal of Clinical Nursing* 16:2149–57.

Meuser, T. M., and S. J. Marwit. 2001. "A Comprehensive, Stage-Sensitive Model of Grief in Dementia Caregiving." *Gerontologist* 41 (5): 658–70.

Moss, S., and M. Moss. 2002. "Nursing Home Staff Reactions to Resident Deaths." In *Disenfranchised Grief: New Directions, Challenges, and Strategies for Practice,* 3rd ed., ed. K. Doka, 197–216. Champaign, Ill.: Research Press.

National Alzheimer's Association 2007. "Facts and Figures." www.alz.org. Accessed March 17, 2008.

Neimeyer, R., ed. 2003. *Meaning Reconstruction and the Experience of Loss.* Washington, D.C.: American Psychological Association.

Novak, M., and N. L. Chappell. 1996. "The Impact of Cognitively Impaired Patients and Shift on Nursing Assistant Stress." *International Journal of Aging and Human Development* 43:235–48.

Ochberg, F. 1998. "When Helping Hurts." http://www.giftfromwithin.org/html/helping.html. Accessed March 15, 2008.

Pines, A. M. 2005. "The Burnout Measure Short Version (BMS)." *International Journal of Stress Management*, 12, 78–88.

Ramirez, M., J. Teresi, and D. Holmes. 2006. "Demoralization and Attitudes Toward Residents Among Certified Nurse Assistants in Relation to Job Stressors and Work Resources: Cultural Diversity in Long-Term Care." *Journal of Cultural Diversity* 13:119–25.

Rodney, V. 2000. "Nurse Stress Associated with Aggression in People with Dementia: Its Relationship to Hardiness, Cognitive Appraisal, and Coping." *Journal of Advanced Nursing* 3:172–80.

Rothschild, B., and M. Rand. 2006. *Help for the Helper: Self-Care Strategies for Managing Burnout and Stress.* New York: Norton.

Sanders, S., and K. B. Adams. 2005. "Grief Reactions and Depression in Caregivers of Individuals with Alzheimer's Disease: Results from a Pilot Study in an Urban Setting." *Health and Social Work* 30:287–95.

Sanders, S., H. Butcher, P. Swails, and J. Power. (In press). "Portraits of Caregivers of End-Stage Dementia Patients Receiving Hospice Care." *Death Studies.*

Schell, E. S., and J. Kayser-Jones. 2007. "'Getting Into the Skin': Empathy and Role Taking in Certified Nursing Assistants' Care of Dying Residents." *Applied Nursing Research* 20:146–51.

Sheets, V. 2000. "Teach Nurses How to Maintain Professional Boundaries, Recognize Potential Problems, and Make Better Patient Care Decisions." *Nursing Management* 31 (9): 28–30, 32–34.

Stamm, B. 2009. "Professional Quality of Life, ProQol Test." http://www.proqol.org?proQol_Test.htm. Accessed January 19, 2009.

Strom-Gottfried, K., and N. D. Mowbray. 2006. "Who Heals the Helper? Facilitating the Social Worker's Grief." *Families in Society* 87:9–15.

Wadensten, B., E. Conden, L. Wahlund, and K. Murray. 2007. "How Nursing Home Staff Deal with Residents who Talk About Death." *International Journal of Older People Nursing* 2:241–49.

Worden, J. 2009. *Grief Counseling and Grief Therapy: A Handbook for the Mental Health Practitioner.* 4th ed. New York: Springer.

The Future of Palliative Psychosocial Care for Nursing Home Residents with Advanced Chronic Illness

MERCEDES BERN-KLUG

The end of this book brings us to a threshold. In this last chapter we look at some of the factors that may affect the provision of palliative care for older adults with advanced chronic illness. The chapter takes a broad view and situates palliative care for people with advanced chronic illness within the context of long-term care. The chapter starts with a discussion of factors at the individual and societal levels that may affect the need for and availability of palliative care in the nursing home and other long-term-care settings over the next four decades. The chapter concludes with two questions, the answers to which will help create the parameters for palliative long-term care during the decades when the baby boom generation reaches advanced old age. Throughout the following pages, programs that have already been started toward improving the experience of older adulthood and advanced chronic illness are highlighted; indeed, there is much reason for hope.

The baby boom cohort includes the 78 million people born in the United States between 1946 and 1964. The cohort seems large, in part, in comparison with the fewer number of babies born during the World War II years. The oldest members of the baby boom cohort will begin reaching age eighty in less than two decades, in the year 2026. All baby boomers who survive long enough will have reached age eighty by the year 2044. Over the next decades, the number of people in the United States age eighty or older is expected to triple from 11.5 million in 2010 to 32 million by 2050 (U.S. Census Bureau 2008).

Age eighty is important because of the increased likelihood of needing assistance that currently accompanies age. But old age is not synonymous with function decline. While the majority of people around the globe with advanced chronic illness in the first half of the twenty-first century will be older adults—especially octogenarians—not all will. As such, it is important to distinguish the concept of "older adult" or "elder" from "frail" or "poor health." Palmore (2000) pleads with readers of *The Gerontologist* to stop using the term "aging" as a substitute for deterioration: "if one means decline or deterioration, it would be more honest and clearer to say so, and instead of aging use deterioration or debilitation when that is what you mean."

The long-term-care scholar Rosalie Kane points to six themes likely to affect the provision of long-term care in the future: workforce issues (recruiting and retaining staff), defining and assuring quality, the balance of autonomy versus safety, ethical issues (such as privacy, confidentiality, proxy decision making, and colliding interests of the family members providing care versus those requiring care), the development of a cross-disability agenda for people with disabilities (while older adults have viewed access to quality care as a healthcare issue, younger people with disabilities see it as a human-rights issue), and social work roles (Kane 2008). These themes will directly and indirectly affect the provision of palliative care in the nursing home setting. For the purposes of this discussion, however, the factors affecting the future of palliative care in long-term-care settings are grouped in two categories: those affecting the number and characteristics of people who will need advanced chronic illness care and those that affect the provision of care. In other words, the remainder of this chapter discusses factors that will likely affect the demand for and supply of palliative long-term care.

Factors Affecting the Need for Long-Term Care for People with Advanced Chronic Illness

The need for palliative care for people with advanced chronic illness in the long-term-care system will depend on the number of people at various stages of advanced illness, available treatments to postpone or prevent disability, and changes in technology and communication that can help to maintain functional abilities despite declines in health status. Even if we are not able to prevent or postpone the physical and mental declines that can accompany advanced chronic illness, we can develop ways to minimize the negative effects. For example, cell phones don't prevent people from falling but can make it easier for people to call for help once they have fallen. Raised toilet seats help people rise from a toilet without the assistance of another person. Alarms on pill containers can remind people to take their medications at the appointed hour. Universally designed living quarters facilitate the use of the kitchen and bathroom so that people with arthritis or mobility limitations can live independently. Social-networking Internet sites can help people remain in touch even if they are bed-bound.

Improvements in the diagnosis, treatment, and prognoses of currently known chronic conditions will shape future care needs. For example, a cure for Alzheimer's disease would radically alter the need for nursing home care because about half of the people currently living in nursing homes have dementia. Even if a cure for Alzheimer's disease is not discovered, if the onset of dementia could be postponed for five years, far fewer people would be affected (Brookmeyer, Gray, and Kawas 1998).

On the other hand, the number of people in need of long-term care may actually increase because people who would have died from cancer or organ failure or another chronic condition may live longer but not necessarily in better health. Because we are mortal, even if the number of people who die from Alzheimer's disease or breast cancer or heart disease decreases, then the numbers dying from other causes will increase. Gruenberg ([1977] 2005) in his essay "The Failure of Success" argues that public-health research emphasizing the alleviation of conditions that result in death contributed to the growing number of people remaining alive but in frail health.

> We have seen how the provision of medical care, while it has served as an important means of postponing death, has done so, to a great extent, by defeating the fatal complications that used to terminate the diseases people were suffering from, thus making those diseases more common in the population.
>
> (Gruenberg [1977] 2005:796)

Gruenberg encouraged clinical researchers to pay attention to conditions with disabling effects, even if they were not directly implicated in death.

Other factors that may affect palliative care for advanced chronic illness include behaviors that people engage in or fail to engage in. For example, we may be looking at the most obese cohort of people to reach older adulthood in U.S. history. Because obesity is related to diabetes and diabetes is related to organ failure, the future effects of current and sustained levels of obesity and diabetes on eventual organ failure are not known. Olshansky and colleagues (2005), writing in the *New England Journal of Medicine*, report that with two-thirds of adults in the United States obese or overweight, it is quite possible that life expectancy at birth and at older ages could "level off or even decline in the first half of this century" (1142). They also point to pollution, lack of regular exercise, ineffective blood-pressure screening, tobacco use, and stress as other forces that could negatively affect life expectancy.

Furthermore, the middle of the twenty-first century may bring new diseases. We may find ourselves dealing with diseases not yet known or mutations of known but little understood diseases. Suffice it to say that most of the people who will need advanced chronic illness care in the near future are with us today, but their actual needs are difficult to predict because of the possibility of new pharmaceutical, technological, and public-health interventions to mitigate the effects of current foes, and also the possibility of negative consequences of current and as yet unknown health problems, some of which will be related to individual behaviors or the environment.

Taking a broad approach to understanding developments that have contributed to rapid improvements in life expectancy over the twentieth century in the United States, Bell and Miller (2005) cite the following:

- Access to primary medical care for the general population
- Improved healthcare provided to mothers and babies
- Availability of immunizations
- Improvements in motor vehicle safety
- Clean water supply and waste removal
- Safer and more nutritious foods
- Rapid rate of growth in the general standard of living.

They write that the following set of factors are among those that will likely affect the rate and age at which Americans die over the coming decades:

- Development and application of new diagnostic, surgical and life sustaining techniques

- Presence of environmental pollutants
- Improvements in exercise and nutrition
- Incidence of violence
- Isolation and treatment of causes of disease
- Emergence of new forms of disease
- Prevalence of cigarette smoking
- Misuse of drugs (including alcohol)
- Extent to which people assume responsibility for their own health
- Education regarding health
- Changes in ideas about the value of life
- Ability and willingness of our society to pay for the development of new treatments and technologies, and to provide these to the population as a whole

The future need for palliative care within the context of long-term care does not affect only the United States. The needs in the United States and other developed countries will be dwarfed by the enormous palliative care needs in developing countries. (The U.N. classifies as "more developed regions" all regions of Europe plus North America, Australia, New Zealand, and Japan; see United Nations [2007]). In general, population aging is happening much faster in developing countries. For example, France had the 115 years between 1855 and 1980 to adjust to the percentage of older adults growing from 7 to 14 percent; the United States will have 69 years (1944–2013). But developing countries will experience population aging in a shorter span of years. Chile's sixty-five and older population is expected to go from 7 to 14 percent during the twenty-seven years between 1996 and 2025, and China—currently the world's most populous country, soon to be second to India—is expected to see the change occur over the twenty-year span starting in 2000 (Kinsella and Phillips 2005:15). Unlike the developed countries, many developing countries will "get old before they get rich" (Weinberger 2007:18). The enormous and rapid changes occurring because of the acceleration of globalization and of population aging are likely to impact developing countries more profoundly (Fry 2005).

Globally, about 850,000 people reach age sixty-five each day (Kinsella and Phillips 2005:6), and most of this growth occurs in developing regions of the world. The fastest-growing age group in the world consists of people age eighty and older; this is also the age group most likely to have long-term-care needs because of advanced chronic illness. The eighty and older population, which was estimated at 87.6 million in 2005, is projected (using the medium variant) to increase to 401,777,000 by 2050 (United Nations 2007). With a projected eighty and older population of 103,018,000 people in 2050, China alone will be home to one-quarter of the earth's population age eighty and older (United Nations 2007). Access to palliative care in advanced chronic illness will soon become a pressing global concern, especially in developing countries. The Open Society Institute/Soros Foundation Network is leading the way in building the case for access to palliative care and framing it as a global human rights issue (Brennan, Gwyther, and Harding 2008).

Factors Affecting the Provision of Long-Term Care in the U.S. for People with Advanced Chronic Illness

Aside from changes in factors that may affect the number of people with advanced chronic illness needs, there are certain to be changes in the provision of long-term care. Family members and friends will continue to provide the majority of care. These informal providers will need support from employers, neighbors, and the community in general. The future role of formal (paid) providers of long-term care will continue to evolve, based in large part on issues related to funding. (For a collection of articles about the economics of long-term care, refer to the AARP Web site, http://www.aarp.org/research/longtermcare/programfunding/, or the National Academy for Social Insurance–sponsored report that looks at the financial provisions for long-term-care services in a selection of developed countries with potential application to the United States, http://www.nasi.org/usr_doc/Merlis_LongTerm_Care_Financing.pdf.)

While this book has focused on the provision of palliative care in the nursing home setting, the nursing home is but one setting for long-term care, and, furthermore, the percentage of older adults who move to nursing homes for long-term care is declining as more people opt for assisted-living options and more states allocate a greater share of long-term-care funds for home- and community-care-based services. Although the *percentage* of older adults using nursing home services for long-term care for advanced chronic illness is expected to continue to decline, the actual *number* of residents will likely increase with the aging of the baby boom cohort. The need for nursing homes and other twenty-four-hour care settings will continue on account of the sheer increase in the number of older adults, although the exact role of the nursing home is yet to be determined.

It is hoped that nursing homes built in the future will look less like minihospitals and more like physical and social neighborhoods within a larger building or smaller standalone settings for ten to twelve people like the Green Houses developed by Dr. William Thomas (http://www. ncbcapitalimpact.org/default.aspx?id=156). However, recent trends in the number of beds in nursing homes (reported in chapter 4) indicate that there is a higher percentage of nursing homes with more than one hundred beds than in the past and that nursing homes with fewer than fifty beds are decreasing in number. With the majority of nursing homes being for-profit, until developers are convinced that small can be just as profitable, the larger facilities, with their implied economies of scale, are likely to remain. Perhaps not-for-profit groups will respond to the demand for human-scale buildings.

It is possible that the concept of intentional communities may take hold over the next decades, and this may be another alternative for some people in need of long-term care. Intentional communities occur when people decide to physically locate close to friends, family, or other people with whom they share a common philosophy about life (religion, environmental philosophy, etc.). Intentional communities can take the form of cooperative living, communes, residential land trusts, and ecovillages (http://www. ic.org/). Intentional communities afford the possibility of a shared vision for living in an age-integrated or age-segregated community.

Two Questions That Reveal Our Values

Much attention and energy have been devoted to projecting the demographic, epidemiologic, and economic factors likely to affect long-term care. Less attention has been devoted to considering the social and cultural factors that will also have profound effects on the experience of long-term care and palliative care during the first half of the twenty-first century. The answers to the following questions will help to shape the future experience of receiving palliative care within the context of advanced chronic illness. These questions invite readers to reflect on our culture. The use of the term "culture" here means "the learned set of behaviors and ideas that are acquired by people as members of society" (Lavenda and Schultz 2007:16).

Because these ideas and behaviors are learned, they can be changed. As a society, we can decide to support policies that encourage some behaviors while discouraging others. These policies can be developed at the family, community, company, state, and federal levels. These policies will reflect societal and personal values embedded in the following questions:

Will Society Embrace "Old Age" as a Stage of Life?

For much of human history, societies could only dream of the day that most of their members would survive long enough to die in old age. Now, as we begin the second decade of the twenty-first century, most babies—especially in developed countries—can expect to live to reach older adulthood, and indeed to spend decades in the phase of life called older adulthood. In the process of pursuing increased longevity, we have set aside the reasons we wanted those extra years and decades in the first place. As we have focused on modernizing and globalizing, our society has overlooked the unique gifts of the last chapter of life. As old age has become medicalized, we have turned away from the real experts on aging—the aged themselves—and instead have come to rely upon medical professionals as the experts on aging (Hirshbein 2001). Greater emphasis on palliative care can help to rebalance power for people affected by advanced chronic illness.

In his book *What Are Old People For: How Elders Will Save the World* (2004:270), William Thomas says, "Our culture declares that adulthood is forever, that old age means decline, and that perfection is lodged in remaining young. These great lies stand behind all the propaganda against aging and longevity. The truth is that old age is difficult, but it is essential because it teaches us how to live like human beings."

One of the largest membership organization in the world, AARP, is working to eliminate ageism and help society understand the benefits of increasing numbers of older adults through the "Reimaging America" project (AARP 2005). They outline how changes in the U.S. healthcare system (including long-term care), changes in the Social Security program, and a new emphasis on "livable communities" can help to usher in a better America for people of all ages.

The physical changes associated with the process of aging have been documented and typically framed as deficits from middle-age. It is becoming clear that some of the physical decline that can accompany aging is not "aging" per se, but the consequence of physical inactivity. Researchers have documented the negative effects of inactivity on older adults (Brown 2000) and confirmed that even wheelchair-bound nursing home residents in their nineties can benefit from exercise (Fiatarone et al. 1994). We have much to learn to be able to distinguish normal aging, inevitable physical decline, and what physical function can be maintained with appropriate exercise.

We are more than our physical bodies. Cohen (2005) pulls together recent research about how aging affects the brain and comes to the conclusion that older brains have enormous potential and can continue to develop throughout life: "Our brain hardware is capable of adapting, growing, and becoming more complex and integrated with age. But at the same time, our minds also grow and evolve. This is psychological development—development of insight, emotional stability, knowledge, creativity, and expressive abilities" (2005:28). These psychological changes help to explain the unique desires and opportunities of older adulthood. As the Roman statesman Cicero wrote in 44 B.C.E., "Boys have their characteristic pursuits, but adolescents do not hanker after them, since they have their own activities. Then these too, in their turn, cease to attract the grown-up and middle-aged, seeing that they also have their special interest—for which, however, when their time comes, old people feel no desire, since they again, finally, have interests peculiar to them." Perhaps the poet Longfellow was tapping into this insight when he wrote, "Old age is opportunity no less than youth—though in a different dress—and as the twilight fades away, the sky is filled with starts, invisible by day." It is time to reclaim older adulthood and to value this time of life on its own merits, rather than gauging old age exclusively through the eyes of youth and middle age.

Part of reclaiming older adulthood is acknowledging a place in society for elders. A key concept behind the notion of "social roles" is that there are expectations that accompany roles (Turner 1990). Social roles, such as being a parent or being a teacher or being sick, have rights and responsibilities. Knowing the parameters of the social role helps to smooth social interactions. With no clear expectations for the rights and responsibilities in older adulthood, elders are deprived of a unique place in society and instead are treated as people who have aged out of middle-age. Yet no one wants to be defined by what they are not, and no life stage should be defined by what it used to be.

Over the twentieth century, as life expectancy increased, so has the "chronologization" of life, which means that the concept of chronological age has been heavily relied upon to determine what activities a person should be involved with (Kohli 1988.). Riley and Riley (2000) write about the need for our society to change the rigid terms of what is expected of a person, based on age (an age-differentiated society), to one in which opportunities to participate in the three main activities of adulthood, that is, education, work, and leisure, are integrated throughout adulthood, including throughout older adulthood. Uhlenberg (2000) suggests that a more age-integrated society can lead to greater productivity and civility.

In Buettner's (2008) study of societies where people live the longest, he found that good social connections (along with consistent physical activity, a good attitude, and a plant-based diet) increase the chances of living a long life. Others have also documented the positive impact of social connections on health (Crooks et al. 2008). We need to build good social skills early in life and then recognize the importance and the pleasure of using these skills throughout life. The United Nations counts the right to social participation as one of the five principles for older persons (http://www.un.org/esa/socdev/ageing/un_principles.html).

A place in society means that society accommodates older adulthood in terms of housing-stock issues (e.g., in universal design); neighborhood issues such as sidewalks and good public transportation; and overall settings that offer opportunities to interact and participate in the community. An effort toward making cities more elder friends is underway through the World Health Organization (see http://www.who.int/ageing/publications/Global_age_friendly_cities_Guide_English.pdf), and they are finding that the same features that make locales more accessible for elders also make communities better places to live for people of all ages.

If we want to improve the experience of older adulthood, we need to start early in life. What happens in youth can affect old age. Poor health in childhood has been shown to be related to increased morbidity in older adulthood (Blackwell, Hayward, and Crimmins 2001). We increase our chances for a better older adulthood tomorrow by investing in children today. Indeed, in the preamble to the U.S. Constitution, the founders of our nation stated that one of the purposes of government is to promote the general welfare. In twenty-first-century terms, promoting the general welfare should include access to health care and education, as both are key to fully participating in our democracy and both can positively affect the experience of old age.

Many people will experience physical dependency as part of old age, and almost all will if they live long enough. One of the challenges our society must face is what does "dependency" mean in older adulthood, or what should dependency mean? Pipher (1999:78) discusses the stigma that accompanies dependency in contemporary American society: "This change in the meaning of dependency, from a natural to a shameful condition, has turned our elders elderly. The old don't want to be dependent in our dependent-phobic culture. And we young are afraid to get sucked in." Our society would do well to emphasize how we are all interdependent.

Included in embracing old age is accepting dying and death. "Approaching death makes life a limited commodity and scarcity confers value" (Pipher 1999:207). If the principles of palliative care are invoked throughout the illness experience, including the final days and hours of life, the social as well as the medical issues are addressed and people are supported in their journey toward death. "It's important not to spare people the experience of their death. Suffering allows people an opportunity to deepen their characters and behave with great courage" (Pipher 1999:216). The experience of dying in older adulthood in the context of advanced chronic illness will continue to be the norm. We must recognize that each trajectory toward dying brings with it unique needs related to how the illness affects the person (Lunney et al. 2002) and the family; each path toward dying requires its own map.

Will Caregivers Be Honored?

A part of rethinking dependency in adulthood is recognizing that our caregivers deserve better. Both the unpaid family and friends and the paid (formal) caregivers employed through nursing homes, home-health agencies, assisted-living centers, and other settings deserve public recognition and appreciation for the important work they do.

For informal caregivers, better treatment includes more role accommodations (e.g., flexible work schedules) and empathy. We cannot and should not perpetuate the expectation that informal, unpaid care giving is the sole responsibility of middle-aged women. Adults in general need to take a more active role in providing care or supporting those who do. In addition to the changes needed within families and places of work, our government policies related to Social Security need to be revisited. Currently, when people (typically women) work part-time or leave the work force for a number of years in order to provide care for a dependent child or an adult with care needs, their earnings record is negatively affected, which means they may be penalized with a smaller Social Security check when they retire. There should not be a financial disincentive to provide care.

For formal caregivers, better treatment includes better compensation and better working conditions. It means being respected for the special set of skills—the science and the art—needed to excel as a caregiver. Respect comes from society valuing the work that caregivers do—and not just what they do, but how they do it. One initiative designed to improve working conditions of direct-care staff is the "Better Jobs, Better Care" project funded by the Robert Wood Johnson Foundation and Atlantic Philanthropies. The Institute for the Future of Aging Services (which is affiliated with the American Association of Homes and Services for the Aging) is investigating changes in long-term-care policy and practice that can help to reduce high vacancy and turnover rates among direct-care staff across the spectrum of long-term-care settings (http://www.bjbc.org/).

The Institute of Medicine's 2008 report "Retooling for an Aging America: Building the Health Care Workforce" draws attention to the urgent need to recruit, train, and retain more geriatric specialists and aides. In order to increase the number of healthcare specialists and paraprofessionals trained in geriatrics the IOM report says that they need to be paid higher salaries and need to work in improved models of care. The report also calls for providing basic geriatrics education to all healthcare providers and to improve models of care provision. Recruiting a workforce committed to working with persons in frail health will be easier if ageism was reduced and if dependency was not stigmatized. As we learn to embrace the stage of life called older adulthood and accept our interdependent circumstances, we also embrace and honor those who provide care.

Summary

The Clinical Practice Guidelines for Quality Palliative Care (National Consensus Project 2004) clearly state that palliative care is appropriate across the lifespan and across the illness trajectory. Although it is appropriate, it is not necessarily available. People with chronic illness, their advocates, and healthcare providers must demand palliative care and must demand that comfort-care issues are addressed throughout the illness. This book is about providing palliative care to people living and dying as nursing home residents, but in order to fully succeed in doing this, consumers, patients, residents, and their family members should have experienced good palliative care well before moving into a nursing home. Palliative care in the nursing home should be a continuation of palliative care experienced throughout the illness, regardless of setting.

While the ideas expressed in this chapter provide fodder for a discussion of what the future may hold, the multiple possible combinations of factors ensures that there will be surprises. We can hope that many of the surprises are pleasant ones, and we see signs of enhanced palliative care in the growing number of hospitals with palliative-care teams, the growing number of Medicare beneficiaries who are accessing palliative care and hospice services, and greater awareness of the principles of palliative care. We are the creators of our future. We must work for a future that honors the meaning of personhood and is grounded in recognizing the importance of human relationships, regardless of age and regardless of health status. The future of palliative psychosocial care for people with advanced chronic illness? It is up to us.

References

AARP. 2005. "Reimagining American: How America Can Grow Older and Prosper. AARP's Blue Print for the Future." http://assets.aarp.org/www.aarp.org_/articles/legpolicy/reimagining_200601.pdf. Accessed December 12, 2008.

Bell, F. C., and M. L. Miller. 2005. "Life Tables for the United States Social Security Area 1900–2100." Actuarial Study #20, Social Security Administration. http://www.socialsecurity.gov/OACT/NOTES/s2000s.html. Accessed February 2, 2009.

Blackwell, D. L., M. D. Hayward, and E. M. Crimmons. 2001. "Does Childhood Health Affect Chronic Morbidity in Later Life?" *Social Science and Medicine* 52:1269–84.

Brennan, F., L. Gwyther, and R. Harding. 2008. "Palliative Care as a Human Right." http://www.soros.org/initiatives/health/focus/ipci/articles_publications/publications/pchumanright_20080101/pchumanright_20080101.pdf. Accessed January 29, 2009.

Brookmeyer, R., S. Gray, and C. Kawas. 1998. "Projections of Alzheimer's Disease in the United States and the Public Health Impact of Delaying the Disease." *American Journal of Public Health* 88 (9): 1337–42.

Rubric322

The Future of Palliative Psychosocial Care

Brown, M. 2000. "Strength Training and Aging." *Topics in Geriatric Rehabilitation* 15 (3): 1–10.

Buettner, D. 2008. *The Blue Zones: Lessons for Living Longer from People Who Have Lived the Longest.* Washington, D.C.: National Geographic Books.

Cicero. 1971. *Selected Works.* Trans. M. Grant. London: Penguin Books.

Cohen, G. D. 2005. *The Mature Mind: The Positive Power of the Aging Brain.* New York: Basic Books.

Crooks, V. C., J. Lubben, D. B. Petitti, D. Little, and V. Chiu. 2008. "Social Network, Cognitive Function, and Dementia Incidence Among Elderly Women." *American Journals of Public Health* 98 (7): 1221–27.

Fiatarone, M. A., E. F. O'Neill, N. D. Ryan, K. M. Clements, G. R. Solares, M. E. Nelson, S. B. Roberts, J. J. Kehayias, L. A. Lipsitz, and W. J. Evans. 1994. "Exercise Training and Nutritional Supplements for Physical Frailty in Very Elderly People." *New England Journal of Medicine* 330:1769–75.

Fry, C. L. 2005. "Globalization and the Experience of Aging." *Gerontology and Geriatrics Education* 26 (6): 9–22.

Gruenberg, E. M. [1977] 2005. "The Failure of Success." *The Milbank Memorial Fund Quarterly* 83 (4): 779–800.

Hirshbein, L. D. 2001. "Popular Views of Old Age in America, 1900–1950." *Journal of the American Geriatrics Society* 49:1555–60.

Institute of Medicine. 2008. "Retooling for an Aging America: Building the Health Care Workforce. Washington, D.C.: Institute of Medicine. http://www.iom.edu/Object.File/Master/53/509/HealthcareWorkforce_FS.pdf. Accessed January 26, 2008.

Kane, R. A. 2008. "Long-Term Care." In *Encyclopedia of Social Work,* ed. T. Mizrahi and L. E. Davis, http://www.oxford-naswsocialwork.com/entry?entry=t203.e229. New York: National Association of Social Workers and Oxford University Press.

Kinsella, K., and D. R. Phillips. 2005. "Global Aging: The Challenge of Success." *Population Bulletin* 60 (1). http://www.prb.org/Publications PopulationBulletins/2005/GlobalAgingTheChallengeofSuccessPDF575KB .aspx. Accessed March 4, 2009.

Kohli, M. L. 1988. "Social Organization and Subjective Construction of the Life Course." In *Human Development and the Life Cycle,* ed. A. B. Sorenson, F. E. Weiner, and L. R. Sherrod, 271–92. Hillsdale, N.J.: Erbaum.

Lavenda, R. H., and E. A. Schultz. 2007. *Core Concepts in Cultural Anthropology.* 3rd ed. Boston: McGraw Hill.

Lunney, J. R., J. Lynn, and C. Hogan. 2002. "Profiles of Older Medicare Decedents." *Journal of the American Geriatrics Society* 50:1108–12.

National Consensus Project for Quality Palliative Care. 2004. "Clinical Practice Guidelines for Quality Palliative Care." http://www.nationalconsensusproject.org.

Olshansky, S. J., D. J. Passaro, R. C. Hershow, J. Layden, B. A. Carnes, J. Brody, L. Hayflick, R. N. Butler, D. B. Allison, and D. S. Ludwig. 2005. "A Potential Decline in Life Expectancy in the United States in the Twenty-first Century." *New England Journal of Medicine* 352 (11): 1138–45.

Palmore, E. 2000. "Guest Editorial: Ageism in Gerontological Language." *Gerontologist* 40 (6): 645.

Pipher, M. 1999. *Another Country: Navigating the Emotional Terrain of Our Elders.* New York: Riverhead Books.

Riley, M. W., and J. W. Riley. 2000. "Age Integration: Conceptual and Historical Background." *Gerontologist* 40 (3): 266–70.

Turner, R. H. 1990. "Role Change." *Annual Review of Sociology* 16:87–110.

Uhlenberg, P. 2000. "Essays on Age Integration." *Gerontologist* 40 (3): 261–308.

United Nations. 2007. "World Population Prospects: The 2006 Revision." In population database. http://www.un.org/esa/population/publications /wpp2006/WPP2006_Highlights_rev.pdf. Accessed February 2, 2009.

U.S. Census Bureau. 2008. "Projections of the Population by Age and Sex for the United States: 2010 to 2050 (NP2008_T12)." Summary table 12. http://www.census.gov/population/www/projections/summarytables.html. Accessed May 2, 2009.

Weinberger, M. B. 2007. "Population Aging: A Global Overview." In *Global Health and Global Aging*, ed. M. Robinson, W. Novelli, C. Pearson, and L. Norris, 15–30. New York: Jossey-Bass.

Appendix

State Operations Manual: Appendix
Guidance to Surveyors for Long Term Care Facilities,
Table of Contents

(Rev. 26, 08–17–07)

§483.15(g) *Social Services*

F250

§483.15(g)(1) The facility must provide medically-related social services to attain or maintain the highest practicable physical, mental, and psychosocial well-being of each resident.

Intent §483.15(g)
To assure that sufficient and appropriate social service are provided to meet the resident's needs.

Interpretive Guidelines §483.15(g)(1)
Regardless of size, all facilities are required to provide for the medically related social services needs of each resident. This requirement specifies that facilities aggressively identify the need for medically-related social services, and pursue the provision of these services. It is not required that a qualified social worker necessarily provide all of these services. Rather, it is the responsibility of the facility to identify the medically-related social service needs of the resident and assure that the needs are met by the appropriate disciplines.

"Medically-related social services" means services provided by the facility's staff to assist residents in maintaining or improving their ability to manage their everyday physical, mental, and psychosocial needs. These services might include, for example:

- Making arrangements for obtaining needed adaptive equipment, clothing, and personal items;
- Maintaining contact with facility (with resident's permission) to report on changes in health, current goals, discharge planning, and encouragement to participate in care planning;
- Assisting staff to inform residents and those they designate about the resident's health status and health care choices and their ramifications;
- Making referrals and obtaining services from outside entities (e.g., talking books, absentee ballots, community wheelchair transportation);
- Assisting residents with financial and legal matters (e.g., applying for pensions, referrals to lawyers, referrals to funeral homes for preplanning arrangements);
- Discharge planning services (e.g., helping to place a resident on a waiting list for community congregate living, arranging intake for home care services for residents returning home, assisting with transfer arrangements to other facilities);
- Providing or arranging provision of needed counseling services;
- Through the assessment and care planning process, identifying and seeking ways to support residents' individual needs;
- Promoting actions by staff that maintain or enhance each resident's dignity in full recognition of each resident's individuality;
- Assisting residents to determine how they would like to make decisions about their health care, and whether or not they would like anyone else to be involved in those decisions;
- Finding options that most meet the physical and emotional needs of each resident;
- Providing alternatives to drug therapy or restraints by understanding and communicating to staff why residents act as they do, what they are attempting to communicate, and what needs the staff must meet;
- Meeting the needs of residents who are grieving; and
- Finding options which most meet their physical and emotional needs

Factors with a potentially negative effect on physical, mental, and psychosocial well being include an unmet need for:

- Dental/denture care;
- Podiatric care;
- Eye care;
- Hearing services
- Equipment for mobility or assistive eating devices; and
- Need for home-like environment, control, dignity, privacy

Where needed services are not covered by the Medicaid State plan, nursing facilities are still required to attempt to obtain these services. For example, if a resident requires transportation services that are not covered under a Medicaid state plan, the facility is required to arrange these services. This could be achieved, for example, through obtaining volunteer assistance.

Types of conditions to which the facility should respond with social services by staff or referral include:

- Lack of an effective family/support system;
- Behavioral symptoms;
- If a resident with dementia strikes out at another resident, the facility should evaluate the resident's behavior. For example, a resident may be re-enacting an activity he or she used to perform at the same time everyday. If that resident senses that another is in the way of his re-enactment, the resident may strike out at the resident impeding his or her progress. The facility is responsible for the safety of any potential resident victims while it assesses the circumstances of the residents' behavior);
- Presence of a chronic disabling medical or psychological condition (e.g., multiple sclerosis, chronic obstructive pulmonary disease, Alzheimer's disease, schizophrenia);
- Depression
- Chronic or acute pain;
- Difficulty with personal interaction and socialization skills;
- Presence of legal or financial problems
- Abuse of alcohol or other drugs;
- Inability to cope with loss of function;
- Need for emotional support;
- Changes in family relationships, living arrangements, and/or resident's condition or functioning; and
- A physical or chemical restraint.
- For residents with or who develop mental disorders as defined by the "Diagnostic and Statistical Manual for Mental Disorders (DSM-IV)," see §483.45, F406.

Probes: §483.15(g)(1)

For residents selected for a comprehensive or focused review as appropriate:

- How do facility staff implement social services interventions to assist the resident in meeting treatment goals?
- How do staff responsible for social work monitor the resident's progress in improving physical, mental and psychosocial functioning? Has goal attainment been evaluated and the care plan changed accordingly?
- How does the care plan link goals to psychosocial functioning/well-being?
- Have the staff responsible for social work established and maintained relationships with the resident's family or legal representative?
- [NFs] What attempts does the facility make to access services for Medicaid recipients when those services are not covered by a Medicaid State Plan?

Look for evidence that social services interventions successfully address residents' needs and link social supports, physical care, and physical environment with residents' needs and individuality.

For sampled residents, review MDS, section H.

F251

§483.15(g)(2) and (3)

(2) A facility with more than 120 beds must employ a qualified social worker on a full-time basis.

(3) Qualifications of a social worker. A qualified social worker is an individual with

   (i) A bachelor's degree in social work or a bachelor's degree in a human services field including bu,t not limited to sociology, special education, rehabilitation counseling, and psychology; and

   (ii) One year of supervised social work experience in a health care setting working directly with individuals

Procedures §483.15(g)(2) and (3)

If there are problems with the provision of social services in a facility with over 120 beds, determine if a qualified social worker is employed on a full time basis.

CHAPTER 6 MATERIAL

Life Review

Childhood

- What do you remember about when you were a young child? What was life like?
- Who took care of you? What were they like?
- Did you have any brothers or sisters? If yes, what was each of them like?
- Where did you live?

Adolescence

- What do you remember about being a teenager?
- Where did you go to school? What was your school like?
- Who were your closest friends?
- Was there someone that you especially admired?
- What was your relationship like with your parents?
- Were there grandparents, aunts, uncles, cousins, etc. who you were close to?
- Who was your "first love"?
- What was the most unpleasant thing about being a teenager?
- What was the best thing about being a teenager?

(Continued on page 334)

Spiritual Needs Inventory (SNI)

COLUMN A	COLUMN B					COLUMN C	COLUMN D
Please rate the items in the column below. For every item in column A for which you answer 2, 3, 4, or 5, please answer yes or no in Columns C and D. *In order to live my life fully I need to...*						Do you consider this activity to be a spiritual activity?	Is this need being met in your life now?
	Never	Rarely	Sometimes	Frequently	Always		
1.[a] See smiles of others	1	2	3	4	5	Yes No	Yes No
2.[a] Think happy thoughts	1	2	3	4	5	Yes No	Yes No
3.[a] Talk about day-to-day things	1	2	3	4	5	Yes No	Yes No
4.[a] Be around children	1	2	3	4	5	Yes No	Yes No
5.[a] Laugh	1	2	3	4	5	Yes No	Yes No
6.[b] Talk with someone about spiritual issues.	1	2	3	4	5	Yes No	Yes No
7.[b] Sing/listen to inspirational music.	1	2	3	4	5	Yes No	Yes No
8.[b] Be with people who share my spiritual beliefs.	1	2	3	4	5	Yes No	Yes No
9.[b] Read a religious text.	1	2	3	4	5	Yes No	Yes No
10.[c] Use inspirational materials.	1	2	3	4	5	Yes No	Yes No

(Continued on next page)

Spiritual Needs Inventory (SNI) *(Continued)*

	COLUMN A	COLUMN B					COLUMN C	COLUMN D
	Please rate the items in the column below. For every item in column A for which you answer 2, 3, 4, or 5, please answer yes or no in Columns C and D. *In order to live my life fully I need to...*	Never	Rarely	Sometimes	Frequently	Always	Do you consider this activity to be a spiritual activity?	Is this need being met in your life now?
11.[c]	Use phrases from religious texts.	1	2	3	4	5	Yes No	Yes No
12.[c]	Read inspirational materials.	1	2	3	4	5	Yes No	Yes No
13.[d]	Pray.	1	2	3	4	5	Yes No	Yes No
14.[d]	Go to religious services.	1	2	3	4	5	Yes No	Yes No
15.[e]	Be with friends.	1	2	3	4	5	Yes No	Yes No
16.[e]	Be with family.	1	2	3	4	5	Yes No	Yes No
17.[e]	Have information about family and friends.	1	2	3	4	5	Yes No	Yes No

[a] Subscale: Outlook
[b] Subscale: Inspiration
[c] Subscale: Spiritual Activities
[d] Subscale: Religion
[e] Subscale: Community

Source: Herman 2006. Reprinted with permission.

Lubben Social Network Scale—Revised (LSNS-R)

FAMILY: CONSIDERING THE PEOPLE TO WHOM YOU ARE RELATED EITHER BY BIRTH OR MARRIAGE . . .

1. How many relatives do you see or hear from at least once a month?
   0 = none 1 = one 2 = two 3 = three or four 4 = five through eight 5 = nine or more

2. How often do you see or hear from the relative with whom you have the most contact?
   0 = less than monthly 1 = monthly 2 = few times a month 3 = weekly 4 = few times a week 5 = daily

3. How many relatives do you feel at ease with that you can talk to about private matters?
   0 = none 1 = one 2 = two 3 = three or four 4 = five through eight 5 = nine or more

4. How many relatives do you feel close to that you could call on them for help?
   0 = none 1 = one 2 = two 3 = three or four 4 = five through eight 5 = nine or more

5. When one of your relatives has an important decision to make, how often do they talk to you about it?
   0 = never 1 = seldom 2 = sometimes 3 = often 4 = very often 5 = always

6. How often is one of your relatives available for you to talk to when you have an important decision to make?
   0 = never 1 = seldom 2 = sometimes 3 = often 4 = very often 5 = always

7. How many of your friends do you see or hear from at least once a month?
   0 = none 1 = one 2 = two 3 = three or four 4 = five through eight 5 = nine or more

8. How often do you see or hear from the friend with whom you have the most contact?
   0 = less than monthly 1 = monthly 2 = few times a month 3 = weekly 4 = few times a week 5 = daily

9. How many friends do you feel at ease with that you can talk to about private matters?
   0 = none 1 = one 2 = two 3 = three or four 4 = five through eight 5 = nine or more

10. How many friends do you feel close to that you could call on them for help?
    0 = none 1 = one 2 = two 3 = three or four 4 = five through eight 5 = nine or more

11. When one of your friends has an important decision to make, how often do they talk to you about it?
    0 = never 1 = seldom 2 = sometime 3 = often 4 = very often 5 = always

12. How often is one of your friends available for you to talk to when you have an important decision to make?
    0 = never 1 = seldom 2 = sometimes 3 = often 4 = very often 5 = always

LSNS-R total score is an equally weighted sum of these twelve items. Scores range from 0 to 60.

Source: Lubben and Gironda 2003. Reprinted with permission.

SM-EOLD

HOW OFTEN IS THE RESIDENT EXPERIENCING THE FOLLOWING SYMPTOMS?

		Never	Once a Month	2 or 3 Days a Month	Once a Week	Several Days a Week	Every Day
1	Pain	0	1	2	3	4	5
2	Shortness of breath	0	1	2	3	4	5
3	Skin breakdown or the development of a pressure ulcer or bedsore	0	1	2	3	4	5
4	Sense of calm	0	1	2	3	4	5
5	Depression	0	1	2	3	4	5
6	Fear	0	1	2	3	4	5
7	Anxiety	0	1	2	3	4	5
8	Agitation	0	1	2	3	4	5
9	Resistiveness to care	0	1	2	3	4	5

Source: Volicer, Hurley, and Blasi 2001. Reprinted with permission.

Quality of Dying in Long-Term Care (QOD-LTC)

Factor scores (range 1–5) for the three factors are obtained by averaging the item scores for each factor: Personhood (items 1, 2, 4 10, 11); Closure (items 3, 6, 9); and Preparatory Tasks (items 5, 7, 8). These factor scores can be averaged to obtain an overall score (range 1–5).

Please think back over the last month of [RESIDENT'S] life. Here are some statements that have been considered important during the dying process. Please indicate how true each statement is for [RESIDENT].	Not at all	A little bit	A moderate amount	Quite a bit	Completely
1. There was a nurse or aide with whom [RESIDENT] felt comfortable.	1	2	3	4	5
2. [RESIDENT] received affectionate touch daily.	1	2	3	4	5
3. [HE/SHE] appeared to be at peace.	1	2	3	4	5
4. [RESIDENT'S] physician knew [HIM/HER] as a whole person including life and personality.	1	2	3	4	5
5. [RESIDENT] had treatment preferences in writing (either his/her own or by a surrogate decision maker).	1	2	3	4	5
6. [RESIDENT] indicated [HE/SHE] was prepared to die.	1	2	3	4	5
7. [RESIDENT'S] funeral was planned.	1	2	3	4	5
8. [RESIDENT] had named a decision maker in the event [HE/SHE] was no longer able to make decisions.	1	2	3	4	5
9. [RESIDENT] maintained [HIS/HER] sense of humor.	1	2	3	4	5
10. [RESIDENT'S] dignity was maintained.	1	2	3	4	5
11. [RESIDENT's] clothes and body were clean.	1	2	3	4	5

Note: This scale was developed as part of an NIH research project so is available for use. No changes should be made without consulting Dr. Jean Munn.

Quality of Dying in Long-Term Care—Cognitively Intact (QOD-LTC)

Factor scores (range 1–5) for the three factors are obtained by averaging the item scores for each factor: Personhood (items 1, 2, 4 10, 11); Closure (items 3, 6, 9); and Preparatory Tasks (items 5, 7, 8). These factor scores can be averaged to obtain an overall score (range 1–5).

Please think back over the last month of [RESIDENT'S] life. Here are some statements that have been considered important during the dying process. Please indicate how true each statement is for [RESIDENT].	Not at all	A little bit	A moderate amount	Quite a bit	Completely
1. Although [HE/SHE] could not control certain aspects of [HIS/HER] illness, [RESIDENT] had a sense of control about [HIS/HER] treatment decisions.	1	2	3	4	5
2. [RESIDENT] participated as much as [HE/SHE] wanted in the decisions about [HIS/HER] care.	1	2	3	4	5
3. In general, [RESIDENT] knew what to expect about the course of [HIS/HER] illness.	1	2	3	4	5
4. As [HIS/HER] illness progressed, [HE/SHE] knew where to go for answers to [HIS/HER] questions.	1	2	3	4	5
5. [RESIDENT] had a physician whom [HE/SHE] trusted.	1	2	3	4	5
6. [HE/SHE] spent as much time as [HE/SHE] wanted with [HIS/HER] family.	1	2	3	4	5
7. There was someone in [HIS/HER] life with whom [HE/SHE] could share [HIS/HER] deepest thoughts.	1	2	3	4	5
8. [RESIDENT] received affectionate touch daily.	1	2	3	4	5
9. [RESIDENT] had regrets about the way [HE/SHE] lived [HIS/HER] life.	1	2	3	4	5
10. Thoughts of dying frightened [HIM/HER]	1	2	3	4	5.
11. [HE/SHE] was able to say important things to those close to [HIM/HER].	1	2	3	4	5
12. [HE/SHE] was able to make a positive difference in the lives of others.	1	2	3	4	5
13. [HE/SHE] was able to help others through time together, gifts or wisdom.	1	2	3	4	5
14. [HE/SHE] was able to share important things with [HIS/HER] family.	1	2	3	4	5
15. Despite [HIS/HER] illness, [HE/SHE] had a sense of meaning in [HIS/HER] life.	1	2	3	4	5
16. [HE/SHE] appeared to be at peace.	1	2	3	4	5
17. [RESIDENT] had treatment preferences in writing (either his/her own or by a surrogate decision maker).	1	2	3	4	5
18. [RESIDENT] indicated [HE/SHE] was prepared to die.	1	2	3	4	5

(Continued on next page)

Quality of Dying in Long-Term Care—Cognitively Intact (QOD-LTC) *(Continued)*

Factor scores (range 1–5) for the three factors are obtained by averaging the item scores for each factor: Personhood (items 1, 2, 4 10, 11); Closure (items 3, 6, 9); and Preparatory Tasks (items 5, 7, 8). These factor scores can be averaged to obtain an overall score (range 1–5).

Please think back over the last month of [RESIDENT'S] life. Here are some statements that have been considered important during the dying process. Please indicate how true each statement is for [RESIDENT].	Not at all	A little bit	A moderate amount	Quite a bit	Completely
18. [RESIDENT] indicated [HE/SHE] was prepared to die.	1	2	3	4	5
19. [RESIDENT's] funeral was planned.	1	2	3	4	5
20. [RESIDENT] had named a decision maker in the event [HE/SHE] was no longer able to make decisions.	1	2	3	4	5
21. [RESIDENT] maintained [HIS/HER] sense of humor.	1	2	3	4	5
22. [RESIDENT's] dignity was maintained.	1	2	3	4	5
23. [RESIDENT] was at peace with God.	1	2	3	4	5

Additional information about these measures is available in Munn et al. 2007.

Note: This scale was developed with NIH funds and is available for use.

(Continued from page 328)

Adulthood

- What was life like for you in your twenties and thirties?
- What kind of person were you?
- What did you enjoy doing?
- Did you go to college?
- Was there someone you shared your life with? How did you meet?
- What kind of work did you do?
- What were some of the challenges you faced in your adult years?
- Who were your closest friends?
- What were some of the "defining moments" in your life?
- Where did you live in your adult years?
- Did you have children? What can you remember about each one?
- Is there a faith tradition that you are a part of? If yes, is this an important part of your life?
- What are some of the significant historical events that you remember?

General

- What are your greatest achievements?
- If you were going to live your life over again, what would you do differently? The same?
- What was the unhappiest period of your life? What did you learn from it?
- What was the happiest period of your life?
- What were the most difficult things that you have had to deal with in your life?
- Tell me about your experience living with a terminal illness or coming to terms with your own mortality.
- Do you have any other words of wisdom that you would like to pass on

Adapted from Barbara Haight's "Life Review and Experiencing Form," from Haight and Webster 1995.

CHAPTER 9 MATERIALS

A List of Things to Do Related to Final Arrangements

A. Secure vital statistics (this helps with the death certificate)
1. Full name of decedent, address, and phone
2. How long has this person lived in this state?
3. Social security number
4. Veteran's serial number
5. Date of birth
6. Place of birth
7. U.S. citizen?
8. Father's name
9. Father's birthplace
10. Mother's maiden name
11. Mother's birthplace
12. Plan to order multiple copies of the death certificate, as originals will be needed for claiming life insurance and other benefits
13. Draft ideas for the obituary and decide which papers to send to; decide if a photo will accompany the obituary; costs vary. The funeral director will likely offer to finalize the obituary

B. Pay all or some of these expenses:
14. Burial space
15. Grave marker
16. Funeral home costs
17. Cemetery costs
18. Clergy
19. Florist
20. Transportation

21. Ceremony costs (see General Price List for estimates of funeral home costs)

C. Collect documents (helps with claiming insurance and pensions)
   22. Will
   23. Legal proof of age or birth certificate
   24. Marriage license
   25. Citizenship papers
   26. Insurance policies (life, health, property)
   27. Bank books
   28. Cancelled checks/income tax returns
   29. Veteran's discharge certificate
   30. Cemetery certificate of ownership

D. Needed for final arrangements
   1. Check the person's will to see if final-arrangement details are included
   2. Burial location
   3. Casket type
   4. Clothing for deceased
   5. Grave liner or vault if required by the cemetery
   6. Sacred or secular readings for ceremony
   7. Selection of funeral home
   8. Desired time and location of funeral ceremony
   9. Charitable organization for memorialization (if desired)
   10. Pallbearers
   11. Flowers (and what to do with flowers after the ceremony)
   12. Music selection and musicians
   13. Transportation for people to attend the funeral or ceremony
   14. Reception following the funeral or memorial ceremony
   15. Locating contact information for people to be notified about the death
   16. Meeting with people who will help with arrangements, for example: funeral director, clergy, cemetery staff
   17. Place to keep track of who sent flowers and notices

E. People to notify as soon as possible:
   18. Religious or spiritual leader
   19. The physician
   20. A funeral director
   21. The cemetery
   22. The body-donation program
   23. Relatives and friends
   24. Pallbearers
   25. Insurance agents
   26. Attorney
   27. Credit card companies to cancel cards

Life-History Grid

YEAR	AGE	LOCATION	FAMILY SYSTEM	SCHOOL	HEALTH	ACTIVITIES	PROBLEMS	PERSONAL EVENTS	HISTORICAL EVENTS

Adapted from: Cashwell and Blake (2002).

F. Considerations involving the nursing home

28. Would family like to have a simple service at the nursing home for residents, nursing home and hospice staff, and family members? Describe examples of previous on-site services

29. What should happen with the resident's belongings?

30. Verify forwarding address for the resident's mail

31. Are there any final discussions about the last days or hours of the resident's life that the family would like to review a with particular staff member?

32. Invite family members to call the nursing home later if they think of anything; suggest that follow-up calls go through the social services office

Examples of Options Available to Minimize the Cost of Final Arrangements

1. Hold the viewing or visitation immediately before the funeral ceremony; some funeral homes will discount the price of the visitation.

2. Get a low-cost casket or purchase an "alternative burial container" made of heavy cardboard or plywood. If concerned about the appearance, drape a quilt or lovely fabric over the container. Any funeral home can order any casket and receive it within a day or two. If the customer would like to purchase a simple casket and one is not available at the funeral home, it can easily be ordered through the funeral home. Ask the funeral director to explain low-cost-casket options. The survivors can purchase a casket online or through a local casket vendor. Survivors may decide to build the casket themselves (directions are available on the Internet). Some families hire a carpenter to make a casket well in advance and use the casket as a shelf until the time of need.

3. Buy a concrete grave liner rather than a sealed vault, and only if the cemetery requires one in the first place.

4. Forego embalming if there will be an immediate burial or direct cremation or if the body will be buried within forty-eight hours. Dry ice or refrigeration can be alternatives to embalming.

5. Handle the final arrangements without hiring a funeral home. This means the family would be responsible for getting the death certificate signed, getting a cremation or burial permit (if appropriate), getting a permit to transfer the body, and any other state- or locale-specific paperwork. Each state has laws about the extent to which people can "bury their own." Check with the county coroner, attorney general's office, or www.funerals.org.

6. Use a temporary grave marker (available from the funeral home or cemetery or made at home). The temporary grave marker can be replaced months or years after the burial.

7. Ask the cemetery about a double-depth burial plot (one grave on top of another) or about the option of more than one set of cremated remains on the same plot. Some

cemeteries will allow multiple remains but may have a limit on the number of grave markers allowed per plot.

8. Consider body donation. Host a memorial service at a time and place that suits the family.

9. Especially if the body is to be transferred ("forwarded") from a local funeral home to a funeral home in a different city (where it will be "received"), compare prices reported on funeral homes' General Price Lists.

10. Hold a memorial service (the body is not present) at a time and location that suits the family, such as at a place of worship, park, or private home.

11. Tell the funeral director that keeping the costs down is a desire or need, and ask for suggestions on how to do that. Bring a friend along if you feel uncomfortable talking about costs upfront.

CHAPTER 10 MATERIAL

Outline for In-Service on Grief and Loss in the Nursing Home

This outline follows the format of this book chapter. The length of this presentation is forty-five to sixty minutes.

I.   Creating a safe environment
    A. Ground rules for training
    B. Confidentiality
II. Overview of Terms
    A. Grief
      1. Definition
      2. Unique process
    B. Bereavement
      1. Definition
      2. Differentiate bereavement from grief
    C. Mourning
      1. Definition
      2. Differentiate this from grief
    D. Disenfranchised grief
      1. Definition
      2. Reasons why this occurs
III. Implications of grief
    A. Burnout
    B. Compassion fatigue
      1. Reasons why this occurs
      2. Long term ramifications
IV. Reasons for grief in the nursing home
    A. Deaths of residents

B. Working with residents who are facing many losses
  1. Loss of possessions
  2. Loss of control
  3. Loss of autonomy
  4. Loss of personhood
  5. Loss of pets
  6. Loss of physical and cognitive health

V. Impact of grief on staff
  A. Emotional
    1. Sadness
    2. Anger
    3. Fear
    4. Depression
    5. Others
  B. Psychological
    1. Feeling presence of resident
    2. Seeing deceased resident
    3. Smelling deceased resident
    4. Others
  C. Physical
    1. Changes in sleeping
    2. Changes in eating
    3. Others
  D. Spiritual
    1. Questioning
    2. Seeking meaning
  E. Behavioral
    1. Need to stay busy
    2. Fidgety
    3. Others
  F. Cognitive
    1. Constant thoughts of residents
    2. Feeling distracted
    3. Others

VI. Strategies for addressing grief of staff
  (**Use this as a brainstorming session with staff)
  A. Setting realistic expectations
  B. Define clear boundaries
  C. Identify opportunities for group remembrance
  D. Promoting self-care and wellness
  E. Developing a work life balance

Source: Anewalt and Sanders.

VARIATION IN FUNERAL HOME PRICES BASED ON A SUMMARY OF GENERAL PRICE LISTS, KANSAS CITY METRO AREA, 2007

		LOW	MEDIAN	HIGH	DIFFERENCE BETWEEN HIGH AND LOW
*1	Basic services of the funeral home generally include the cost of the funeral director and staff as well as overhead (this is a non-declinable charge—which means that all customers will be charged this amount for the privilege of using this funeral home)	500	1,698	3,095	2,595
*2	Embalming	215	650	995	780
3	Other preparation of body (aside from embalming	45	275	425	380
*4	Transfer body from local place of death to this funeral home	100	275	495	395
*5	Hosting a viewing or visitation at the funeral home (staff and space)	100	343	625	525
*6	Hosting a funeral service at funeral home (staff and space)	125	425	695	570
7	Hosting a funeral ceremony at a place other than the funeral home (funeral home staff charge) [Note: there may be a separate charge for the use of the place of worship or other facility.]	125	395	695	570
8	Memorial service (the body is not present) at the funeral home (staff and space)	125	475	695	570
9	Graveside service (although the FTC defines what this is, there is wide variation among funeral homes as to what this term means)	150	350	695	545
*10	Hearse (funeral coach)	195	314	550	355
*11	Family car (limousine or sedan)	100	250	500	400

Caskets

		LOW	MEDIAN	HIGH	DIFFERENCE BETWEEN HIGH AND LOW
*12	Lowest-priced casket	269	650	1,495	1,226
13	Highest-price casket	2,995	9,995	39,000	36,005

(Continued on next page)

VARIATION IN FUNERAL HOME PRICES BASED ON A SUMMARY OF
GENERAL PRICE LISTS, KANSAS CITY METRO AREA, 2007 *(Continued)*

		LOW	MEDIAN	HIGH	DIFFERENCE BETWEEN HIGH AND LOW
14	Rental casket—if available. Sometimes listed as if only for cremation options, however should be available to anyone	350	950	1,375	1,025
15	Alternative container (lowest price) [alternative to a casket—could be made of heavy cardboard or plywood or other material]	85	150	325	240

Outer Burial Containers (OBC)— to encase the casket

		LOW	MEDIAN	HIGH	DIFFERENCE
*16	Lowest priced OBC	250	648	989	739
17	Highest price OBC	1,045	9,995	16,377	15,332
18	Forward remains from this funeral home to another funeral home (usually in a different city—does not include transportation costs)	795	2,168	3,478	2,683
19	Receive remains at this funeral home from a different funeral home	515	1,555	2,748	2,233
20	Direct cremation (in an alternative container). The body is cremated before a public ceremony occurs	525	1,746	2,690	2,165
21	Cremation fee (sometimes is included in the "direct cremation" fee)	160	395	695	535
22	Immediate burial (in a minimum casket). The body is buried before a public ceremony occurs	889	2,895	4,182	3,293
Cost for set of 9 items with *		**3,215**	**5,355**	**7,280**	**4,065**
23	Body donation to a local program (the FTC does not require funeral homes to include this cost on the GPL)	225	795	1,500	1,275

Note: The data in this table were culled from more than sixty Kansas City–area General Price Lists. The price lists were collected and tabulated by volunteers associated with the Funeral Consumers Alliance of Greater Kansas City.

Appendix

Outline for In-Service on Boundary Setting in Nursing Homes

The purpose of this presentation is to assist care staff in considering the types of relationships that they should develop with residents and their families and explore areas where they have been challenged with boundary issues. Length of this presentation is 60–90 minutes. This presentation will be most effective if it is interactive. The use of case studies will aid in engaging staff in self-reflection about their own boundaries.

I. Creating a safe atmosphere
   A. Overview of presentation
   B. Ground rules for presentation
      1. Respect cultural differences
      2. Respect value differences
      3. Respect different life experiences
      4. Confidentiality

II. Work in nursing homes
   A. Residents with multiple physical and emotional needs
      1. Facing multiple chronic conditions
      2. Not accepting of health status or location of care
      3. Facing multiple losses
      4. Preparing for death
      5. May not have family support
      6. Are in a position of vulnerability
   B. Staff
      1. Multiple work demands
      2. High stress
      3. Motivated for type of work for different reasons
         a. Transition position
         b. Extra money through school
         c. Primary source of income
         d. Interested in older adults
      4. Long term relationships with residents, encouragement to treat "like family"

III. Forming personal vs. professional relationships with residents
   A. Personal relationships
      1. Mutual
      2. Free exchange of information and communication
      3. Possess degree of emotional, psychological, and possibly physical intimacy
      4. Minimal limit on what is discussed and views expressed
   B. Professional relationships
      1. Resident/family-driven relationship
      2. Resident/family-focused relationship
      3. Based on addressing resident's/family's emotional and physical needs
      4. Based on self-determination, empowerment, and respect of diversity of beliefs or values (NASW Code of Ethics?)

C. Blurring of relationships
  1. Implications for staff
     a. Diminished professional judgment and expertise; emotions can get in the way
     b. Compassion fatigue and burnout
     c. Decreased resident/family care
     d. Professional compromises can occur
     e. Lack of self-care
  2. Effects on resident/family
     a. May expect care (emotional or physical) that cannot be provided
     b. Become dependent on staff
     c. Disempowered—lose voice out of fear of displeasing staff
     d. Emotionally scarred or abandoned when relationships ends or care decisions have to be made
IV. Self-care inventory
  A. Using the compassion-fatigue scale
  B. Measuring your level of burnout
V. Strategies for promoting professional relationships
  A. Limit self-disclosure—keep it focused on the resident/family
  B. Address unmet needs in your own life and areas of personal vulnerability
  C. Be aware of transference
  D. Know your style of coping with stress and loss
  E. Understand concept of Larson's "helper's pit"
  F. Recognize your "triggers"
  G. Practice self-care
  H. Find outlets and mentors for addressing issues that arise with residents/families
VI. Topics for discussion with group
  A. Is this appropriate?
     1. Crying with residents/staff
     2. Accepting gifts or other personal belongs from residents
     3. Visiting residents/families on personal time, even when they are dying
     4. Calling facility to check resident's status
     5. How much self-disclosure is appropriate to residents/families?
  B. Stress management strategies—how to survive and thrive
  C. Identifying and sharing personal rituals

Source: Anewalt and Sanders.

Outline for In-Service on Self-Care and Coping Strategies for Nursing Home Staff

The goal of this presentation is to assist staff in identifying ways to practice self-care in a nursing home environment. If possible, make this presentation interactive and have staff brainstorm ways that self-care can be promoted individually and in the facility. Length of this presentation is thirty to forty-five minutes.

I. What is self-care?
   A. Definition
   B. Why is this important?
      1. Work in an environment of high stress
      2. Multiple work-related demands
      3. Grief and loss are prominent
      4. Others need us to be emotionally, psychologically, and physically available to take care of them

II. What prevents us from practicing self-care?
   A. Time
   B. Energy
   C. Ways that we manage stress
      1. Focus on self-destructive strategies
      2. Long-term impact of this
   D. Other demands in our life
      1. Children
      2. Spouse/partner
      3. Other jobs and commitments
   E. Lack of recognition of its importance until it is too late
   F. Other factors that prevent self-care?

III. Types of self-care activities?
   A. Physical activities
   B. Dietary changes
   C. Spirituality and meditating
   D. Keeping a journal
   E. Hobbies and socializing
   F. Reading
   G. Others?

Ideas for Interaction with Group

1. Do relaxation exercises as a way to model a self-care activity. Could include guided imagery or progressive relaxation; provide soothing music upon arrival to create calm, relaxing environment
2. Have staff identify on a scale from 1–10 (1 = poor and 10 = excellent) their current score for self-care.
   a. Have them identify three barriers they face to practicing self-care.
   b. Identify three self-care goals that they would like to meet in next three months.
   c. Follow up individually with staff on progress with these goals over the course of the three months.

3. Brainstorming session: ways to promote self-care within the facility.
   a. Have administrator or human-resource representative present to provide feedback on feasibility of each option.
   b. Keep this positive.
   c. Recognize that morale improves when staff members feel empowered and have a voice in how organizational culture can support self-care.
4. In pairs or small groups, have staff identify two or three resident deaths they were affected by in the last six months
   a. Facilitate discussion on: why they were difficult, what helped, what to do for self-care the next time this happens

Source: Anewalt and Sanders.

Professional Quality of Life Scale, Compassion Satisfaction, and Fatigue Subscales—Revision 5 (ProQOL R-V)

When you *[help]* people you have direct contact with their lives. As you may have found, your compassion for those you *[help]* can affect you in positive and negative ways. Below are some questions about your experiences, both positive and negative, as a *[helper]*. Consider each of the following questions about you and your current work situation. Select the number that honestly reflects how frequently you experienced these things in the *last 30 days.*

o = Never 1= Rarely   2 = A Few Times   3 = Somewhat Often 4 = Often 5 = Very Often

1. I am happy.
2. I am preoccupied with more than one person I *[help]*.
3. I get satisfaction from being able to *[help]* people.
4. I feel connected to others.
5. I jump or am startled by unexpected sounds.
6. I feel invigorated after working with those I *[help]*.
7. I find it difficult to separate my personal life from my life as a *[helper]*.
8. I am not as productive at work because I am losing sleep over traumatic experiences of a person I *[help]*.
9. I think that I might have been affected by the traumatic stress of those I *[help]*.
10. I feel trapped by my job as a *[helper]*.
11. Because of my *[helping]*, I have felt "on edge" about various things.
12. I like my work as a *[helper]*.
13. I feel depressed because of the traumatic experiences of the people I *[help]*.
14. I feel as though I am experiencing the trauma of someone I have *[helped]*.
15. I have beliefs that sustain me.
16. I am pleased with how I am able to keep up with *[helping]* techniques and protocols.
17. I am the person I always wanted to be.
18. My work makes me feel satisfied.
19. I feel worn out because of my work as a *[helper]*.

20. I have happy thoughts and feelings about those I *[help]* and how I could help them.
21. I feel overwhelmed because my case [work] load seems endless.
22. I believe I can make a difference through my work.
23. I avoid certain activities or situations because they remind me of frightening experiences of the people I *[help]*.
24. I am proud of what I can do to *[help]*.
25. As a result of my *[helping]*, I have intrusive, frightening thoughts.
26. I feel "bogged down" by the system.
27. I have thoughts that I am a "success" as a *[helper]*.
28. I can't recall important parts of my work with trauma victims.
29. I am a very caring person.
30. I am happy that I chose to do this work.

Disclaimer

This information is presented for educational purposes only. It is not a substitute for informed medical advice or training. Do not use this information to diagnose or treat a health problem without consulting a qualified health or mental health care provider. If you have concerns, contact your health care provider, mental health professional, or your community mental health center.

Self-scoring directions, if used as a self test

1. Be certain you respond to all items.
2. On some items the scores need to be reversed. Next to your response write the reverse of that score (i.e. $0 = 0, 1 = 5, 2 = 4, 3 = 3$). Reverse the scores on these 5 items: 1, 4, 15, 17, and 29. Please note that the value of 0 is not reversed, as its value is always null.
3. Mark the items for scoring:
4. Add the numbers you wrote next to the items for each set of items and compare with the theoretical scores.

Copyright information

B. Hudnall Stamm, 2009. "Professional Quality of Life: Compassion Satisfaction and Fatigue Version 5 (ProQOL)." http://www.isu.edu/~bhstamm or www.proqol.org. This test may be freely copied as long as (a) author is credited, (b) no changes are made, and (c) it is not sold.

The Burnout Measure

Please use the following scale to answer the question:
When you think about your work overall, how often do you feel the following?

1	2	3	4	5	6	7
never	almost never	rarely	sometimes	often	very often	always

Tired ___
Disappointed with people ___
Hopeless ___
Trapped ___
Helpless ___
Depressed ___
Physically weak/Sickly ___
Worthless/Like a failure ___
Difficulties sleeping ___
"I've had it" ___

In order to calculate your burnout score add your responses to the 10 items and divide by 10

_____.

A score up to 2.4 indicates a very low level of burnout; a score between 2.5 and 3.4 indicates danger signs of burnout; a score between 3.5 and 4,4 indicates burnout; a score between 4.5 and 5.4 indicates a very serious problem of burnout. A score of 5.5 requires immediate professional help.

Source: Pines, A. M. 2005. "The Burnout Measure Short Version (BMS)." *International Journal of Stress Management* 12:78–88. Copyright Ayala Pines, reprinted with permission.

Contributors

ANN ALLEGRE, M.D., F.A.C.P., F.A.A.H.P.M. Director of Medical Programs, Kansas City Hospice and Palliative Care, Kansas City, Missouri.

PATTI ANEWALT, Ph.D., L.P.C., F.T. Bereavement professional section leader, National Council of Hospice and Palliative Professionals, and director and program director, Pathways Center for Loss and Grief Hospice of Lancaster County, Lancaster, Pennsylvania.

MERCEDES BERN-KLUG, Ph.D., M.S.W., M.A. John A. Hartford Geriatric Social Work Faculty Scholar and assistant professor, School of Social Work and the UI Aging Studies Program, University of Iowa, Iowa City.

LISA CHURCH, R.N., M.S.N. College of Nursing. University of Nebraska Medical Center.

CHARLES E. GESSERT, M.D., M.P.H. Senior research scientist, Division of Education and Research, St. Mary's/Duluth Clinic Health System, Duluth, Minnesota.

MICHAEL J. KLUG, J.D. Senior program director, Training Health Assistance Partnership, Washington, D.C.

PATRICIA J. KOLB, Ph.D. Associate professor, Department of Social Work, Lehman College, City University of New York, Bronx, New York.

JEAN C. MUNN, Ph.D., M.S.W. John A. Hartford Geriatric Social Work Faculty Scholar and assistant professor, College of Social Work, Florida State University.

Don F. Reynolds, J.D. Director, Office for Responsible Research, MU Center for Health Ethics and Research; assistant professor of internal medicine, University of Missouri School of Medicine, Columbia, Missouri.

Sara Sanders, Ph.D., M.S.W. John A. Hartford Geriatric Social Work Faculty Scholar and assistant professor, School of Social Work, University of Iowa, Iowa City.

Peggy Sharr, M.S.W. Research associate, School of Social Work, University of Iowa, Iowa City.

Sarah Thompson, R.N., Ph.D. Niedfelt Distinguished Professor and associate dean, College of Nursing, University of Nebraska Medical Center, Omaha.

Index